PELICAN BOOKS

THE PELICAN HISTORY OF GREECE

Andrew Robert Burn was born in Shropshire in 1902. He was educated at Uppingham and Christ Church, Oxford, where he took a First in Greats. His enthusiasm for Greece dates from earliest childhood, and while still an undergraduate he won the Charles Oldham Prize with an essay on the early Greek lyric poets.

During the war he was the British Council's representative in Greece, 1940–41. He then served in the Intelligence Corps, and from 1944 to 1946 was Second Secretary in the British Embassy in Athens. His former outdoor interests include mountaineering and gliding, and he is still an enthusiastic traveller in the remoter parts of Greece and the Aegean. His other books include *The World of Hesiod*, *The Lyric Age of Greece*, and *Persia and the Greeks*, subtitled *The Defence of the West*; also *The Modern Greeks*, which he wrote in the intervals of duty at G.H.Q., Middle East, in 1941–2. He taught ancient history at the University of Glasgow, 1946–69, and to young Americans in Athens, 1969–72.

Mr Burn is married and lives near Oxford.

D0051237

A. R. BURN

THE PELICAN HISTORY
OF GREECE

PENGUIN BOOKS

Penguin Books Ltd, Harmondsworth, Middlesex, England
Penguin Books, 625 Madison Avenue, New York, New York 10022, U.S.A.
Penguin Books Australia Ltd, Ringwood, Victoria, Australia
Penguin Books Canada Ltd, 2801 John Street, Markham, Ontario, Canada L3R 1B4
Penguin Books (N.Z.) Ltd, 182–190 Wairau Road, Auckland 10, New Zealand

—

First published as *A Traveller's History of Greece* by Hodder and Stoughton 1965
Published by Pelican Books 1966
Reprinted 1968, 1970, 1971, 1973
Reprinted with revisions 1974
Reprinted 1975, 1976, 1977
Reprinted with revisions 1978, 1979, 1981

—

—

Made and printed in Great Britain by
Hazell Watson & Viney Ltd,
Aylesbury, Bucks
Set in Linotype Times

TO HESTER
and all Young Travellers

PLAINS AND MOUNTAINS
Early immigrants & the Bronze Age
Chief alluvial plains (irrespective of height) left untinted.

R. Danube

R. Hebros

Rhodope Mts.
7143

FIRST FARMERS IN EUROPE *c. 8000 B.C.*

Undulating Lowland

Nea Nikomedeia

Axios/Vardar

Servia

SAMOTHRACE

Athos 6350

5250

2625

Pindos

Olympos 9571

Ossa 6410

Pelion 5308

Poliochni

Troy

Ida 5807

LEMNOS

Plateau 3000–4000 ft

5067

Dhimini Sesklo

Othrys 5669

LESBOS

Thermi

7609

Mesa

Parnassos 8064

5726

SKYROS

Krisa (TIN?)

Orchomenos

Thebes

4628

Nisa

CHIOS

7727

Corinth

Athens

PROSPECTORS TO CYCLADES *c. 3000 B.C.*

SAMOS

PELOPONNESE

ARCADIA

Mycenae

Argos Tiryns

Lerna

Troizen

Miletos

Lakedaimon (Sparta) 6355

CYCLADES

NAXOS (EMERY) 3294

Pylos 7194

KOS

MELOS (OBSIDIAN)

THERA

IALYSOS

KYTHERA

RHODES

Ida 8061

Knosós Mallia

Gournia & Vasilikí

8100

7103

Zakro

Phaistós

Praisos

SETTLERS FROM LEVANT TO CRETE BEFORE 5000 B.C.

CRETE

Miles

0   100

CONTENTS

1 PREHISTORY

2 CRETE, MYCENAE AND THE HEROIC AGE

3 THE GREEK MIDDLE AGES
c. 1100–700 B.C.

4 EXPANSION AND RENAISSANCE

15 THE MACEDONIANS

16 THE LEGACY OF ALEXANDER

17 THE SHADOW OF ROME

MAPS

CHRONOLOGICAL TABLES*

For these tables see fold-out at end of book

FOREWORD

MOST existing text-books of Greek history are concerned primarily with the political and military affairs which have traditionally been considered the stuff of history proper; and not unfairly, since they were written for classical students, who were devoting much time to reading the literature (much less to art and science) and studied public affairs chiefly as a background. In an age in which Greek and Latin are no longer the basis of a common culture for most educated western citizens, there is a need of new books to present this great chapter in the evolution of our own way of life to a new reading public, often a travelling public, whose education has been in science or modern studies; though, since even young classical scholars must be beginners at some time, it may be hoped that the book may be of use also to them.

The narrative runs from the age of the neolithic pioneers to the closing of the philosophic schools of Athens under the Christian empire. The appreciation of the classical Athenian achievement has often suffered, through classical Athens being studied too much in isolation. At the same time, it was in Athens that all that had been achieved earlier came to its full flowering; and here the seeds were shed, which fertilised most of what was valuable in the sequel. That Athens, from about 500 to 300 B.C., occupies half the book, is not due to lack of material for a much fuller treatment of the earlier and later centuries; it is as it should be. Likewise the Persian Invasions are singled out to receive the only detailed military history in this work, for the reasons, not only that they are a great story, part of the western heritage and one that must not be left to Hollywood and the nursery books, but also that they were of such unique importance, one of the very few occasions on which so much has depended for so many on the issue of a day.

My warmest thanks are due to the kind friends who read this book in typescript, chapter by chapter: to Miss Hester

13

Fellowes, now Mrs M. C. Greenstock, B.A. Cantab., recent science graduate and traveller to Greece; to my colleague Dr Robert Morrison, representing scientists of more mature years; to my wife, as always; and to Dr D. M. Lewis, of Christ Church, Oxford, who, as one of the most learned professional Greek historians and forthright critics of this generation, saved me from a number of errors in detail, and must not be considered responsible for the views adopted, with some of which, indeed, he disagrees. I would also thank Professors George Huxley and J. N. Coldstream who (appropriately, at sea off Crete) together gave me reason to modify my concluding paragraph on the 'Linear B' controversy; and Messrs Edward Arnold, for permission to use translations written for my *Lyric Age of Greece* and *Persia and the Greeks*.

Finally, a note on spelling: I do not use the letter Z, foreign to the Latin alphabet, in words of Latin origin, such as 'civilise', 'colonise'; though it is acceptable in Greek words, such as 'organize'. Greek names are given in their Greek forms, not Latinised; so *-os*, *-on*, not the less euphonious *-us*, *-um*; Kimon, not Cimo. Only some familiar names are given in their familiar forms; so Socrates, Aeschylus. Long vowels are marked, ē, ō, etc., at first appearance and in the index, except personal name-endings, -e, -o, -on, -es, which are always long.

The Greek vowels were probably pronounced much as in modern Italian. Modern Greek pronunciation is no guide to ancient; for instance, fifth-century Athenians spelt all names ending in -e or -es with an epsilon.

Glasgow, October 1969   A. R. BURN

In the 1981 reprint the section now entitled 'The Last Mycenaeans and the Dorian Problem', Chapter 2:7 (pp. 56–60) has been completely rewritten to take account of recent publications; and other additions and alterations have been made in the text and bibliography.

Oxford, August 1980   A. R. B.

14

ILLYRIA

MACEDONIA
(MAKEDHONÍA)

Thessaloníki
(Salonica)

CHALKIDIKÉ

Olymbos
(Mt Olympos)

Mt Athos
(Áyion Óros)
or Holy Mountain

KÉRKYRA
(CORFU)

Iánnina

EPEIROS
(EPÍROS)

Arti
(Arta)

THESSALY
(THESSALÍA)

MAGNESIA

Volos

SKÝROS

LEVKÁS
(LEUKAS)

AKARNANIA

AITŌLIA

E. LOKRIS

DORIS

W. LOKRIS

PHOKIS

EVVIA
(EUBOIA)

KEPHALLĒNIA

ITHAKI

BOIOTIA
(VIOTÍA)

ZÁKYNTHOS
(ZANTE)

ACHAIA

ATTICA
(ATTIKÍ)

Athēnai

ELIS

Kórinthos

ARCADIA
(ARKADHÍA)

ARGOLIS

AIGHINA
(AEGINA)

MESSĒNIA

Kalámai
(Kalamáta)

LACŌNIA

MĒLOS
(MILO)

THE REGIONS OF
GREECE

*with some modern
Key-points*

KÝTHERA
(KYTHĒRA)

Miles

0   50   100   150

Khania
(Canea)

Suda
Bay

K

THRACE
(THRÁKI)

Própontis
(Sea of Marmara)

THÁSOS

Thracian
Chersonese
Gallipoli

SAMOTHRÁKI
(SAMOTHRACE)

PHRYGIA

LÉMNOS
•Troy (Hisarlik)
Mudros
Bay
TROAD

LESVOS
MYSIA
AIOLIS
Mytilénē

LYDIA
CHÍOS
Izmir
(Smyrna)

ANDHROS
SÁMOS

TÉNOS   IKARÍA
IONIA
SYRA   MÝKONOS
DHÉLOS
YKLÁDHES (Cyclades)
KARIA
PÁROS   NAXOS
Bodrum (Halikarnassos)

KÓS

THÉRA
(SANTORIN)

RHODHOS
(RHODES)
Líndhos

Héráklion (Candia)
RÉTĒ

Epidamnos c.625
(Durazzo)

L.Ochrid

MACEDONIA

ILLYRIA

L.Prespa

Philippoi
(357)

Valona
Bay

Apollonia

Pella

Therma
later
Thessalonika
Olynthos

Amphipolis
(437)

Stageiros

Drikos

Methone
Pydna

Akanthos
c.650

Mt Olympos

Poteidaia
c.594

Torone

Mt
Athos

EPEIROS

THESSALY

Tempe
Pass

Mende

Skione

Kerkyra
733

Dodona
("rediscovered"
636 tr)

MtOssa

Larisa
Krannon
Pherai

MtPelion

Demetrias

SPORADES

Colonial
Empire of
Corinth

Ambrakia
c.625

Pharsalos

Pagasai

Battle of
Actium·31

Aktion Cape

Leukas

AITŌLIA

Thermon

Thermopylai

Histiaia

EUBOIA

KEPHALLENIA

ITHAKA

Amphissa

Delphoi

PHOKIS

Elateia

Orchomenos

Chalkis

Thebes

Eretria

BOIOTIA

ATTICA

Styra

Patrai

Aigion

ACHAIA
City of Elis c.470

Sikyon

Megara

Karystos

ZAKYNTHOS

ELIS

Mantineia

Corinth

ARGOLIS

Athens

AIGINA

KEOS

Olympia

ARCADIA

Argos

Epidauros

Nauplia

Troizen

KYTHNOS

Tegea
c.6

MtPartnon

Megalopolis
c.369

Mt Taygetos

SERIPHOS

SIPHNOS

Messene

Sparta

LACONIA

MELOS

M = Colony of Miletos
MG= Colony of Megara
tr = traditionally

Cape Tainaron
(Matapan)

Cape Malea

KYTHĒRA

GREECE
AND THE AEGEAN

Cities founded
after 750 BC
underlined

KR

Kydonia

Eleutherna

CHAPTER 1

PREHISTORY

1 BEGINNINGS

ANCIENT Greece yielded in 1976, from the cave of the Petrá-
lona in Chalkidike, much the oldest human skeleton yet found in
Europe (*c.* 400,000 B.C.?) and evidence of the use of fire much
earlier still. This epoch-making discovery affects our general
view of the emergence of Man; but, far later, yet still pre-
Neolithic, a startlingly *Greek* note is struck by finds on Kythnos
Island and at the Franchthi Cave in Argolis of obsidian blades,
which must have come from Melos. Greece had its seafarers
even before agriculture made possible any density of population!

Agriculture probably began in south-west Asia. There,
astride an axis running from Syria to the Caspian, are found
wild barley and emmer (ancestral to our wheat), and wild
goats and sheep, ancestral to our domestic species; and there,
'eastward in Eden', in centuries perhaps about 10,000 B.C.,
took place the 'Neolithic Revolution'; first, perhaps, the herding
of the horned beasts, leading to full domestication, and then,
arising out of concern for fodder, the search for and care of the
'noble grasses', the basis of western agriculture. Thereafter,
though the children of Adam might ask, in the sweat of their
brow, what sin they had committed that they should have to
work so hard, the new way of life spread steadily. By 6500,
farmer pioneers had entered Europe at the Bosporus and
established a substantial hamlet north-west of Thessalonika, at
Nea Nikomēdeia. Others spread to central Europe by way of the
Danube. From Macedonia the farmers spread south into
Greece. In Thessaly, the earliest type-site is Sesklo, near the
Bay of Volos.

These people already made good pottery, though without
the wheel. At Sesklo their cabins were brick-built, on stone
foundations; and they made little clay female statuettes of a
fantastic but evidently admired plumpness. At Nea Niko-

21

medeia, five of these were found in a building that was perhaps a shrine. Already, we infer, like peasants in classical Greece, they conceived of the power which could give or withhold fertility, in the likeness of a goddess. They maintained the fertility of their fields by sound farming too (perhaps rotation of grain crops with peas and beans); for their small settlements were durable, rising with repeated rebuilding of the cabins into mounds or 'tells', as in western Asia. For 500 years they remained unfortified. There was room for all on the good soil of the alluvial plains between the limestone hills. As Greek legend said, ages later, things began with a Golden Age when war was not yet.

Other neolithic settlers reached Crete from the Levant, bringing with them pigs, sheep and cattle (presumably in the form of young creatures; but it was no small feat). They too made plump clay figurines, and lived without fortifications – inland, often in caves, no doubt more comfortable than most huts. They settled mainly in the eastern half of the island, warmer and drier than the west. Radioactive carbon from Knosós seems to show settlement as early as 5000 B.C.

Others again had reached the Cyclades by about 4000. Their descendants, by about 2750, were the first men in Greece to have some copper daggers and spearheads; and in the islands they found and worked copper and other minerals. They made their female statuettes of the island marble – spare and geometric, these; much admired (and some forged) in modern times. Their metal-workers, jewellers and stone-cutters must, it would seem, have been specialists (a development still unknown in Crete and the mainland); and their island settlements, though still with populations of only a few hundred at the largest, begin to look more like little towns. Their pottery-decoration includes conventionalised representations of men in boats; they buried their dead in rock-cut or stone-built chamber-tombs; and the prominence of weapons among the grave-goods is ominous. From Phylakopí in Mēlos, they traded obsidian blades and cores for working, to Crete and the Greek mainland; and on the mainland their culture blended during the third millennium with that of the spreading peasant settlements, in what is called the Early Helladic culture.

The knowledge of metals and the practice of deliberate prospecting for minerals had no doubt reached the Cyclades from the east by way of Asia Minor. In Mesopotamia by 3000 B.C. there were already cities and ordered governments, based on the necessity for organizing irrigation and regulating the use of water-supplies; and since metals and precious stones were to be found in stony regions, while population grew dense on the alluvial soil along the great rivers, trade covered long distances. Also, as Gordon Childe pointed out, while copper was not very much better than stone for agricultural implements, it made very much better weapons. Therefore, governments which could organize and protect the trade in metals had the power to dominate large populations. The demand for copper became inexhaustible with the development of war in the east, where Sumerian cities fought for tracts of the rich but limited alluvial land, and then attempted to secure their position by dominating their neighbours and terrorising adjacent barbarians. Later it was reinforced by the demand for tin, the rare and precious metal, 10 per cent of which, as the Sumerians knew by 2500, could alloy copper to make the hard and tough bronze. Traders and prospectors from Assyria established in Cappadocia, north of the Taurus mountains, regular mining colonies, from which caravans and correspondence, including cheques and letters of credit, on baked clay tablets, kept up communication with the business centres of Babylonia. Bronze weapons, and the long-distance trade necessary to obtain them, and to go on obtaining them in greater plenty than one's rivals, were the basis of the precocious imperialism and royal splendours of the Bronze Age. With copper spear-heads Menes from Upper Egypt (c. 2900?) conquered the Delta, to found the First Dynasty of united Egypt; and later, Sargon, overlord of Sumer and Akkad, marched as far as 'the cedar forest and the silver mountain' (Taurus) and may even have crossed the 'Upper Sea' to the copper isle of Cyprus.

Now through Asia Minor, from east to west, a route running parallel to the northern and southern mountain chains offers few natural obstacles. With minor variations, it must have been followed by the farmer-colonists; ages later, it was the Royal Road of the Persian Empire, followed thereafter by Macedonians, Romans and Turks. By this same highway the knowledge of metal would have reached the Cyclades.

As in later ages, prospectors for metals made voyages of astonishing length and daring. Especially after the discovery of the importance of tin, the Cycladic islanders may have made coasting voyages that would have taken many weeks; but the suggestion that at this and later times the Aegean bronze age strongly influenced western Europe has been overtaken by new developments in carbon-14 dating. Since the 'calibration' of carbon-14 dates after comparison with tree-ring dating (see Colin Renfrew's book (below, pp. 37, 379)) it has appeared that many developments took place in the west too early to have resulted from 'diffusion' from the Near East. For the present at least, theories of independent, parallel developments of culture hold the field.

The metal trade also stimulated the foundation of a stronghold at a famous site, commanding the Dardanelles: the first fortress of Troy. A neolithic settlement in the plain near the mouth of the Scamander is succeeded in the early copper age by a fortress on the hill of Hisarlik, 'the castle-place', made famous by Heinrich Schliemann. A promontory of the high ground, overlooking the plain, was surrounded by a massive stone ring-wall, enclosing an area about 100 yards in diameter. 'Within the citadel', says C. W. Blegen, the latest excavator, 'stood a small number of relatively large free-standing houses, obviously the homes of a ruler and his entourage.' They were built with stone foundations and superstructure of crude brick. One of these buildings, long and narrow, with a portico and entrance at one end and a hearth in the principal room, has the unmistakable plan of a *megaron* – a 'hall', such as Mycenaean and Homeric chiefs were to inhabit later in Greece. Rebuilt and replanned through some four centuries, the houses of Troy II ultimately raised the ground-level by about fifteen feet in places. Copper was in use throughout this time, as well as stone tools and weapons. The pottery, polished black, grey or brown monochrome, is quite different from the fine painted ware of Thessaly. (Trojan chiefs probably already drank out of gold and silver.) The Trojan culture did not only dominate the Troad. It crossed the water to Lesbos and Lemnos to found the early towns of Thermí and Polióchni, and to the Gallipoli peninsula; and its influence seems to appear as far afield as Macedonia.

Before 2750 B.C., also, new immigrants entered the Aegean lands at several points; perhaps part of a 'chain-reaction' started by events further east. Bronze weapons, brought by broad-skulled 'Armenoids' from Asia Minor, appear in Crete, where metal had hitherto been almost unknown. The newcomers, apparently in no great numbers, soon intermarried with the first inhabitants, who were narrow-skulled, small and probably black-haired; the 'Mediterranean' type. Broad-skulled mingled with narrow-skulled people also in the Cyclades, and there was increased impact of Cycladic culture on the Greek mainland. New settlements in Argolis included those on the rocky knolls of Tiryns and Mycenae (Gk. Mykēnai), with a good land hard by, and at Lerna on the west coast of the Argolic gulf. The mingling of cultures and ideas (not to speculate on the possible genetic effects) was followed by a marked quickening in cultural development.

In the north there was immigration, too. A northern settlement of the Thessalian Sesklo culture (p. 21) at Servia on the Haliakmon was destroyed and burnt (c. 2500?), and its red or painted pottery gives place to black, polished wares, with incised or painted geometric decoration, including spirals. Clay phalli (one of them found among grave-goods in a burial of the new period at Servia) indicate a new emphasis on the male life-principle. War, still on a small scale, had come, bringing the domination of the male sex, and an end to the age of innocence. When the newcomers, here too mingling with their predecessors, settled at Sesklo and at Dhimíni (the type-site of the new period) in south-east Thessaly, their villages were walled. Copper and gold, represented respectively by two axeheads and a pendant, all found at Dhimíni, appear in a context still mainly neolithic; later, oblong houses with a porch and entrance at one end recall the *megaron* type at Troy. The new, mixed culture influenced that of Macedonia, which spread far up the Vardar; but compared with that of the Aegean world, it remained backward.

2 MINOAN CIVILISATION

It was in Crete that bronze age Aegean culture developed most precociously and reached its greatest height. Sir Arthur Evans's suggestion that a sudden upswing was stimulated by Egyptian immigrants, fleeing before Menes, has been abandoned, though the beginning of the Aegean bronze age, synchronized with Dynasty I, is now again dated by carbon-14 about 2900. The bringers of an alien culture, which appears around Phaistós, on the south coast, perhaps about 2500, perhaps from Libya, soon adopted the ways of the island. The remarkable and artistic Cretan civilisation, though its basic skills in metals, pottery and other crafts were brought from the east, was a native development.

The name 'Minoan', it must be noted, is modern; it was invented by Evans, whose excavations at Knosós first revealed it in 1899, on the basis of the name of Minos of Knosós, the sea-king famous in Greek legend. It was at once objected that Minos, according to Homer, was the grandfather of a Greek hero who fought at Troy many centuries later, and that to divide the centuries before 1600 into Early and Middle Minoan was like calling our own early and late middle ages Early and Middle Victorian. There is now a move to divide Cretan bronze age rather into Pre-Palace, First Palace and Later Palace periods. However, 'Minoan' has long had international currency.

The Early Minoan ('E.M.') period, then, was probably not so long as its discoverer believed. Evans distinguished within it three sub-periods, E.M. I, II and III; for, in any temporal series, any object or event must be rather near the beginning, or rather near the middle, or rather near the end. Evans's E.M. I culture, R. W. Hutchinson (in *Prehistoric Crete*, Penguin Books,

1962) says, 'is not a unity at all'. Not even any copper tools *certainly* dated to this time have yet been found, though they were probably in use. One has to remember that copper and bronze, unless accidentally lost, were regularly melted down. What we see rather is a new stirring of experimentation, in vase-painting, in the use of stone as well as clay for figurines, in more ambitious house-building. It is 'the day of small things' for many processes, interesting because of their sequels. Knosós itself, half way along the north coast, with good lowlands to cultivate and access to the best passes across the centre of the island, is one place where remains of the new age overlie the neolithic. At many sites in east Crete the Copper Age appears ready-made; population was expanding. In the wetter and cooler west, less attractive to the settlers, it remained much thinner.

In E.M. II and III (*c.* 2600 to 2100?) the island civilisation is clearly in being. Faience (blue paste) beads and ornaments from Egypt, ivory from Egypt (or Syria, where there were still elephants), imported and worked in Crete, give evidence of trade; jewellers worked in gold; but the most attractive of all Early Minoan products are vases cut in local marble, steatite and other stones, with a keen eye for 'graining' or colour variations; an art first stimulated perhaps by imported vases from Egypt, the home of many masterpieces in this genre. The olive, basic, with grain, to Greek diet ever since, was already known. At Vasilikí in east Crete the many-roomed, L-shaped 'House on the Hill', measuring thirty yards each way, is notably larger than its neighbours; it suggests emerging class differences, and is a forerunner of the famous Minoan palaces.

At nearby Myrtós a ninety-room (classless, extended-family?) rabbit-warren settlement was burnt, *c.* 2200, while life went on on another hill with a revered tomb. Copper is now common, but alloyed with little, if any, tin. Pottery-painting, vigorous and attractive, still confines itself to abstract designs; but a taste of what was to come – the famous Minoan feeling for nature – appears in isolated cases, as where the potter, with charming humour, has turned a jug into a small but greedy bird, with wide-open beak, nascent wings and tail, standing on four apparently human feet; or on the lids of cosmetic-boxes, where a handle (though the lid is also pierced for two strings) is provided in the form of a delightful, sprawling but restless, long-legged and long-tailed dog.

Then, about the twentieth century B.C., Crete had, in Childe's phrase, its urban revolution. Almost suddenly, as it appears to us now, the progress of six centuries comes to the boil in an epoch of rapid change. Political events, of which we know nothing, seem to be presupposed by a shift in the centre of gravity of Cretan life, from the east of the island to its centre. At Knosós, which had a port at Amnisos, at Mallia, some twenty miles to the east, and at Phaistós near the south coast, real towns arise, with houses packed tight along narrow streets; and in each there is a palace, a vast complex of rooms with paved corridors and stone stairways, grouped round a central court, but exhibiting no trace of planning for architectural effect. Rather, rooms and ranges of rooms were added piece-meal, as they were wanted; Minoan architecture has been described as 'agglutinative'. There is also apparent absence of rooms large enough for entertainment or court functions in winter, such as we might expect; but these may have been on an upper floor, reached by the stairs whose lower treads sur-vive. At smaller towns in east Crete, Gournia and Palaikastro (the names are modern), complete street-plans have been re-covered; at Gournia a smaller 'big house' has been described as the residence of a local lord of the manor. In the Middle Minoan period (c. 1950–1550) roads were engineered, especi-ally over the passes from Knosós to Phaistós, with police-posts at intervals; and a hieroglyphic system of writing, perhaps adapted from that of Egypt, was adopted; from it later developed a simpler syllabary, called Minoan Linear A.

True bronze was now in use. The dagger lengthens into a bronze thrusting sword; but more striking than this develop-ment of weapons is the fact that they are relatively rare, and that the rich and prosperous towns are still unfortified. The palaces, indeed, have narrow entrances, protected by a massive keep or guard-house, defensible against a riot; but the whole impression is of a land at peace. If the various palaces suggest that there was, as yet, no centralised monarchy ruling the whole island, the absence of fortifications suggests that the city princes, perhaps priest-kings or the consorts of divine queens (for the chief deity was a mother-goddess, and art shows that the status of court ladies was high), kept the peace with one another, having indeed a common interest in the maintenance of their privileged position. The unprivileged were probably held in subjection and taxed in kind (especially in oil, of which the later palace at Knosós held huge stores) by the artifices of religion and for its upkeep; the upkeep of the august personages who kept things right between gods and men. Like Roman emperors, the rulers also provided games; some of the famous Middle Minoan miniature frescoes delight in showing great crowds of people assembled at a spectacle. In one case it is a dance of noble ladies under huge olive trees; in another, probably bull-baiting or rather bull-vaulting (a game fraught with dire peril for the athletes) before a pillared shrine. The crowd, red, sunburnt men, white-skinned women, is summarily rendered. More care is expended on the court ladies seated in a grandstand near the shrine, in their elaborate dresses – flounced skirts, puffed sleeves, breasts exposed – but the artist reveals that they are not attending, but engaged in conversation.

Meanwhile culture in the Cyclades wilted; but one southern island, Thera (perhaps more spacious then), had a prosperous city, including comfortable houses with frescoed rooms. One room, not large or specially pretentious, has swallows flying and 'kissing' in mid-air, above conventional rocks and wind-blown red lilies – an artist's impression of a windy day in spring. One, quite narrow, band seems to depict a sea-fight. Furniture, utensils, much painted pottery, in a style rougher than the Cretan but with a charm of its own, are among other foretastes of what may yet be to come; for Thera became (we shall see) a bronze-age Herculaneum. Melos too had its frescoed rooms and painted pottery; but in contrast to Crete its town, Phylakopí II, has a massive wall.

On the mainland, the early culture developed more slowly; though at Lerna, before 2000, there was a great house, roofed with tiles, clearly that of a chief. Here as in Crete, the rainier west was backward, and more thinly populated.

3 PEOPLES AND LANGUAGES, AND THE COMING OF THE GREEKS

Before about 1950 B.C., the Greek language, or its ancestor, had probably never been heard in the Aegean world. The tongues in use, as many surviving pre-Hellenic place-names show, were akin to those of Asia Minor. Classical Greek writers numbered among the first inhabitants of their country, before the Hellenes, the Leleges, a people of Karia in south-west Asia Minor. Further north appear the Pelasgoi, of whom remnants survived in historic times in Lemnos, in the peninsulas of the north-west Aegean, and on the sea of Marmara, and whose name survived in that of a district of Thessaly, and of a 'Pelasgian Argos' on Thessaly's southern borders. A complex 'Pelasgian question' was started by classical Greeks, through the practice of using 'Pelasgian', in any part of the Aegean world, as a synonym of aborigines.

But the Karian or Lelegian tradition is in full accord with the findings of archaeology; an observation already made in the Cyclades by the historian Thucydides, who noted the Karian weapons found in ancient graves on Dēlos, dug up in an Athenian purification of that sacred islet. It is supported also by linguistic facts. Very few of the ancient place-names of Greece belong to the Greek language; and among the non-Greek majority, some classes, especially those ending in -nthos and -sos (also written -ssos, with a variant -ttos in Attica) recall the many names ending in -sa and -nda in Karia. Among them are Knosós, Amnisós, Parnasós (Parnassus), Hymettós, Lárisa ('King's place'? – a name of many citadels), Halikarnassós and many others; Corinth, Tiryns (accusative Tiryntha), Olynthos, Mount Kynthos (in Dēlos); Lindos in Rhodes, Alabanda, Labraunda, home of a war-god famous for his *labrys* or sacred axe, of which more hereafter; -nda is the commonest Karian place-name termination. The accent denoting a higher pitch of the voice, on the Greek -sós terminations, is often found in Greek in adjectival terminations. *Argos* is another recurrent name, on which a Greek geographer remarks that it always seems to denote a plain by the sea; and the termination -ēne, seen in Messene, Athēnai (Athens), Mytilene, Priene, also appears in a constellation of names, such as Melitene, astride the Taurus.

The -s and -nth terminations also appear, very interestingly, in a range of Greek common nouns, unconnected with Greek roots. They fall into two groups: country words, mostly names of plants, and a smaller group of words connected with civilisation. All of them, in short, are 'native' words, such as invaders would pick up, to denote things new to them. A few of these words have even come down to us today, though sometimes with changed meanings: hyacinth (iris?), narcissus; mint (from *mintha*); terebinth (whence 'turpentine'); absinthe, acanthus, cypress; and among the civilisation-terms, plinth, from Greek *plinthos*, a brick. Among other old Aegean words in Greek are *thálassa*, sea; *nēsós*, island; nearly all the Greek words for metals; and *asaminthos*, a bath.

The people who brought the Greek language into Greece, then, appear to have arrived as relatively primitive people, coming into contact with a more advanced civilisation and with the sea. Also, the Greek language belongs to the far-flung Indo-European family along with the Celtic, Germanic, Slavonic and Italic (with Romance) language groups; old Persian; more than one language spoken in Asia Minor in the second millennium B.C.; and Sanskrit, introduced into north India, perhaps about 1600, by barbarian invaders, who called themselves Arya, 'the noble people'. (Hence modern 'Aryans'; the term, emphasised by Brahmans in the interest of what gradually became the caste system and found convenient by nineteenth-century German philologists, has been taken up with pathological enthusiasm by some modern Europeans, to justify a theory of a master-race.)

This far-flung group of languages, replacing older tongues, of which traces remain in the Aegean and other areas, must clearly have been spread by the migrations, often conquering migrations, of people who spoke 'Aryan'; but the attempt to identify by archaeology the 'cradle of the Aryan folk' has proved difficult. Theory after theory has encountered factual objections. However, the vast migrations and the points at which these languages enter history, impinging upon the civilised world from the north, suggest an origin in the northern plains. Here movement is easy; and here a barbaric culture, or group of cultures, distinguished by certain types of stone battle-axe, seems at present to provide the best clue. These cultures seem to emerge as a secondary development, when the ways of life of northern savages, descended from the palaeolithic hunters, had been irradiated from the civilised east with the introduction of sheep, hoe-cultivation, and a few rare objects of metal. Even the battle-axes, though perhaps derived from antler picks, seem to imitate copper forms; and the word 'star' (Greek *astēr*) may, it has been thought, be derived from the name of the goddess Ishtar.

In the third millennium these northern peoples had domesticated horses and cattle, and had learned from the civilised world the use of the wheel. This gave them formidable mobility. The necessity of defending cattle on the move between summer and winter pastures produced a warlike society, with domination of the male in small family groups; and the group of mutually intelligible dialects (Gordon Childe suggested, following Russian philologists) 'might result from the adjustment of language to the requirements of intercourse under the new social order'; intercourse among mobile peoples, over a wide area. The people and their herds increased in numbers and spread (like Abraham and Lot) in diverse directions. Often aggressive against peasant peoples who came in their way, they did not (being neither Brahmans nor Nazis) have any inhibitions about mingling their blood; skeletal remains of probable early Aryan-speakers exhibit much diversity. Before 2000, horse-bones and the cord-decorated pottery of the steppe appear in Macedonia; an infiltration, in Childe's phrase, 'of warrior bands'. It was probably their descendants who introduced a speech, ancestral to classical Greek, into Thessaly, in the twentieth century B.C. A little later, some of their kindred occupied Troy.

The Middle Bronze Age ('Middle Helladic') certainly is inaugurated by something like an invasion. Southward from Thessaly through eastern Greece, some old sites are deserted, others resettled after the houses on them had been burnt. The attractive Early Helladic painted pottery comes to an end. The new dominant people were accustomed to the grey ware from Asia Minor, found already in the Balkans; though it seems to have been in eastern Greece itself that they developed the characteristic Middle Helladic ware; a technically excellent pottery, wheel-made, evidently by professionals, highly polished and smooth to the touch. It is known as 'Minyan', a now time-honoured but none too happy name, given because it was first found by Schliemann at the city of the Minyai of legend, Orchomenos in Boiotia.

'Minyan' pottery spread through Greece, even to the Peloponnese, where it is sometimes yellow and not grey. It was not only traded, but manufactured there; some of the kilns and heaps of 'spoilers' have been found. And with it, it is reasonable to assume, came the Greek language; for Greek was certainly spoken throughout Greece *before* the next invasion, at the end of the bronze age (p. 59). As elsewhere, older languages gave way before Aryan speech; how quickly, in Greece, we cannot say. Perhaps the Aryan tongues, developed for communication over wide areas, really were superior in clarity – through the well-developed tense-system of their verbs, for example. Certainly they had the social prestige of being the languages of chiefs and their companions.

The spread of the Hellenes (as their descendants called themselves) may not always have been by direct conquest. Sometimes they may have been invited, as often in Greek legends, by local chiefs to help them against enemies; Thucydides believed that this was how 'the children of Hellēn' spread from Thessaly. In the legends, the hero arrives alone or with one or a few faithful companions: that is poetic convention; he delivers the land from enemies or monsters, and marries the king's daughter: as a modern writer has said, it is 'the recognized rate for the job'. He may then also succeed to the kingdom; and it is not impossible that such things actually happened, for in the old Aegean (as still in historic times, in a few old-fashioned corners), descent probably was traced and property passed in the female line. Menelaos in Homer (a suitor accepted because he is brother to the powerful king of Mycenae) holds the kingship of Sparta as husband of Helen, daughter of the old king, although (as Helen says in the *Iliad*) when she left Sparta her brothers were living. One is reminded of the spread of the Normans – 'tamers of horses', like Homer's heroes – by conquest indeed to Normandy, England, Sicily and Syria; but by invitation of the king of Scots to Scotland and of the Pope to Italy.

Through four centuries, about 1950 to 1550, the peoples of Greece spread out and mingled. By the end of this time Greek-speaking chiefs dominated from their castles almost every good plain, even to south-western Pylos, near the splendid Navarino Bay. Sometimes what look like the results of local political events can be distinguished. At Lerna, the great House of the Tiles was burnt (*c.* 1650?) and later a wide tumulus was piled over the ruins, as though to give them honourable burial. Not much later again, a shaft-grave was dug into the tumulus. The local capital moved north into the plain of Argos; but not to the central position of Argos itself. *Two* major fortresses, Tiryns near the sea and Mycenae 'in the inner corner' as Homer says, guarding the northern passes, seem as though ready to dispute the plain. In Homer, whose *Iliad*, close on 1,000 years later, so remarkably reproduces the 'map' of the later bronze age, the High King of 'Mycenae rich in gold' exercises direct rule over the lands north and west, to the Corinthian Gulf, while 'Tiryns of the mighty walls', with Argos and most of Argolis, is under a faithful baron and two local chiefs. Greek tradition had it that, long before then, this division of the land had resulted from a compromise between two warring brothers. Like many political frontiers, this one is so odd and uneconomic that one feels the story might well be true.

CHAPTER 2

CRETE, MYCENAE AND
THE HEROIC AGE

1 CRETE AND MYCENAE

IN the islands the age from about 1950 to 1400 B.C. was a golden age punctuated by cataclysms. Twice, *c.* 1730 and 1570, the palace at Knosós was shattered by earthquakes; it stands, we now know, on a fault, an earthquake line. But the people apparently still felt solidarity with their rulers; they did not revolt, but cleared the wreckage and built again. In Thera, *c.* 1520, a volcanic eruption buried the town in lava (its people had fled in time); and *c.* 1480 there was a huge consequent disaster. Probably the volcanic cone collapsed, causing tidal waves greater than those of Krakatoa in A.D. 1883. Coastal sites in Crete suffered fearful damage. Many were abandoned; but Knosós, on its rising ground, survived again. It grew and spread, with its two-storey, flat-roofed houses, to a size comparable to the great cities of Babylonia. With its harbour-town of Amnisós, Evans conjectured a population of about 100,000 souls.

The basis of so much prosperity and such a population was not only the agriculture of a great island at peace, but a far-flung trade. Cretan goods reached Syria and Egypt (whence we can date Middle Minoan phases with some accuracy; e.g. M.M. II metal vases in Egypt under Amenemhat II, 1929–1895, and 'eggshell' fine pottery in a tomb sealed *c.* 1840). Westward, they reached Ischia, off the Bay of Naples, and the Lipari islands; western metal was no doubt still a magnet. But the closest contacts, especially after about 1600, were with the Greek mainland.

Here, 'rich Mycenae' too owed its wealth clearly not only to agriculture but to position. Its kings were middlemen on a route to Europe; and the wealth which they took with them to the grave is truly amazing. Already in the earlier shaft-graves (the more recently discovered grave-circle, outside the later walls of the fortress) there were ornaments of gold, silver and electrum (the alloy of gold and silver); silver and bronze jugs and vases, bronze swords and daggers with gold and ivory handles; while an electrum death-mask in one grave is the first of a series. After 1600, in the grave-circle which Schliemann discovered (perhaps graves of a new dynasty), the wealth is even greater and the art, as in the ivories and the inlaid dagger-blades – linked spirals, silver lilies, on one blade a whole lion-hunt – is more delicate. Pottery-painting goes over completely to Cretan styles; palaces were probably (Thebes at least gives us direct evidence) already frescoed, like the best houses in Thera before the disaster, and we may suspect the hands of Cretan artists in the metal-work, as in the bull-hunting scenes on the famous cups found at Vaphío near Sparta.

But Mycenaean Greece was no Cretan colony. The kings were of another race; taller – one, from the earlier grave-circle, stood well over six feet; bearded and moustached, as in the fine death-mask from the later circle, in contrast to the clean-shaven Minoans. Unlike the Cretans, they valued ornaments of the northern amber, probably thought, because of its electrical qualities, to have magic virtue. They rode to war or to hunt in horse-drawn chariots, known in Crete only later; and scenes of war or hunting were carved in relief on standing stones over their shaft-graves; a fashion unknown in Crete, and the first monumental stone sculpture in Greek lands.

Through Greece, influences from the near east reached bronze-age Europe. In central Europe, through which ran the amber-route (used no doubt also for goods less easy to identify), there had arisen 'higher barbarian' cultures, dominated by warlike chiefs, trading east, west, north and south along the great rivers. A bronze helmet from Brandenburg resembles one, perhaps Mycenaean, from Knosós of around 1425. Whether by central Europe or (more probably) by the western Mediterranean, Egyptian blue faience beads reached bronze age

Wessex. On Salisbury Plain, a chief's grave contained an inlaid sceptre 'paralleled only', says Professor Piggott, 'in one of the early shaft-graves' of Mycenae. 'In Britain too,' he adds, 'the final monument of Stonehenge, with its architectural competence and sophistication, is best explained in terms of the momentary introduction of superior skills from an area of higher culture, which in the circumstances can hardly be other than Mycenae.' This, however, is disputed by Professor Colin Renfrew and others on the ground that carbon-14 datings make the culmination of the Wessex culture older than the Mycenaean; which is conclusive if there are no unknown factors complicating Carbon-14 dating.

Thus Crete and the mainland stood face to face, headed, we may guess, the one by the priest-king of Knosós, now lord of the island, the other by the king of Mycenae, *primus inter pares*; his social 'peers' being, as long after in Homer, the lords of Tiryns, Pylos, Lakedaimon (Sparta), Thebes, Orchomenos, and other baronies. The mainland had access to the riches of the virgin north; Crete, until the mainlanders took to the sea, monopolized the trade with Egypt and the Levant. Across the water they also interchanged their own products; for Mycenae, after absorbing the lessons of Minoan art and perhaps many craftsmen, was not slow to develop the export of her own wares to Crete. The argument that bronze-age kings would not concern themselves with trade is not valid; they were very much concerned with the tolls that could be levied on it, and with precious goods, and with war materials. Personal and diplomatic relations must often have been close, as they were between Egyptians and Hittites and other kings of the east. Islanders and mainlanders were trade partners, trade rivals, of different traditions, and not necessarily friends.

Among the differences we may infer, from the visible remains and the literary evidence of later times, two contrasting religions; no necessary source of enmity, since men had not yet been taught to hate each other's religions, but still significant. That of the mainlanders, as of the Arabian and northern herdsmen, we may infer was patriarchal. After assimilating many local gods, and having then been reduced to order by the epic poets, it became the familiar Olympian polytheism. Head of the family was Father Zeus, a sky-god, whose messenger was the rainbow, his weapon the thunderbolt, and his home on the highest mountain, Olympos in the ancestral home in Thessaly; all other gods were subordinate to him, though just how subordinate was uncertain. But the ancient agrarian religion of the farmers was far from dead. It survives, present but not conspicuous, in Homer, who sang for warrior noblemen; and it emerges again in history exactly when the farmers themselves gained political importance (p. 125). Annually celebrated, vitally important for the crops on which all depended, was the return of Persephone, daughter of the Great Mother, carried off into the underworld for half the year by the dark god Hades. In many places, as at Eleusis in Attica, where it was in classical times revealed as a Mystery to the initiated, there was also a Divine Birth, that of the daughter's Son. At Mycenae itself, it is possible that the divine triad of Mother, Daughter and daughter's Son is represented in an exquisite little ivory group, discovered in 1939, which is one of the treasures of the Athens National Museum. But in Minoan Crete, so far as we can see from works of art, the Olympian system is absent; the Great Goddess is the chief deity, and a young god, perhaps her son, perhaps her consort, like Adonis 'the Lord' in Syria, is subordinate to her. In Crete in classical times, we are told, the Birth and the preservation of the divine Child from enemies who would destroy him were mimed annually as part not of a mystery for initiates but of a public liturgy. It was this young god whom, as the chief male deity, the first Greeks in Crete called Zeus; a scandal to religious Greeks later. For this 'Cretan Zeus', like Adonis, was a Dying God, and Cretans pointed out not only his birthplace but also his tomb.

There may have been a colossal statue of the Great Mother in the palace at Knosós, mainly in painted wood; for what seem to be bronze locks of hair were found in a hall there, along with masses of charred wood. The hall was decorated with high reliefs in plaster, representing sports, especially the (probably sacred) bull-leaping game. But only small statuettes of her have been preserved. Other Cretan religious symbols were bulls' horns and the double-axe, both common in decoration. *Labrys*, as we have seen, was a word meaning 'axe', used still in Karia in historic times, and the sanctuary of a war-god there was called Labraunda. Probably the word *Labyrinth*, which the Greeks preserved with the meaning of a maze, is the same word, the name of the palace of Knosós, and meant Place of the Double Axe.

Already in Middle Minoan Crete, says Childe, 'the distinction between province and metropolis becomes prominent. The provincial potters of eastern Crete could not compete with the experts employed in the palaces . . . in turning out polychrome ware of eggshell thinness.' The palace of Knosós in 'M.M.I' consisted of a number of free-standing blocks round a central court; it already had its celebrated main drainage system. In the following Minoan period, after a slight re-building, the blocks were linked up into one vast, rather amorphous, 'labyrinthine' complex, with light-wells to serve its internal rooms and corridors; and here and at Phaistós (now, we may guess, the southern or winter residence of a dynasty ruling the whole island) the court lived in a refined luxury hardly to be paralleled west of China, before our era. The finest rooms were probably those, now lost, on the upper floors, reached by the splendid Grand Staircases, and extending above the range of magazines, where the huge oil-jars of Knosós stood and still stand; but a good idea of Minoan comfort may be obtained from the secluded little apartment east of the Great Court, which Evans christened 'the Queen's Megaron'; a 'drawing-room', open on one side to a light-well, its walls decorated with a fresco of blue dolphins and fish, and probably another of dancing-girls, with its private bathroom adjoining and flushable water-closet down a passage. Water-supply was laid on with much ingenuity; the lengths of clay pipe tapered, so that the outgoing end of each fitted into the intake end of the next, with a raised collar to prevent it from slipping too far and splitting its neighbour. Water may even have been led uphill in places, to 'find its level'. Gullies to lead rain-water off down the east slope (where, Evans suggested, there may have been the palace laundry) conduct it down in a series of short paraboloid curves, so that it falls in its natural trajectory down each one, rather than rushing straight and uncontrollably down the slope. The contrast with later Greeks, whose sanitation was elementary, is very marked.

Fragments of fresco, preserved in the Heraklion museum but many with colours now sadly faded, may still be studied in careful restorations on the palace walls, and enable us to see its inhabitants: ladies with their flounced skirts, puffed sleeves and open bosoms; men in loin-cloth only (a cloak could be worn out of doors in cold weather), with tight belt and boots. The best preserved is the famous Cup-Bearer, with his curly hair and his seal strapped on his wrist; he could be a modern Cretan. The cup which he carries is like some of those borne by foreign bringers of gifts to Pharaoh, represented in the tomb-paintings of officials of the XVIIIth Dynasty. Other large vessels which they carry reproduce the shapes of the little Vaphío cups, or of a fine bull's-head cup also found, carved in steatite, in Crete. The caption to the latest of these Egyptian paintings, from the tomb of Rekhmire, closed about 1450, reads 'Coming in peace of the great ones of Keftiu [and ?] the isles [or 'coasts'] of the Green Sea'. Some differences in the style of their loin-cloths from those of the Minoan paintings, and the presence of some vases also of Asian and Syrian shapes, have suggested doubts as to whether the Keftiu (cf. biblical Caphtor) are from Crete, or represent a kindred civilisation in Cilicia; but no such rival 'Caphtor' has been discovered, and the above-mentioned goods are Minoan; indeed identifiable as of the period, Late Minoan I.

2 KING MINOS, AND THE
LINEAR B TABLETS OF KNOSÓS

Homer, as was said above, knew traditions of a great king Minos of Knosós. He 'reigned for nine seasons, and held familiar converse with great Zeus'; a priest-king, apparently, who like Moses 'knew God face to face'. Homer puts him two generations before the fall of Troy, which would date him about 1250; but this should not be pressed. Epic tradition often runs together stories of different ages; the German heroic cycle, dating from the fall of the Roman Empire, brings Eormenric the Goth (fourth century), Attila (fifth) and Theodoric (early sixth) into the same story. Minos, the law-giver of Crete, whose brother Rhadamanthys became one of the judges of the dead, must surely be connected with Crete's greatest days, before 1400. Later tradition also associated him with the earliest Aegean sea-power, a 'thalassocracy' which suppressed pirates, 'naturally', says Thucydides, 'so that his revenues might come in better'. Eight places called Minoa – two in Crete, two on the mainland coast, three in the Cyclades and one in Western Sicily – were thought to preserve his name. It all fits in well with the facts of Knosós' widespread trade and that, while so wealthy, it could remain unfortified.

It remains a disputed question: Was Minos a Greek? Evans thought of him as a pre-Hellenic 'true-Cretan', of a race still extant in parts of the island in Greek times; but mainland archaeologists, notably A. J. B. Wace, who did much work at Mycenae, have produced evidence for counter-influence of the mainland upon the island culture, even before 1400. (Archaeologists, according to the field of their main interest, have appeared quite capable of developing a Minoan or a Mycenaean patriotism; we note also that Evans and Wace, in this and other disputes, received the almost unanimous support of their respective universities, Oxford and Cambridge.) It appears quite possible, on the archaeological evidence alone, that some of the masterful Greek 'heroes' had infiltrated Cretan as well as Peloponnesian society and taken over the government. But there was no catastrophe to make a break in the sequence of remains, and the intimate mutual influence across the water makes it impossible to be positive.

The matter is settled in favour of Greek rulers at Knosós if we accept two premises, both connected with the writing in which the scribes of the palace kept their detailed accounts. (There is no evidence that it was used for literature.) The syllabic writing, known as Linear A, used in 'M.M.' times, gives place in 'L.M.' to Linear B; and it was this script which

Michael Ventris, after preliminary work by many scholars, deciphered, finding, to his own surprise, that it yielded Greek. Ventris' hypothesis produced striking positive results on some tablets unknown to him when he formed it; e.g. the syllables *ti-ri-po-de*, 'tripods', on a tablet with a sketch or ideogram of three-footed pots, from Pylos on the mainland; *qe-to-ro*, where the numeral *four* would make sense (*quattuor*?! – whereas later Greek lost the Q-sound); *i-qo* (*equus*?!) and *o-no,* 'horse' and 'ass', on a Knosós tablet with a drawing of equine heads. There are still many difficulties; *inter alia*, if the new script was introduced in order to write the Greek language, it is striking that it fits it rather badly. Nor, indeed, does it fit 'Minoan' well; e.g. the *-nth-* termination has to be written *ni-to*. The 'early Greek' of the translations proposed for some texts is odd, in the appearance or non-appearance of the W-sound, which was still known to Homer, but disappeared later. Nevertheless, it is agreed by nearly all scholars who have worked on it that the Ventris decipherment represents an important 'breakthrough', leading to good readings of many texts, though much work (just as in the early stages of the decipherment of Egyptian or Hittite) remains to be done. It may therefore be assumed that the language really is Greek.

The famous tripod-tablet from Pylos

But there is also a controversy about the date of the Knosós tablets. It appears that Evans and his professional assistant, Duncan Mackenzie, both at first believed, from the context in which the tablets were found, that they belonged to the period after 1400; but that later they came to believe that Minoan writing, a startling discovery when first made, must date from the most flourishing days of the palace, and not from its later, impoverished period. (It is now also clear that Evans over-stressed the impoverishment of the years after

1400.) Both he and Mackenzie seem to have come to believe that some of their observations, made during the excavations of 1900 and recorded in their log-books at the time, were wrong. Now Linear B (or, as they are also called, Mycenaean) tablets have since been found both at Mycenae and, in greater plenty, at Pylos. They are securely dated about 1200; and they are identical in script and 'spelling' or word-groups with those from Knosós. This would be more natural if they were contemporary than if they were 200 years later. In favour of Evans's published second thoughts, it is pointed out that the tablets owe their preservation to having been hard-baked (like those of Pylos) in a conflagration, which burnt the palace over them. But, it is pointed out by archaeologists of today, while there was such a conflagration at Knosós about 1400, no later fire, such as must be postulated in support of the later date, has left recorded traces. The controversy has, unfortunately, generated some heat of its own. Most specialists, remain, however, convinced that the Knosós tablets date, at latest, from the early fourteenth century.

3 THE FALL OF KNOSÓS

Be that as it may, the palace of Knosós in the late fifteenth century was at the height of its wealth and luxury; but there are also some signs which we, with hind-sight, can recognize as ominous. The trade with Syria wilts, though it is kept up with Egypt. The civilisation is growing more warlike, or at least more aware of war. Swords, spears and helmets appear more commonly. The horse, used for war-chariots, seems to have been introduced only in L.M.I; a seal-impression with a large horse superimposed upon a many-oared boat perhaps commemorates the event. Was it introduced by Greeks? The art itself, at the height of its luxury, begins to call to mind the somewhat over-used word 'decadent'; the luxuriating plant-ornament on the great palace-style vases becomes almost rococo; and worse, both at Knosós and Phaistós, some vases begin to grow knobs and 'ornamental' excrescences, apparently for no other reason than to demonstrate virtuosity; in fact, as a status-symbol. One is reminded of the prostitution of wonderful technical skill in some late Venetian glass. The gulf between governing class and people yawns wider; indeed, the last palace style, Late Minoan II (c. 1450–1400), has proved, since Evans named it, to be a style peculiar to Knosós and unknown in the rest of the island. Such has been the artistic prelude to disaster in more than one wealthy monarchy. Of the social situation, we have perhaps a hint in some fragments of a fresco, in which a young captain leads a file of spearmen who are coal-black. Are they Nubians, slave mamelukes bought from Pharaoh by a 'Minos' who can no longer trust his own subjects?

There is no evidence whatever of disaster foreseen; for example, still no fortifications. In the fifteenth century, Knosós seems to have planted colonies abroad, from Kythera to Milētos and Rhodes; but in Rhodes a mainland, Mycenaean settlement appears at Ialysos, about 1450, and the Minoan afterwards declines. Is Mycenae, already exporting to Knosós and to Egypt, growing restive in the embrace of the Minoan octopus?

Greek legend told of a Minos who destroyed Nisa, near later Megara, and forced Athens, for the murder of a Cretan prince, to yield tribute of youths and maidens to be fed to the monstrous Minotaur (which means literally, simply Bull of Minos), housed in the Labyrinth. Is it a mythologized reminiscence of the truly 'labyrinthine' palace (especially as it must have seemed to simple mainlanders), and of a tribute of young people to 'make sport' in the bull-leaping game? It used to be thought that perhaps the end of the matter was that the mainland turned against Crete, as in some late and rationalised versions of the Theseus story. In these, Theseus of Athens, after killing the Minotaur and escaping, built ships secretly in his other kingdom of Troizen and invaded the island and killed the king's son in the gate of the palace. Minos himself had meanwhile been murdered (so Herodotos heard from the Cretan aborigines of Praisos) on an expedition to Sicily. But Evans, after careful examination of the ruins, and with experience of earthquakes locally, came to the belief that it was an earthquake which once more destroyed the palace, and was followed by an uprising of 'submerged elements within the island'. If the Late Minoan dynasty was Greek, this would be a rising of the native Cretans against them; but there is no hint of that in the tradition. What is certain is that the palace was not only burnt – that can easily follow an earthquake, when beams fall across cooking fires – but thoroughly looted of all gold and silver. And there is a hint of invaders at least taking advantage of the catastrophe, in the fact that practically all the provincial coastal settlements were burnt and looted at about the same time.

Whether or not they took part in the destruction, it was Mycenae and the mainland which profited by it. Mycenae received a consignment of blue faience marked with the royal names, in the usual 'cartouche', of Amenhotep III (c. 1411– 1375); perhaps a trace of diplomatic relations. In the short-lived capital of his son, Amenhotep IV (1375–1360) – the monotheist 'heretic Pharaoh', who changed his name to Ikhnaton and moved to a new city at Tell-el-Amarna – were found fragments of much Mycenaean pottery, and such Cretan as appears is of the more chastened style characteristic of Knosós, after the sack (L.M. III A). This is the best evidence for dating the catastrophe about, or soon after, 1400.

4 MYCENAE AND THE HEROIC AGE

Mycenaean trade and colonisation now burst out into the Levant, as though with the fall of Knosós an impediment had been removed. Cyprus, hitherto rather a backwater despite its wealth in copper, suddenly receives mature Mycenaean culture *en bloc*, apparently by colonisation; it has been Greek ever since. Princes of Cyprus built themselves courtyarded palaces in the Aegean style, where their descendants still lived long after this way of life had disappeared from Greece. Trade became active again with the south coast of Asia Minor and with north Syria, where that of Crete had wilted, and mainland Greek merchants even resided in the Syrian city of Ugarit (Ras Shamra). The importance of Cyprus at this time reminds one of that which it had again after the Crusades. In the west,

Mycenaeans may have taken over the Cretan *pieds-à-terre* on Lipari and Ischia (p. 35) (the *facts* are simply that pottery of both kinds is found there). Signs of what looks like colonisation appear in southern Sicily and near the 'heel' of Italy, with considerable quantities of pottery and the appearance near Syracuse and Agrigento of domed tombs, such as chieftains were now using on the Greek mainland.

At home the principal chiefs reigned in considerable splendour, imitated, so far as their means allowed, by local lords, now in every lowland area of the mainland, and also in the western isles, Kephallenia, Ithaca (small, but with a fine harbour) and the all-but-island of Leukas. The centre of every palace was a hall or *megaron*, with pillared porch at one end and a central hearth, surrounded by four pillars which presumably supported a louvred roof over the smoke-hole. The bathroom was normally near the front door, so that, as in the epic tradition, the master of the house or his guests might be bathed on arrival. Its stone floor, slanting to a drainage-hole in the corner, is well seen at Tiryns. Around grew up a complex of store-rooms, quarters for servants and the chief's companions or housecarles, chariot-sheds, sometimes across the front courtyard past the altar of Zeus of the House; but none of them approached in size the Labyrinth at Knosós. The domed 'beehive' tombs in which kings and chiefs were now buried (a tradition perhaps descended from the rock-cut tombs of the Cyclades) increased in size and splendour. They were cut into a hillside, approached by an unroofed passageway or *dromos*, and roofed with skilfully constructed though keystoneless vaults. There is a fine example at the Minyan Orchomenos; but none approaches for splendour the largest one at Mycenae, built perhaps *c*. 1330, with its well-fitting ashlar masonry; its dome is forty feet high, and the lintel-stone of its door calculated to weigh about 100 tons. Too conspicuous to escape notice, it was looted in early Greek times, and later Greeks, mistaking its purpose, called it the Treasury of Atreus. Some moderns have called it the Tomb of Agamemnon, but that is an equally baseless guess.

Outside the citadel at Mycenae (not only the most important

site, but the one most intensively explored) were the houses of a prosperous *bourgeoisie*. One had a pottery store; others have yielded tablets with inventories, like those of the palaces, in Linear B script.

Mycenaean culture extended only later to the Cyclades; but there was some trade with 'Troy VI', now a fine and considerably enlarged castle, which drew riches presumably from trade between Europe and Asia, and between the Black Sea, where there are a few Asianic-looking names (Odessos, Salmydessos) and the Aegean. In Crete, now certainly under Greek lords at the chief centres, there was reconstruction, and some survival of Minoan religious traditions; but Crete never regained the lead. She still had her natural and human resources, but she had lost her 'special position'.

This is essentially the age to which Greek legend looks back; legend preserved partly in Homer's epics, partly in later authors who drew extensively on epics now lost. The 'map' is essentially the same. Every place important in Homer's list of the contingents at Troy has yielded Mycenaean and usually palatial remains; Mycenae more important than Tiryns or Argos; Pylos important, though its very site was forgotten later; Boiotia important, Athens (only one of many Mycenaean sites in Attica) not very; Crete important, but less so than Mycenae; Rhodes and Kos, outposts, Troy and Lesbos alien, Cyprus in 'diplomatic relations'. Even many features of Homeric life appear in Mycenaean culture, or of that culture in the poems; the chariots, the porched 'halls' with other buildings round about; though the hall in which Odysseus fights, using his bow, against several scores of suitors, is a product of epic imagination. The long leather shield, reaching to the feet, is familiar from Minoan and Mycenaean art; the round shield, covered with bronze, appears later, like the Homeric slashing sword; but both might have been observed on battlefields by about 1250. Homer is aware of the contrast, and once depicts two heroes in a fencing-match, using the contrasted shields.

On the other hand, there are also great differences. Mycenaean chiefs buried their dead, with costly grave-goods; Homer's heroes invariably use cremation, followed by urn-burial of the ashes under a barrow, which may be marked by a standing stone. This rite is also known from archaeology, but only from the iron age, after the splendours of Mycenae had passed away. It appears that the epics are indeed based on a real, continuous tradition, handed down from Mycenaean times, but that, being an oral tradition, it has not only become contaminated with folk-tales and marvels in the interests of entertainment, but also has unconsciously assimilated the customs and equipment of daily life to those of successive poets' and reciters' own times. Only the story, and sometimes whole passages of traditional verse, passed on with little change, have prevented a change out of all recognition. The same has happened in other ages. The *Nibelungenlied* has turned dark-age warriors into medieval knights. Likewise in art, King Arthur or Joshua or Goliath will wear medieval armour; but David will still have his sling; that was part of the story; and in like manner Ajax (Aias) in Homer has still his famous leather shield 'like a tower'; one of the two standard Mycenaean shapes, a rectangle with sides curved back. One feature of the bronze age that has all but disappeared in Homer is the art of writing – though a letter 'on a folded tablet' is mentioned once, in the old story of Bellerophon. It was essential to the story; it included the message, 'Please execute bearer'. And if we may trust the picture of Mycenaean society derived from readings of the Linear B tablets, especially those of Pylos, not only the economics of Mycenaean society but its social organization was of a surprising and entirely un-Homeric complexity.

5 THE SEA-RAIDERS

The cause which led to the simplification, or in other words the decline and fall, of Mycenaean civilisation, is not in doubt; it was war. The mainland Greeks had been warlike from the first; and with the removal of whatever restraint may have been imposed by Cretan sea-power, it became altogether too tempting to supplement the revenues gained from 'protection' of trade by quicker if riskier gains from sheer piracy. Gradually the seas first, and then the land, became too unsafe for trade to survive. The trade that had brought Mycenaean pottery to Lipari, Ischia and Sicily ceases by about 1300; Troy received less of it thereafter than formerly. In the Levant, already in the time of Amenhotep III, before 1375, piracy was a serious nuisance; a king of Alasiya (Cyprus) writes to Pharaoh denying that any of *his* people were concerned in the depredations of the Lukki, or promising, alternatively, that if any *are* proved to have taken part, they shall be punished. Actually, he says, the Lukki make annual descents on one of his ports too. The Lukki are pretty certainly the Lykians of Homer, occupying the coats east of Karia. They are in touch with Greece in the *Iliad*; it is to their court that King Proitos sends Bellerophon in order to get rid of him, with the 'many baleful signs on a folded tablet' above-mentioned.

One of the great powers of the east in the Mycenaean age was that of Khatti: the Hittite Empire, which dominated Asia Minor and in the days of the pacific Pharaoh Ikhnaton, more interested in religion than in empire, overran north Syria. It is in the archives of the Hittite capital, Khattu-sas, near the modern Turkish village of Boghaz-keui, that we find our first contemporary reference to Mycenaean Greece. For Greece, with its 'High King' at Mycenae, is almost certainly to be recognized in a kingdom apparently in the west and connected with the sea; the kingdom of Ahhiawa, earlier once called Ahhaïwa, whose name recalls that of the Akhaiwoi (in our texts, Achaioi), Homer's most frequent name for the Greeks of the Trojan War. The king of Ahhiawa is called 'brother' by the Hittite king; that is, he was an independent monarch. He is not necessarily recognized as equal in power; Pharaoh uses the same term in addressing the king of Alasiya (Cyprus). A character named Piyamaradus has committed depredations in the region round Millawanda or Milawata; possibly Miletos, where Minoan Cretans and later Mycenaean Greeks had settled. The Lukki appealed to the Hittite king to help them, as also to one Tawagalawas (is this the Greek name Ete[w]okles?), who was in the neighbourhood and was known to the king of Ahhiawa. The king of Ahhiawa ordered Atpas, his agent at Millawanda, to hand over Piyamaradus; but when the Hittite king reached the city, Piyamaradus had escaped by sea. The king (not named; so datable any time under the empire) now requests the king of Ahhiawa to extradite Piyamaradus, or failing that to see that he stays inside Ahhiawan territories.

Names known from Homer may also be recognized, some more, some less confidently, in Egyptian records. When the young Rameses II tried to recover Syria, he was met by a Hittite imperial army including contingents with names known from Homer as Trojan allies, among them the Dardanoi, whose name survives in the Dardanelles, and Kilikes, who are in the Troad in Homer and only migrate to the historic Cilicia later.

After 1300, here too conditions change for the worse. Less Mycenaean pottery abroad indicates shrinking trade; Cyprus develops its own provincial style; and at Mycenae itself vase-painting grows slovenly. The palaces still contained considerable stores of treasure; it has been observed that Homer's heroes sometimes estimate it in terms of how many generations it would last. The late Mycenaean world was living on its capital, and to Homer's heroes, among whom 'sacker of cities' was a title of honour, the best way of increasing one's wealth appeared to be to seize someone else's. 'Cattle may be had for the raiding,' says Achilles quite casually; adding that life, on the other hand, comes only once. The 'Heroic Age', like the heroic ages of other countries, was an age of brutal and destructive war. Homer loved the stories and admired the heroic virtues of courage and loyalty; but he knew quite well how brutal it was. His Trojan Hector expects that if the city falls his wife will be enslaved and her baby thrown off the battlements; and Odysseus, hearing a minstrel sing of his own name and deeds (in fact, of the Wooden Horse and the sack of Troy) in a foreign court, where his face was unknown,

broke down and wept, as a woman weeps, falling down and embracing her dear husband, who has fallen defending city and people ... when she sees him dying, gasping for breath, and falls upon him and cries aloud; but the foe behind her beat her with their spears on back and shoulders, and lead her into slavery, to have toil and grief, and her face is marred with most piteous woe.

Another Hittite file tells how Attarissiyas or Attarsiyas, 'a man of Ahhiā', campaigned in Karia with 100 chariots as well as foot-soldiers, expelling a prince Wadduwattas (Adyattes), who fled to the Hittite king. The king gave him another fief; but later Wadduwattas joined forces with Attarsiyas, and they attacked Alasiya. From archaeology, a second wave of Mycenaean immigrants does appear to have overrun Cyprus and the plain of Tarsus by violence about 1200 B.C. Some have identified this raider with Atreus, father of Homer's Agamemnon, in a supposed uncontracted form of his name, 'Atresas', 'Undismayed'; but he is not called *king* of Ahhia, and others have compared his name to that of Perseus (Pterseus, 'Sacker'), or Teiresias! The fact is that we do not know. But the amount of coming and going across the Aegean does suggest that the legend that Pelops, father of Atreus, came from Asia Minor to give his name to the Peloponnese and to supplant the House of Perseus at Mycenae, could preserve a fact.

In 1221 a name, K-W-SH, which *could* be vocalised as 'Akaiwasha' appears (for the only time) in Egyptian records; these and other sea-peoples, including Lykians and T-r-sh (Hittite Taroisa, Trojans?), joined with Libyans in an attempt to invade Egypt, only to be slaughtered by Egyptian archers and chariotry in the battle of the Horns of the Earth. (Was it near Hellfire Pass?) From a detail of how the Egyptians counted the bodies – 6,500 Libyans and 2,500 sea-raiders – by bringing in detachable portions thereof, it rather appears that the K-W-SH were circumcised; which is surprising, if they were European Achaioi.

It is certainly not impossible that Achaians took part in such a raid. Odysseus in Homer, passing himself off in Ithaca as a Cretan prince who had fallen on evil days, says that he had taken part in a small (nine-ship) raid on the Delta, and been captured there. The Pharaoh Merenptah, successor of the long-lived Rameses II, describes these raiders as hungry men, 'fighting to fill their bellies daily'. There had lately been a famine in the Hittite Empire; Egypt, now at peace with that state, sent shiploads of grain to help to relieve it. Too late, the civilised powers, which had weakened one another in their old wars, had drawn together; for about 1200 the Hittite archives come to an end. The great empire fell; when we next have information, centuries later, Phrygians, from the Balkans, hold the central plateau; and the Hittite kings and mercenaries (like Uriah) in the Old Testament come only from city-states in their old province in Syria.

About 1190 Egypt had to face the consequences of the collapse.

'The isles were restless, disturbed among themselves,' says a great inscription of Rameses III on the temple-walls of Medinet Habu: 'They poured out their people all together. No land stood before them, beginning from Khatti, Cilicia, Carchemish, Arvad and Alasya; they destroyed them and assembled in one camp in the midst of the Amorite country.'

Rameses defeated first another attack from Libya, supported by sea-raiders, and then, in two great battles, on sea and land, the main force; a migration of peoples, bringing their women and children in heavy, solid-wheeled ox-carts, and supported by a fleet of ships with crows'-nests on their masts, crowded with warriors in horned helmets or with feather crowns, with round shields and flexible body-armour, curiously like a primitive form of that of Roman legionaries. But they were outmatched once more by the deadly Egyptian archery, as we see in the vivid relief-sculptures on the temple walls. The Egyptians had also fighting for them as mercenaries men similarly armoured, the Shardana, themselves one of the sea-peoples, who may, it seems from the similarity of name and of their horned helmets, have settled in Sardinia and produced the stone towers and bronze statuettes of the later *nuraghe* culture. Among the invading peoples, with others less convincingly identified, appear the D-n-y-n, perhaps Homer's Danaoi – a name which he uses almost interchangeably with Achaioi – and a name which also appears later in Cilicia, round Tarsus. The sub-Mycenaean kingdom there is called, in a bilingual inscription, Hittite and Phoenician, D-n-y-n and also 'House of

Mopsos'; and Mopsos is a hero and prophet known also to Greek poetry. But the most famous name is that of P-l-s-t, the Philistines, who were then settled on the coast under Egyptian supervision; who gave Palestine its Greek name; who later, now independent, warred with chariots and armoured men (Goliath's armour is Homeric) against the Israelites of the hill-country, and whose pottery is a remote but recognizable descendant of Mycenaean. Their name, not certainly but in the opinion of many philologists, might be that of the Pelasgoi.

6 THE WARS WITH THEBES AND TROY

With the great sea-raids, all recorded contact between the Aegean and the east comes to an end for centuries; and the greatness of Mycenae ended about the same time. To the age of the sea-raids, it appears, we must assign the exploits which Greece remembered through epic poetry as the most famous achievements of the Heroic Age, and among the last: the sieges of Thebes and Troy. We cannot date them precisely. If the dates computed by Greek scholars for the fall of Troy (ranging from 1334 to 1127, with 1183 the most popular) were approximately correct, it was largely by luck; for the genealogies, by which those scholars bridged the Dark Age, were 'heraldically' linked up with the names of epic heroes and the sons of Hellen, the eponymous ancestor of the race. Those of the kings of Sparta (in two lines) seem to have enough authentic generations to take us back to about the ninth century, and thence to be poetically joined up to their heroic ancestor, Herakles; and to do it, their earlier generations are given the improbably long average length of thirty-nine years; Spartan reigns, in historic times, average about twenty-five. However, it seems reasonable to assign these wars to the age when Mycenae really was the leading city of Greece, and when the chief sites known from archaeology correspond closely to the chief places in the *Iliad*'s List of Contingents. Greek tradition may be perfectly right in saying that in the second generation after the siege of Troy, the heroic dynasties fell.

The expedition of the Seven against Thebes was traditionally a generation before that to Troy; as was the very much more mythical expedition of Jason and the *Argo* to the Black Sea (this tale seems to be a semi-rationalised version of a myth derived from a fertility ritual). Legend said that the Theban war started with a quarrel between the two sons of the ill-fated Oedipus, of the house of Kadmos, said to have come long before from the east. Polyneikes ('Much Strife'), driven out by his brother Eteokles ('True Glory'), resorted to the Achaians of the Peloponnese, who, nothing loth, set out to sack the city for him. They drove the Kadmeians within their walls, but then, attempting an assault with ladders, met with disaster, in which six of the seven champions, including Polyneikes, fell. The Kadmeians thereafter strengthened their walls; and indeed, in the thirteenth century, fortifications were being strengthened everywhere. The vast walls of Tiryns were completed then; at Mycenae the great eastern tower was added, and at each fortress a secret passage was excavated, running out under the walls to reach a secure water-supply from a spring. Nevertheless, against that stronger wall (as a hero of Argos, whose father was killed in the first expedition, reminds Agamemnon at Troy) the sons of the original Seven captured Thebes, while the remnant of the Kadmeians fled north. The natural result was that other and less civilised people moved in. Homer is remarkably consistent about this; he always refers to Kadmeians at Thebes in earlier times, but to Boiōtians at the time of the Trojan War. These send to Agamemnon's army large contingents of troops but only minor chiefs; they are newcomers, and their chiefs are not fully admitted to equality with the Achaian kings.

The war with Troy is placed a little later than the fall of Thebes; Diomedes fights in both. The poems still describe some peaceful intercourse with the Levant. Paris, 'on the same voyage, from which he brought back Helen', visited Sidon and brought back rich eastern robes for his mother; and Menelaos with Helen visits Egypt in peace just after the war. He brings back from there 'two silver bath-tubs', among other riches; and Helen a silver work-basket that ran on wheels and (entirely in character) a supply of nēpenthē, the celebrated tranquilliser.

The Sixth City of Troy, according to the archaeological record, was ruined by an earthquake about 1300. Troy VIIa, which represents the immediate rebuilding, never achieved the same standards of life; but that does not imply (though it has been suggested) that it would not have seemed worth looting. It was still on the trade route to Europe; King Priam's allies come not only from Asia, as far as Karia and Lykia, but from Europe as far as the Vardar or Axios. What gives especially the impression of 'an abject, uncomfortable Troy', in Sir Denys Page's expression, looks like the direct result of preparations for war. There was squalor enough in London, when people slept in the Underground stations during the bombing. Page describes vividly the scene laid bare by Blegen's excavations: 'A network of unworthy lodgings spreads to the right and left and climbs inward over the foundations of the great houses of yesterday ... gloomy little bungalows, thin-walled, party-walled, one-roomed, barely furnished, backed on ... the fortification wall itself.' And what marks out the Seventh City most particularly is the extraordinary number, under every floor, of storage pits and bins. The country people have crowded into the fortress; every available yard of space is very properly occupied by shelters which, their residents hoped, would be temporary; and they brought their reserve grain inside the walls with them, while they could.

What relation the famous war bore to Hittite history we cannot say; one theory is that (discounting Homer's famous ten years) it took place when the Hittites were engaged in a known war, after 1250, against an eastern neighbour. There is even a mention, in the *Odyssey*, of an attempt to relieve Troy at the eleventh hour, by Eurypylos, a prince of the Kēteioi. If this is for earlier Greek Kāteioi, which is likely, it could actually be the name Khatti; and even the name Eurypylos could be a Hittite name, Urpalla. That the Greeks took Troy at all, we are reminded by M. I. Finley, it would be rash to claim as certain, when we remember that Charlemagne, as a matter of cold fact, won no victory and fought no Saracens at Roncesvalles. Homer himself tells us that the Achaians did not occupy Troy; on the contrary, having sacked it, they went home – some, like Agamemnon, to find their wives living with other men. The great war was not a colonising venture, but a viking raid. Aineias (Aeneas), a cousin of King Priam, was, according to a god, destined to rule in Troy when the invaders had gone. The final destruction of the city, according to a later Greek account, with which archaeology is entirely consistent, was due to a new wave of invaders from Thrace.

7 THE LAST MYCENAEANS AND THE DORIAN PROBLEM

The Mycenaean palaces themselves did not last much longer. For their fall, we should not blame the strain of the Trojan War in particular; rather, it was the continual indulgence in war in general; also, probably, the fact that the palace-people, the chiefs and their house-carles, had become so far removed from the peasantry that they could no longer trust them as soldiers. Thus they would be in a parlous plight if attacked by a tribal people, among whom every man was still a warrior. The tradition says that indeed, when attacked by rougher Greek-speakers, the Dorians, from their northern borders, led by Mycenaean exiles, they fell.

These exiles were said to have been descendants of Herakles, expelled long since by Herakles' jealous cousin Eurystheus of Mycenae, whose dynasty was then supplanted by Atreus. But Herakles is a much more mythical figure than Atreus or Agamemnon. Some tales told of him belong to a culture-hero; some may be of eastern origin. A Hittite seal, for example, shows a hero fighting a seven-headed monster, three of whose heads are severed, four still up and fighting (Herakles and the Hydra, located, with two more heads, at the waters of Lerna?). Possibly the whole story of the *Return* of the Herakleidai, requiring their previous expulsion, was invented to reconcile the claim of Dorian kings to descent from Herakles with traditions that he was born at Tiryns (or Thebes) in Achaian times.

They attacked first, it was said, before the Trojan War, by the Isthmus of Corinth. Here they were defeated and Hyllos, son of Herakles, was killed by the Arcadian king of Tegéa. They came again when Tisamenos ('Avenger'; the appropriately named son of Orestes, who avenged his father Agamemnon by slaying his mother) was king of Mycenae. This time they crossed the Corinthian Gulf in the west, to reach Messenia and Laconia; and Mycenae fell last, to an attack from the south. Tisamenos, in one version, survived to lead a migration of his people to the historical Achaia.

Archaeology supports some of these details. There *was* a Mycenaean wall across the Isthmus; also a fortress, Teichos Dymaiōn, near modern Patras; it was burned around 1200 B.C. So was the palace at Pylos, where oil stores seem actually to have exploded, blowing a wall over bodily; and so were the houses outside the walls at Mycenae. At Sparta a large settlement on the defensible ridge of Therapne (now much eroded), where later Greeks venerated Menelaos and Helen, suffered damage; and occupation ends on scores of Messenian and Laconian village sites, to be replaced by – nothing; a problem. Meanwhile, there *was* a Mycenaean migration to Achaia and Kephallenia.

This major disaster, contemporary with the catastrophes in the Levant, was not the end. In Argolis and at Sparta there was partial recovery; some final Mycenaean pottery is not without verve. Mycenaean life continued too in eastern Attica and the islands, from Euboia to Naxos, Rhodes and Kos; but in this phase, called Late Helladic IIIC, local art styles appear. Mycenae no longer dominates; and her own art was dispirited even before final disaster came, about 1100. Teichos Dymaiōn, refortified, fell again, and, at last, Mycenae citadel. The island sites were abandoned, and there was new migration to Crete and Cyprus. Argos survived, now practising individual cist-burial; the old family tombs required social stability.

But there are no visible traces of the invading Dorians; so much so that some recent writers have dismissed the invasion as a myth, postulating internal feuds and risings of the oppressed to destroy the palaces; or raiders who came, ravaged and went (where?); or a prolonged drought, after which the Dorians came into an empty land. But it is a strange (though not impossible) drought that depopulates rich Messenia and Laconia but not notoriously 'thirsty' Argos and the Cyclades; and the Dorians, so important in historic times but absent from Homer (save for one stray mention), were distinguished later not only by their dialect, with north-western connexions, but by a division, in cities from Rhodes to Sicily, into three 'tribes', the Hylleis, Pamphüloi and Dymānes; surely a characteristic of a 'nation' antedating the cities, rather than of insurgent serfs. Finally, if the south lay empty for many years, it is surprising that the Achaians did not move back into it. Rather, there were people there, who left little evidence for archaeology, but whom they did not want to meet. The Slavs in south Greece, after A.D. 600, are attested by history and by a scatter of place-names; but they left only destruction to mark their coming. The historic Dorians believed that they were a people long migrant, and had come last from Pindos, where a small classical Dōris represented those who stayed behind. If so, what would their prehistoric culture have been like?

Conspicuous among the people of those mountains today are trans-humant shepherds, who drive their flocks to the plains in winter and to high 'alps' in summer, reconditioning their round, thatched huts at each journey's end; the fine Greek Sarakatsanaioi and the Romanian-speaking Vlachs, post-Roman incomers from further north. For travelling, crockery is inconvenient. Leather bottles are better, and wooden cups, such as are still made by the Arcadians of Mount Mainalos. *If* the Dorians were like modern Pindos highlanders, they would not have made distinctive pottery nor built solid houses, until slowly, maybe grudgingly, they learned lowland ways; and their early camps, if ever detected, will not be found *in* the burnt ruins. As to metal, 'northern bronzes', including slashing swords and safety-pins for securing looser clothing, are found on Mycenaean sites even before the disaster; brought by soldiers of fortune? They are not numerous; most bronze of any sort gets melted down; and when *not* found in a Mycenaean context they are not closely datable. But we may claim that there is no ground for denying that the invasion is at least as 'historical' as the fall of Thebes or Troy; though a century is, as usual, foreshortened in folk-memory.

Doric spread overseas, still before the dawn of history, to Crete, Melos, Thera, Rhodes, Kos, Knidos and Halikarnassos; and it clearly came after an earlier form of Greek; for an archaic dialect, said to resemble the Mycenaean of Linear B, survived in inland Arcadia and in remote Cyprus. This makes sense if Doric broke a Mycenaean continuum, leaving its fragments only in a land that even Sparta could not conquer, and an island which the Dorians did not reach.

Athens alone on the mainland, she claimed with pride, out-rode the storm, harbouring exiled chiefs of Pylos. But it is found that *before* 1200 new people, using cist-graves and long, straight dress-pins, came into western Attica and Salamis. At Athens the lower town was abandoned in haste and panic; but the Acropolis held out, with access to water by a secret stair, ingeniously fitted between the north face of the rock and a huge, split-off flake. Now Athens did have a legend of an *early* invasion. Eleusis (in the west!) 'fought with Eumolpos against Erechtheus'; Thucydides mentions it as well known. Later writers add that Eumolpos headed a band of sea-raiders from Thrace; and if his name (Hellenized?) sounds unconvincing, he had a son, Immarados, which is not Greek.

Coming to terms, perhaps, Athens long after (*c.* 1065?) fought off a Dorian thrust from the Isthmus, though a new Dorian city, Megara, 'Big Houses', one of the few in Greece to bear a Greek name, was planted on her western border. Legend said that good King Kodros, descended from kings of Pylos, gave his life for the city. Having heard of an oracle given to the Dorians, that they would take Athens if they did *not* kill the king, he walked into a Dorian camp disguised as a woodcutter and got himself killed; evidence at least of ideas of sacred kingship, and of the merit of self-sacrifice.

Athens survived; moreover Athens survived *alone* in Attica.

There had been 'beehive' tombs, indicating local princes, at other Attic sites; but all were abandoned during the bad times. At the dawn of history Athens is already the unquestioned capital of an area of 2,500 km², one of the largest Greek states, and one where in the ninth century, after a dark-age 'low', population, indicated by the number of new settlements, increased rapidly. By this stubborn survival, the foundations of much future glory had been cemented.

POSTSCRIPTS:

Kadmos from the east (p. 54): The sensational find in 1963, in the burnt layer of the Kadmeian palace, of a collection of thirty-six Babylonian and other oriental seals, fourteen of them with cuneiform inscriptions, together with thirteenth-century Linear B tablets, indicates – although the owner probably could not read the seals, which are rather a miscellaneous collection – at least that some Kadmeian princes took a lively interest in oriental curios!

The cataclysm of Thera (p. 35): On proposals to connect this with the disappearance of legendary Atlantis, see note on Plato's account, p. 304.

CHAPTER 3

THE GREEK MIDDLE AGES

c. 1100–700 B.C.

1 THE DARK AGE

THE Dark Age is dark both in its poverty and in our ignorance
of it, which archaeologists are now working to remedy.
Palaces and writing had gone; but the techniques of daily life
survived, augmented c. 1000 B.C. by iron-working, introduced
probably from Cyprus. There had no doubt been a fall in
population; indeed, a poet, perhaps of Cyprus, who, after
Homer had written the *Iliad*, set out to write an 'introduction'
to it, on the beginnings of the war (it was called the *Cyprian
Lays*), said that it began because there were too many people
in the world. Mother Earth groaned under them, and Zeus
decided to ease her burden.... It is not impossible, either,
that the Mycenaean world, like imperial Athens and imperial
Rome, may have been weakened by epidemics, moving along
the trade-routes. Plagues have their place in the legends, too;
e.g. in the camp of the Achaians at Troy, and at Thebes in the
time of King Oedipus.

2 MIGRATIONS OVERSEA

However, there were enough people in Greece for even the
fugitives to carry out a notable work of colonisation. A sequel
to the coming of the Dorians was the Greek occupation of the
west coast of Asia Minor and of the islands, except a few in
the north Aegean which long remained Pelasgian. The coast
just south of the Troad (not occupied at first) and the island of
Lesbos were taken by migrants from northern and central
Greece, displaced by the incoming of Thessalians from the
north-west into historic Thessaly and of Boiotians, displaced by
the Thessalians, into historic Boiotia. Their dialect, called

61

Aiolic, is consistent with this tradition. The middle section, Ionia, was taken perhaps rather later by refugees from central Greece and the Peloponnese, who also occupied the Cyclades.

Ionia was to become for a time the most civilised and progressive region of the Greek world. Among its twelve cities (including those on the islands of Chios and Samos) were Miletos and Ephesos; Teos and Klazomenai on the central peninsula; and Smyrna in the north, which Ionians, under chiefs descended from the kings of Pylos, took from the Aiolians. One form of the tradition of Ionian origins represented their migration as an organized expedition, setting out from Athens, now recovered from the turmoil, with all the formalities observed by later Greek colonists; but Herodotos, who knew Ionia well, knew of less systematized traditions which made the founders a very mixed multitude. Even, he says, the founders of Miletos, 'who set out from the City Hall of Athens and consider themselves the most nobly-born of the Ionians – these very people brought no women with them, but took to wife Karian women, whose parents they had slain'. Greek tradition usually made these migrations an immediate consequence of the folk-wanderings on the Greek mainland.

Dorians, as we have seen, took to the sea in turn, and occupied Melos with its fine harbour, volcanic Thera, Rhodes, Kos and the adjacent islands, and the peninsular cities of Knidos and Halikarnassos, forming, with Rhodes and Kos, an Asian Dōris. And in Crete, Dorian bands took over Knosós and nearly all the coastal cities with their adjacent plains. Here they ruled as aristocracies, exacting tribute in kind from a peasantry long accustomed to servitude, whom they called Mnōïtes; a word in which some have seen a reminiscence of the name of Minos. Only in the east of the island, in hill-settlements, did some gallant Eteocretans ('True Cretans') still make an attempt, as the forms of their shrines show, to preserve Minoan ways. Here, at Praisos, was preserved the legend of how King Minos perished in Sicily and of the disasters that followed; and at Praisos too, far on in historic times, the classical Greek alphabet was used for inscriptions in a non-Greek language.

With the completion of these movements, the ethnic map of historic Greece had now taken shape.

3 THE CITY-STATES

Politically, classical Greece is a land much more minutely fragmented even than Greece in the bronze age. It is customary to blame the Greeks for their failure to form a national state or United States of Greece; though the record of the disunited national states of Europe hardly suggests that we are in a strong moral position for doing so. It must be added that our maps usually *under*emphasize the disunity of classical Greece, since the appearance of the Greek names of *regions*, such as Arcadia, Boiotia, Ionia, with boundaries drawn between them, but not between the cities within them, gives the impression to a superficial glance that these regions at least *are* states. Except Laconia, under the rule of Sparta, and Attica, they were not. Achaia contained twelve small *poleis* or cities, Phokis as many as thirty (we should call them rather 'walled villages'), Boiotia fourteen, some of which had over ten thousand inhabitants, no insignificant figure by Greek standards. Arcadia contained both walled cities and highland tribes. Even where, as in Boiotia, the communities not only shared in common worship and festivals, but developed a rudimentary federal organization, the 'cities' still sometimes fought each other.

The great factor which made for continued disunity – which made it possible for the defence of local autonomy always to triumph in the end over the attempts of the more powerful states to impose unity by force – was the nature of the country. Since Greece is not only a mountainous country but a *limestone* mountain country, by no means all moisture, other than that which evaporates, finds its way to the sea by way of rivers. Much finds its way downwards through swallow-holes or cracks in the limestone, after soaking through the surface earth and depositing in the process much silt, brought down from the mountains. In ancient times, when the mountains were forested, much of the rain-water, which now often descends in destructive floods from the bare hillsides, came down gently through the foliage and roots of the trees, to enrich the plains, flat-surfaced pockets of earth caught in folds of the rock; and these plains, unevenly distributed between the mountains of Greece, and filling only a small fraction of its area, were, even more than the sea, the economic basis of Greek life. The plains are fertile; when people speak of the infertility of Greece, they are referring, or should be referring, not to the quality of the agricultural land, but to the fact that its whole area is small in proportion to that of the peninsula, which is about the size of Scotland. When ancient Athenian writers themselves refer to Attica as 'thin-soiled' (as Thucydides does), they are writing at a time when the population had long since overflowed the limits of the plains, so that most Athenian farmers were farming hill-foot land, which was thin-soiled indeed.

Every considerable plain contained a city, or, if large enough, as in Boiotia, sometimes more than one. The cities were walled fortresses, occupying the best available site for defence which had adequate water-supply. Often a citadel on a mountain spur was the original *polis*, and from it, except in times of secure peace, men walked out daily to till their fields. Wars arose usually out of quarrels over border-lands; and in the early days too there was probably frequent need to repel raids by hungry highlanders or belated migrants. This accounts for the curious fact that in early Greek history chariots and, when horses that could carry a man were introduced, cavalry or rather mounted infantry were important in warfare. They were useless in the mountainous majority of the country; but that was not what mattered. What they were useful for was carrying armoured warriors – men of the richer families, who could afford both armour and horses – swiftly and untired over the plain, to repel raiders trying to lift cattle or reap the corn (as classical Greeks still sometimes did, under cover of an army) from its outlying portions. In many cities the ability to provide oneself with horse and armour was for a long time the minimum qualification for recognition as one of the 'best people' or *aristoi*.

The 'best people' belonged to families which had been on the scene early enough to possess good land, in the plain which was the reason for the city's existence, and the nearer the walls, the better for security. As population increased, poorer peasants (and who were they? Descendants of dependants of the old families, younger sons of younger sons, whom the estate could not support?) took up land farther away, sometimes too far away to come back to the city every night. If this happened, if such people formed outlying villages and took to living there, they dropped out of city society. People in town ceased to know them, and it ceased to be the custom (*nomos*, the original meaning of the Greek word for 'law') that they should attend town-meetings. They became known as *perioikoi*, 'dwellers round about'; there were also ruder words for them, such as 'sheepskin-wearers' and 'dusty-feet', applied to them by smart citizens in woven garments when they came into town. Other 'dwellers-around', in some places, were the inhabitants of smaller communities, originally independent, which had asked their more powerful neighbours for protection, or been defeated in border war themselves. It suited the more powerful cities, and was a good way of securing the home plain from raiders, to be surrounded by a ring of dependent communities, bound in alliance to 'have the same friends and enemies'. The old-established families with land near the city thus not only had the best land; they were also the best protected against trouble, and controlled or indeed consituted the full-citizen body. In these circumstances the gulf between richer and poorer farmers, the 'best families' and second-class citizens, tended to grow wide.

Another way of promoting regional security was for a group of neighbouring and more or less kindred communities to form a league, as in Phokis and Boiotia, for mutual protection, and such a league could discourage though not always prevent wars between its members. But the league itself still had outer frontiers, on which there might be trouble, especially through competition between these little power-blocks to dominate border communities. The history of Greek inter-state relations is largely a history of rival powers in search of security through imposing their will upon neighbours. Ultimately it became a rivalry of the most powerful cities, Athens, Sparta and for a time Boiotian Thebes, to dominate the Greek world. But no unity was found that way; for the walled cities were usually too strong to take by storm, and to form a siege and reduce an enemy by starvation meant keeping an army in the field, away from its own farms, for long periods. The distances over rough country between the plains also helped the relatively weak to survive. Ancient Greece never achieved political union.

Kingship, the universal form of government in Homer, had disappeared from most cities before the dawn of history, towards 700. With the collapse of trade, kings could no longer maintain a retinue of 'companions'. Where they remained, as at Argos and at Sparta (where there was the anomaly of two royal houses; some think, through a fusion between two Dorian bands), it was with limited powers. The typical governing body of a city at the end of the dark age is a Council of the 'Best Men', sometimes limited to the heads of families, which later Greeks thought extraordinary; sometimes, as at Corinth, all claiming descent from the last kings. The Council appointed executive officers, at first sometimes for life or for long periods, later usually for one year; and an assembly, or town-meeting of all warriors, might be called, as in Homer, chiefly to be told what the Best People had decided. The best position on the citadel, as at Mycenae and on the Acropolis at Athens, where there had once been a palace, was now usually occupied by a temple of the state's chief patron deity.

4 ATHENS AND GEOMETRIC ART

Athens, thanks to antiquarian researches by some Athenians in classical times, is the city where we have the best or at least most systematic account of the abolition of a monarchy. Reasoning back from the institutions of their own time, and making some use of oral tradition, which preserved some mythologized stories of ancient kings, the Athenian equivalents of King Lud, King Lear and King Arthur (not all *equally* mythical), these scholars 'restored' a 'history' preserved in such works as Plutarch's *Life of Theseus*. But when they describe the origins of the Nine Archons, the chief magistrates of early historic Athens, they are worthy of some respect. The first blow to the royal power is said to have been the *election* by the nobles, at a time when the king was not a great fighting man, of a separate War-Chief; and then, the decisive step, the appointment over the king of The Archon, whose title is a participial form and means Regent. The first Archon is said to have been named Medon; he held office for life, and his family continued to hold the position for some time. The king thus became a *roi fainéant*; but he continued to be the city's chief priest. With the usual conservatism of religion, it was felt that the gods were accustomed to a king, and that they might not like it if the city's prayers and sacrifices were not offered by someone bearing that sacred title.

Thus a 'king' still existed, even in classical, democratic Athens. For ceremonial purposes, he was the second man in the state; the Archon ranked over him, the War-Chief (striking evidence of the *civil* character of the Athenian state) third. The Archon was, especially, chief judge in law-cases concerning property; the king, in cases concerning religion, and also homicide – for blood-guilt unexpiated might incur the wrath of heaven, expressed in pestilence, as at Thebes in the Oedipus legend. The king's wife, still under the democracy, was called the queen, and had some religious duties; she was annually united to the vegetation-god Dionysos (represented probably by her husband, thought to be 'possessed' by the god) in the seasonal Sacred Marriage, celebrated for the fertility both of the crops and of the people; an interesting survival of prehistoric fertility-magic. In historic times, all these three were annually appointed, and there had been added, as population and judicial work increased, six Judges, Thesmothetai or Layers Down of the Law. The nine together were collectively called the Nine Archons or Rulers; the name of the Archon, the first citizen, was used for dating the year; and a king was chairman of the jury-court at the trial of Socrates.

Athens, already, early in the dark age, also took a leading part in the development of art. Probably before 1000 B.C. (though, as we have seen, precise dating is impossible) there was an artistic revolution. Vase-painters at Athens abandoned the decadent and slipshod imitation of late Mycenaean proto-types, and – almost overnight as it seems to us – went over to abstract pattern. Concentric circles are a favourite *motif*; a series of such patterns, bold and dark on the pale clay, may encircle the vase, decorating a broad band of its surface between two continuous dark bands; or concentric semicircles may 'hang' downwards from a dark band, or rise from it. Necks, shoulders and bases are most often singled out for decoration; otherwise the whole surface may be left plain, or encircled only by a single band or group of three narrow bands, about half-way up. New shapes are used, stable, symmetrical (*e.g.* deep cups with two small handles), very satisfactory to the eye. Though all is so simple, the very simplicity and formality are full of promise. From Athens, it seems, this new art spread rather rapidly, to Argolis, to southern Thessaly, to some of the islands. Athens definitely seems to have taken the lead; though, when the early iron-age art of some other regions has been more studied, the picture may be modified.

Through the next two or three centuries this proto-geometric pottery develops into a more elaborate style, the mature Geometric. The early simplicity is lost; it becomes a point of honour with painters to cover every inch of surface with decoration: cross-hatched triangles and lozenges ('diamonds'), squares and oblongs filled with chequer-board pattern minutely executed, or a continuing, square-cornered meander, the famous 'Greek key pattern'. But the sense of form and eye for pure design is as much in evidence as ever. Late in the series – not, it is thought, before the eighth century – animal figures, tiny, highly formalised and in solid black, begin to appear; and right at the end, perhaps not till after 750, just before the dawn of history, there appear on huge vases, between bands of the old geometric ornament, principal bands showing scenes of human life and death. Many show ships: ships of war, of a new type, long and lean, with many oars and a sharp ram on the waterline. Sometimes they are in action; men brandish spears, and corpses sink in the sea. But commonest of all are scenes showing funerals: chariots process (according to the convention, both wheels of each chariot, the heads of both horses and all their legs are carefully and separately shown); mourners beat their foreheads or tear their hair, and in the midst, the corpse, stiff in geometric *rigor mortis*, is likewise *shown* (to remove all doubt about the subject) *above* the hangings (also shown) which would have covered it. The choice of subject has a reason: for these great vases, some of them 1½ metres high, stood as monuments on the graves of rich men (now once more usually inhumed, not cremated), in the cemetery where later stood Athens' Dipylon or Double Gate. The practice had grown out of that of placing vessels of food- or drink-offerings on the grave. Some of the great Dipylon vases are even pierced with a hole in the bottom, so that drink-offerings might flow through into the earth for the presumed enjoyment of the deceased.

Geometric art, 'this small, bleak, thrifty art', as Sir John Beazley called it, has superficially a strong resemblance to some of the oldest pottery-painting in the world, in pre-dynastic Egypt and in Elam. Highly conventional, it still looks primitive; it is in fact neo-primitive. Also the small black figures, as well as the geometrical patterns, look so like decoration woven or embroidered in textiles as to suggest the question whether such textiles – like that which Helen worked at Troy in the *Iliad*, adorned with battle-scenes – gave a style to the vase-painters.

There is no great mystery (such as has sometimes been made) of the origins of Geometric. After the palaces had fallen, vase-painters went on for a couple of generations reproducing, without much conviction, imitations of the style to which men were accustomed. This is the length of time which it usually takes for a people, after a far-reaching social change, to get habits which are no longer relevant thoroughly out of their system; for the first generation of survivors are still people brought up under the old order, and the second generation are people brought up by people who were brought up under the old order. This is one reason why a *century*, a period of about three generations, so often seems to have a distinctive character. In the third generation, vase-painters at Athens and perhaps elsewhere had at last lost the feeling that the decadent sub-Mycenaean was in some way the 'right' style, and a fresh start is made with proto-geometric, the folk-art of a vigorous and talented people. By the eighth century, the great Dipylon vases gave evidence of competitive expenditure by men of some wealth.

5 IONIA AND THE EPIC

Among the eastern Greeks, art lagged behind that of the 'old country'. Colonial conditions presumably gave little scope for it. But, like some other colonists – for instance, the 'hill-billies' of the Appalachian mountains, among whom Cecil Sharp collected ballads and folk-songs that had been lost in Britain – the Greeks in Asia had carried with them a part of their culture, which weighed nothing in the baggage: their own ballads and songs, and stories of gods and heroes going back to the Mycenaean age. The favourite stories were always of the 'good' old days in Greece; never of Ionia. Towards the end of the prehistoric period – Herodotos believed 'not more than 400 years' before his time, or about 850, and many modern scholars would say a hundred years later than that – this poetic capital was inherited by a man of genius. Perhaps there was more than one, but Greece remembered only one name, that of Homer.

As Hellenic art proper begins with the proto-geometric, so, but at the level of genius, Hellenic literature begins with the epics of the Trojan War as Homer remade them. Epics on the subject no doubt existed before him; sometimes Homer uses whole blocks of older material; for instance, the List of Contingents, which Homer, introducing it into his story of an episode towards the end of the war, when it clearly was meant to stand at the beginning of a chronicle-epic, has to adapt, telling us that this or that chief mentioned in it was now dead, wounded or absent. Sometimes too he has apparently tinkered with an episode of the fighting, bringing the armour up to date. But if we had Homer's sources, we should probably find that Homer is to them as Shakespeare to Holinshed.

Homer did not write a chronicle. With artistic sophistication or native genius, he plunges, as Horace said of him, into the middle of his story, *in medias res.* Out of the long war he chooses, like a modern novelist, a manageable episode: the quarrel, over allocation of captive women, between the High King of Mycenae and his best northern fighting man. Agamemnon was forced to restore his favourite captive to her father, because that father was a priest of Apollo, at Chryse on the Dardanelles, and his prayers to his god for a pestilence, when Agamemnon refused to ransom her, were being answered.* Agamemnon consoles himself by taking a girl who had been assigned to Achilles, who had taken the lead in pressing him to release the priest's daughter. Achilles withdraws to his huts in anger. For lack of him, the Achaians are defeated, and Agamemnon has to yield again.

But this is not all. After one-third of the poem (which is of the length of a longish novel, 437 pages in Rieu's prose translation) there is a great turning-point. After one defeat, Agamemnon offers Achilles restitution: an apology, his girl back again, ample gifts in addition, and the offer of the hand of his daughter. But Achilles refuses. He does not want Agamemnon's gift, he says; he wants to see him further humbled. Achilles, the hero of the poem, thus puts himself in the wrong. He has his way. In the next and greatest of the battles Agamemnon himself, leading the attack, is wounded; so are Odysseus and other chiefs; the Greeks are driven back to the water's edge among their beached ships. Achilles' friend Patroklos at last persuades him to let Patroklos lead out his Myrmidons to the rescue. By their attack the ships and camp are saved; but Patroklos is killed. Achilles' anger against Agamemnon is now swallowed up in his fury against Hector, the slayer of his

*The girl's name is not given; she is simply called Chryseïs, Daughter of the Man of Chryse; but this appellation, Latinised, in its accusative form, Chryseïda, in a much later romance, was to have its own fame. A passive victim of Homer, she becomes the Criseyde of medieval romance and of Chaucer and the Cressida of Shakespeare.

friend; Agamemnon's offers of restitution are accepted now, too late. Next day, Achilles drives the Trojans with great slaughter into the town, and kills Hector, though his goddess mother has told him that if he does so his own fate is to be killed soon after.

Achilles, the brilliant young hero, whose sense of his own dignity (*to philótimon*, still a key word in modern Greek) has led him *to go too far* and to lose his best friend, is the proto-type of Greek tragic heroes. But the plot is only a small part of the greatness of the poem. In its first lines Homer defines his subject as the Wrath of Achilles and what came of it; but it was as the *Iliad*, the Tale of Ilion, the city of the Trojans, that the work was always known. Homer expands his work to make it so. Delaying his climax, he brings in a great gallery of sec-ondary characters, not least the Trojans, destined victims of vindictive gods: Hector, the brave fighter for home and family, and his wife; Paris his brother, selfish and spectacular, who had brought on the war; Helen herself, full of emotional revulsions, on the city wall in tears, come to witness an attempt (foiled by the gods) to settle the matter by a duel between Paris and her husband Menelaos; while the old Trojan councillors of King Priam whisper to each other that they cannot blame the young men for fighting for one such as she is. Homer describes his battles with gusto, and feasts and athletics and horsemanship with insatiable joy in life; but he is as full of pity over the waste and misery of war as Vergil himself.

The epic has been called the Bible of the Greeks, and not unjustly; for not only did it fix for Greeks the picture of the Olympic gods, their characters and relationships, it also had a powerful influence on Greek popular ethics. The ideal of Greek manhood was fixed for ever in Achilles, loyal and pas-sionate in friendship (though the idea that his relationship with Patroklos, an older man, was homosexual is a later invention), and refusing to prolong his life at the cost of honour. There was a warning too, against pressing even a justifiable quarrel too far. Centuries later in Athens, in the conversations of Soc-rates as reported by Plato, men will try to settle an ethical question with a quotation from Homer; and not only men who wish to be saved the trouble of thinking. Socrates on trial for his life, explaining why he cannot change his ways, quotes the example of Achilles when his mother told him 'Straight after Hector, death is assured for thee.'

But if the *Iliad* is perhaps the greatest poem ever composed, and in Greece was the most revered, its companion and sequel the *Odyssey* has been, perhaps in Greece and certainly ever after, more loved. For all its giants and monsters and fantastic adventures (some of them, like that with the man-eating Cyclops, derived from folk-tales) its main theme is unromantic: the story of a middle-aged soldier, escaping from enemies and shipwreck to make his way home; arriving alone, disguised, recognized only by his old and dying hound and his old nurse; finding out carefully how things stand, before, with the help of his young son and two herdsmen, making a clean sweep of the suitors who had wished to presume his death and take his wife and his kingdom. Cool, resourceful and indomitable, Odysseus was a less glamorous hero than Achilles; but he embodied the kind of man that many a Greek wished to be.

Many modern and some ancient readers of the two poems have felt, from differences in some of the stock phrases, in the whole tone, and in some of the views implied – Olympos, for instance, seems to have turned from a mountain into a kind of heaven – that they cannot be by the same hand. The differences certainly are there; but tradition preserved only one name, not two; and it would be hard to disprove the view that the 'different' author of the *Odyssey* is the same man, now passed from fiery youth into middle age. Another puzzle about the poet was that so many cities, mostly in Ionia, claimed him. If he was a travelling rhapsodist who chanted his poems at many festivals and great houses, that might account for it. As a later Greek epigram said,

> Seven wealthy towns contend for Homer dead,
> Through which the living Homer begged his bread.

However, the best claim was certainly that of Chios, where a guild of poets and rhapsodists, called the Homēridai, long claimed physical or professional descent from him.

Living when he did, one of the most startling things about Homer is that he is irreligious. True, the gods are always at hand in his stories. Zeus holds the scales of battle; Athena is the constant friend of Odysseus, and helps Achilles to slay Hector, to modern taste sadly spoiling the story. That was epic convention. But what is startling is that the gods are inferior to the heroes, not exactly in morals, but in dignity. Agamemnon indeed was murdered by his wife; but Zeus is henpecked. The heroes have as many bedfellows, usually slaves, as they choose (there is one standard for them and another for their wives); but Ares the War-god not only has an intrigue with Aphrodite (the Latin Venus), who is married to Hēphaistos the lame smith-god, but is caught in adultery with her, in a snare set by the cunning of the outraged husband. Hēphaistos then invites the other gods to come and have a hearty laugh at them. And it is the goddesses Hera, wife of Zeus, and Athena, who, from sheer vindictiveness against Troy, prevent peace from being made and procure the breaking of the truce, when men had tried to settle the quarrel by the duel between Paris and Menelaos.

This is not only the poet's choice; it must have been acceptable to his audience. Homer's use of the gods *for comic relief* is a fact about Ionian society in his time, and about Greek cultured society in general thereafter. His irreverent tales of Olympos were not only told; they were preserved.

The fact is that Homer's Olympians are the gods of bronze age war-lords, made in the likeness of their original worshippers and preserved by poetic tradition into an age to which they do not belong. Homer's ribaldry is like that of Elijah, when he suggests to the worshippers of Baal that if Baal does not answer a call he must be away from home, or asleep, or out hunting. But Homer has no better alternative to offer. Much mental stress was to result for thinking people, from the fact that, in this middle age between two civilisations, this view of the gods became fixed. The ultimate effect was to leave a field open, precisely in Ionia, Homer's country, for the rise of philosophy.

In the meantime, the outlook of Homer's heroes and so presumably of Homer's audience is sombre. There is a life after death, but it is not comforting; a life of ghosts under earth in the sunless House of Hades, where the ghost of Achilles cries 'Better be a hired man on a poor farm on earth than king over all the strengthless dead.' The one poor comfort is to be well remembered. The heroic code is summed up in the famous words of the Lykian king to his fellow-chief at Troy (words which were paraphrased by A. E. Housman):

Oh friend, if, once we had escaped this war, we should never grow old nor die, then I would neither fight in the foremost ranks nor urge you on to battle, the glory of men; but now, since anyhow the fates of death stand over us, that no mortal may escape or avoid – let us go on!

However, even Homer's Olympians are not completely un-ethical; his Zeus may send rainstorms at harvest time upon men who do not do justice in their assemblies. Nor are his people always (though they are quite often) thinking about death and fate. *Because* life is short and youth still shorter, Greek life was what it was, both for good and ill, and the word 'Homeric' rightly stands to us for all healthy physical joy in living. The preservation of the City, too, offered Greeks a kind of immortality. Hector, spurning an unfavourable omen (with disastrous results – that is *his* tragedy), produces the splendid line 'One omen is best – to fight for your country'; a favourite quotation in modern Greek schools. The basic fact is that these Greeks of the Iron Age, especially the uprooted Ionians, have been *detribalised*. The city is not merely the tribe over again, with a wall round it. In the dialectic of history, it has the in-dividualism of the Homeric age within it. A whole civilisation had died to produce Homer's situation. In thought as well as in techniques, historic Greece did not begin again where the Bronze Age began, but where the Heroic Age ended.

6 HESIOD

How true this is may be seen in Hesiod, a poet not to be com-pared with Homer, but with a special interest of his own; he is the first farmer and working man in Europe whose voice we hear. He farmed at Askra, up a valley under the south side of Mount Helikōn in Boiotia, probably about 725–700. His most famous poem, called *Works and Days*, is an address to an unsatisfactory brother, who according to Hesiod, spent time scheming to get more than his share of their father's property instead of getting on with his work; and it develops into an account of how that work should be done, what positions of the stars to look for, to know when ploughing is due, what days of the month are lucky or unlucky for various purposes. Hesiod's great lesson is always to be in good time with things; then 'you will buy another man's farm, not he buy yours'; to waste time and get behind-hand is the road to ruin. And while he is about it, he gives us a fascinating description of the work of a middle-sized farm throughout the year. Hesiod has an ox (the early-iron-age tractor) and a few slaves, and takes on an extra, hired man at harvest time. He is not very poor; and he is very far from being a 'primitive peasant', though he may look like one to a superficial modern view. He lives in a world in which *land* can be bought and sold; he is rightly proud of his star-lore; and his world is not bounded by his mountain horizon. He is not even of a family that has been 'always', since the conquest, in the same place. His father had been a sea-farer, trading from Kyme in Aiolis, an important city, in touch with the east (*cf.* p. 83). Failing in this business, he had 'retromigrated' and either bought his farm or, perhaps, cleared it himself on unoccupied 'marginal land' in the Askra valley-head. Hesiod became a poet, he tells us, by inspiration; 'the Muses spoke to him', when he was minding sheep on Helikon. But his metre comes from Asia. It is no other than the Homeric hexameter, which he turns to new uses; and he composes not in his own vernacular, but in the Ionic which epic poets had already developed as an artificial literary language.

According to tradition, Hesiod was also the author of poems on mythology. The most important of these, called the *Theogony* or *Genesis of the Gods*, made an attempt to systematize the legends on the birth of the gods and emergence of an ordered cosmos out of chaos (emptiness or space). It was not a creation of the world by God, as in the Hebrew Genesis.

Other poems went on to set in order the genealogies of heroic families. Some scholars have denied that any of these poems are by the author of the *Works and Days*, but more from a nineteenth-century passion for 'criticism' than on any definite evidence. An important recent discovery has been that of a prose Theogony in Hittite texts, several hundred years earlier, including struggles between the gods. In its main outline and many of its barbarous details, it bears a strong resemblance to Hesiod's. Either the Aegean world had a version of these legends already or Hesiod knew of them from Kyme. Hesiod, the original, inspired and self-made poet, clearly had a passion for systematizing and explaining things; and it seems quite possible that, after settling the fraternal quarrel, he had time to set in order all that he 'knew' about his world and its origins, during the spring pause in farm-work that comes before the Greek harvest (in May) or in the dead time of winter.

Hesiod's version of the origins of gods and men survived to be the basis of all later Greek mythology and to scandalize serious religious thinkers, and something must therefore be said about it. The king of the gods is Father Zeus, lord of the thunder. He has a wife, Hēra ('Noble Lady'), mother of Hēphaistos and Ares, and an innumerable progeny by other ladies, both immortal, like Lētō, mother of the twins Apollo and Artemis, and mortal, like Alkmēna, mother of Hērakles. Often his mistresses are persecuted by his jealous consort. Poseidon, lord of the sea, and Hades, euphemistically called Pluto, 'the Wealthy One', lord of the underworld, are his brothers. But Zeus was not always king. Long ago, he dethroned his father Kronos, who in fear of such an event had made a practice of swallowing his children; but his wife Rhea hid Zeus, giving Kronos a stone instead, which he swallowed without noticing the difference; and when Zeus was grown up, he forced Kronos to cough his immortal brothers up again (as well as the stone, which was preserved at Delphoi). Kronos was relegated to an earthly paradise, the Isles of the Blest, in the distant Ocean, where he reigns over some favoured heroes.

But even Kronos was not there at the very beginning. In the very beginning there was Space (Chaos) and then Earth and

Hell (Tartara) and Love, Erōs. This Erōs is more a life-force than an anthropomorphic god, and quite different from the boy-Erōs or Cupid, the child of Aphrodite. Earth brought forth the starry sky, Ouranos (Uranus, Heaven), her son and consort; and Ouranos, like Kronos after him, used to put away his sons, burying them in the earth. Earth, in considerable discomfort, urged them to rebel; but none dared, before Kronos, her youngest. To him, Earth gave a sickle, with which he castrated Ouranos when he was about to unite with Earth again; and Kronos reigned in his stead. This barbarous legend, which looks as if it had emerged from an agricultural fertility ritual, is that which has the most notable analogies in Hittite myth. There too Kumarbi castrated his predecessor Anu (Heaven) and was the father of the later gods, including a weather-god who dethroned him in turn.

Hesiod also, in the *Works and Days*, has a theory of human history. He knows that he lives in the Iron Age, and he finds it bad. Old poems told him that before it there had been a Bronze Age, when iron was unknown. Poets had been unable to substitute iron for bronze in the traditional epics, because the word for iron had one more syllable, and would have upset the metre. Then, seeing that in the course of human degeneration the baser metal had replaced the nobler one, either Hesiod or a predecessor had the bright idea of extrapolating a Golden and a Silver Age before the Bronze. The Golden Age was in the time of Kronos, when men were innocent food-gatherers and there was neither work nor war. The Silver Age men were inferior, but still innocents, having a long childhood and a short adult life; the Bronze men were terrible and warlike. Between them and the Iron Age, Hesiod puts (correctly) the Heroes who fell at Thebes and Troy; they too were warlike, but, anomalously, they were better than their immediate predecessors. Hesiod is apparently combining two traditions, one favourable (epic and aristocratic?) and the other less starry-eyed, about the warlike Achaian period.

7 THE ALPHABET

Hesiod collects and systematizes the legends, as he systematized his star-lore and hints for farmers; he encyclopaedizes, like a man conscious of long vistas of time behind him. If to us Homer and he come at the beginning, it is because theirs are the first works in Europe to be preserved in writing.

Homer's epics, it has been common form to say since the work of Milman Parry, have the characteristics of oral poetry, such as has existed down to our own century among many keen-witted but illiterate peoples; in Bosnia, for instance, and still in some parts of Soviet Asia. The Mycenaean writing had disappeared except in Cyprus, where, as in a little Byzantium over against barbarian Europe, the old ways – kings, palaces, chariots, writing, even the Minoan loin-cloth as men's dress, all survived. But in the commercial world of the Levant, while Greece lay fallow, there had been a whole series of experiments aimed at producing a simpler writing than the old system, with their syllabic spelling combined with ideograms denoting whole words. Ugarit (Ras Shamra), which traded with Mycenae, had already had what has been called an 'alphabetic' cuneiform system; in Cyprus, men had reduced the 200 signs of Linear B to about forty syllables, in which they wrote Greek – though rather clumsily since, with every syllable ending in a vowel, they had no good arrangement for writing double consonants. It was the Phoenicians who produced the best script, with only twenty-two characters; it is employed, already mature, in the famous inscription of Mesha, King of Moab, who fought against Ahab of Israel around 850; and it was this which Ionians and islanders trading with the Levant (pp. 83, 88 f.) took over, at latest before 750.

The Phoenicians employed their writing for business purposes. So did the Greeks, but they also applied it to poetry. The new letters were so few that anyone could learn them. Some of the earliest Greek writing is in deeply cut letters on rocks on the island of Thera, in which boys appear to have inscribed names and opprobrious comments on their schoolfellows, at the back of the gymnasium. A great step forward was made when some Greeks invented what the Phoenicians lacked, a set of pure vowels. For these they appropriated a few letters representing sounds which Greek did not have. It is quite likely that Homer and Hesiod themselves could write; it may have been the possibilities opened up by writing that stimulated them to their ambitious flights; and it is certain that their works were written down not long after their composition. For this reason, as well as for their merits, their works survived, while all those of the long tradition leading up to them have perished.

The Greeks called their letters 'Phoenician characters'. Later they attributed them, quite wrongly, to Kadmos, the alleged Phoenician founder of Thebes (p. 54). But we also notice that whereas the names of the letters in Greek, alpha, beta, gamma, delta, are a mere jingle, in Phoenician they have meaning, as the illustration below demonstrates. *Aleph* = ox; put in two dots for eyes, and the fact that it is an adapted ideogram is obvious. It was the Greeks, not knowing the meaning, who thought (characteristically) that ⊲ would look better 'standing up'. Beta, *beth* = house, and was originally angular; perhaps, at first, actually a triangle upon a square. Gamma, *gimel* = camel (represented by that animal's most characteristic feature?), delta is *daleth*, a tent door; and so on.

aleph beth gimel daleth

Reproduced from *Writing* by David Diringer (Thames and Hudson)

8 THE DAWN OF HISTORY

Literacy spread rapidly. Whole alphabets, painted on pottery, are common in its early days. And so here prehistory ends and history begins; though for some 200 years it is proto-history rather than history proper, in that such contemporary literature as we have is poetry, not history, and such history as we have is not contemporary. The dates, before about 500, given by later Greeks, with many variations, are probably calculated from genealogies. These include the date of oversea colonies, whereby archaeologists date the earliest pottery found in them, and then date other finds by means of the pottery. The colonial dates are thus not always reliable. Some *may* be derived from an officially-kept count of years; but many are variously given. Cyrēne, for instance, is dated 759 *and* 631. Since the grandson of its founder fought against Pharaoh Hophra, who reigned *c.* 588–570, there is no doubt which is right. But usually we have no such 'control'.

Greece in the eighth century, then, was a settled country, and in parts of it pressure of population was again beginning to be felt. It was to explode in a vigorous movement of expansion, the effects of which were to revolutionise society in turn, even at home. In Ionia, the cities were still able to extend their boundaries inland; and there, there was much opulence. A long and beautiful *Hymn to the Delian Apollo*, traditionally ascribed to Homer, gives a famous picture of an Ionian holiday:

... Lord, archer Apollo, ... many are thy temples and wooded groves; and all places of wide view are dear to thee, and sheer buttresses of high mountains, and streams that flow to the sea; but in Delos, O Phoibos, dost thou most delight, where the long-robed Ionians come together for thee, with their children and their honoured wives. With boxing, dancing and song they remember thee for thy pleasure, when they celebrate the games. A man would say they were immortal and youthful for ever, who should come then, when the Ionians are assembled, and see the men, and the women with their beautiful figures, and their swift ships and all their possessions....

The poet goes on to celebrate the maidens of Delos, his choristers, and to bid them say, if anyone should ask who is their favourite poet: 'He is a blind man, and dwells in craggy Chios.' The tradition of the blind Homer of Chios is based on this line.

In Elis, in western Greece, too, there were games at a holy place, sacred in the bronze age to the Great Goddess, now identified with Hera. Taken over in honour of Olympian Zeus, it was called Olympia. The establishment, or re-establishment, of the Olympic Games is traditionally dated 776 B.C.; but only by a much later calculation. Hippias, a scholar of Elis, some 350 years later, collected all the names of traditional victors in the games which he could find, arranged them in a reasonable order and found they extended so far; but we cannot be sure that the list is complete, or that all are genuine, or that the festival was originally (as it was in classical times) four-yearly. Hippias did his best with what material he had; later people 'canonized' his results. Here too, however, there was 'boxing, dancing and song', foot-racing and merriment. It was held at the second full moon after midsummer. Pindar of Thebes in the fifth century imagines the scene when Herakles held the games in ancient times, after defeating the local king. Heroes were the victors

and all the host of his allies raised a cheer; and the light of the fair-faced moon made bright the evening, and the holy place was loud with feasting and song.

At Olympia women were excluded from watching the Games, a significant difference from Delos; though there survived a separate, very minor, women's festival with a girls' foot-race.

CHAPTER 4

EXPANSION AND RENAISSANCE

1 THE GREEKS AND THE WEST

KYME in Asian Aiolis, whence Hesiod's father had returned, weary of sea-faring, was already a commercial city. It traded oversea products, especially metal, for the wool and corn of Phrygia. A daughter of King Agamemnon of Kyme married Midas, King of Phrygia, and a sea-captain named Midakritos ('approved of Midas' – probably a man of Kyme, named for his father's patron) is named as the first man to bring tin from a 'Tin Island' in the west. An ancient throne at Delphoi was said to have been a gift of Midas. Eastward, a Midas (it was the name of several kings) fought the Assyrians in the Taurus mountains; and Phrygia probably supplied tin to the kingdom of Urartu (Ararat), which also fought the Assyrians at the height of their power, and was famous for its bronze and iron work. Midas was a great name in its time. The legends of Midas the Rich Fool probably come from later Greek comedy, which at one time relied largely on 'Ancient History' for its subjects.

Also interested in the west were the Greeks of central Euboia, where Chalkis (pronounced Hal-kís), 'Bronze-city', has one of the few Greek place-names that have a Greek meaning; and about 750, Kyme, Chalkis and its neighbour Eretria went into partnership in a new venture, to establish a permanent advanced base in western waters. The place selected was on the western promontory of what is now the Bay of Naples (Neapolis, New City, a later foundation which outgrew the old one). Named after Kyme, this first Greek colony in the west is better known by its Latin name; it is the Cumae of Vergil. Through it the alphabet came into central Italy, and so to the Romans, in the Chalkidian form, a little different from the Ionic of our Greek texts.

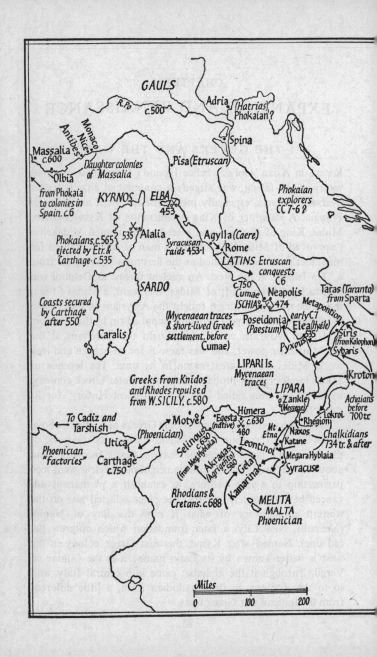

GAULS

R. Po
c.500

Adria (Hatrias)
Phokaian?

Monaco, Nice,
Antibes

Spina

Massalia
c.600

Pisa (Etruscan)

Olbia

Phokaian
explorers
CC 7-6?

from Phokaia
to colonies in
Spain. c.6

KYRNOS

ELBA
453

Daughter colonies
of Massalia

Phokaians, c.565
ejected by Etr. &
Carthage c.535

X
535

Alalia

Syracusan
raids 453-1

Agylla (Caere)

Rome

LATINS Etruscan
conquests
C6

SARDO

c.750
Cumae
Neapolis

Coasts secured
by Carthage
after 550

ISCHIA
474

Taras (Taranto)
from Sparta

Metapontion

Caralis

(Mycenaean traces
& short-lived Greek
settlement, before
Cumae)

Poseidonia
(Paestum)

early C7
Elea (Hyéle)
535

Pyxous

Siris
(from Kolophon)

Sybaris

LIPARI Is.
Mycenaean
traces

Krotor

Greeks from Knidos
and Rhodes repulsed
from W. SICILY, c.580

LIPARA

Achaians
before
700 tr.

To Cadiz and
Tarshish

Motyé
(Phoenician)

Himera
c.630
480

Egesta
(native)

Zankle
(Messene)

Lokroi

Rhegion

Mt
Etna

Naxos

Katane

Chalkidians
734 tr. & after

Phoenician
"factories"

Utica

Selinous
c.630
(from Meg. Hyblaia)

Leontinoi

Megara Hyblaia

Carthage
c.750

Akragas
(Agrigento)
c.580

Gela
c.690

Syracuse

Rhodians &
Cretans, c.688

Kamarina

MELITA
MALTA
Phoenician

Miles

0   100   200

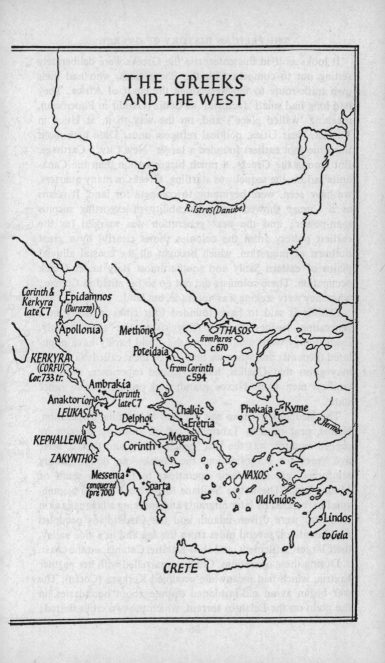

THE GREEKS
AND THE WEST

R.Istros(Danube)

Corinth &
Kerkyra
late C7

Epidamnos
(Durazzo)

Apollonia

Methōne

THASOS
from Paros
c.670

KERKYRA
(CORFU)
Cor.733 tr.

Poteidaia

from Corinth
c.594

Ambrakia
Corinth
late C7

Anaktorion

LEUKAS

Chalkis

Phokaia

Kyme

R.Hermos

Delphoi

Eretria

KEPHALLENIA

Megara

ZAKYNTHOS

Corinth

NAXOS

Messenia
conquered
(pre 700)

Sparta

Old Knidos

Lindos

to Gela

CRETE

It looks as if in this enterprise the Greeks were deliberately setting out to compete with the Phoenicians, who had their own trade-route to the west along the coast of Africa. They had long had small 'factories' at Cadiz (Gaddir in Phoenician, meaning 'walled place') and, on the way to it, at Utica in Tunisia. Near Utica, political refugees under Dido had about this time (not earlier) founded a larger 'New City': Carthage. But among the Greeks, a much bigger nation than the Canaanite sailors, the sequel was startling. Greeks in many quarters, we have seen, were beginning to compete for land. It seems as if Cumae showed the practicability of exporting surplus man-power; and the next generation was marked (as the earliest pottery from the colonies shows clearly) by a great outburst of migration, which brought all the coastal alluvial plains of eastern Sicily and southernmost Italy under Greek occupation. These colonists did not go so far afield as Cumae; what they were seeking was not trade, but land.

Chalkis is said to have founded four cities in Sicily in a generation, besides Rhegion (Reggio) on the 'toe' of Italy. Even if they were small at first, she could hardly have populated them all; and when we find one of them called Naxos, we may guess that Chalkis, having gained experience, recruited landless men from Naxos island, and probably from other states.

The Sicilian enterprise was planned as a military operation. Naxos, near modern Taormina, cut off from the interior by rugged country, was the first 'beach-head'; and thence, after five years for consolidation, the Greeks, no doubt heavily reinforced, extended their operations to the plain south of Mount Etna. The native Sicilians (bronze-age farmers, somewhat barbarized by later migrants and speaking a language akin to Latin) were driven inland, and the Chalkidians occupied *first* Leontinoi, several miles from the sea and in a side valley, their largest settlement, and *then* Katáne, Catania, on the coast.

During these operations, Chalkis quarrelled with her partner Eretria, which had meanwhile occupied Kerkyra (Corfu). The war began as an old-fashioned dispute about boundaries, in the plain on the Lelantos torrent, which the two cities shared;

but, with oversea enterprises now much in view, the Lelantine War became linked up with other neighbourly enmities in the first widespread general war of Greek history. Samos and Miletos, enemies at home in Ionia, fought as allies of Chalkis and Eretria respectively. Corinth, which also lent a naval architect to Samos, to direct the building of a new type of warship, drove the Eretrians from Kerkyra; she also took over the finest harbour-site in all east Sicily at Syracuse. The Chalkidians had probably visited it; for the famous spring Arethusa, on the inshore island, whence the Corinthians 'first drove the Sicilians', was first named after a spring near Chalkis. Syracuse too had from the first a farming population. A contingent came from the inland Corinthian village of Tenea; and a story became proverbial, of an improvident emigrant who ran short of food on the boat and was constrained to barter his prospective allotment for a 'mess of pottage', in the form of a honey-cake.

Syracuse became the greatest city of Greek Sicily. In the next century she extended her territory over the south-east corner of the island, subduing native villages and planting three daughter-colonies, until her boundaries marched with those of Gela. Gela, founded by Cretans and men of Lindos in Rhodes, on the south coast about 688, was the last Greek colony here for two generations.

In Italy, the Achaians, who preserved their ancient name between the Arcadian mountains and the Corinthian Gulf, produced from their restricted territories a flood of emigrants, and occupied the best alluvial plains of the south coast. Small as it seems to us, this new world appeared inexhaustible as America to the little towns of Greece, and became known as Great Greece, Megále Hellas. Sybaris, in particular, with a wide plain under the 'instep' of Italy and valleys leading inland, spread out like Syracuse and more rapidly, with daughter-colonies and native subjects. Reaching the western sea, the Sybarites very soon launched out again, to found Poseidonia (the Latin Paestum, near Salerno). Here, half-way to Cumae, trade may well have been in view from the first. On this site, flooded by the sea in the middle ages and malarious later, a splendid series of early temples has escaped the stone-robber and stands to this day.

As in the modern world, much colonisation resulted from particular crises at home. Sparta about this time satisfied her land-hunger by subduing her neighbours in Messenia, an event destined to poison much subsequent history. Some Messenians withdrew to join the Chalkidians at Reggio; descendants of theirs later gave their name to the city across the straits, now Messina. Sparta after the war had some internal troubles, and a faction, treated as second-class citizens and suspected of plotting revolution, finally were sent to found a colony at Taranto. Lokrians from north of the Corinthian Gulf, with other 'displaced persons' from the same upheaval, founded a western Lokroi near Reggio. The Achaians tried to secure everything between Taranto and Lokroi, but were not numerous enough, and an Ionian band, their lands at home cut short by the rise of a new native power, Lydia, seized the good land at the mouth of the Siris river. The Achaians regarded them with jealousy as interlopers.

The west was by far the most important area of Greek expansion; it really was like America to Greece's Europe. Here grew up cities often more populous than those which had founded them, and very much richer; and Greeks in the west made major contributions to literature, philosophy and art. Such developments were rare in other colonial areas. The word colony, it must be noticed, is here used in its original sense, of a *settlement* abroad, not in that which has come to be a 'dirty word' in our time, of a foreign possession under despotic rule. Greek colonies kept up ties of religion and sentiment with their mother cities, and might help or be helped by them in war; but as a rule mere distance made it impossible to think of keeping them in subjection; and when Corinth tried to maintain her rule over Kerkyra, the result was a war of independence, and long hostility.

2 COLONISATION IN THE EAST

As early as the foundation of Cumae, Ionians were beginning to trade and settle in the Levant. There were new settlements in the plain of Tarsus and one, called Poseideion, at Al Mina north of Ras Shamra. Geometric pottery reached Hamath (Hamah), which was sacked by the Assyrians in 720; but the Assyrians also severely checked Greek aggression. King Sargon, in a famous boast, says that he 'dragged the Ionians like fish from the sea', in operations near Tarsus, and 'gave peace to Cilicia and Tyre'. Greek trade with the Levant remained important, and influenced Greek culture; but for lands to settle, especially when Corinthians and Achaians monopolized the west so far as they could, other Greeks had to look elsewhere.

The north Aegean, where there were still remnants of the ancient Pelasgians, notably on Lemnos, was less obviously attractive; but this way, *after* the first great rush to the west, overcrowded islanders now turned. The Eretrians driven from Kerkyra by Corinth returned home; but they found that they were not welcome, and at last settled at Methone in the northwest Aegean. Euboians and others founded many cities, mostly small, in the neighbouring three-pronged peninsula; Chalkis organized many of them, and the whole area came to be called Chalkidiké. They had reason to confine themselves mainly to peninsulas, for the people of central Thrace were formidable: large, blond barbarians, whose word for a town was *bria* (*burgh*?) while their word for making beer, their local drink, resembled *brew*. They fought with the slashing sword, and by them more than one strong Greek expedition was destroyed.

But now Greek ships began to force their way, with difficulty against the strong current, up the Dardanelles. Somehow, perhaps using inshore back-eddies and at awkward places towing from the shore, they reached easier waters in the Marmara. Men of Lesbos had already spread up the coast of the Troad, and they secured the constricted but important stronghold of Sestos, on the European shore of the Narrows. Then new actors appear on the scene. Megara, a dependency of Corinth, had founded a new Megara in Sicily, just north of Syracuse; but, boxed in between the Corinthians and Chalkidians, it was

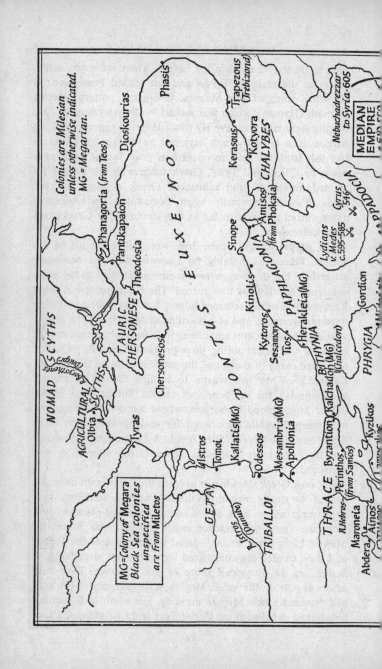

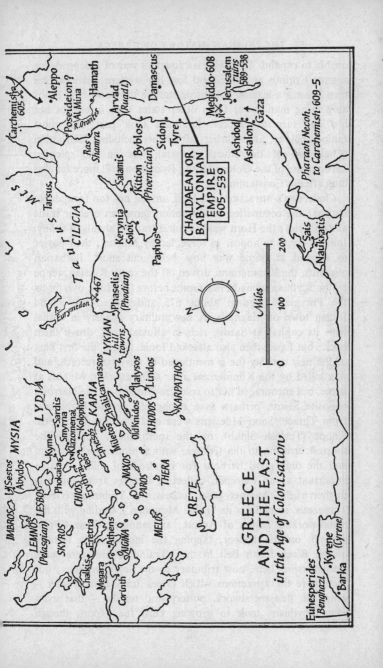

GREECE
AND THE EAST
in the Age of Colonisation

CHALDAEAN OR
BABYLONIAN
EMPIRE
605–539

unable to expand. Then Megara fought a war of independence against Corinth at home, and lost her western chances. She then became a leading colonising state in the north-east, probably using man-power from other states too; in one of her last and largest ventures, Boiotians took part. Her most famous colony, after earlier settlements including Kalchādōn (Chalcedon of the church fathers), was on the splendid harbour-site of the Golden Horn; Byzantion, still more famous long after as Constantinople.

Chalcedon's attraction was land, among not too formidable natives; the occupation of Byzantion shows an eye for trade and fisheries; the Horn was a natural trap for shoals of tunny. Ionians began to appear in force, led by Miletos; their power to expand at home was now being cut short. Barbarian migrants, the Kimmerians, driven off the south Russian steppe by the Scythian nomads, like Goths before the Huns, overthrew the Phrygian kingdom about 675 and sacked the inland Ionian town of Magnesia. A new military dynasty in Lydia, with its capital at Sardis, rich in alluvial gold, drove them back; but Lydia then also attacked Ionia. Gyges, the first king of the new dynasty (he is mentioned in Assyrian records, and was killed by the Kimmerians after 650), attacked Miletos at home, but encouraged her to colonize Abydos, on the Narrows opposite Sestos, perhaps as a stronghold against barbarians from Thrace. Soon Milesians were exploring the Black Sea. Sinope (Turkish Sinub), on the south coast, opposite the shortest crossing to the Crimea, with a promontory position and the only good harbour for hundreds of miles, became important as an *entrepôt*, collecting cargoes from outposts further afield. Another great success was Trebizond (Greek Trapezous, named for its 'Table Mountain'), trading with the metal-working region of Ararat; and another, Olbia ('Prosperity'), on the Dniepr, tapping the inexhaustible fertility of the Black Earth Belt in the Ukraine. There were some peasant tribes here, now tributary to the Scythian kings; but such were the attractions which Greek trade had to offer – wine, oil, fine metalwork, pottery and textiles – that even some Scythians took to growing corn for export, though living on meat and milk themselves. Even under the fierce Caucasus mineral wealth made it worth while to have out-posts. One such was Dioskourias, dedicated to the Great Twin Brethren, protectors of sailors, where, with the typical linguistic diversity of mountain country, it was said that seventy languages might be heard on market days. Greeks were fond of describing the strange customs of the peoples of the Euxine, or 'Hospitable Sea', as they euphemistically called it: the Scythians with their covered wagons and their invention of the 'Russian' vapour bath; the mountaineers, tattooed, extremely dirty (it was too cold to make washing attractive), and using *crampons* for snow-walking; also the climate, described as 'four months cold and eight months winter', when (though really it was only true of some winters) the very sea froze, and metal wine-amphoras had been known to crack, leaving the contents standing up. 'If you pour water on the ground, you will not make mud,' says Herodotos, 'but if you light a fire, you will.' He also notes that in Scythia an earthquake was considered a portent, but rain in summer was not.

Miletos was said to have organized seventy colonies, all round the Euxine; other Ionian cities added a few, and Megara several; her largest, with many Boiotian farming settlers, was Herakleia (Turkish Eregli), which founded daughter colonies in the Crimea and on the Thracian coast. The vast resources of the region, especially in grain, dried fish, leather and slaves, made it of immense importance to the Greek economy, and the Straits area correspondingly important strategically.

In formidable and alien surroundings, among coastal tribes, some of whom became pirates or wreckers, the settlers clung stoutly to their Hellenic heritage. Achilles, imagined as a pioneer who had fallen fighting to open these waters, became as it were a patron saint; and Homer had no stronger devotees than in Sinope and Olbia. Another legend which was adapted to the interests of Black Sea Greeks was that of Jason and the Golden Fleece.

Originally this story belonged to a myth and ritual of rain-making kings in the northern Achaia (southern Thessaly), who might be sacrificed for the good of the crops. King Athamas married Nephele, the Cloud; and when he was unfaithful to her, the clouds fled away and there was famine. The king's children, Phrixos and Helle, were about to be sacrificed when the Flying Ram, with its golden or (in one early poet) purple fleece, sent by the Cloud-Queen, their mother, appeared and carried them off. Helle fell off and was drowned off Helle's Cape (hence Helles-pontos, the Greek name of the Dardanelles); Phrixos got safe to the land (*Aia*) of sunrise, where he sacrificed the ram and dedicated its fleece. Later Athamas was going to be sacrificed himself, when Kytissōros, son of Phrixos, came back from the east and rescued him; but it remained necessary, for reasons variously given, to bring back the Fleece. This was done at last by Jason ('the Healer'?), great-nephew of Athamas, against the will of King Aiētes ('the Man of Aia'), son of the sun, by the help of Mēdeia (the 'Wise Woman' or Witch), Aietes' daughter; but Jason was unable to return on his tracks, and had to go round the back of the world (the way the sun goes?).

This old tale was rationalised by poets, after the opening of the Black Sea, into a story of exploration. Aia was identified with Kolchis, the country round Trebizond; Jason's journey 'round the back' was made into a journey round Europe, up one river and down another, with a portage between, thus bringing in Homer's reference to the ship *Argo* in *western* waters; and the Golden Fleece itself was explained by reference to a method of collecting alluvial gold, known in the Caucasus both in ancient and modern times, by pegging out fleeces in the shallows of gold-bearing streams.

But the culture of the Black Sea settlers remained conservative and provincial. The climate was not really suited to the Greek outdoor way of life. They got their art from old Greece; and in classical times intellectuals from this region tended to go to Athens for their higher education and, if they became established in the literary world, to stay there. In later pages we shall hear much of the western colonies; of those in the Euxine, little, for all their vital importance economically.

3 EGYPT AND CYRENAICA

In Egypt, Greeks were already trading in the time of the Pharaoh Bokkhoris, before 700. After an interval, when Egypt was occupied by Nubians and then by Assyria, they returned, and were welcomed as mercenaries by Psamatik, founder of Dynasty XXVI, who revolted from Assyria about 650, defeated his rivals and had relations with Gyges. Here too Greeks obtained corn in exchange for wine and oil, while works of art, such as scarabs and Greek pottery, went both ways.

Egypt had a unique influence on Greek culture. Greeks were quite ready to overestimate the wisdom of the Egyptians, and to trace imaginary Egyptian influences on Greek religion. But the reality was impressive enough: the huge temples and sculpture stimulated Greeks to undertake their own first monumental works; in the earliest Greek statues, before 600, the wig-like treatment of the hair is unmistakably Egyptian. The unique character of the country, with the Nile and its annual burden of fertilising silt, stimulated Ionians to geological speculations; rules of land-measurement after each flood (geometria) became geometry; and the antiquity of Egyptian civilisation amazed men of a young culture, whose longest pedigrees went back only about sixteen generations.

The Greek soldiers were perhaps secretly no less impressed; but in their comments, after the manner of soldiers, they were less reverent. Our word for the pyramids is their Greek word, and meant 'buns'; 'obelisk' meant 'skewer' or 'needle' (like 'Cleopatra's Needle'); crocodiles, which were worshipped in some parts of Egypt and honoured with ceremonious mummification, they called crocodiles, after the lizards on the stone walls at home, and ostriches 'sparrows'. Some of them also commemorated an expedition far up the Nile by a historic piece of vandalism, when they cut their names on the legs of Rameses II's rock-cut colossi at Abu Simbel:

When King Psamatichos came to Elephantinē, this they wrote, who sailed with Psammatichos son of Theokles. They went beyond Kerkis, as far as the river let them; Potasimto led the foreigners and Amasis the Egyptians. And Archon, son of Amoibichos, and Peleqos, son of Eudamos, wrote us.

'Us' = the letters; the stone speaks, as in many early inscriptions. The last words should perhaps be rendered 'Axe, son of Nobody', i.e. Archon did it with his hatchet. Other soldiers add their names and cities: Teos, Kolophon, Ialysos in Rhodes. The sarcophagus of the Egyptian general Potasimto, who led the 'foreigners' (Karians?), has been found; he lived under Psamatichos II, who reigned 594–589. Psammatichos (sic), the son of Theokles, is probably a second-generation Greek mercenary, whose father named him after his royal patron, Psamatik I.

Greek humour at the expense of the Egyptians appears also in a superbly comic Ionian vase-painting, showing a great ruddy-skinned Herakles making havoc of an Egyptian king and priests (some black and some yellow), who, according to a story, had tried to sacrifice him. Round the back of the vase hurry five strong negroes with sticks; the police – too late. Naturally the Greeks were not popular in Egypt, and about 570 there was a nationalist reaction. The Egyptians overthrew Pharaoh Hophra and his foreign guards, and made king a general, another Amasis. He restricted the movements of the Greeks; but he continued to employ Greek soldiers, quartering them largely at Daphne, in the modern 'Canal Zone'; and, not wishing to lose the Greek trade, he confined it to a 'treaty port' at Naukratis in the western delta, where the chief cities of Asian Greece had temples. Dorians, Ionians and Aiolic Mytilene united in founding the Hellenion, a 'precinct', both for business and worship, and in electing 'rulers of the market'. Only one city west of the Aegean was represented: the island of Aigina, with a separate temple.

West of Egypt, the fertile land 'about Cyrene' received colonists from Thera (Santorini) in a time of famine; later they were reinforced from many parts of the Aegean, and daughter-colonies spread westward to Euhesperides (Benghazi). There were wars with the (white-skinned) Libyans, but also intermarriage; wars with Egypt (one of them set off the revolution against Pharaoh Hophra) and later with Carthage;

internal struggles between old and new settlers; but through them all Cyrene remained a monarchy under descendants of the first Founder, from Thera, until classical times. The chariot of a king of Cyrene won a victory at Delphoi in 462, celebrated in the most elaborate of the odes of Pindar. This king's grandfather is depicted and named on a famous vase, a masterwork from a Sparta not yet turned 'Spartan', sitting under an awning, supervising the weighing and stowing of his produce, while a monkey sits on the spar over his head, and a lizard (a gekko) climbs on the wall. Cyrene was yet another source of grain for Greece, and exported also the herb silphion (now extinct), a laxative. Through it, too, Greeks visited a revered oracle in the oasis, still sacred today, of Siva; the oracle of Ammon or Amon, identified with Zeus. Here Herodotos heard the tale of western Libyans who had crossed the great desert, to a land of pigmies, much addicted to sorcery, living in a town beside a great river with crocodiles in it. The river flowed east. It must have been the Niger, though Herodotos guessed that it was the upper course of the Nile.

4 AN AGE OF REVOLUTION

Colonisation, then, had arisen out of trade in valuable commodities, such as ivory and tin. But it *led to* trade on a far more massive scale. The colonies, planted on relatively spacious plains, had corn to spare. It became possible to import food instead of exporting men: and this is why the impulse to colonisation presently slackens. In classical times not only Athens but the Peloponnese imported grain. In exchange, the new cities provided an insatiable market for luxury goods; painted pottery, surviving when other goods have perished, enables us to trace the course of this trade. There was also even a tourist-traffic, when rich westerners took to visiting Olympia and Delphoi for the festivals. The seventh and sixth centuries were thus a period of exuberant growth in Old Greece itself; the time of a rise both in population and in standards of living, and of revolutionary developments in art, in literature, and also in politics.

Colonisation had been organized by the land-owning aristocracies; a fact, at first sight, surprising. But what the land-
owners were concerned about was agrarian unrest. There seems
to have been a widespread myth among Greek peasants that
once, in the days of good king X, the land had been fairly
divided; and the standard Greek revolutionary cry was for a
'redivision'. To avert this, the land-owners were prepared to
take a good deal of trouble. But the effects of colonisation on
the trading and colonising cities themselves were revolutionary
in a more far-reaching way. New social classes arose. Ship-
owning traders, manufacturers using two or three scores of
slaves (such a workshop would be large by Greek standards),
resented the old families' monopoly of government. Middle-
class farmers, with more elbow-room, prospered till they could
equip themselves with full armour and claimed full citizen
rights. Money, a Lydian invention, introduced in Europe first
at Aigina about 625, made property more fluid, with commodity
production and the unsettling possibility of debt. Also the
aristocracies, which might have preserved their privileges
longer if they had both admitted new members and preserved
class-solidarity, were usually split by personal and family
rivalries.

The result was a crop of revolutions in the mercantile
cities. Leaders, often though not always dissident nobles
themselves, headed risings of the discontented and, if successful, wielded supreme power for as long as they could, usually
with an armed bodyguard, but with popular support as well.
A normal feature of the operation was the carrying out of the
Redivision of Land, at least to the extent of dividing the
estates of the leader's enemies among his supporters. These
leaders were the *tyrannoi* or tyrants, a non-Greek word (and
apparently not Lydian either, though Gyges is the first man to
whom we find it applied). It was not originally pejorative. It
was an informal title meaning 'Boss' or 'Chief', and was
properly used of revolutionary despots; it would be applicable
to Cromwell, Napoleon, Stalin or Idi Amin, but not to even
the most blood-thirsty of hereditary kings.

There were many tyrants in Ionia, and later in Sicily; but

the best recorded of the early ones are those of cities near Athens. Theagenes of Megara 'slaughtered the cattle of the rich, when out grazing beside the river'; perhaps there had been strife between poor peasants and rich cattle-keepers. He brought running water into town by an aqueduct, a boon to working-class wives; such public works were a service rendered by many 'tyrants'. But the attempt of a young Athenian aristocrat, who had married Theagenes' daughter, to make himself tyrant of Athens, seizing the Acropolis with his friends and some Megarian troops, was a failure; the Athenian peasants still stood by their government; and before the end of his life Theagenes himself was driven into exile by a coalition of his disillusioned countrymen. Many despotisms, among a people so devoted to free speech as the Greeks, were equally short-lived. On the other hand, the dynasty founded at Sikyon by Orthagoras, said to have been the son of a cook, lasted a century (about 650 to 550?), the longest 'tyranny' on record, and left as its legacy the 'integration' of Dorians and a pre-Dorian peasantry.

Fairly typical of what was happening is the history of Corinth. Corinth under the close oligarchy of descendants of her last kings had colonised successfully, and in the seventh century her pottery (and presumably her trade in general) dominated the western market. But the attempt to keep political control over Kerkyra was met by rebellion. A battle at sea about 664, the earliest on record known to Thucydides, left Kerkyra independent; and within ten years, if we may trust the traditional dates, the oligarchy at Corinth fell. Kypselos, the tyrant who overthrew it, is said to have been son of a daughter of the governing clan by a non-Dorian father, to whom she had been married off because she was lame and no nobleman would take her. Kypselos made havoc of his mother's relations, but was popular with the people, and never had a bodyguard. His son Periandros, who reigned for forty-four years, did keep a bodyguard and lived in royal state. Ruthless and able – legend counted him among the 'Seven Wise Men' of his time – he subdued Kerkyra, planted colonies in north-west Greece, which long remained Corinthian dependencies, planned (vainly) a Corinth canal, and did establish a slipway, over which ships were hauled on wheeled transporters from sea to sea. But his despotism became increasingly unpopular; his sons died before him, one in a chariot crash, one of sickness in a colony (Poteidaia in Chalkidike), one by violence after a bitter family quarrel; and his successor, a nephew named Psammetichos – interesting evidence of relations with Egypt – was soon overthrown. The dynasty had lasted seventy-seven years – the second longest tyranny known to Aristotle. Corinth then passed under a more moderate *bourgeois* government, based on property qualifications. Kerkyra, independent once more, was usually hostile.

But Athens and Sparta, the two states which were to dominate the history of the classical period, both had rather *un*usual histories at this time; and their histories must be considered later.

5 THE NEW ART

Meanwhile art went through a revolution of its own. The first Greek pottery in the western colonies was still geometric. Greeks were already importing oriental decorated textiles and metalwork; but so far their traditional art had held its own. Then, in the mood of confidence and ambition brought on by the feeling that the world had room and plenty for all, very quickly it disappears. All Greece, it seems, looked with new eyes at geometric art and decided that it was 'square'.

The new 'orientalising' styles drew motives from eastern art; not eastern painted pottery, for there was none worth importing, but from the ivories, jewellery, metalwork and textiles. Rosettes, used for ornament in the new vase-painting, resemble those on court dresses in Assyrian sculpture. The ornament that was to become the 'egg and tongue' or 'egg and dart' pattern, familiar in classical architecture, is derived from an Egyptian pattern of alternating lotus flowers and buds; when its origin was forgotten, the buds became the 'eggs', while the 'tongues' represent the stamens of wide-open flowers, each originally flanked by two petals, which curve back parallel to the sides of the adjacent buds. The palmette derives from the top of the Mesopotamian Tree of Life, with ribbons adorning and connecting the ends of its branches, like tinsel on a Christmas tree; a religious symbol in Babylonia, though to the Greeks just an attractive pattern. Sometimes the whole tree, in varied colours, adorns a vase-handle; sometimes the palmette is used separately. The pillar-capital with symmetrical volutes, which in its later classical form is called Ionic, was borrowed from Syria in an earlier form, with a spike between the volutes, representing a stem between curled fronds. On a vase from Rhodes, a palmette rises from such a spike between volutes, and two agreeably vivacious goats are browsing on it. Animals – wild goats, lions (first a Syrian Hittite, later an Assyrian type), human-headed sphinxes, dogs coursing hares – form friezes round the vases. Men, plump and muscular, appear, often as armoured warriors fighting; then names, often from Homer, are written beside them, and the art begins to deal largely in scenes from saga.

Competence in the new styles was attained swiftly, but still not in a day. At Athens, where large, ambitious figures were at once attempted, one might think – if we did not know the sequel – that this is just another case of a decent, peasant art ruined by commerce. Corinth began more cautiously, and in the mid seventh century 'Protocorinthian' attained wonderful skill. The lion-headed scent-bottle (aryballos) presented by George Macmillan to the British Museum has in three zones a battle-scene, a horse-race and a hare-hunt, thirty-three separate figures in all, in a space less than two inches high. Corinth did not capture the western markets through geographical advantages alone. Later, however, the insatiable demand for their products did tempt the Corinthians into commercialism. In 'ripe Corinthian' the drawing is sometimes slovenly; some of the workers are second-rate; all are under pressure to work fast; they even resort to such unworthy expedients as elongating their lions in order to get round the vase in three lions instead of four! Then Athens, now producing the fine Attic Black-figure ware, invaded the western market in her turn. In a last attempt at a 'come-back', the Corinthians imitated the Athenian style. Then, after 550, they went out of business.

Vase-painting was, after all, a minor art; only, it is the one which we know best, because pottery, in fragments, is almost indestructible. Of major Greek painting very little survives, and even of sculpture relatively little. The bronze statues, more highly regarded than stone, have mostly been melted down, and even marble has often been burnt for lime. However, we have enough early Greek major sculpture to be able to see it gradually shaking off Egyptian influence and achieving great dignity long before it reached what the sculptors (unfashionable as it may be to say it) were continuously seeking, realistic verisimilitude. Typical are the statues of young men in athletic nudity, set up at temples, perhaps in commemoration of athletic successes, or over graves; a high proportion of early Athenian grave monuments seem to be those of young men dead before their time, set up by parents. Fine work was being produced in Ionia, the islands and the Peloponnese; but Athens, with such achievements as the eleven-foot *kouros* (youth) of Sounion and others in the Athens National Museum, was already taking the lead. Later begins the charming series of *korai* (maidens) of the Acropolis, perhaps girls of leading families who had been acolytes before their early marriages. They were found, with a good deal of their original paint still on them – red lips, brown eyes, frocks patterned in green and gold – in the pits in which they were laid away by the Athenians, tidying up after their city had been sacked by the Persians in 480.

The appearance of a Greek city in archaic times was not like our idea of a Greek city, full of marble-pillared façades. That kind of acropolis and city-centre was first achieved in Athens and Sicily after the Persian Wars, and spread to eastern Greece later still. The first temples, torn down and replaced in stone later, were of timber and brick, brightly painted, on stone foundations. Early stone temples known include that of Kerkyra, with its powerful pedimental (gable-end) sculptures, preserved in Corfu, though unfortunately not *in situ*: the Gorgon with her children Chrysaor (Golden-Sword) and the horse Pegasos, flanked by two huge panthers, their spots neatly executed with a drill and compass. The idea of having just *this* group perhaps emerges from an idea of adorning buildings with a hideous, tusked face, to scare away evil influences. The Gorgon (Glaring-Eyes) probably meant or *was* just such a face, represented on gables or on shields, before the name was attached to the legend of Perseus the monster-slayer. The Corfu sculptures would be even more horrific if they had kept their paint.

The Kerkyra temple, early sixth century, was built perhaps to celebrate the recovery of civic independence. The temple at Corinth itself, of which a few sturdy monolithic pillars remain, much photographed, is dated by pottery fragments, found under its foundations, about 540 or 530; and by that time many others were in existence or in building; one, for instance, built by enlightened tyrants at Athens. It had in its gable-end the agreeable and smiling three-bodied monster, now in the Acropolis Museum. But for the most part, our impression of a Greek city about 650 or even 550 would be of something rather barbaric; a huddle of little cubical or (still) apsidal-ended houses, flat-roofed in the islands, gabled and thatched in most of the mainland, where there is more rain, nestling under an acropolis, as the white houses still do (only not so closely) at Lindos in Rhodes. Tiles are said to have been introduced at Corinth, under the tyrants, and at first were used mainly for temples and large buildings. Decoration was largely in paint, on wood, on stone, on terracotta; for instance, on terracotta slabs used for blocking the holes between beam-ends along the side-walls of a temple, to keep the birds from getting in and nesting; for, once they did get in, they were 'in sanctuary', and could not be disturbed. Between the houses wound little alleys, barely wide enough for a loaded donkey; Greek town-planning was still in the future. The 'wide ways' that Homer mentions were outside the gates, where tracks from the country converged. Irregular and colourful, the archaic Greek cities seem an entirely suitable home for some of the irregular and colourful personalities who lived in them.

CHAPTER 5

THE AGE OF THE LYRIC POETS

1 ARCHILOCHOS OF PAROS

WITH the new art came a new poetry.

It is not that short, personal, 'occasional' poems had not existed before. Hymns to the gods, work-songs, battle-songs, love-songs, in dactylic (–··) or anapaest (··–) metres must have existed for ages; also short pieces satirising the neighbours, in iambics, like English blank verse lines but two syllables longer. On some festal occasions, satire was a tradition, 'for luck', to take people down, lest too great happiness might provoke the envy of heaven. As in many preliterate societies, they were not only produced by professionals. But in the time of Gyges (whom he mentions) there lived a poet so great that, for the first time, people wrote down and preserved his short poems, as professional reciters had already written down the epics. We, unfortunately, have only later writers' quotations from them. This was Archilochos, from the island of Paros, soldier, sailor, gold-digger, vagrant and genius, whom Greeks did not hesitate to mention in the same breath with Homer. His father was a leading citizen, but his mother a slave; so he was on the edge of aristocratic society, but not in it. Fiercely sensitive, his poetry is as bitter and salty as the sea, which he knew well from earning his living on it, and did not romanticise.

His father was deputed to lead a colony to Thasos island, off the Thracian coast, and offered Archilochos a place in it. He left home without regret ('Good-bye to Paros and those figs and a sailor's life'); but he did not think much of Thasos when he saw it. 'This place sticks up like a donkey's back, crowned with wild woods.' 'There is no good land here ... as on the Siris river.' Perhaps he had been to Italy on trading ships. Nor did he think much of his fellow-colonists, a mixed lot. He was hard to please, and he never could control his tongue.

He did not stay many years in Thasos. One reason for this was his almost inevitably unhappy love-affair. He remembers the girl, Neoboule, 'playing with a sprig of myrtle and a rose, while her hair shaded her back and shoulders'. He fell deeply in love, and they became engaged, or at least so he says; but something happened, and they did not marry. Archilochos tries to reason, and pleads, and finally storms, using language unknown to the Homeric epic. His barbed iambics – and the very word iambic was connected with a word meaning 'shoot' – were so hideously telling that, according to legend at least, Neoboule and her father and sisters all hanged themselves. He had the egoism of his kind of genius in full measure, and when Thasos was startled by an eclipse, turning day into night, he says that after the way he has been treated, that is the sort of thing that would happen nowadays. This was by no means his only quarrel; and nothing, according to him, was ever his fault.

We do not know, but it may be that the breaking-off of his engagement had something to do with the other most famous episode in his story; and that was on this wise:

There was gold in Thasos – no doubt one of the objects of the operation; but earlier miners proved to have had most of it out. But there was more on the mainland opposite, and thither an expedition from Thasos shortly went – and was defeated by the Thracians. Archilochos ran with the rest, throwing away his heavy shield. A shield was a sore impediment in a rout, but to lose it was serious; to be able to 'provide armour', as the phrase ran, was a title to status in the community. It was the sort of thing one did not talk about; but Archilochos did, writing in a verse letter to a friend:

> Some Thracian flaunts the shield I left behind,
> My trusty shield – I had to – in a wood.
> Well, I have saved my life; so never mind
> That shield; I'll get another just as good.

It is the first appearance of the anti-heroic note; and, naturally, it is not sounded by a coward; on the contrary, when he finally made Thasos too hot to hold him he became a soldier by profession; 'a mercenary – like a Karian', as he says in his usual

ruthless way. The Ionians affected to regard the Karians, neighbours whom they could not conquer, as the lowest form of
life. 'With my spear I win my bread, and with my spear the
Thracian wine, and on my spear I learn to drink.' Again, 'I am
the servant of the God of War, and skilled too in the Muses'
lovely gift'. 'Tossing his Karian plume' – the well-known
Greek horse-hair plume, adopted, like the large round shield,
painted with a blazon, from the east – he is every inch a soldier; and he writes of soldiering with anti-romantic realism.
'Seven men died – we ran them down – a thousand we the
slayers.' Wine and women and lice; and the captain of his
choice, not 'tall and handsome, flaunting love-locks'; no,
'Give me a little man and bandy-legged, firmly planted on his
feet, and full of guts'. It sounds like a portrait.

In the end, still in vigorous middle-age, he went back to
Paros. In an age that valued poetry, so that many tyrants kept
poets at their courts, his father's family may have been prepared to welcome him for his poetry's sake. He could write to
please when he chose: lines for dedications, epitaphs, beast-
fables. Also he could be useful in the recurrent neighbourly
wars with Naxos. In what may be some of his last lines he
speaks as an old soldier: 'Bid the young men be cheerful;
victory is in the hands of the gods.' Fighting for his own city,
a man of Naxos killed him.

2 SAPPHO AND HER TIMES

Fifty years after Archilochos, the most vivid picture that we
have of a Greek city in this age of revolution comes from
Mytilene, in the poetry of Sappho and Alkaios.

Lesbos, large and green, hilly but not mountainous, with a
1928 population of 140,000, had six cities in early Greek
times; one was soon wiped out in a war with a neighbour, leaving a sense of guilt. Mytilene, on the east coast, was the largest.
With settlements on the mainland, where surplus peasants
could go and colonise, it was a prosperous city. Its aristocrats
traded with Egypt, not disdaining to go as shipmasters themselves; one of Sappho's poems was a reprimand to a brother

of hers for spending his money on a slave-courtesan of Naukratis, whom he bought and set free. At home, Mytilene struck coins of great beauty; and the composition of lyric poetry, that is to say, in Greece, *song*, accompanied on the lyre, was an accomplishment common to many cultivated people, not only that of a few professionals. People sent poems in complex lyric metres to each other as letters, and many of the poems that we have are of this kind. Sappho, no great beauty – she was little and dark, typically Greek in fact, whereas the ideal was to be tall and fair – enjoyed fame for her poetic genius, and parents even from Ionia would send their girls to be taught by her. They left, normally, to be married; Sappho herself was married and had a daughter of her own; music was considered a desirable accomplishment for a lady and mistress of a household. Sappho's circle gives the first glimpse that we have, after the pictures of home-life in the *Odyssey*, of women's life in a part of the Greek world where it was notably free.

It is an outdoor world. The city was the centre of all things, but it was small, close-packed, and the country never far away. Groves, not temples, are the places where she and her maidens worship on high days, as when she invokes Aphrodite:

> Come hither, come, out of the Cretan land
> To this thy shrine, within whose orchard glade
> Of apple-trees thy altars fragrant stand
>   With frankincense.
> Cold water falls between the apple-trees
> And climbing roses over-arch their shade,
> And rustling in the leafy boughs the breeze
>   Lulls every sense.

The girls would garland each other, and Sappho dwells lovingly on all the flowers that they wove in. A wedding-song (probably; Housman imitated it in his *Epithalamium*) calls up the picture of evening outside a village, when all creatures stream home: 'Evening star, thou bringest all that the bright dawn scattered; thou bringest the lamb and the kid, and the child to its mother.' In another fragment, perhaps two choruses are answering each other, one at least with a touch of jealousy that marriage is taking away their playmate:

As the apple reddens and ripens, up on the tree so high,
High on the topmost twig – and the pickers have passed it by –
No, not that; but they never could reach it however they try!

As the bluebell grows on the hills, till the shepherds' trampling feet
Beat it down; and bright on the ground is the flower so sweet. . . .

Jealousy; Sappho was passionately devoted to many of her
pupils, and she did not attempt to disguise her feelings when
marriage took them away. However, it was the course of nature, and Sappho duly produced the required songs, and some
traditional heavy humour, such as jokes about the size of the
bridegroom's feet. What was really intolerable, but happened
occasionally, was for a girl to leave Sappho and resort to
another teacher.

But it must be added that the later tradition, which made
Sappho nothing less than a pervert, is probably a piece of literary silliness; a caricature of Sappho, produced on the comic
stage of late-classical Athens, having been taken seriously by
solemn scholars in late antiquity. Sappho in love became a
'pantomime' character; and how far it deserves to be taken
seriously may be seen, when we are told that in one play two
other poets, Archilochos, who was probably dead before she
was born, and another who *may* not have been born when she
died, were represented as her suitors.

When the girls married, she could still keep in touch with
them. There is a poem addressed to Anaktoria, who had gone
to live in Sardis – there would be no feeling against intermarriage with the civilised Lydians – perhaps in answer to a letter
about the splendour of the Lydian army. We are reminded of
the armies on vases.

> Some call a host of cavalry
> And some of foot the finest sight
> Of all, and some a fleet at sea;
> But I would say, the heart's delight.

Look, she goes on rather inconsequently, at what Helen did
for love! But now, she ends, I will remember Anaktoria,

The marvel of whose living grace
And laughing eyes I'd rather see
Than chariots all of Lydian race
And armoured lines of infantry.

Not so was it with little Timas, who died before her wedding, 'and all the girls of her year cut their hair short for mourning'.

Sappho, even more than most poets, is strictly untranslatable', and one must apologize for even trying. There is nothing out of the ordinary in her thought; and the fire is lost, like the bouquet of a delicate wine, that 'will not travel'. The Aiolic dialect of Greek, rural and conservative, keeping old forms, has an archaic attractiveness; and in Sappho it found genius to exploit it. Plato the philosopher, himself a poet, called her the Tenth Muse; and the later poet who first collected 'epigrams', that is *inscription*-poems (epitaphs, dedications, etc.), comparing the work of each of his poets to a different flower, calls his pieces from Sappho 'few – but roses'.

But the delicate life of this society was rudely interrupted. The people rioted against the arrogance of an aristocratic governing class. More than one popular leader or 'tyrant' was killed, and Alkaios, a great poet and a friend of Sappho, betrays the extent of his political thought in the opening of a song, 'Now to get drunk, for Myrsilos is dead'! But some nobles were more discriminating. One, Pittakos – his name seems to be Thracian – who had acted with Alkaios' brothers, when Alkaios was a boy, to kill an earlier *tyrannos*, sided *with* Myrsilos; and after Myrsilos' death the people elected Pittakos dictator (Alkaios says 'tyrant') to reform the state. Alkaios and his friends were furious at this disloyalty to their class; but the new government was too strong for them and they had to flee abroad. Alkaios, puzzled, compares the storm-tossed state to a ship in a gale; the phrase, 'the ship of state', is probably his invention.

Sappho is said to have visited Sicily. The men took service with the kings of the east. It was a stirring age. Nineveh, capital of Assyria, had fallen in 612 to the Medes, an Aryan-speaking people of Iran, and insurgent Babylon; Egyptians and Babylonians crossed swords in Syria. At Carchemish on the Euphrates, where Nebuchadnezzar of Babylon routed Pharaoh Necoh in 605, D. G. Hogarth and T. E. Lawrence found among the burnt ruins of the city a Greek gorgon-faced shield, lying among the charred wood of a doorway shot full of arrow-heads. Probably later than this, Alkaios' brother Antimenidas served with the Babylonian army. Alkaios himself went to Egypt; perhaps in defeat the exiles had quarrelled. A tattered papyrus scroll of his poems, preserved among the rubbish-heaps of much later Greeks in Egypt, included a poem which mentioned sea-faring ... war ... Babylon ... Askalon (in the Philistine country); but unhappily only a word or two at the end of each line is preserved. It is rather typical of our evidence on archaic Greece.

Presently the exiles gathered again in Lydia, to make one more attempt to 'liberate' their country. Antimenidas was there, displaying an ivory-hilted sword of honour, given to him for slaying a gigantic enemy champion. Perhaps there were some signs of a reaction against Pittakos, who had been trying to reform morals; one of his laws provided double penalties for acts of violence if committed under the influence of drink. But he again proved far too strong for the émigrés. He captured the whole gang and, with the saying, startling in early Greece, 'Forgiveness is better than vengeance', granted them pardon. After ten years in power, he resigned and is said to have lived for ten years longer in honoured retirement. Alkaios too, perhaps in somewhat reduced circumstances, lived to be old.

3 PROGRESS IN THE WEST

If Sappho had meanwhile visited the west, she very likely travelled in a ship of Phōkaia. This city, the Ionian neighbour of Aiolic Kyme, had close relations with Mytilene, including a convention for a common coinage, and replaces Kyme (we do not know why) in western pioneering. Coming on the scene late, and following the old tin-route, beyond the area of Greek primary colonisation, Phokaians reached and even colonised on the coasts of France and Spain. Their greatest achievement, about 600, was the foundation of Marseilles.

Greek Sicily also, after a long pause (about 690–630), was expanding. Two new cities, founded almost simultaneously, are pushed forward as though with imperialist ambitions, hard up against the corner of western Sicily held by the Phoenicians and their civilised native allies, the Elymoi of the city of Egesta or Segesta. Both had a stormy history, but also made notable contributions to Greek culture. Selinous, on the south coast, with noble temples (shaken down by earthquakes), wide streets and a 'town-planned' city centre, produced some of the finest early Greek sculpture; archaic followed by exquisite early classical architectural reliefs in the Palermo Museum, and an archaic bronze boy, jealously guarded in the local township. Selinous was organized by the Sicilian Megara, with its con- stricted territory (p. 89). Himera, on the north coast, founded by Chalkidians of Sicily with some Syracusan political exiles, produced the earliest coins in the west, and the west's first famous poet: Tisias, surnamed Stēsichoros, 'stablisher of the chorus', who greatly advanced one of the most splendid Greek art-forms, the choral lyric, later to form an essential part of classical tragedy. Stesichoros was a man around whom stories clustered. He was said to have been struck blind by the deified Helen for an unkind reference to her, but cured when he wrote his *Recantation*, saying that she had really been spirited away by Aphrodite to Egypt, while the Trojan War was fought for a phantom of her! Perhaps the blindness, of which he repented in his famous poem, was only spiritual. He also told, perhaps with mimetic dancing, the fable of the Horse, driven off his pasture by the Stag, who called in a Man to help him and then could not get rid of him. It was said to have been a warning to Himera, at war with her non-Greek neighbours, against calling in Phalaris, tyrant of Akragas.

Phalaris was the ideal Wicked Tyrant of Greek popular his- tory, the favourite story about him being of how he used to roast his enemies alive in a brazen bull. What truth there may be in the story, if any, we do not know. His city of Akragas (now Agrigento) was the last major foundation of the Greeks in Sicily, established by Gela (p. 87) about 580 to secure the land half-way to Selinous. Phalaris (c. 570–555?) belongs to its first generation. In a splendid situation, in a 'saucer' of rocky hills two miles from the sea, it was hailed by Pindar as 'fairest of the cities of mortal men'. The unrivalled line of temples still standing along the ridge, within its southern walls, dates from Pindar's time, in the fifth century.

About 580, also, an expedition from the Asian Doris tried to seize the western point of Sicily – a direct attack on the Phoenicians there; but they and their Elymian allies succeeded in destroying the new colony. Its survivors then occupied the Lipari Islands (pp. 35, 49). There they formed an interesting semi-communist state, in which the land was re-divided every twenty years. The harmony of this state and its freedom from class-conflict won it some admiration from other Greeks; but towards non-Greeks it was frankly piratical. The advance of the Greeks and their aggressiveness was by this time causing the Phoenicians to draw together, under the leadership of Carthage, and to make alliance with other non-Greeks, notably the Etruscans. Already at the time of the founding of Marseilles the Phokaians had fought Phoenicians; and Herodotos says that they regularly carried on their voyages 'not in merchant vessels but in ships of war'. The Greeks were certainly not innocent in the increasing hostility that developed in the west from this time on; and their enemies succeeded in limiting their advance. The Phokaians were driven back from southeastern Spain, leaving Ampurias (Emporiai, 'the Trading-Posts'), on the Costa Brava, as the westernmost outpost where Greek walls remain; and likewise a Phokaian half-way house in Corsica, founded about 565, was made untenable by the fleets of Carthage and Etruria twenty years later. Its colonists withdrew to Elea, south of Paestum, which was to be famous in the annals of Greek philosophy (p. 142).

4 SPARTA AND REACTION

By no means all Greek cities emerged from their revolutionary period as successfully as Mytilene or even Corinth. At Megara, for instance, after the fall of the tyranny, there was first a conservative (coalition?) government, then a radical one; the poor turned on the *bourgeoisie* with such demands as that all who had lent money at usury must repay all the interest they had received; and then the democracy, with few educated leaders, fell into such confusion that the numerous *émigrés* were able to return and overthrow it. On this sad story we have firsthand and highly personal comments in the poems of Theognis, a nobleman, whose poems (or perhaps a collection, based on his poems) survive because old-fashioned gentlemen, groaning under the democracy of classical Athens, thought them suitable for school reading. To this end a number of amatory pieces addressed to boys were taken out and relegated to a separate book. By arranging the poems in a suitable order (quite arbitrarily, it must be admitted) we may imagine ourselves going through an autobiography: youth, with love, wine and agonies of jealousy; political frustration, with indignation that mere peasants, who used to 'dress in skins and keep out of town', should demand human rights; some tory observations on the neglect of eugenics; exile, escaping with one's skin, 'like a dog out of a torrent'; and finally ('Trample the foolish people!'), the pleasure of revenge.

Megara under a restored, reactionary government then joined the Peloponnesian League organized, latish in the sixth century, by Sparta, which became the champion of all reactionary forces in Greece.

Sparta had not always been 'Spartan' in the sense of being austere and 'fascist'; but she was military from the beginning of her history. Dominating all Laconia, she ruled over many subject villages and townships, in some of which the people kept their personal freedom as *perioikoi* or neighbours, while in others, which had resisted too fiercely, they became serfs, attached to the soil (not slaves, who could be sold), called helots. The name was said to come from Helos, a town on the south coast, which was treated in this way. After the conquest of Messenia (p. 88), with more land and more helots, Sparta's aristocracy was among the richest in Greece. They imported eastern ivory, Egyptian scarabs, northern amber, Lydian dresses for ladies, whose social life was as free as in Lesbos; their craftsmen were skilled in vase-painting and in fine bronze-work. Late in the seventh century (not earlier, as a recent papyrus discovery has shown) lived Alkmān, a master of choral lyric as delicate as any in Greece. Many of his songs were for choirs of girls. A quoted fragment evokes the view over the vale of Sparta at evening:

Now lie sleeping the peaks of the mountains and the gullies,
Buttresses and water-courses;
The creatures, even all that the dark earth nurses;
Wild beasts in the mountain caves, and honey-bees,
And monsters in the deep of the purple sea;
And now sleep all the birds,
The race of the slender wings.

But already before Alkman's time, the Spartans had been starkly faced with the fact that if they were to hold their wide lands, they must above all be strong. In 669 (traditionally) they were defeated by Argos, the senior Dorian power, which Sparta had grown to rival; and, six kings' reigns before 480 (about 630?), Messenia rose in desperate rebellion, with help from Arcadia, and for a time the Spartans were fighting for their lives. Tyrtaios, a Spartan nobleman (the tale that he was a lame Athenian schoolmaster is another fantasy from the Athenian theatre), was the poet who helped to steel their spirits in this war; and in some of his poems there is also talk of the proper ordering of the state. What came of it was that, just when most of the Greek world was 'modernising' its ways, Sparta reaffirmed many stern, archaic customs; that, at least, is a theory which reconciles the facts of the early promise of Spartan art and poetry, and the grim archaism of Spartan society in classical times.

The revolt was crushed; an Arcadian king betrayed his allies – his own people stoned him for it afterwards – and the Messenians, except some who fled abroad, were forced back into helotry, required to hand over half of all their produce to Spartan landlords; it was intended to be physically and morally crushing. But the Messenians never forgot that they had been a free people; and the Spartans knew that they had not forgotten.

At home, the Spartans overhauled their constitution. The power of the kings was limited. They were watched by five annually elected Ephors ('Overseers'), to whom they annually swore an oath to govern according to the (unwritten) laws. This magistracy dated from the time of the first conquest of Messenia. They were also required to consult a council of twenty-eight elders, elected for life from men over sixty, of certain noble families only. The kings remained war-leaders and guardians of property; judges, notably, of the question which kinsman had the right to marry an heiress left without brothers. Important decisions, including that of peace or war, had to be voted by the Assembly of all males over thirty, of the few thousand full citizen or Spartiate families. It had been confirmed as a right, sanctioned by the Delphic Oracle, that the People had 'decisive power'; but in a reactionary mood, this was limited by provisions that they must give (Tyrtaios says) 'straight answers' (not introducing amendments?) and that if they did not do so the kings and elders could apply the closure. The assembly thus had no initiative. Also the method of voting remained primitive; it was by acclamation, and a group of men shut up in a building near by had to decide which shouts were the loudest, not only as between Aye and No, but even between candidates for the ephorship.

There could be differences within the Spartan governing class, but the grounds for solidarity, as against Messenians and even the more peaceful, loyal and satisfied helots in Laconia, were so strong that governments seldom had difficulty in getting their way. More important than the nominally democratic political machinery were the social customs under which every Spartan was brought up as a soldier. Spartiate babies, it is said, had to be shown to the ephors, and if they appeared weakly were put out to die on Taÿgetos. Those who were reared left their mothers at the age of seven, and were brought up in 'packs', led by older boys, for whom they 'fagged', under the supervision of a carefully chosen Spartiate as 'headmaster'. They wore one tunic summer and winter; their beds were of reeds, which they plucked (not cut) from the river Eurōtas; their food was monotonous (its staple, a blackish wheat-porridge, a method of treating corn more primitive than leavened bread) and barely sufficient. They were expected to supplement it by stealing from the farms, and beaten if caught, not for dishonesty but for bad scouting. They were taught to read and count, and traditional songs and dances, calculated to inculcate patriotism and to give training in ordered movement; and the packs met in tough ball-games and organized fights. Among the older youths, the training became more definitely military, while athletics and choral music and dancing continued. The object of every boy was, on reaching the age of twenty, to win election to a club or mess, of about fifteen members, which would thenceforth be his section in the army, and in whose house he would dine and normally sleep, even after marrying, which he was expected to do at thirty. Election had to be unanimous; and not to get elected somewhere was social death. The terror of this must have kept every boy desperately resolved not to show the white feather under any trial. Girls also received some athletic training, running and wrestling in short 'gym frocks', which other Greeks thought immodest.

(Some, by the way, have thought that Dr Arnold introduced from his classical reading some of the leading features of the English public school, but this does not seem to be so. Rather, Arnold made opportunist use of features of a largely unsupervised boys' society which he found existing.)

In all this, classical Spartans believed that they were living under the Laws of Lykourgos (Lycurgus). Many Greek codes of law, written down (unlike Sparta's) fairly early in the age of literacy, were ascribed to known codifiers; but as to when Lykourgos lived, or to which (presumably royal) family he belonged, there was hopeless disagreement; even the Delphic Oracle did not know whether to address him as man or god, but 'rather thought' the latter. Hence, though Plutarch wrote a Life of him, and the latest learned work on early Sparta is prepared to date him about 700, there are grounds for suspecting that he was an ancient god, identified before the dawn of history probably with Apollo, but always associated with Sparta's almost entirely unwritten laws. It is hardly ever possible to say when any feature of Spartan life was introduced, because, whereas in many other states later antiquaries traced the evolution of their customs, in Sparta everything was ascribed to the one lawgiver, just as the Jews ascribed Deuteronomy to Moses. Spartan realities are difficult to discern through the mists of the great Spartan patriotic myth. It is merely a reasonable theory that Sparta turned her back on progress in the crisis of the great rebellion. She rejected the invention of money, which other states were then adopting. She did not intentionally reject art and poetry; Alkman, and the best Spartan art, were still to come; but in about a century – three generations; the time that it usually takes for a new climate of culture to permeate a society – Spartan art was dead.

There was a belief at Sparta, Herodotos tells us, that Lykourgos introduced the characteristic Spartan usages, political, military and social, from Crete. This too was a reasonable theory. In the cities of Dorian Crete, too, there were powerful magistrates like the ephors – more powerful, indeed, since they also replaced the early kings; there was a similar military society, in which the soldier-citizens took their meals in messes; and there was a similar rejection of the growing individualism of the rest of Greece. There was also the same effect on culture. Crete had been quick to adopt orientalising art, and Cretan sculptors had influenced the mainland; then, earlier than at Sparta, the promise fades, and Crete contributes practically nothing more to the Greek achievement. This decline is surely not so mysterious as some have thought it. In Crete as at Sparta, Dorian landlords ruled a serf population. In the seventh century, that age of unrest, they held their position only by adopting a régime of militarism; and their civilisation paid the price.

In the meantime, these Dorian aristocracies 'had their reward'. Military training, hunting, athletics, and the choral song and dance which was the main Dorian contribution to Greek poetry, and was *preserved* even when it had ceased to be created, filled up a life which many found satisfying. There was also the supervision of their estates. Some Spartiates were on excellent terms with some helots; some had been nursed by helot foster-mothers, and foster-brothers were sometimes admitted to the boys' training and then to the messes and the citizen body; whatever its faults, that body was not a caste. In Crete, the cities might fight each other, but there was a gentlemen's agreement that none would ever tamper with another city's serfs.

Sparta did better than that. After being defeated by the brave Arcadians of Tegea on their own ground, she gave up conquest – she had already as many helots as she could manage – and, after avenging the defeat, admitted Tegea to honourable alliance. She brought home from Tegea (by theft, between the wars) the alleged bones of Orestes, son of Agamemnon, and honoured him as a hero, thus claiming continuity with the pre-Dorian heroes; were not her kings descended from Herakles? She thus turned her back on narrowly Dorian racialism. She defeated Argos, and made alliance with the smaller cities of Argolis, which Argos under her last powerful king, Pheidon (late seventh century?), had dominated; she made similar alliances with Elis, which owned the sanctuary of Olympia, and with other Arcadians, though they were sometimes restive, and sometimes fought among themselves. She made it a policy to suppress tyrants and support upper-class governments. By about 540 she dominated the Peloponnese, and 'the Lakedaimonians and their allies' were a force for reaction, indeed, but also for stability.

5 THE RISE OF ATHENS

Athens, without whose achievement all that other Greeks did would have much less significance for us, has no early history, only archaeology and legend. That is because, until after 600, she sent out no colonies and had no tyrant. Her peasants could still find room in her (by Greek standards) extensive territory; in 600 she was still exporting grain to the neighbouring commercial cities; and, a generation before that, when Kylon, the Athenian son-in-law of Theagenes of Megara, tried to make himself tyrant, the people did not move, and he failed. There was no revolutionary situation – yet. But he was only a little too soon; for by that time, many peasants were trying to farm hill-foot 'marginal land', and having difficulty in making ends meet. In bad years they had to borrow from richer neighbours; but with the coming of money, this meant that, instead of borrowing a sack of corn in the old, neighbourly way, one had to borrow the *price* of enough food to tide one over, before the harvest, when it was dear, and sell grain enough to repay the loan after harvest, when it was cheap; or alternatively, to pay heavy interest, of the kind that raised such indignation at Megara. By 600, while rich men exported to good markets in Aigina or Corinth, poor men were going hungry. Many, too, were losing their land, pledged as security for debts, and even their liberty; for the creditor's last recourse against the insolvent debtor was to seize him and his family as slaves.

The law was harsh; it was rich-man's law. Moreover, it was sacred, primeval custom, its secrets locked in the breast of noble judges; and when at last, with the spread of writing and in answer to popular clamour, the Laws were reduced to writing, under the supervision of one Drakon, people were not much comforted. It appeared that under the 'draconic' code, death could be the penalty for almost anything. Those laws, said a later Athenian, seemed to be written in blood. Under them, rich and noble Athenians, in fierce, late-Renaissance, social competition for wealth and splendour, 'joined house to house and laid field to field', until the question 'Will you live *alone* in the midst of the earth?' began to worry the more far-sighted among them, as it had worried Isaiah. It was not so much the danger of revolt, for the rich had the best weapons; but what would become of a state with a dwindling army?

In this situation, the Athenians showed more wisdom than many Greeks. It was agreed to give dictatorial powers to a man commanding the confidence of all classes for his fair-mindedness and integrity: Solon, a man descended from the ancient kings, but only moderately rich; a man who had seen the world as a merchant, and who had attracted attention by outspoken poems condemning the rich for their greed, as well as by patriotic verse, scourging the Athenians into making one more effort in a war in which they captured the island of Salamis from Megara.

In 594 or 592 – the accounts vary – Solon took office and, amid acute tension and excitement, announced his programme. To the bitter disappointment of the poor, he did not proclaim a redivision of the land. Probably his fellow-nobles, when they accepted him as a dictator, knew very well that he was no revolutionary. But he forbade once and for all the enslavement of any free Athenian for debt; he cancelled all debts outstanding, and there was a joyful sweeping away of boundary-markers on the many mortgaged holdings; and he organized the re-purchase (an expensive operation, and we do not know how it was financed) of all Athenians who could be traced, who had been sold abroad. The rich must have paid heavily. Solon also placed an embargo on the export of agricultural produce, except olive oil, of which Athens had a surplus. There should be no more selling of grain in richer markets while men at home went hungry. Athens was given a decisive push in the direction in which the rise of population was driving her. She was soon importing grain from the Black Sea, and fought a war with Mytilene for a foothold on the Dardanelles near Troy, to secure her trade-route; the poet Alkaios recorded, like Archilochos, how he had thrown away his shield in a defeat in that war. Athens must import grain – and pay for it. The rise of a great export trade in Attic pottery, found throughout the Mediterranean, and presumably also of more perishable manufactures, is a feature of the following century.

Solon also took in hand the Athenian constitution. This had the usual essential elements of the city-state: the elected executive, the nine Archons (p. 67); the Council of the 'Best Men', Eupatridai or 'patricians', who met, as they had done since Athens was a village, to discuss all public questions; and the Assembly of the people (*ekklēsia*, later the word for 'Church', *église*), which had to agree on important decisions. This was not a pure formality; even the chiefs in the *Iliad* recognize that you cannot make war if the troops will not fight. But the Assembly had no prestige, no organization, and no initiative. The 'best people', meeting at the rock called Areopagus, discussed who should be Archons for next year, and any other matters to be put to the Assembly, and any counter-proposals from the 'floor', if made, which we do not know, had little chance of acceptance against those of the Council.

It was Solon who made the Assembly, not yet indeed supreme in Athens, but a reality, with which influential men would henceforth have to reckon. He laid down that all freemen were to be admitted to it, even those who had little or no land. With the rise in the importance of tradesmen, this was important. He laid down that all men possessing enough *landed* property to support a war-horse might become archons; that archons, after their year, must give an account of their actions, financial and general, to the Assembly; and that only if this was passed might they, and no others, become members of the Areopagite Council. Rich merchants who bought land *could* therefore become Areopagites, though this was probably rare for a long time; and even noblemen could only reach that influential position if they secured election to office, and carried out their duties to the satisfaction of the people.

To make this a reality Solon introduced his most far-reaching innovation, the creation of a second or People's Council, usually called The Council in distinction from the Areopagus. It consisted of a hundred men from each of the four Tribes found (residentially mingled) in Attica and in all Ionian cities. Admission to it was open probably to the middle-class farmers or 'owners of a yoke of oxen', defined as those with half (or, *aliter,* two-thirds) the qualification for a 'knight', and roughly equalling the class of armoured infantry; and election was by lot, so that one did not have to be well known in order to secure a place. To this body was transferred the discussion and presentation of business for the Assembly, including presumably the acceptance of candidates for the archonships. The Areopagus, a council of elder statesmen and a supreme court, allegedly founded by the goddess Athena herself, had great prestige. Solon left it, with vague powers, as 'Guardian of the Laws', in which capacity it could presumably arraign and punish anyone whose behaviour, public or private, was not according to custom. It thus had formidable power to _veto_ drastic innovations. But, a matter all-important for the future of Athens, it lost the initiative.

A People's Council (so-called in an official document and therefore probably existing beside another Council which was not the people's) appears also in an early inscription from Chios; but the inscription is later than Solon, and whether the Council at Chios is earlier is therefore uncertain.

Solon had tried to do justice to all classes; naturally he satisfied no one. He was no democrat; he claimed to have given the people 'power _enough_', and his later poems, or verse pamphlets, show exasperation at their ingratitude. Badgered on all sides – 'like a wolf among many dogs', as he says – he declined to suppress criticism by force, as a tyrant; that, he says, would have meant bloodshed. Finally he laid down his office and went abroad again 'to trade and see the world', leaving the Athenians, still bound by powerful oaths to obey his enactments for ten years, to learn to administer his constitution without him. He allegedly visited Egypt, hearing tales from the priests about a lost kingdom of Atlantis, which may possibly have been Thera. In Cyprus he gave advice to a young king, Philokypros, who was modernising his city. The most famous of all the Solon-stories, that of his visit to Croesus, the rich king of Lydia, rests only on saga; indeed, unless there is something very wrong with the traditional chronology (which there probably is, but it would take too long to discuss it here), Croesus' name must have been substituted for that of his father. Croesus showed Solon all his treasures, and then asked him, who was the happiest man in all his experience? Solon named an old Athenian, whom Croesus had never heard of; a man, he explained, rich by Greek standards, who saw his sons' sons, and died gloriously, repelling a border raid. Croesus, still hoping to be placed second if not first, asked, who next? But Solon named two young Argives, whom Croesus had never heard of; brothers, both victors in the great games, who had died in their sleep after a mighty act of piety. They dragged their mother, who was priestess of Hera, for five miles in a waggon to the temple on a festal day, when she had to ride, and 'their oxen had not arrived in time from the farm'. Solon explained that all these men had lived and *died* well; before pronouncing on Croesus' claim, one had better wait.

There were statues of the two young Argives, Kleobis and Biton, at Delphoi; one of them is still there. Whether Solon really told their story to Croesus, we may doubt; but the tale, told by Herodotos, embodies two pieces of Greek 'proverbial philosophy'; that *heaven is envious* of too great prosperity among men, and that one should *look to the end*. Croesus, as we shall see, did not end happily.

At home in Athens, Solon's constitution emphatically did not bring peace. Rather, by giving defined rights to the middle and poorer classes, he had introduced a new type of political struggle, in which old-fashioned rivalries between great families blended with class-struggles in factions partly, at least, local. Sometimes elections were so fierce that no archon could be elected at all. About 570 Megakles, head of the great family of the Alkmeonidai, whose grandfather, another Megakles, had massacred the supporters of Kylon, violating sanctuary, and was alleged to have incurred a family curse, was faced by a coalition of other nobles. Against them, he took the side of those who supported Solon's constitution, the liberals as it were; a 'Coast' party against the conservatives of the Plain. But there then appeared on the scene a third party, led by another ambitious nobleman, Peisistratos, a successful general in the wars with Megara, who took up the cause of the Hill-men: the crofters of the uplands, especially in northern Attica, whom Solon had left free, and with votes, but still miserably poor. After an attempt on his life – his enemies said that he had faked it, but this we may take leave to doubt – his supporters voted him a bodyguard, fifty men with cudgels; the nucleus of a private army, with which, in 561 traditionally, he seized the Acropolis. He was driven from Athens for a time; returned in coalition with Megakles; quarrelled with him, and was driven out again; and went off with a band of his supporters to seek wealth, gold-mining in Thrace. He spent ten years there; and having accumulated the sinews of war, and made friends with Athens' enemies in Thebes and Euboia, came back, scattered the government forces by a surprise attack between Athens and Marathon, and ruled as tyrant till his death (546–528).

But he was no tyrannical tyrant. He administered the constitution of Solon, 'merely seeing to it that reliable supporters always held the chief offices'. He even went into court once, before the Areopagus, to answer a charge of murder; but the accuser lost his nerve and did not appear. He levied a modest direct tax of 10 per cent of produce, and used it to make loans on easy terms to his crofter supporters, to provide themselves with good ploughs and oxen to draw them. Production soared, and the debts were easily repaid. A charming story describes him taking a walk in the country, as he often did, to see how things were going, and seeing a peasant working hard with his mattock, excavating a croft among 'absolute stones'. Peisistratos sent his one attendant to ask him what he was getting out of that field. 'Only aches and pains', said the peasant, who had not recognized the Boss, 'and of those, Peisistratos will be wanting his 10 per cent.' Peisistratos, delighted, replied that he could do without those, and the croft should be registered as tax-free.

His sons ruled after him till 511. The long generation of peace which the tyrants gave Athens saw the laying of deep and strong economic foundations; a great increase in the planting of olive trees, for example – always a sign of security; for the olive, which gives little return for thirty years, is a long-term investment. Under Peisistratos the fine Athenian pottery captured world markets (p. 101); sculpture increased in delicacy and skill; temples and water-conduits increased the beauty and amenities of the city. About 535 came the artistic invention of red-figure vase-painting; instead of painting black figures, with incised details, the artist blacked-in the whole surface, reserving the figures in the natural red. Details of features or clothing could then be painted in, giving scope for much more variety and realism.

About the same time, too, society began to take notice of certain peasant rituals, with choral song and mimic dancing, celebrating the sufferings of Dionysos, god of the vine, whose blood is shed for the service of men. This art-form begins to receive notice, naturally, just when the peasants were achieving political status and growing more civilised. Goats were sacrificed in the worship of Dionysos, wherefore the ritual was called *trag-ōdia*, Goat-Song. In a generation, transformed out of all recognition, it was to become Attic tragedy. At present, it was still a purely religious celebration. A participant called the Answerer or Responder (see p. 205) narrated the Birth of the Divine Child and the machinations of his enemies, who wished to destroy him, and the passion and triumph of the Dying God; and between these 'lessons', the chorus sang and danced traditional or newly composed *chorales*, or carols.

CHAPTER 6

THE AGE OF THE FIRST PHILOSOPHERS

1 THE LIFE AND TIMES OF THALES, AND THE COMING OF CYRUS

GREEK philosophy was not worked out by cloistered scholars. Some of the great thinkers were scientists, without laboratories and at first without any established method; some were contemplatives, some were both. All were citizens, involved in the intense life of small communities. What is recognizable as philosophy begins in Miletos, in times of turmoil and violence. It culminates in Athens, just when Athens too was falling upon evil days.

Miletos had her great tyrant, before and after 600: Thrasyboulos, who led the defence against Alyattes of Lydia, the father of Croesus. Beaten in the field, their farms harried for eleven years on end, the Milesians held out, getting food by sea; and when a Lydian embassy was expected, Thrasyboulos bade the people feast and make merry, disguising any need for economy for the moment. The stratagem worked; Alyattes, who was ill, and thought it was because his troops had burnt a Greek temple, made peace and an alliance. Thrasyboulos was also said to have given advice on how to be a tyrant to the young Periandros of Corinth, taking his messenger for a walk by a cornfield, and thoughtfully lopping off with his walking-stick the head of any stalk that looked superior to the average; and it was Periandros who forewarned the Milesian that Alyattes had consulted Delphoi about his illness and would be sending ambassadors.

Soon after this, Alyattes called upon his Milesian allies to join his army further east. The Medes after the fall of Assyria (p. 109) had pushed west into Asia Minor, but Alyattes held them to a draw in several stubborn campaigns. The war is said to have ended after an eclipse had interrupted a battle (traditionally in 585 or 584, but no eclipse at a suitable time of day seems to be available; possibly 21 September 582, three-quarters total about 10.0 a.m.). It may have suggested to two kings, already finding the war unprofitable, an occasion for peace with honour.

The fact that there would be an eclipse that year is said to have been predicted by a young Milesian named Thales; and this, if true, marks the birthday of western science. Babylonians and Sumerians had observed eclipses for many centuries, recorded their dates, noted their cyclic recurrence, and been glad to record the *non*-occurrence of a bad omen when one was not visible in Mesopotamia. Thales might conceivably have got hold of one of their tables, and if he simply predicted an eclipse, i.e. treated it as a natural event (and was lucky in its being visible), he deserves credit for taking a scientific view of it. But it must be noted with regret that O. Neugebauer, astronomer and orientalist, denies that even the Babylonians could yet have predicted with sufficient precision, and doubts the whole story.

Many stories of Thales in fact belong to saga rather than history, like many told of Roger Bacon and Michael Scott. He was said to have measured the height of the Great Pyramid by measuring its shadow, cast when the shadow of a vertical rod was equal to its height, which could well be true; also to have measured the distance of a ship off-shore, which is usually doubted, but might have been achieved by means of a diagram, without his having anticipated Euclid. One story told how, while observing the stars, he fell into a well, the prototype of all stories about absent-minded professors; and another, pro-intellectual this time, that he 'cornered oil', paying a deposit, out of season, for the use of every olive-press in Miletos and Chios (her ally), and then raising the price slightly when sub-letting. That he had foreseen an exceptionally good crop 'through his knowledge of the stars', as this story adds, is impossible; but possibly he thought he could.

Thales was numbered among the Seven Sages, as were

127

Periandros, Pittakos and Solon, and of all these legends were told. As to what in fact got Thales his reputation, no tradition is better attested than that he thought all matter was water. The earth (a flat earth), he believed, floated in water – perhaps influenced by Babylonian cosmology, with its 'waters under the earth'. Poets like Hesiod had long been repeating and embellishing stories of how the universe came to be; the Milesians now dropped the stories and asked 'What is it?'.

During Thales' life, which lasted till about 540, Miletos, having ejected the successors of Thrasyboulos, fell into savage class-struggles like those which ruined Megara. Two parties, called the Rich and the Workers, fought for power, and committed atrocities. At last foreign arbitration was called in, that of the islanders of Paros; and they put the government, as a remedy for urban discord, into the hands of the landed interest; 'those whose fields were best tilled'.

There had been those, throughout, who had been disgusted at the violence and slaughter. A poet, Phokylides, wrote 'Would you be wealthy? – Tend your fertile field!' He praised moderation, and middling wealth; scorned noble birth without good wits; and summed up his proverbial philosophy in the saying: 'A little city on a rock, with order, is better than madness in Nineveh.' He also said 'All virtue is summed up in justice', which was original in his time. Virtue in Homer, *arete*, was quite compatible with aggression. A horse or a sword could have *arete* as well as a man. What Phokylides was saying is that human virtue is moral virtue.

Thales lived through all this, and through another catastrophe, in or about 546. Cyrus the Persian, king of a nation kindred and till now vassals to the Medes, overthrew the Median high king and made Persia supreme. Croesus, whose sister, under his father's alliance with Media, had married the last Median king, marched to avenge him, and to extend his own borders – encouraged, we are told, by the Delphic oracle, which in a celebrated piece of ambiguity gave him the answer 'If Croesus crosses the Halys, he will destroy a mighty empire'. Thales, now elderly, went with him again, and was said (though Herodotos doubted the story) to have helped him to cross the Halys by diverting part of that river's water into another channel.

But Cyrus was a genius, and his men were tough. Croesus, an experienced soldier, held his own in the first campaign; but when Croesus withdrew to demobilise for the winter, Cyrus gave him a short start and, braving the cold of Anatolia, marched after him. Croesus had to fight before Sardis, without his allies; the famous Lydian lancers were foiled when their horses shied and reared at the unfamiliar sight and smell of a long line of baggage camels, driven before the Persian ranks; and within a fortnight the 'impregnable' citadel of Sardis itself had fallen to the prowess of the Persians in rock-climbing. Croesus probably perished; though at Delphoi, which had received many benefactions from him, stories were told of how he was miraculously delivered. A poem tells us that Apollo carried him off to the earthly paradise of the Hyperboreans, 'beyond the north wind'; Herodotos, later, has a rationalised version of his deliverance. It was the most startling overthrow of 'a mighty empire' that the Greek world had ever seen.

Sparta, which had been in alliance with Croesus, attempted a *démarche*, bidding Cyrus keep his hands off the Greeks. Cyrus asked, 'Who *are* the Spartans?' Thales proposed, at an Ionian congress, that the cities should form a federal state; but he was in advance of his time, and also Cyrus split the resistance by offering Miletos an alliance, such as it had had with Lydia. Then, leaving a general to subdue Ionia, he returned east to deal with more important matters. Many Ionians emigrated, singly or in mass; but the cities, placed under Greek governors or 'tyrants', were unmolested as long as they paid their tribute. At Miletos, it was exactly the generation after the coming of Cyrus which witnessed the most brilliant speculations of the 'Natural Philosophers'.

2 SCIENCE AND RELIGION

Anaximandros, a disciple of Thales, was an intellectual giant. Rejecting Thales' notion of water as the primal substance, he would describe this only negatively, as the Boundless or

Undefined; a long step towards the general concept of 'matter'. General concepts are the last to appear in the evolution of language, and some of the major struggles of pioneer thinkers have been directed to framing them, often by giving a new sense to a common word. (Our word 'matter' or 'material' is simply Latin for the Greek '*hylē*', 'wood'; timber for building.) Anaximandros believed that the earth, which he still thought of as cylindrical, with a flat top on which we live, 'floated free in space, held by nothing, because of its equal distance from all things'. There was no *need* for support. It sounds almost like an adumbration of gravitation. Within the Boundless, which is in perpetual motion, worlds, including our world, come into being and pass away. They come into being by the separating out of opposites, such as the hot and cold, moist and dry (a pointer to the later 'four elements'). In our earth, cold and moist elements sink to the centre, and outside the atmosphere it is surrounded by a sphere of fire; this is mostly concealed from us by opaque mist (*aer*, not yet simply 'air', which was a concept not yet formed); the heavenly bodies are fire, seen through holes in the *aer*. At first the earth was covered by water, and the first living creatures were marine creatures, covered with spiny shells; then, as the sea was partly dried up by the sun, some of them emerged on to the land and, 'their shells breaking, they shortly changed their manner of life'. Men are descended from fish, perhaps of the shark or dogfish type. It looks as though he had made observations on embryos and also on fossils, as one of his successors certainly did; but we are not positively told this.

Anaximandros also called his worlds 'gods'; but they are not eternal. The action and reaction of the opposites is a kind of aggression or *injustice*. So 'the source of the genesis of things must also be the source of their destruction; for they render judgment and requital to each other for their injustice in the process of time, as he says in his rather poetic language'. The quotation is from a late Greek historian of philosophy, quoting Theophrastos, a pupil of Aristotle. It looks as if Theophrastos had before him Anaximandros' book; probably the first work of European prose.

Prose had long been known in the east; in Syria, kings had their chronicles before Greece had the alphabet. Borrowing is as evident in Anaximandros as in Thales. He was also credited with having set up the first sundial in Ionia, like that by which Babylonians had first 'divided the day into twelve parts', and having made the first map; a Sumerian map, of a sort, scratched on metal, nearly 2,000 years earlier than his time, has actually been found. The originality of the Greeks lies not in owing no man anything – their debts were heavier than used to be thought – but in what they did with it.

Anaximandros' successor, Anaximenes, on the other hand, wrote, we are told, in 'a simple and unpretentious Ionic'; and he proposed the doctrine that the primary substance is *aer*; still not just 'air' but rather 'a mist'. It is not a mere falling-back from the great abstraction of Anaximandros; rather, Anaximenes considers the primary matter to have definite qualities. Also, he tries to give a quantitative basis to qualities; he considers that the denser substances are formed from his *aer* by condensation. For this, interestingly, he uses a term taken from an industrial process, literally 'felting', as of wool; a process which Milesians had observed among the Scythians. The concept of air as a substance, not a mere no-thing (as when we still say that there is nothing in the bucket), emerges directly *from* Anaximenes' theory. 'When most uniform,' says a later summary, 'it is invisible to the eye. . . .Winds arise when the *aer* is dense, and moves under pressure. When it becomes denser still, clouds are formed, and so it changes into water. Hail occurs when the water descending from the clouds solidifies, and snow when it solidifies in a wetter condition.' He also made observations on phosphorescence at sea.

Anaximenes thus regards 'air' as matter in its simplest form; and, as Erwin Schrödinger has said, 'had he said "dissociated hydrogen gas", (which he could hardly be expected to say), he would not be far from our present view'. Later Greeks considered his work the culmination of that of the Milesian school. To him, especially, later Ionian materialists looked up; among them, Dēmokritos of Abdēra in Thrace, who a century later developed an atomic theory.

More obviously interesting perhaps is Xenophanes, from the neighbouring city of Kolophōn, who, after probably hearing Anaximandros discourse, emigrated to the west. He was a poet, and perhaps made a living out of it, wandering from city to city; but he is rightly numbered among the philosophers. He made observations of marine fossils at Malta (a Phoenician outpost) and Syracuse, and gave the correct explanation of them. He wrote lighter verses, including some lines satirising the already extravagant adulation of athletes, and some on how to behave at a party, remembering to thank the gods for good cheer, not drinking more than one can carry home unassisted, and not singing party-political songs, or 'old fables' about wars in heaven. But also, in dead earnest, he is the first Greek known to have asserted that the time-honoured stories of the gods would not do:

Homer and Hesiod have ascribed to the gods every deed that is shameful and dishonourable among men: stealing and adultery and deceiving each other.... The Ethiopians make their gods black and snub-nosed, and the Thracians theirs grey-eyed and red-haired. ... If animals could paint and make things, like men, horses and oxen too would fashion the gods in their own image.

Xenophanes asserts the existence of one supreme God:

Greatest among gods and men; not like mortals either in body or mind.... He is all sight and all mind and all hearing ... and he remains in one place, not moving at all ... it is not seemly that he should be now here and now there.... And he sways all things without effort, by his thought.

In the Milesian manner, he lays down that 'all things are arisen from earth and water'. Iris (the goddess of the rainbow) is 'a bright cloud'. Our perceptions of quality are relative: 'If God had not made the yellow honey, men would have thought figs much sweeter.'

No one has seen, nor shall there ever be one who *knows* about the gods and the things that I say about the universe. Even if a man should happen to say what is exactly right – still, he himself does not know; but opinion is over all.

It is interesting that no one seems to have thought of persecuting him. Finally he is said to have settled at Elea, a new colony south of Paestum. In a last poem he speaks of himself as having reached the age of ninety-two – 'if I can reckon rightly of these matters'.

3 THE MYSTERY-RELIGIONS

The age of the first philosophers was by no means an irreligious age. It was, in fact, just then, and in Ionia, that many Greeks *began* giving their children names compounded with that of a patron god; such names as Hērodotos ('Given by Hera'), Apollodōros ('Gift of Apollo'), Dionysios, Dēmētrios; the last two very common later, for reasons which will appear. Nor did the Olympic gods, despite such criticisms as those of Xenophanes, lose their hold on the belief of classical Greeks. They were bound up with the life of the city and its bright and joyful festivals; and even a much later and highly intelligent Athenian, whom we know from his own writings – Xenophon (pp. 309 f.), soldier and historian, who in youth had listened to Socrates – derived comfort from sacrificing and praying to them. This was, however, perhaps rather an upper-class religion. To some, especially the humbler, the Olympians perhaps did seem rather remote; especially, they gave little comfort in the face of death, either one's own or that of loved ones. Just in this age, as we have seen (p. 125), we begin to hear more of the peasants' gods, Dēmēter and Dionysos, the givers of bread and wine, little mentioned in Homer. Their cults were no doubt primitive in the Aegean, but were now often blended with new rites and legends introduced from foreign lands, from Thrace, from Asia Minor and perhaps from Egypt.

These deities had their public cults, including the mimetic dancing and choral song of early tragedy; but they also had, in many places, secret rites, called *Mysteries,* from a verb *myo* meaning to keep one's mouth shut, which were only revealed to worshippers duly initiated. The original reason for this was probably to prevent enemies from learning the secrets of the community's fertility-magic, including the holy 'real' name of its chief god, lest they should work destructive black magic against it. Associated with the worship of these gods of the vegetation, and its death and rebirth, were beliefs in a happy after-life for those initiated into the fellowship of the god and who kept his (or her) laws; sometimes these included the demand for clean hands and a pure heart.

Among the most impressive local mysteries were those of Demeter the corn-goddess at Eleusis in Attica. Naturally we do not know much about what was done; but a Christian writer says that the climax of the second initiation, taken in a later year and by relatively few worshippers, was the elevation by the priest of an ear of wheat, such as 'falls into the ground and dies'. Admission even to the first initiation demanded prior sanctification and an exhausting day of pilgrimage, taken fasting, for fifteen miles along the Sacred Way from Athens, with many stops for worship at wayside shrines. Thousands were glad to accept the privilege, which was opened to Athenians after the union of Attica, and soon to all men and women 'of intelligible speech and free from blood-guiltiness'; not unintelligible 'bar-bar-ians', though Romans were later admitted.

The basic legend of Demeter was not secret; it is told in a long and exquisite 'Homeric' hexameter Hymn. Her daughter Persephone was carried off, while out gathering flowers, by the grim Hades, lord of the underworld. Demeter sought her, sorrowing, a *mater dolorosa*, and in the guise of an old woman, unrecognized, was kindly treated by the King of Eleusis and his daughters, who found her when they went to draw water from the village well. For reward she later revealed to them her works, her *orgia*. Finally Zeus, who was afraid that mankind would perish (for Demeter, while wandering, was neglecting her duties) prevailed upon Hades to let Persephone go; but she had taken food in his house, and so was bound to him; so for the four winter months each year she returns underground.

Within the context of the Mysteries, there seems to have been enacted a Sacred Marriage; a Christian writer makes a great scandal of 'the descent into darkness of the Expositor and the priestess'. There was also a birth of a divine child. Some verbal explanation of the rites seems to have been given, but never to have become standardised. The essential matter was what was *done*. Eleusis kept its magnetism through an impressive ritual, which men, through the changing centuries, could interpret according to their lights.

Mysteries of Dionysos tended to be wilder, connected as they were with wine. His female votaries, Maenads ('wild women'), were said to go, or at least to have gone, in ancient times, out on the mountains, where they tore beasts in pieces, and also, in a Theban legend, the king Pentheus, who tried to suppress them. Dionysos was said to have wandered over the whole earth; later rationalisers made him into a conquering king. There were also many and various stories of his birth. One was that his mortal mother Semele begged Zeus, her divine lover, to reveal himself in his full glory; he did, and it burned her up. But Zeus rescued her unborn child, sewed it up in his own thigh, and brought it forth afterwards. Another legend seems to have given an account of human origins and an original sin, of such a kind as to encourage asceticism; a doctrine and a way of life in sharp contrast with the earth-bound cheerfulness and even the earth-bound pessimism of most Greeks. The divine child Dionysos, son of Zeus and Persephone, said this story, was torn to pieces and devoured by the wicked Titans. Zeus blasted the Titans with his thunderbolts, ate the heart of the Child, and then begot the young god over again, as son of Semele. From the smouldering remains of the Titans sprang the human race; we are therefore evil, sprung from the ashes of primeval sinners; but inasmuch as the Titans had just eaten the Divine Child, there was within them a portion of the god; and in us too there is a trace of the divine, which the properly instructed will foster and make ready to return to heaven by mortifying the flesh.

This barbarous myth was, we are told, commemorated in a public ritual in Crete, but elsewhere revealed only in mysteries. Other accretions to the Dionysos mythology were introduced from Thrace; and with them came the figure of Orpheus (whose name, by the way, has two syllables and should not be pronounced 'Orphius'). Orpheus first appears in Greek art and literature about 540. On an early relief preserved at Delphoi, he stands, lyre in hand, in a ship, with his name, spelt ORPHAS, written beside him. From the first he was associated with the Argonaut legend, which, as we have seen, was connected with the discontinuance of human sacrifice. Aeschylus, the first great poet of Attic tragedy, devoted a trilogy of plays (unfortunately lost) to the subject of Dionysos in Thrace; in the second of them Orpheus figured, and was torn to pieces by the Maenads. And already before Aeschylus' time, poems and prophecies attributed to Orpheus and his son Mousaios ('friend of the Muses') were circulating and being avidly collected. The sons of Peisistratos at Athens had a collection, and their court expert on oracles was caught in the act of forging additions to them. These poems were in Homeric metre and style; but if Orpheus lived in the heroic age, it naturally followed that they were much older than Homer, and when phrases and whole lines had been 'lifted', it was alleged that Homer had copied Orpheus. Herodotos was among those who were not deceived.

However, such poems had a great vogue. The uncritical religious believed in them, and were duly terrified by accounts of hell, a hell of mud – Orpheus should know, for he had been to the underworld in his unsuccessful attempt to rescue his wife, Eurydike. People with a sense of sin resorted to self-employed practitioners called 'Orphic initiators'. Classical philosophers refer to them with contempt, as peddlers of absolution for a modest fee. Some, perhaps, may have been sincere. Certainly they did not preach 'pay me and do as you like'; on the contrary, the severer Orphic doctrines taught (not always consistently, for there was no organized Orphic church) respect for all life, with its corollary, vegetarianism, and sexual abstinence. The movement did not capture the allegiance of any of the great classical writers or statesmen; but it remained part of the sub-rational underworld of Greece, far into Christian times. Mystery-religions (greatly increased in numbers and variety by that time) aroused the especial ire of the Christian Fathers, and formed part of the variegated phantasmagoria known as Gnosticism; but Orpheus even appears, a symbolic figure, in the art of the catacombs.

We have now seen why Demetrios and Dionysios (whence

western 'Denys') are the commonest late Greek names; it is because Demeter and Dionysos were the most loved of Greek gods. Initiation into their mysteries offered participation and a promise of divine favour. Besides, for those whom the Homeric gods did not satisfy, Demeter, who wandered sorrowfully, Dionysos, who was persecuted – these were gods who had been on earth and had suffered; they would understand.

4 PYTHAGORAS

Pythagoras, one of the first Greeks to be given a religious name (connected with the Pythian, i.e. Delphic, oracle of Apollo), exhibits the phenomenon of a fine mind deeply influenced by the superstitions of his age.

Pythagoras grew up in Samos, where, after Persia had subdued the mainland, Polykrates, a pirate king, remained independent and dominated the Cyclades. 'He robbed all men indiscriminately,' says Herodotus; 'for he said that his friends were more grateful if he gave them their property back than they would have been if he had never taken it.' He was one of the greatest of the tyrants. He equipped Samos with strong walls and harbour-moles, and with a water-conduit (still visible) tunnelled through a hill from both ends, to meet with a very slight error in the middle. It is a marvel of early Greek engineering, and speaks volumes for the capacity of Greek surveyors. He introduced the best breeds of domestic animals into the island, and also artists and poets: Ibykos, from Reggio, the first writer known to have mentioned Orpheus, and Anakreon of Teos, poet of love and wine (whose fame in modern times, however, rests largely on some much later poems, falsely ascribed to him). Polykrates also enticed to Samos with a huge salary a great doctor, Dēmokēdes, from the court of the Peisistratids at Athens, who had previously enticed him from Aigina; he came from Achaian Kroton in Italy, already famous for its medical school, and left home after quarrelling with his father. Pythagoras, however, left Samos and went *to* Kroton, in order – at least, so his biographers said – to escape from the dissolute court of Polykrates.

Pythagoras was then already a man of some reputation for 'wisdom', including both mathematics and Orphic theology. He himself said that only God was wise, and claimed only the status of a 'lover of wisdom'; whence the word *philo-sóphos*. His modern fame rests largely on his famous theorem. He generalised the empirical fact, long known to the Egyptians, that by constructing a triangle with sides in the ratio of 3, 4 and 5, you get a right-angle (important for building), into the *theorem* (meaning an *object of contemplation*) about the square on the hypotenuse. But, believing also in the transmigration of souls and in the need to purify the soul to win through from this process to heaven, he apparently also taught as important various *taboos*, on a level with the modern superstitions about not walking under a ladder, or breaking a mirror. Such were: Do not poke the fire with a knife (Do not *hurt* the fire?); do not cut your nails at a sacrifice (Hesiod would have understood); always spit upon your nail-parings (rejecting them, lest magic be worked against you through them); when getting up, roll the bed-clothes together (Frazer compared the almost world-wide belief that you may lame an enemy by stabbing his foot-prints; so it would be most unwise to leave the imprint of your whole body at the mercy of occult powers). He was above all a *religious* figure. In number he found, like many mathematicians, the thrilling proof of the rationality of the universe.

How much of oriental mathematics Pythagoras learned at Samos we do not know; but the men who engineered the tunnel must have known, practically, a good deal. He is said to have studied also the connexion between number and music; probably he noted that, by stopping a lyre-string at three-fourths, two-thirds and half of its length, one obtained the fourth, fifth and octave of its note. Seeing that number controlled both sound and shape, he leapt to the intuition that this was the secret of the universe; that numbers (unity perhaps thought of materially, as a minimal, atomic particle) are the elements of things, rather than water or any other substance known to sense; though, being in no position to anticipate mathematical physics (which he would have loved), most of his school's identifications of numbers with things or institutions are purely fanciful.

Even in pure mathematics, he met with one bitter disappointment. The hypotenuse of an isosceles right-angled triangle, the diagonal of a square, ought surely to have produced some great revelation; and he could not get a rational value for it at all. In TWO, which had no square root, in duality, division, lurked, it appeared, the secret of evil. Pythagoras identified it with the female, and ONE with what was male and strong. THREE, consequently, was marriage. EIGHT was justice (perhaps the cube, with its 'equal measures'?); TEN, represented by the pattern

.

. .

. . .

. . . .

(the best available notation), was Number itself, and the pattern, called the *tetraktys*, was to later Pythagoreans a sacred symbol, by which oaths were sworn.

Pythagorean boldness appears to better advantage in astronomy. Eight moving heavenly bodies were visible to the eye: the sun, moon, five other 'wandering stars' or planets, and the 'sphere of the fixed stars'. Pythagoras, or someone under his influence, had the audacity to make the earth itself a moving body; not a sphere, indeed, but a disc, near the centre of things, revolving with its inhabited face towards the stars, producing day and night by its movement relative to the sun, and with its 'back' to a central fire at the heart of the universe. The sacred number ten was completed, assuming a 'counter earth' revolving on the other side of the fire. Claiming to have found that 'their speeds, judged by their distances, are in the same ratio as the musical concordances', Pythagoreans said that the sound of their movement formed a harmony, the 'music of the spheres', which to our ears, accustomed to it from birth, is silence.

South Italy, when Pythagoras reached it, had been rent by war. Achaian Kroton and Sybaris, still greedy to monopolize the land, had destroyed Ionian Siris; but Kroton had then sustained a humiliating defeat in attacking her smaller neighbour Lokroi. To a rich but demoralised 'post-war' Kroton, Pythagoras' austere teaching attracted a band of earnest disciples, of the leisured class. With their secret doctrines and sworn loyalty to each other and to the Master (known as Himself, as though his name were too sacred to be lightly used) they formed something like a freemasonry. Soon they dominated the Krotonian ruling aristocracy. Pythagoras spent many fruitful years at Kroton; but when, inevitably, political questions divided the fraternity itself, between a conservative and a reformist wing, he withdrew to end his days in quieter, corn-growing Metapontion. Without him, the conservative party closed its ranks and remained in power.

Meanwhile Sybaris, even richer and more powerful than Kroton, was moving to revolution. A tyrant, Telys, with the support of the masses, gained power; opponents of his fled to Kroton; a demand for their extradition led to war; and in that war the great Sybarite army, presumably with some internal disloyalty, went down in a shattering disaster. The victors pressed on and, after a campaign of seventy days, captured the city. They destroyed it, turning the local river across its site, while survivors scattered, largely to the west coast. The particular savagery of this war is more easily understood when it is seen as a class war.

The accounts of this war, and of Sybaris, come, like most history, from the victorious side. We are told of Sybaris corrupted by luxury – of the young Sybarite who complained of a crumpled rose-leaf in his bed. They piped their wine to the quay; they segregated industrial and residential quarters; when we hear that one of their luxury-inventions was that of chamber-pots, we get a glimpse of the level of discomfort from which such 'luxury' was escaping. If Sybaris, like Athens, had survived to write her own history, we should no doubt get another picture. Sybaris was a great commercial town overwhelmed by disaster in a moment of instability; far away in Ionian Miletos, men went into mourning for her.

The early promise of 'Greater Greece' was ruined; but the influence of Pythagoras remained strong. The Fraternity dominated Kroton until they were massacred in a riot, long after the death of the sage; and even later, Archÿtas, a Pythagorean, was the trusted 'prime minister' of the democracy of Taranto. Votive paintings from a temple of Persephone at Lokroi also show the persistence of a religion much interested in the fate of the soul; some small gold plates buried in tombs, several of them from the territory once ruled by Sybaris, bear something unexpected – texts from a Greek equivalent of the Egyptian Book of the Dead. They instruct the soul how to direct her journey; how to avoid drinking of Lēthē, the Water of Oblivion, how to answer the guards of the Water of Memory, how to address Queen Persephone herself and win admittance to the abode of the saints. There is reference to having 'won free from the sorrowful, weary wheel'; a striking parallel to the Indian 'wheel of rebirth'. That Pythagoras had learned this doctrine from India was alleged in later Greek times, but is improbable; the extent to which men can independently follow the same trains of original thought has often been astonishing.

Out of the same *milieu*, influenced by Pythagoras, emerged in the next century, in Sicily, Empedokles, no inconsiderable poet and thinker, but also a religious charlatan. He, in his own poetry (whereas Pythagoras left no writings), claims to remember his past lives: 'I have been ere now both a boy and a girl; yes, and a bird and a bush, and a dumb fish in the sea.' He claimed to have worked miracles, even raising the dead; he entered cities triumphally, robed as a priest-king; at the end, his followers seem to have claimed that he had been caught up to heaven. The story that he really jumped into the crater of Etna, in order to give that impression by his disappearance, and that the volcano spoilt the plan by spewing up one of his bronze sandals, is probably one of the parodies of comic drama.

5 THE ONE AND THE STREAM

Probably there was a real danger that Greek thought might be side-tracked into theosophy and occultism. That it was not, was due to Greeks no less bold in speculation, but more ruthless in criticism. The first recorded criticism of Pythagoras comes from his contemporary, Xenophanes; he told a story of Pythagoras asking a neighbour to stop beating a puppy, saying that he recognized in its cries the voice of a deceased friend. In his old age at Elea, Xenophanes is said (though it has been seriously doubted) to have taught another profound thinker, Parmenides, who may have lived till about 450.

Parmenides, to whom a brief summary can do scant justice, is essentially another religious writer. He had been hit by the experience of an intense consciousness of Reality itself, the sense that IT IS, and of the wonder of it. In a hexameter poem, he describes, in mythological, physical terms (the only terms possible) his experience of rapture. He was swept up from earth in a divine chariot to the closed gates of 'the paths of night and day'. The goddess Dikē – Justice, 'who punishes', but also more than justice; the Way and the Truth, almost the Chinese Tao – opened to him and taught him that IT IS, and there is no beginning and no end, nor past nor future, but an unchanging present; nor anything outside it, nor any not-being (identified with empty space). Unflinching thought, for Parmenides, must lead to truth; 'for to think is the same as to be'. Since this Being is corporeal (no one, not even Pythagoras, having conceived any other), and since there is no empty space, there is also no possibility of real motion.

Since Parmenides, like other mystics, still had to live in the world of phenomena, he continues (still professing to quote the revelation of the divine Dikē) to give an account of these; but the Goddess warns him that this is the way of Seeming, not of Truth. Even here, if the senses give impressions contrary to reason, so much the worse for the senses. Achilles can never overtake the tortoise; for whenever he reaches the place where the tortoise was, the tortoise will have moved on a little. This famous puzzle is said to have been invented by Parmenides himself, counter-attacking the devotees of common sense; it was sharpened, and reinforced with more paradoxes, by his disciple Zenon. His cosmology is more or less Pythagorean. He may have *read* Xenophanes, even if he did not know him; but his personal *guru* is said to have been an obscure

Pythagorean named Ameinias, to whom he built a shrine as to a 'hero' or saint. But he lifted Pythagorean thought, for those prepared to take a great deal of trouble, out of the morass of superstition.

Opposite to Parmenides in his conclusions, but as relentless in reasoning, was his older contemporary, Herakleitos of Ephesos. Starting, in the intellectual climate of Ionia, from the material and not from the mystical, what struck him was the *im*permanence of phenomena. 'You cannot step twice into the same river' – for the water is always changing; a doctrine later summed up in the aphorism 'All things flow', or 'are a flux'. The primary substance, in primitive Ionian style, he found in fire; a fruitful conception, since it suggests more nearly the concept of energy. The world itself is eternal: 'This world, the same for all, no one made, either of gods or men; but it was always and is and shall be an everliving fire, measures kindling and measures going out.' 'The same for all' is a key phrase; the real is the 'public' or 'common': 'Men awake have one common world, but in sleep they turn aside, each into a world of his own.' 'Wherefore one must follow the common; but though the word [*logos*] is common, most men live as if they had private insight of their own.' Within the eternal *cosmos*, all is change: 'All things are exchanged for fire, and fire for all things, as are goods for gold and gold for goods.' What keeps the streaming world from being a chaos is Measure: 'The sun will not overstep his measures, or the Furies, the servants of Zeus, will find him out.' The mythic language is used allegorically, as by Parmenides; God is not really anthropomorphic: 'That which alone is wise both wishes and does not wish to be called Zeus'; not the Zeus of mythology, certainly, but personal or rather super-personal. As an ape is to man, so 'the wisest of men is an ape compared to God, both in wisdom and beauty and in everything else'. Herakleitos is in part pantheistic, also: 'God is day and night, summer and winter, war and peace, fullness and want.'

In these pairs there appears another of his most fruitful concepts, that of the unity of opposites. As has been seen, there are traces of it already in Anaximandros; and one would dearly like to know whether there is any connexion between it and the dualism of Persian religion. (Herakleitos mentions the Magi, the Levites of Iran, but did not think much of them.) The cosmos is held together in 'a harmony of opposite tensions, as in the lyre and the bow.' 'The way up and the way down are the same way.' Our judgements are partial and relative, just as 'donkeys prefer chaff to gold'; and they are all poised between opposites. 'Sickness makes health pleasurable and good; hunger, fullness; weariness, rest.' (We should know nothing of pleasure without antecedent pains.) The relations of opposites in the physical world may be compared to a war, in which sometimes one element gets the upper hand. Our age, which (the mythology said, and Herakleitos may have accepted it) began with a flood, will end in a fire: 'Fire will come and judge and overtake all things'; a pronouncement quoted with approval by the Christian Bishop Hippolytos. So too among men, strife is fundamental; 'War is the father and king of all things, and has made some men and some gods and some slaves and some free.' 'Justice is strife, and all things happen through strife and must do so.' 'Men would not have known the name of justice, had this not been so.' The doctrine of unity of opposites, taken up by Hegel (he explicitly says) from Herakleitos, passed by way of Hegel to Karl Marx, and is prominent in his and Lenin's philosophical writing. None of the intuitions of the Ionians has been more influential.

Like Parmenides, he is more intuitive than scientific; he derided Xenophanes and Pythagoras for their interest in details: 'Learning many things does not teach wisdom.' 'Pythagoras made a selection of these writings' [Orphic poems?] 'and then claimed a wisdom of his own ... a mischievous lore.' Herakleitos took a poor view of popular religion. To purify one's self with blood is 'as though after stepping in some mud, one were to wash in mud'. 'And they pray to images, as though a man were to talk with the walls of his house, not knowing what gods and heroes really are.' (The evidence *from a Greek* that Greek religion could be a naïve idolatry is striking.) He lumped together in one condemnation 'night-walkers, Magi, Bacchic celebrants, mystai', threatening them with trouble after death, for their mysteries are evil and misconceived. 'There await men after death such things as they neither hope nor expect.' But – a cryptic and impressive saying: 'If a man hope not, he shall not find what he did not hope, that is beyond search and reaching.' As for burial rites, they are nonsense. 'Corpses ought to be thrown out like the muck, or more so.' The soul is what matters; and the soul, too, is fire. 'It is death to souls to become water'; and the souls of the drunken and incontinent can positively be seen drowning. 'A dry soul is best and wisest.' The souls of the wise and the brave do not drown, but leave the body with their fire undimmed; he mentions specifically men killed in battle. Bishop Hippolytos, who preferred Hērakleitos to the heretics of his own day, attributes to him the doctrine that such heroes enjoyed an after-life of service: 'to rise up again and become waking guardians of the living and the dead'.

In this belief he was, for once, not alone. This view of the destiny of the heroic man was shared by Empedokles and by Pindar (pp. 198 f.) after him. A thorough aristocrat (he came of the old royal family of Ephesos, whose head was hereditary priest of Demeter Eleusinia), he despised the people; but still, Law, representing again what is 'common to all', is the bulwark of society. 'The people must fight for its law, as for its walls'; and 'human laws have their sustenance from one law divine'. *Hubris* – arrogance, the characteristic of a tyrant – is 'more to be suppressed than a conflagration'. Fatalism is contemptible. 'A man's *daimon*' (the tutelary spirit, in virtue of which a man was said to be *eudaimon*, happy, or the reverse) is, he says finely, 'his character'.

Hērakleitos represents the last fine flowering of that Ionian civilisation which had produced both Homer and the Milesian philosophers. But in his time, disaster was impending for the eastern Greek world.

CHAPTER 7

THE RISE OF PERSIA, AND THE ATHENIAN REVOLUTION

1 PERSIA AND THE WEST

THE Persian conquest of Ionia made little difference to the Greek world for a generation. Art, poetry and the new philosophy flourished not least in Ionia. Persia had many other preoccupations. Cyrus conquered Babylon, united the whole of Iran, and was killed in central Asia in 529, attacking nomads, who were still in the bronze age. His son Cambyses conquered Egypt. The old king Amasis had done what he could, recruiting more Greek mercenaries, securing Cyprus and making alliance with Polykrates; but when the eastern colossus moved, Cyprus and Polykrates promptly defected. Supplied with water by camel caravans, organized by the local Arab ruler, Cambyses negotiated the Sinai desert and defeated Amasis' successor; his Phoenician and eastern Greek fleets entered the Nile; and Egypt was soon conquered, though an expedition against the 'Ethiopian' kingdom in Nubia broke down through supply difficulties.

Cambyses, like an Egyptian Pharaoh, married his sisters. He was turning himself from a national leader like Cyrus into a despot, and the blood-royal was to be separate from that of common mortals. He is said also, after his disaster in upper Egypt, to have gone finally mad; and he died in mysterious circumstances. Meanwhile his brother, or according to later official history an impostor, impersonating the brother, whom Cambyses had murdered, had risen against him, with the support of the Magi, and announced a peace-policy: no more wars or war-levies for three years. There was great enthusiasm, and when he was killed by a group of nobles, headed by Darius, a distant cousin of Cambyses, there were revolts throughout the empire; but they were suppressed in bloody fighting by

146

the war-seasoned Persian army (522–1). Darius, a tremendous worker and master of detail, then reorganized the empire, divided into twenty great Satrapies under Persian princes or noblemen, with a central and provincial secretariat (the secretaries being able to keep an eye on the Satraps), travelling inspectors, called the King's Eyes, and regular assessment of taxes. Persians, whose education, according to a famous phrase of Herodotos, taught them only 'to ride, to shoot and to tell the truth', said that Cyrus was a father, Cambyses a master and Darius a shopkeeper; but Darius' work gave the Middle East a seldom broken peace for nearly 200 years.

Later Greeks affect to despise the Persians as soft barbarians, formidable only through their numbers. Herodotos makes no such mistake. Born a Persian subject (at Halikarnassos, opposite Rhodes, about 484) and widely travelled, he represents them, even when they are 'the enemy', as brave, dignified, efficient and devoted to their king. He also has some interesting observations on Persian religion:

They make no cult-statues or temples or altars, and think those who do this foolish, because, as I gather, they do not think the gods are anthropomorphic, as the Greeks do. Their custom is to sacrifice to Zeus upon the tops of mountains; they call the whole circle of the heavens 'Zeus'. They also sacrifice to the sun, moon, earth, fire and water. These were originally their only gods . . .

– though, he goes on, they had later supplemented these with some of the gods of Babylonia. And, he adds,

When he sacrifices, no man may pray for benefits for himself alone; but he prays that it may be well for all the Persians, and for the King.

In that age of Greek, Hebrew, Indian and Chinese prophets and philosophers, Iran too had had its stirring of the waters; the great name is that of Zarathustra, in its Latinised form Zoroaster. His religion is based on the same Aryan polytheism as that of north India; but in the more bracing air of Iran its issue was very different – practical, this-worldly, optimistic. Where the Indian sought Nirvana or worshipped Shiva the Destroyer, the Persian prided himself, 'next to prowess in

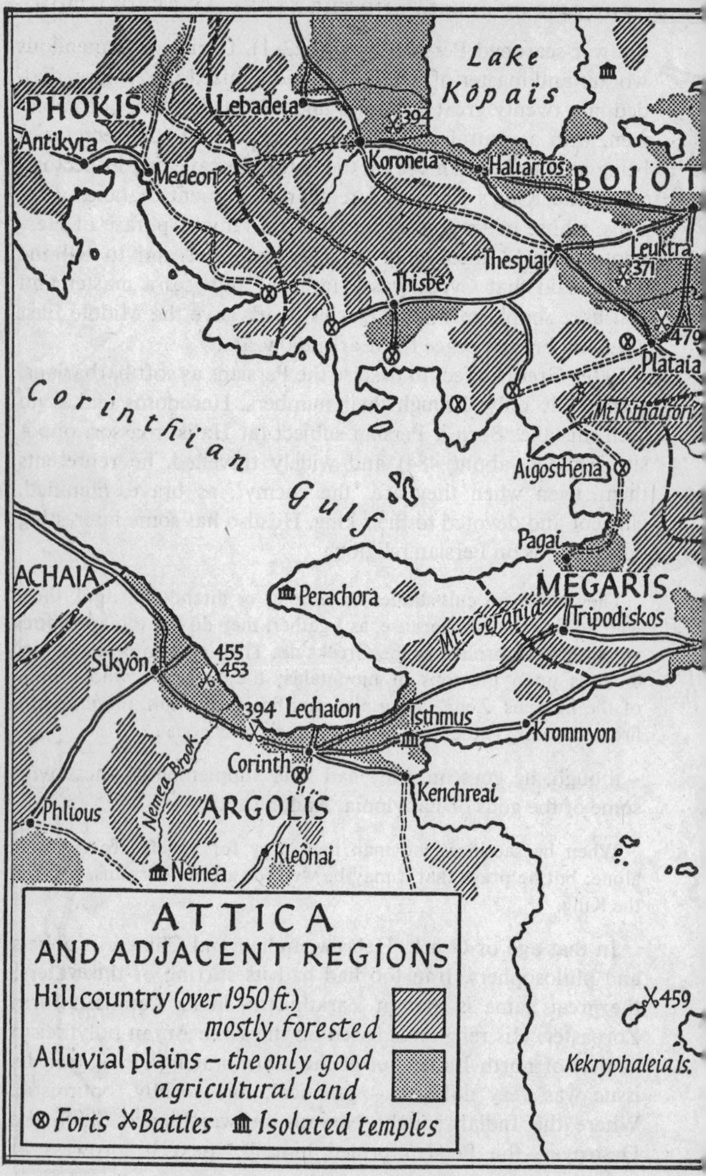
Lake Kôpaïs
PHOKIS
Lebadeia
394
Antikyra
Koroneia
Haliartos
BOIOT
Medeon
Leuktra
371
Thespiai
Thisbe
479
Plataia
Corinthian Gulf
Mt Kithairon
Aigosthena
Pagai
ACHAIA
Perachora
MEGARIS
Mt. Gerania
Tripodiskos
455
453
Sikyôn
394 Lechaion
Isthmus
Krommyon
Corinth
Kenchreai
Phlious
Nemea Brook
ARGOLIS
Kleônai
Nemea
459
Kekryphaleia Is.
ATTICA
AND ADJACENT REGIONS
Hill country (over 1950 ft.) mostly forested
Alluvial plains – the only good agricultural land
Forts
Battles
Isolated temples

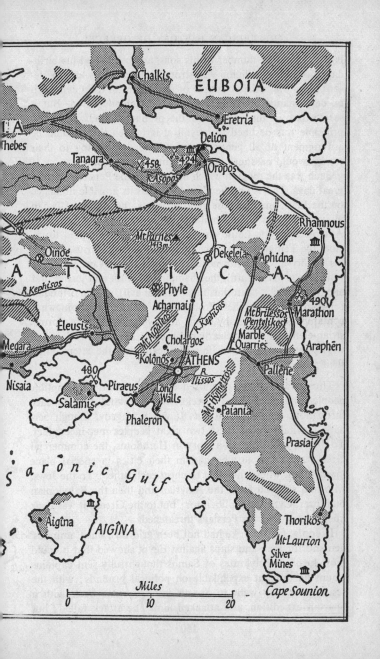

battle', upon the number of his sons, and celebrated his birthday. Zoroaster's religion was strongly ethical. It is usually described as the classic example of a dualism; in it an evil spirit or devil stands embattled against the righteous God. But it seems that, in the thought of the prophet himself, the good principle was destined to prevail at last; then there would be a Judgment of all generations, and men, according to their works, would pass into heaven or into a hell of fire.

Such was the religion which invigorated the Persians in their great days. This is not the place to discuss its possible influence on the Jews, one of whose great prophets, the author of Isaiah xl–lv, represents God as hailing Cyrus by name (xlv, 1) as 'My Anointed' (in the Latin version, *Christo meo*), destined to restore the Temple; nor yet the question how far Darius, who in his victory-inscription proclaims himself the servant of Ahura Mazda (the Wise Lord), the champion of truth and justice and enemy of the Lie (Zarathustra's word for evil), was an orthodox follower of the prophet. Probably his religion was somewhat contaminated with Babylonian and with Persian pre-Zoroastrian elements; but it clearly did provide him and his Persians with an ethic, as well as with a justification for the extension of their power.

Thus it was a well-organized empire, and no contemptible people, with which the Greeks were to stand face to face throughout their classical age. It was a tragedy, though perhaps inevitable, that these two great peoples met in conflict. To Cyrus, according to a story in Herodotos, the commercial Greeks were people who had in their cities 'a special place marked out, where they met to cheat each other'. To the Jews, who had suffered from the Assyrian and then the Babylonian bulldozer, Cyrus was a liberator; but to the Greeks it was their liberty itself that the Persians threatened.

In Ionia, Cyrus' yoke had not been grievous, but Cambyses' demand for men and ships against Egypt showed that it could grow heavier. Polykrates of Samos thoughtfully sent captains whom he thought expendable on political grounds; with the result that they went to Sparta instead, came back with a Spartan expedition, and attacked him. The attack failed; but

Polykrates, having made enemies everywhere, did not long survive it. He was decoyed to the mainland by the Persian satrap, seized and put to death. Samos itself fell about 517 to a Persian expedition accompanied by an exiled brother of Polykrates; and about 513 Darius in person came with a great army to invade Europe. He subdued eastern Thrace, but an expedition beyond the Danube was nearly a disaster. Harassed by the nomad Scythians, whom he could not catch, he narrowly escaped the fate of Cyrus. The tyrants of Ionia, who owed their position to Persia, rejected a proposal to demolish his bridge of boats over the Danube, formed of their ships, and to leave him marooned; but Byzantion and Chalkedon revolted and destroyed the similar bridge over the Bosporus. Darius had to return by sea over the Dardanelles. He left his army in Thrace, to show by more conquests that Persia was still formidable, before bringing it back to deal with the revolt. However, European conquests were, for the time, suspended; the king had, as always, many other preoccupations. It was a precious respite; for during it there arose in Greece the democracy of Athens.

2 THE ATHENIAN REVOLUTION

Out of the wreck of Polykrates' fortunes, the sons of Peisistratos at Athens rescued the poet Anakreon, sending a warship to pick him up. To acquire such a poet, always a ground for satisfaction, must have had added piquancy after being outbid by the Samian in the matter of Demokedes. Demokedes himself was not available; he had been in attendance on Polykrates, and was among the prisoners. He reappeared after a few years, accompanying a Persian reconnaissance of the west in two Phoenician warships; and at Taranto he succeeded in 'jumping his ship', and went home to Kroton.

Thus far, then, all was still well with the Peisistratids; but while Darius was planning his Scythian expedition, trouble began. The arrogance of a younger member of the family provoked a plot, as a result of which Hipparchos, the chief Peisistratid patron of poets and artists, was stabbed to death while organizing the Panathenaic procession. The only immediate effect was to make Hippias, the eldest brother, who managed the government, suspicious of plots everywhere; there was a reign of terror, and he made more and more enemies. But in the folk-memory of later Athens the two young tyrant-slayers, whose names were Harmodios and Aristogeiton, became martyrs of the democracy. Statues of them were set up, and a popular song celebrated them as the men 'who slew the tyrant Hipparchos and set Athens free'. Historians knew that this was nonsense; but once the song and saga had taken hold, research toiled after them in vain.

But the tyranny, increasingly unpopular, did not last much longer. Kleisthenes, head of the Alkmeonid family, had been a friend of Hippias and even held the archonship under him; but he had since fled into exile with his family. After failing in a rebellion in the hill country, they settled at Delphoi, where they had old family friendships. They undertook the contract for rebuilding the temple, which had been burnt down (noblemen in business, once more), and by generosity in exceeding the terms of their contract acquired great prestige. They used their influence (or, in a less friendly version of the story, bribery) to affect policy. Whenever the Spartans consulted the oracle the reply (for Apollo was under no obligation to confine himself to the question asked) was 'First, liberate Athens'. They were embarrassed, for Hippias had always been their friend; but finally (510) they did so. Their young and able king, Kleomenes, an original and sceptical person, may have been influenced by the feeling that Hippias was compromised with Persia. His outpost on the Dardanelles was within the Persian empire. To that outpost of Sigeion Hippias retired under an armistice, and looked to the extension of Persian power to restore him to Athens.

Kleisthenes came home in triumph; but, like his father before him, he found himself opposed by a coalition of other influential families, who carried their candidate to the chief archonship in 508.

The question of the day was that of citizenship. Under the laws of Solon desirable immigrants, especially skilled workers, if they moved to Athens with their families, could become citizens. Many had come, probably especially since the Persian conquest of Ionia, and had passed for citizens under the tyrants. But the aristocrats, who wanted a limited and docile citizen body, now proposed to conduct a scrutiny of the citizen rolls, probably hoping to exclude many of the immigrants for not having (under the tyranny, when it seemed not to matter) gone through the formalities of getting themselves attached to one of the Athenian clans. Ancient law, it seems, was on their side; thousands were struck off, and more feared to be.

At this point Kleisthenes proposed that the franchise question be settled once for all by an amendment to the constitution, making all free men permanently domiciled in Attica citizens by 'act of parliament'. It could be done by scrapping the old Ionic tribes and instituting new ones; a measure often adopted by Greek states, when it was desired to take in large numbers of immigrants. There was apparently still a majority in the Assembly who saw with anxiety the prospect of power going back into the hands of the gentry, the chief men in the old clans; and against the Archon and his supporters the measure was carried. Kleisthenes, his enemies grumbled, having found himself too weak in political friendships, was now taking the common people for his friends.

Isagoras the Archon cried that this was revolution; and he appealed to his friend Kleomenes to come back and restore order. Kleomenes came, with a bodyguard, and with his backing Isagoras took proceedings against Kleisthenes. He brought up, not for the last time in history, the family curse of the Alkmeonidai, for the massacre of the supporters of Kylon (p. 123), 'some of them at the sanctuary of the Furies'. The Alkmeonidai always claimed that they had received absolution for this, but after the manner of such questions it remained controversial. Kleisthenes did not stay to argue it. It did not suit him either to submit to being denounced as a probable lightning-conductor before the Areopagus, full of men jealous of his family, or to become a cause of bloodshed. He left, and waited for his opponents to overreach themselves, which they proceeded to do.

Backed by Kleomenes, Isagoras and the aristocrats (the Areopagus, sitting as a court?) pronounced the exile of no less than

700 households, the entire Alkmeonid faction. Then, having deprived the populace of its leaders, he went on, in total illegality, to dissolve the People's Council, which must have accepted Kleisthenes' bill before it could go to the Assembly. But then it was seen what eighty years of conducting their own routine business under the Laws of Solon, plus economic prosperity under the tyrants, had made of the Athenian commons. The Council simply refused to go; the people came out in arms; and Kleomenes and Isagoras, enormously outnumbered, fell back on the Acropolis. There the people blockaded them. The citadel was not provisioned, and on the third morning Kleomenes, seeing that it was no mere mob that faced him, agreed to go, with his Spartans, leaving behind their arms and their Athenian partisans. Among his men he also smuggled out Isagoras, who was bound to him by the tie of hospitality; but the Athenians secured a number of other reactionaries. There was no Kylonian massacre this time; they tried them regularly, no doubt before the People's Court (the Hēliaia, which was the Assembly convened for judicial purposes), and executed them in proper form.

A siege of two days may not sound a tremendous achievement; but as an operation by an army deprived of all its regular leaders, it was not inconsiderable. But even more impressive was their initial defiance of their own Archon backed by the prestige of a king of Sparta. A century later, the Old Men in Aristophanes' Lysistrata recall it, when the women's Peace Movement has seized the Acropolis:

> Shall women have the laugh of me? – Oh, by Our Lady, NO!
> For not Kleomenes himself who seized it long ago,
> > Got off so lightly; woe betide
> > The snorting Spartan in his pride!
> > He left his arms with me,
> > And, barely decent, in his shirt,
> > Unkempt, unshaved, in six years' dirt
> > Unwashed, we saw him flee;
> So fierce a watch and ward did we upon that hero keep,
> With seventeen-deep embattled shields before the doors asleep!

A minor action, really – like the fall of the Bastille.

Kleomenes was furious. Moreover, this democratic revolution was dangerous. He determined to crush it. In the next spring he and his fellow-king Dāmarātos led out the armies of the Peloponnesian League to restore order – 'to make Isagoras tyrant', Athenian democrats said – while the men of Boiotia and Chalkis attacked from the north. Desperately resolved to stand against all odds, the Athenians faced the main enemy, who had reached Eleusis; and then it must have seemed that a miracle happened. The enemy did not advance. At the sight, perhaps, of what was clearly neither a mob nor a faction, but the Athenian army in array, the Corinthians, old allies of Athens against Megara and Aigina, pleaded qualms of conscience and withdrew. Then King Damaratos himself also queried the object of the campaign; 'and seeing the kings at variance, the other allies also broke off and went away'. Without a blow struck the great Peloponnesian army went home.

The Athenians did not wait; they went straight after the Chalkidians, who had been ravaging north-eastern Attica unopposed. The Boiotians marched east to join their allies; but the Athenians got between them. They smote the Boiotians hip and thigh, taking 700 prisoners for ransom, and on the same day crossed the Euripos and routed the Chalkidians; a defeat so shattering that it broke the Chalkidian oligarchy. Athens annexed their lands and settled on them 4,000 Athenians as small-holders.

This was Athens' revolutionary war, on which Herodotos comments:

It shows how splendid a thing is political equality; the Athenians under the tyrants were no better soldiers than their neighbours, but once they were rid of them they were far the best of all.... Once they were free, every man was zealous, in his own interest.

Kleisthenes, recalled after the siege of the Acropolis, was now free to implement his reform; and in it he showed no less originality than Solon. Citizenship was henceforth to depend on membership of a dēmos or civil parish. There were 168 of these; and Kleisthenes divided them into thirty groups, ten each of the city and district, the inland region and the coast.

These he called Thirds ('Ridings'); and to each of his new Tribes he allotted three non-contiguous Thirds, one from each area, so that each tribal body was not local, but contained a sample of the whole Athenian people. Like the French revolutionaries, he was concerned to unify the country. Under his system, any differences of interest would cut across each tribe, minimizing the danger that they might, as in the old struggles of Coast, Plain and Upland, become identified with local units and threaten civil war. Each tribe provided a regiment for the army, and new officers, the Generals, were elected to command them under the War Archon. The tribes were as artificial as 'houses' in a day school; but like these, they developed some *esprit de corps* through competition in the athletic and musical contests of the city's festivals.

The People's Council, increased from 400 to 500, was also overhauled. It had a large and increasing load of work to carry (*cf.*, below, pp. 238ff.); and to spread this load, and also because the Council was itself rather large for detailed committee work, the fifty Councillors of each tribe took it in turn, drawing lots to decide the order, to be, as it was called, 'in Presidency' for a tenth of the year. During this time they were called 'the Presidents', *prytaneis*, and the period itself was called a *prytaneia*. They acted as a steering committee at meetings of the full Council and of the Assembly, and every afternoon they appointed by lot a Duty Officer from among their number, who held office from sunset to sunset, with a chain of office and custody of the state seal and the keys of the Treasury. During this time he, with sixteen other *prytaneis* whom he nominated, lived in the 'Round House' or presidents' mess, next to the Council Chamber, leaving it only for meetings of the Council or Assembly. The post of Duty Officer was never held twice by the same man; nor might one even be a member of Council more than twice in a lifetime, and not in successive years. Thus at any time in classical Athens there were thousands of citizens who had experience of day-to-day administration; and thus, too, there was always, at any hour, a duty officer and committee to be found if news of an emergency came in, who could decide whether to summon immediate meetings of the Council and Assembly and to alert the military authorities.

This was not yet complete democracy. The Nine Archons were still elected from among 'knights' only and, if 'passed' by the Assembly at the end of their year, entered the Areopagite Council for life. That council was still a supreme court, and as Guardian of the Laws, under Solon's arrangement, could indict proceedings as unconstitutional; and since it contained all Athens' chief political, military and religious experts, its voice was always heard with respect. Later Athenian conservatives called this constitution aristocracy, the Rule of the Best.

Kleisthenes' memory was never revered like that of Solon; perhaps people knew too much about him as an astute, aristocratic, 'whig' politician. He passes from the scene in silence soon after his legislation. Perhaps he simply died; but perhaps also he was made a scapegoat for his Persian policy. In the dire crisis before Kleomenes' invasion in force, Athens, then under the guidance of Kleisthenes, had made overtures to the Satrap at Sardis for Persian protection, and received the inevitable answer: Yes, if Athens would give earth and water, symbolising the surrender of all her territories to the Great King. In desperation, the ambassadors promised this; but when they got home, they found the crisis over, and were repudiated. It was an episode which Athens would have been glad to forget. But Persia's memory was long.

3 FROM SARDIS TO MARATHON

Then, in 499, Ionian discontent with Persian taxes and tyrants blew up in rebellion. A Persian expedition, conveyed on Ionian ships, had failed to reduce Naxos and restore a government of the rich, expelled by a revolution. The fleet mutinied and seized the tyrants (one was lynched by his own people, but most were let go); and Aristagoras of Miletos, who (in trouble with the Persians for having sponsored the expedition) had resigned the tyranny to lead the revolt, came over to seek aid from Sparta and Athens. Sparta refused; she had trouble in the Peloponnese, where Kleomenes inflicted a smashing defeat upon Argos, five years later. Athens had her troubles too ; she was still in a state of desultory, raiding war with Boiotia and Aigina. Yet she agreed to send twenty ships to Ionia. Her Euboian ally Eretria added five, and may have sent more to join the Ionian fleet in the Levant. The satrap Artaphernes, Darius' half-brother, had sent his available troops against Miletos ; and the Ionians and allies pushed up country from Ephesos and captured Sardis behind their back (498). But the thatched city caught fire, which made the Lydians hostile ; with the Persians closing in on them, the Greeks had to retreat ; they were overtaken and defeated before Ephesos, with heavy loss, including the Eretrian commander ; and the allies went home and took no further part in the campaign. Even so, the revolt now spread, as far as Cyprus and the Bosporus ; but with no further support from Greece, with the forces of the empire mustering, and spread out, as the insurgents were, round the coast against an enemy in the centre, it was doomed to fail. A Persian army and Phoenician fleet subdued Cyprus ; another army, the Asian coast of the Marmara ; a third, in Ionia itself, broke through to the sea. In 494 the Levantine fleets entered the Aegean ; and in the Battle of Ladē, off Miletos, the Samians, Miletos' old enemies, having been offered easy terms of surrender through their late tyrant (a nephew of Polykrates), started a débâcle by hoisting sail and making off.

Miletos was sacked, and there were savage reprisals at many towns, especially by the Phoenicians, who hated the Greeks as pirates. But afterwards the Persians showed remarkable breadth of view. They abolished the tyrannies, at least in Ionia itself, and permitted democracies. They insisted on commercial treaties between the cities, to prevent disputes leading to commerce-raiding, which was common in Greece ; and they conducted a land-survey as a basis for more equitable assessment of tribute. Nevertheless, city life in Ionia remained, archaeologists find, poor and undistinguished throughout the fifth century.

While Ionia was slowly beaten down, the question of intervention or non-intervention kept Athens painfully divided. There was a strong peace party, which thought resistance to Persia useless ; better to come to terms with the King and with his protégé, old Hippias; there were still many who thought quite kindly of the late dictatorship. In 496 they actually carried their candidate for the archonship, another Hipparchos, brother-in-law to Hippias and son of Peisistratos' favourite general; a man who, with no common-law charge against him, had stayed quietly in Athens. In 493 a poet named Phrynichos produced a tragedy (still something like an oratorio with the singers in costume), not on a mythological subject but on *The Fall of Miletos*: the triumph of Persians and Phoenicians, the lamentations of the women doomed to be taken as slaves. It created a tremendous sensation; but a court fined the poet and banned the piece from further production; the legal ground was probably 'impiety' in introducing a modern and a jarring note on a sacred occasion. But there was already a sign that public opinion was changing; for the archon elected that same spring stood for no surrender.

This was Themistokles, a man of the Kleisthenic revolution; for his mother was non-Athenian, some said not Greek, so that but for the reforms he would have been excluded from politics. A democrat and a radical, he gets a rather poor 'press' from our authorities, even from the honest Herodotos, who got his information largely in Alkmeonid circles. He was said to have enriched himself in politics, and he probably did. But he was the most brilliant strategist and politician that Athens ever had.

One of his proceedings this year, it is said, was the first step in constructing a fortified naval base among the hitherto neglected rocks of the headland of Piraeus.

While Themistokles was in office there arrived, among the refugees from Ionia, one who was different; a chief, with four shiploads of his people and their portable wealth – a fifth had been captured by the Phoenicians in a stern chase. This was Miltiades, of a family claiming descent from Homer's Ajax, some of whose chiefs had for two adventurous generations been lords of the Gallipoli Peninsula. The first of them, another Miltiades, had gone there in the time of Peisistratos, with his blessing (glad both to see the back of a formidable aristocrat and to secure Athens' hold on the straits) and at the invitation of the natives, threatened by the tribes of the mainland.

Arriving in Athens, the younger Miltiades was prosecuted on a charge of having ruled as a tyrant (as he had, with a private army of 500 mercenaries) over Greek colonists as well as over Thracians. However, he was acquitted. He had a reputation as a soldier, he was irretrievably committed against Persia, as a rebel; and it is a reasonable guess that influence was exerted for him by the archon Themistokles. Earlier, it was true, he had served under Darius in the Scythian expedition; but he met this with a claim, which it is rather difficult to believe, that he himself had proposed to destroy the Danube bridge and leave the king stranded in Scythia. From the Chersonese, moreover, he had conquered the Pelasgians of Lemnos and Imbros, opening those islands to Athenian settlers. This gained him considerable favour. Shortly afterwards, he was elected general of his tribal regiment.

Athens needed a good general, for the danger was coming closer. Mardonios, a brilliant young general, son of one of Darius' first supporters and married to the king's daughter, had arrived in Ionia with fresh troops, and had carried through the suppression of the tyrannies. He then resumed the advance along the north coast of the Aegean. His fleet was wrecked by a north-easterly gale in trying to round Mount Athos, and he himself was wounded in a night attack by the Thracians, though 'he did not withdraw till he had subdued them'. When, however, he did return to Asia, somewhat injured both physically and in reputation, the only result was that new commanders, Datis and Artaphernes, son of the old Artaphernes of Sardis, set out in 490 by the sea-route across the central Aegean. With them they had the now aged Hippias. The burning of Sardis had not saved Ionia; but it had put Athens and Eretria high on Darius' agenda.

Before this armament, much larger than the last, the men of Naxos fled from their town to their wooded valleys; other islanders, with no punishment to fear, hastened to submit and join the expedition. Karystos in Euboia closed its gates, but submitted in time to avert the worst; and the Persians reached Eretria. Here they had to open full-scale siege operations; but after a week, as happened often in Greek sieges, a gate was opened by a dissident faction; the city fell, and its people were put on inshore islands pending deportation. After a few days for reorganization, the Persians crossed the water to Marathon, where Hippias had landed with his father on their victorious home-coming, over fifty years before. Then, they had been able to advance on Athens, gathering their partisans; but this time the citizen army, convinced by Miltiades in the Assembly that passive defence was not best, came out in force and occupied the south end of the plain.

The runner Philippides was already on the way to Sparta, covering the 150 miles in two days; but he returned with the unwelcome news that, owing to a festival, the Spartans could not march before the full moon, still some days ahead. (The superstition was no doubt perfectly genuine.) There followed, therefore, several days of anxious waiting. The Persians, clearly not in overwhelming numbers – not enough to tackle Athens and Eretria simultaneously – and in touch, through Hippias, with members of the Peisistratid and Alkmeonid factions, were waiting for political warfare to help them, as in Samos and Eretria; but the democracy proved more solid than Hippias expected. Finally, on the very day when the Spartans were due to march (Hippias had probably had word of that, too), they seem to have embarked some troops by night, including their modest force of cavalry, to sail round Sounion, in the hope that when they landed at Phaleron their supporters would at last move. Some Ionians stole over to the entanglement of felled trees before the Athenian lines and gave news of this. There was now no time to lose; and at first light the war-archon Kallimachos, advised by Miltiades, led out his ar-moured force – perhaps 10,000, including some 600 from brave Plataia, a Boiotian city which Athens had protected against Thebes – to attack the Persians in their position a mile away.

It must be added that the deep water-course which now bi-sects the plain and forms a serious obstacle was *not there* in antiquity. Its sides consist of silt, washed down from the hills since they were deforested; pottery-fragments of the Christian era have been found in them, over a metre down. When the hills were wooded, the drainage would have come down more gently. Modern censures on Herodotos for failing to mention this obstacle have, here as often, been proved unjustified.

There were not enough armoured Athenians to cover the whole length of the enemy line in depth; but Miltiades knew that the Persians put their best troops in the centre; also that these were archers, more mobile than his pikemen, though not equal to them in close fight. To deal a decisive blow, he must get the 'outside station', and avoid the arrows as far as possible. So the Athenian generals led their regiments outwards on both flanks; their centre, a thin screen, perhaps hung back. Moving fast, they closed up on the enemy flank divisions; charged, crashing through half-hearted Ionians, and converged, to join hands behind the Persian centre, which had broken the thin Athenian line and was pursuing it. The Persians stampeded to reach their original naval station at the north end of the plain; but many were caught, trampling each other under foot, as an Athenian mural painting of the battle showed, at a point where only a narrow passage separated the sea from a marsh. 6,400 were killed, a number which seemed enormous to the Athenians; but its accuracy is assured, because, under a vow made by Kallimachos, every dead enemy had to be paid for by the sacrifice of a kid. The Athenians could not find so many kids at that season, and were constrained to 'fund' the debt at 500 kids a year, which they went on paying for a century. Kallimachos himself was killed in the moment of victory, trying to capture one of the ships which had stayed to take off fugitives. The Athenians did capture seven, at the cost of a number of their bravest men; but all the rest of the fleet got away.

Then they saw something to remind them of danger within. Someone was flashing a shield from high up on Mount Pentelikos. (So the sun must have been still well east of south.) Was it traitors, signalling at last, 'we are ready?' Everyone guessed so, and the name of the Alkmeonidai was mentioned; but there was no evidence. The regiments reorganized, and through the heat of the day they marched for Athens 'as fast as their feet could carry them'. There would have been no need for such haste unless some of the enemy ships had a long start; this is the reason for believing that some had started overnight.

That evening they camped south of the city walls; and the Persians, having entered Phaleron Bay and seen them, made sail for Asia.

4 BETWEEN TWO INVASIONS: PARTY POLITICS IN ATHENS

Such was the finely conducted campaign of Marathon, by which Athens was saved and her morale raised to even greater heights; but her internal politics were still fierce. Miltiades was the man of the hour, and his advice was to strike at once and win back the Cyclades. He refused to say how he would operate if entrusted with the fleet, which was strategically sensible, but the assembly did not like it; however, he assured them that he would make the campaign pay (through indemnities), and was allowed *carte blanche*. But he failed. He was held up at Paros, and returned wounded, leaving the state heavily out of pocket. His autocratic ways had already made many afraid that he was in a fair way to set himself above the laws, a tyrant; and his costly failure gave them their chance. He was prosecuted again, by one Xanthippos, of whom more will be heard, and who had married a niece of Kleisthenes. The charge was 'deceiving the People', which ranked as treason; the penalty demanded, death.

In the end, 'in view of his past services' it was commuted for a huge fine: fifty talents, or 300,000 drachmas; a drachma was a good day's wage for a skilled man. But it made little difference to Miltiades; his wound had gangrened, and he lay on a stretcher in court while the fierce speeches raged over him. He died, leaving his young son Kimon financially crippled. But there is a helmet in the museum at Olympia, with the curt inscription on it, MILTIADES DEDICATED – very likely that which he wore at Marathon; and that is his monument.

Archon in 489 was Aristeides the Just, also an old supporter of Kleisthenes, and a general at Marathon. Friends of the Alkmeonidai were making a come-back. The man they now most wanted to get rid of was Themistokles; but that did not happen.

Kleisthenes is said to have written into his constitution another original provision: that the Assembly should decide every winter, whether there was a man who should be exiled for the city's good. If the vote was affirmative, an 'election' was held in the spring to decide who it was. Every voter wrote the name of his choice on an *ostrakon*, a fragment of pottery (the 'waste paper' of Greece), whence the process was called unofficially *ostrakismós;* and the top 'scorer', subject to a minimum of 6,000 votes, was banished for ten years, without loss of property or status. Kleisthenes is said to have devised this as a method of getting rid of the blameless Hipparchos, against whom no criminal charge would lie; but then many people had begun to think that Hipparchos might be useful for 'appeasement', and the act had remained dormant. Now it was applied; and Hipparchos went. Next year went Megakles the Alkmeonid, nephew of Kleisthenes and brother-in-law of Xanthippos; two years later, Xanthippos himself. Among the *ostraka* from these elections, many hundreds of which have been found, by far the most frequent name is that of Themistokles, presumably because he was a target, though not the victim, year after year. At least once, half a dozen people, to judge by the hand-writing, sat down to write his name on hundreds of sherds, obtained from the 'spoilers' at a pottery, as an aid to voters who found writing a struggle; but the party workers were left with 190 of these on their hands, and dumped them in an old well, where they were found by an American excavator. Themistokles, for his part, evidently controlled a party well enough organized to be able to concentrate votes against his opponents one at a time, instead of scattering them.

During the same years (in 487) a reform was carried, for which Themistokles was probably responsible, though no name is mentioned. Archons, instead of being directly elected, were henceforth chosen by lot from among 500 candidates, fifty from each tribe, still of equestrian taxation-class and passed by the Council as in good standing. It could be represented as democratic, opening the chance of office to modest land-owners and not only to the well known; also it would take the archon-ships out of politics, eliminating the elections, which had often been fierce. But it also had long-term consequences, which Themistokles, renowned as the most far-sighted of politicians, probably foresaw. The ordinary, respectable 'knights', who would now usually hold office, would lack the prestige of the political leaders formerly elected; in particular the War-Archon would become dependent on the tribal Generals, who were elected for their military talents, and could be re-elected, thus gaining experience. It was not customary to hold an archonship more than once. Further (and did Themistokles foresee this too?), as the distinguished ex-archons, now sitting for life in the Areopagus, grew old and died, the prestige of that august and conservative body must, after a time, decline.

By 484 Themistokles was left face to face with Aristeides, archon in 489, the last hope of the conservatives. Both are said to have sought popularity by making themselves useful to their fellow citizens in the informal settlement of disputes, and to have been attacked by their political opponents for 'setting themselves up as judges', and by-passing the law-courts. There was probably less difference between their methods than we would gather from the literary tradition, which contrasts Aristeides the Just with Themistokles the slippery rascal. Themistokles was for developing the navy, a policy more popular with the poor than with the rich, who would have to pay for it. He was among those who never doubted that the Persians would come again; and even if they came round the Aegean by land, their weakest point would still be at sea, for sea-transport would be the best way of supplying a large army. Aristeides represented the land forces, the men of substance, who provided their own armour and were not paid. This was a method of financing land warfare which worked well enough in Greek border-wars. Also it suited the well-to-do politically, since it meant that arms, and training in arms, were kept in the hands of the Best People. With a navy, which needed state organization and state finance, one could not be sure what might happen.

Aristeides thus had the backing of those who questioned the need for heavy additional expenditure, maintaining that the spears of Marathon could do again what they had done before, and that anyhow the new invasion, of which Themistokles spoke, might never happen. This view was so widely attractive that Themistokles himself was constrained to lay more emphasis on a nearer enemy, Aigina. That island state, more predominantly maritime in its interests than Athens, seems to have kept an establishment of sixty galleys to Athens' fifty, and in the recent hostilities Aiginetans had harried the Attic coast, and even burnt Phaleron and the ships beached there.

This propaganda-line met with success, and when, in 483, the small operators who worked the state-owned silver-mines at Laurion near Sounion, paying royalties to the treasury, ran into an immensely rich vein, Themistokles seized his opportunity. Royalties for the year reached the unprecedented figure of 100 talents, and it was proposed to share these out, at a rate of ten drachmas to every citizen. This would indicate an adult male population of 60,000, which is consistent with the size of the armaments that Athens succeeded in raising. Themistokles persuaded the Assembly, which deserves credit for listening to him, to forgo this windfall and devote the money to building 100 new warships: triremes, requiring crews of 200 men apiece; a new type of ship, first heard of in the sixth century, in which, by an ingenious method of arranging the rowers in *échelon*, 150 oars could be fitted in, in three tiers, without making the galley so long as to risk breaking her back. Altogether, the navy was built up to a strength of 200 triremes in the course of three years. But the bill was not passed without opposition. 'Ostracism' was decided on again, and Aristeides went into exile, after a campaign in which, according to a celebrated anecdote, Aristeides meekly wrote his own name on a sherd, to oblige a rural voter, who did not know him, but said he was bored with all this talk about Aristeides the Just.

The ships were ready only just in time; for in 481 it became clear to all that the invasion was imminent.

CHAPTER 8

THE INVASION OF XERXES

1 THE STORM GATHERS

XERXES, son of Darius by the elder daughter of Cyrus and widow of Cambyses, had long been 'groomed' as crown prince; he is depicted as such in the great reliefs, with their long files of guardsmen and tribute-bearers, of the palace at Persepolis: he succeeded his father in 486, without incident. Older half-brothers by a daughter of Darius' friend Gobryas, noble but not royal, had been set aside; two of them held commands in Xerxes' forces. Altogether, eleven sons of Darius, most of them younger than Xerxes, who was born about 519, took part in the Greek expedition, and three were killed in it. The invasion of Europe was a young man's adventure.

Xerxes, the great enemy, naturally gets a bad press from the Greeks; even the honest Herodotos represents him as cowardly, sensual, generous indeed by fits and starts, but often cruel. There may be some truth in this; but it is clear that he took his duties seriously. He even undertook some suppression of pre-Zoroastrian 'false gods' still lurking in Iran. He was a hard master and a dangerous enemy.

Xerxes inherited a revolt in Egypt; but it was crushed within a year, and by 483 preparations to 'take in' Greece were resumed on a massive scale. Immense cables were ordered from Egypt and Phoenicia, to secure two bridges of boats across the Dardanelles. Rope-making was highly developed in the ancient east; one piece actually found in an Egyptian quarry was 18 inches in circumference and attached to a 68-ton stone block; its breaking strain when new is calculated as 75 tons, and its weight about 28 lb. per yard. Rope-walks half a mile long are known; so, for a military operation, cables such as Herodotos describes, four times that weight per yard and a mile long, seem hardly impossible. Mardonios was back in favour, and all

THE GREEK
PENINSULA
IN CLASSICAL TIMES

preparations were made to suit his strategy. A canal was dug through the isthmus north of Mount Athos, to avoid the dangerous cape; the river Strymon was bridged; great food-dumps were put down along the route. The canal and the Hellespont bridge are regularly quoted in classical literature as products of megalomania – 'marching over the sea, and sailing ships through the land'; but in fact both, especially the bridges, which were supported on old warships, were not unpractical. One need only compare the labour of construction with the trouble and waiting-time (with food-consumption) necessary for loading and unloading tens of thousands of men, horses, mules, camels, wagons and miscellaneous equipment on to and off boats operating from beaches and a few small harbours.

These preparations, especially the canal, could not be kept secret, and Greeks of the homeland at last awoke to their danger. A congress was called at Corinth, under the presidency of Sparta. Most states of the mainland were represented, and from the congress invitations were sent to others; but the results were disappointing. The Cretan cities remained isolationist; Argos, broken and isolated, with her neighbours and some-time subjects – even little Tiryns and Mykenai (Mycenae) – independent and allied to Sparta, refused to place her forces under Sparta, and demanded an equal share in the high command, whereat negotiations broke down. Gelon, tyrant of Syracuse, who, with his friend Theron of Akragas, dominated most of Sicily, demanded the high command either by land or sea, which Sparta and Athens would not concede; but he would in any case have been prevented from intervening; for Carthage was planning an invasion of Sicily. Almost certainly, though Herodotos does not say so, this had been concerted with Persia through Tyre and Sidon.

Athens might have hoped for the command at sea; but seeing that the Dorian naval states would not serve under her (especially Aigina and Megara, which is understandable), she agreed to serve under a Spartan admiral. Themistokles deserves much credit for this, though from Herodotos' aristocratic friends he does not get it. Essentially, the forces that defended

Greece in the end were those of Sparta's Peloponnesian League, Athens and a few islands.

Kleomenes of Sparta was no longer available; he was dead. Like Miltiades, he had aroused the suspicion of his people that he aimed at supreme power. He had got rid of the rival king, Damaratos, by casting doubts on his legitimacy, and replaced him by a compliant cousin; and Damaratos was now with Xerxes. Then, it is said, he was found to have bribed the Delphic oracle in the Damaratos affair, and himself banished from Sparta; but as Damaratos was not invited back, the story sounds dubious. He visited Thessaly, now the frontier region of free Greece; then Arcadia, where he tried to form a league of chieftains, bound by oaths to him personally. If he had succeeded in winning supreme power, breaking the privileged position of the Spartiates and giving wider opportunities to Arcadians and helots under his personal rule, which could not last for ever, it might have been a turning-point in Greek history; but a might-have-been it remained. The Spartans invited him to return, as king. It looked like victory for Kleomenes. But when he returned he went mad, so said the story; he had long been drinking heavily. He became violent, lashing out at respected noblemen with his stick. (Was he goaded by frustration, finding himself faced by a silent conspiracy of non-cooperation?) He was put in irons by his half-brothers, the elder of whom, Leonidas, became regent. Then one morning his body was found, hideously mangled 'from the feet upwards' with a knife. It was officially said that he had intimidated his helot jailer into giving him the knife, and had so mangled himself. The story reeks of the dark mystery of what went on behind the austere, Doric façade of Sparta. Leonidas, a brave, conventional soldier, more acceptable to the Spartiates, was now king.

Greece was indeed in no happy condition. The hardness and lack of chivalry (essentially a Christian virtue) which were characteristic of Greek life – poisoning relations even between rivals in sport, and almost always in politics – meant that everywhere defeated factions and defeated states were liable to prefer a remoter overlord to a nearer, victorious enemy. It was no small achievement that Athens and Aigina were reconciled in the national cause; and the north, where Persian agents had long been active – not disdaining the use of beautiful women among other weapons – was rotten with enemy propaganda. The Aleuadai, the great family of Larisa who aspired to make themselves kings of Thessaly, had been chased out by their peers, and were with Xerxes. Consequently the other barons were now nationalist; but the Aleuadai had a considerable following, and the Thessalian peasantry had no reason to suppose that things would be any worse under Persia and the Aleuads than under the barons. Thessaly, then, was shaky; but if she did join the nationalists, there would be something less than enthusiasm for the cause in Phokis, which had suffered much under Thessalian invasions. Thebes, defeated by Athens and prevented from annexing Plataia, was no better disposed to Athens than Argos to Sparta. And so on.

Worst of all, the Delphic oracle came out on the side of those who thought resistance useless. Datis in 490 had protected Apollo's shrine at Delos; Darius had once actually reprimanded a governor in Ionia who, in Zoroastrian zeal for agriculture, had made priests of the 'truth-telling god' cultivate sacred land. This policy now 'paid off'. Doubters were encouraged to remain neutral, which meant submission, and those bent on resistance received gloomy oracles.

In May 480, as soon as the spring rains were over, Xerxes marched from Sardis. For seven days and nights troops, animals, wagons streamed over the Hellespont bridges. Through the month of June they forged slowly ahead through Thrace, felling the forest and making their own roads, passable for an army with baggage. The Thracians watched with awe. Persian envoys, with considerable courage, entered Greece ahead of the army, demanding the symbolic earth and water of submission; and, especially in northern Greece, many gave it. Athens and Sparta consulted Delphoi, and received deliberately terrifying responses. The Spartans were told that either their city or a Spartan king must perish. (Was it meant as a hint that Sparta might survive under Xerxes' protégé, Damaratos, at the price of the life of the cousin who had replaced him?) But they refused to be dismayed, and put themselves deliberately beyond the pale of pardon by killing the ambassadors. Athens, in a rather suspiciously parallel story, claimed to have done the same.

When the Athenians' consultants came to Delphoi, the Medium (the Pythia, or 'Delphic Woman'), evidently carefully rehearsed in her part, did not even let them put their question. She received them with a shriek – in hexameter verse – bidding them 'flee to the ends of the earth' (to 'go west' like the Phokaians). But they were not to be so easily put off. On the advice of a Delphian, they took olive branches as suppliants and returned to the temple, threatening to stay there till they died unless the god gave them 'some better oracle about our country'. Thus they extorted a response, at worst ambiguous, saying that a Wooden Wall would survive the general destruction in Attica, and that 'divine Salamis would destroy the children of women'. It looks as if they had extorted permission to put their prepared question, naming Salamis. If so, it shows the hand of Themistokles. Having studied the problem for years, he had probably determined that, if invaded in overwhelming force by land, the Athenian government and army must withdraw to Salamis, and that in the narrow waters his young, mass-produced navy would have its best chance. In the Assembly, he argued that the Wooden Wall meant the fleet, not the palisades of the Acropolis as others thought, and that the epithet 'divine', not, for instance, 'cruel Salamis', portended victory.

The more far-sighted citizens sent their families to the Peloponnese, where the little city of Troizen (birthplace of King Theseus of Athens according to legend) showed them noble hospitality. A recently discovered inscription from Troizen, belonging to a memorial of much later date, purports to give the actual words of Themistokles' Decree, moved in the Assembly: recalling exiles, mobilising the fleet, evacuating women and children (the city's future) to Troizen, old people and goods (second priority) to Salamis. Such a decree was quoted for patriotic purposes by a fourth-century orator; probably the same text. But it is *not* likely that the original text was preserved; we have many contemporary inscriptions from Persian War memorials, and they are all short, and in verse. Long prose inscriptions become customary only later. Also the Troizen inscription gives the number of marines per ship (ten men-at-arms, four archers) which was standard later, when, we are told, the number had been drastically reduced; and the time for the recall of exiles was surely long before the time for general mobilisation and evacuation. The Decree is therefore probably a literary 'reconstruction', like the speeches which Greek historians put into the mouths of their characters. It remains interesting as a copy of what classical Athens thought Themistokles said or might have said.

The oracles also, it must be added, have been dismissed by many critics as later inventions. The reason for accepting them as genuine is precisely their pessimism. If they had been made up after the war, Apollo really ought to have done better than that.

Of the exiles, Aristeides and Xanthippos came home, to render distinguished service. Hipparchos did not. He joined the five sons of Hippias and other Peisistratids in Xerxes' camp; and that was the end of Peisistratid influence in Athens.

2 FORCES AND STRATEGY

The high command at Corinth was meanwhile studying its strategy. Themistokles had to devote time also to persuading the Assembly at Athens. However, he did persuade the Peloponnesians, whose instinct was to dig in at Corinth against the world in arms, that this would be useless if they lost command of the sea. For this, they must save Athens, Aigina, Megara, if possible Euboia, and their fleets. His own conviction was that they must start fighting as far forward as possible, and exploit the enemy's difficulties; and that with his new navy, exceeding in strength those of all the other allies, a victory might be won at sea. For preference, the decisive battle should be fought in narrow waters, where the stoutly-built Greek ships with their armoured marines, might be a match for the sleek, skilfully-handled but lighter ships of the Levantines.

That the Greek ships were the heavier and those of the Persian fleet the better sailers, is, by the way, the statement of Herodotos, in two passages (VIII, chapters 10 and 60). Some later Greek authors, desiring to find in the national struggle a triumph of skill over brute force, reversed the adjectives, and have regrettably been followed by many moderns.

To defeat Xerxes in a pitched battle on land was reckoned impossible, not merely because of his numbers, but because of the Persian superiority in cavalry and archers. The armoured Greeks could hold defiles against them, but an offensive, it was felt, would be suicidal. Marathon was the only victory to date won by Greeks against Persians in the open field, and against this, from Egypt to Ionia, there had been a record of defeats.

How large Xerxes' army was, we cannot say; the earliest Greek estimates are the most outrageous, beginning with the almost contemporary war-memorial at Thermopylai, which spoke of three million. To the Greeks, for whom 'myriad', the word for ten thousand, was popularly used to mean 'countless numbers', such figures were clearly meaningless. The water-supplies along their route were not sufficient for them, says Herodotos, except at the major rivers; a statement 'improved' by later rhetoric into the saying that they 'drank rivers dry'. Actually this statement, without the rhetoric, gives a useful limiting factor. General Sir Frederick Maurice, who went over the ground at the end of World War I and applied the data collected by British intelligence to Herodotos' story, found that water-supplies along the route would barely suffice for about 200,000 men (including the non-combatant transport and supply services) with some 70,000 horses, mules and camels. The army may have been smaller; but probably, in this great royal campaign, the Persians brought the largest force that they could. The mounting and supply of the expedition was a remarkable feat.

The backbone of the army was the Iranian infantry and (much less numerous) cavalry, Persians, Medes, Bactrians and others, armed with bow, spear (not as long as the six-foot Greek weapon) and short sword. The infantry carried large wicker shields with a spike below, which could be stuck in the ground, forming a shield-wall, while shooting. The Persian Guards, the 10,000 'Immortals', so-called because there was never a vacancy in their ranks, also had body-armour of metal scales sewn on to leather tunics, but few others had any. But Herodotos' list also includes other troops, ranging from Lydians, armed in the Greek manner, to Caucasian mountaineers with javelins and small targets, and even 'Ethiopians from beyond Egypt', who painted themselves half white and half red before battle and whose arrow- and spear-heads were of stone. It is usually doubted whether Xerxes would have found these savages worth their food; and yet, the Roman imperial army, as shown on Trajan's Column, includes some very wild-looking barbarian 'auxiliaries', stripped to their trousers and armed only with clubs and stones for throwing. Savages, expendable and possibly terrifying, may perhaps have been similarly attached to Iranian 'legions'. Among the mounted troops we hear of an Arab camel-corps, north African Libyans with the archaic chariot, and the Sagartian horsemen of central Iran, armed with lassos. None of these picturesque units appear to have proved useful as the campaign developed; but they conceivably might have, if the Greeks had given battle in open country.

Herodotos gives, from some Persian source, a detailed list of the contingents, but he remarks that no numbers were given. Perhaps they were secret. For the fleet, he does give figures for contingents: Phoenicians, Egyptians, Cilicians and subject Greeks add up to 1,207 ships, exclusive of supply-craft. These figures may represent the estimates of the capacity of each region, formed by the Greek intelligence; if they represent, even so, a great over-estimate of the forces actually raised, it would not be surprising, nor unparalleled in modern times.

The Greek strategy was firmly based on the facts of geography. The east coast of central Greece is covered for over 100 miles by the long, natural breakwater of the island of Euboia; but Karystos, at the south end of Euboia, and the next island,

Andros, owned Persian suzerainty – solid Persian gains from the campaign of 490. North of Euboia opens the Strait of Artemision, so-called from a temple of Artemis (not a town), on the northern tip of the island. North of this, the inhospitable mountain coast of Thessaly runs for another eighty miles, exposed to the north-east, before reaching the Gulf of Therma (predecessor of Thessalonica). Here Xerxes' fleet concentrated, in contact with the army, in accordance with the landsman's strategy of Mardonios. If the Greeks held Artemision in force, as they did, initially with 100 Athenian and 100 Peloponnesian ships, the enemy would be unable to come down the Thessalian coast by squadrons, to draw up on the few small beaches if the weather turned bad, or the Greeks would destroy them in detail as they arrived. They would have to come down that coast, too far to row in a day without arriving exhausted, in mass; and then, well might the Greeks – as Apollo was said to have advised his own Delphic people – 'Pray to the Winds'.

Meanwhile, the land front had to be held; and long before Xerxes reached Macedonia, 10,000 southern Greek men-at-arms (which implies also more than 10,000 light-armed soldiers' servants) under a Spartan officer, Themistokles himself leading the Athenian contingent, were sent by sea to Thessaly, to join hands with local forces and hold the Olympos line at the coastal pass of Tempē. It was a large army by Greek standards. But then came a shock. There were other practicable passes inland; and the mountain peoples, penetrated by Persian propaganda, had no intention of helping to defend them and getting their villages burnt. Alexander I, the young king of Macedonia, who had once nearly won an Olympic crown in the 200 yards, but also was brother-in-law to the Persian officer in charge of the Canal, asked the Spartan Euainetos 'as a friend', was it really wise to stay and be trampled under the feet of the host that was coming? And, with inside knowledge, he gave details of it. Euainetos finally lost his nerve and withdrew; and the Thessalian gentry hastened to make their peace with the Aleuadai and with Xerxes.

3 THERMOPYLAI AND ARTEMISION

It was a moment of deep gloom and alarm. Moreover, if the land front was not held, the fleet could not stay long at the all-important Artemision position. Also, it was now again a sacred season, that of the full-moon Karneian festival of Apollo at Sparta and of the Olympic Games for all Greece; and to march out during the month, without waiting for the climax of the festival, was reckoned in the highest degree unlucky. Most Peloponnesians probably welcomed the excuse for not sending their main armies north; they had never wanted to. But King Leonidas appreciated, if Spartan Elders did not, the urgency of the crisis; and while two-thirds of Xerxes' army rested in Macedonia, and one-third again cut roads through the forest above the vale of the Haliakmon, Leonidas marched to hold the last position that could protect Artemision: the Pass of the Hot Springs, Thermopylai ('Hot Gates'), where the road followed the coast, and the sea then came nearly to the foot of the fierce cliffs of Kallidromos. Leonidas had with him his royal guard of 300 men and seven helots apiece (three apiece perhaps armed), 2,120 Arcadians, 680 men from Argolis, 4,000 Peloponnesian armoured men in all. With 1,100 Boiotians and the forces of Phokis and Lokris, he may have had over 7,000 armoured men; enough, he gave out, to hold the pass until they were reinforced after the full moon (18 August). But he knew very well that it was a dangerous mission. For his 300 Spartiates, he had brought not the usual young men, but men who had sons living, so that their families would not perish if the worst should occur.

Xerxes came down through Thessaly, while his fleet, by order, waited for the army to secure the Gulf of Pagasai ahead of them; for triremes, built for speed, were very dependent on water-points for their rowers. Phoenician scouts caught and destroyed three Greek look-out ships off Skiathos island. On land, a Persian horseman saw and counted the Greek picket, out in front of the wall that guarded the pass. They were Spartiates, and he marvelled that they seemed to be behaving frivolously, doing athletic exercises or carefully combing their long hair. Damaratos is said to have explained the point to Xerxes: Spartans considered it important to die with their heads tidy. But no attack developed for three days. 'Waiting for us to run away,' murmured the Greeks. More probably it took that long for the infantry to come up. Meanwhile the main fleet set out; and then – fifty days after midsummer, a contingency well known to Greek weather-lore – the weather, which had been calm, suddenly broke. What happens is that the air over the Mediterranean heats up till it lifts, and is replaced from the Black Sea in violent nor'-easters.

Such a storm had wrecked Mardonios' fleet off Athos twelve years before. Now, it got up at dawn, catching most of the ships riding at anchor overnight – a proceeding which the captains of the long, narrow triremes always disliked – several rows deep, off beaches on which only a fraction of the fleet could get ashore. There was enormous loss; 400 triremes it was said, besides countless supply boats. Castaways built barricades of wreckage, in fear of attack by the hillmen. It blew for three days, before the Magi, by spells and incantations, stopped it; or perhaps, says Herodotos, it just stopped. Then the armada got under way again. The Greeks, who had sheltered under the lee of Euboia, were rather dismayed to see how many had survived. They got back to their station only in time to cut off fifteen stragglers as they rounded the corner. The rest got safe into the bay of Pagasai.

The Greeks had so far kept a second fleet, including the second hundred Athenian ships, based on Attica, Aigina, and Pōgōn (Poros Sound), in case of a thrust through the Andros channel. From it, as more ships came in and the danger loomed from the north, they reinforced the northern fleet, keeping the southern at 80 or 100. Deducting losses, 146 Athenian ships, including twenty manned by their settlers at Chalkis, and 122 others were now at Artemision; and while the enemy reorganized, on two successive evenings the Greeks attacked their anchorages, inflicting losses and getting away under cover of the swift Mediterranean dusk. More important, a detachment sent to turn the Greek position by the Andros channel was piled up by a second storm on the Hollows (meaning the southern 'thin part') of Euboia. The entire fleet of 200 galleys is said to have perished; heaven itself, says Herodotos, seemed to be working to reduce the enemy to a strength not excessively greater than that of the Greeks. (Having started with 1,207, Greek tradition had to get them down somehow.) With this danger removed, the whole remaining fifty-three Athenian ships now joined the main fleet.

On the same two days, Xerxes' army assaulted Thermopylai; but the Greeks, fighting in relays, threw them back with heavy loss, and were showing no sign of exhaustion. The whole invasion was at a standstill when, on the third morning, the entire oriental fleet came out in battle array to break the deadlock. The Greeks, still outnumbered, drew back their wings in a defensive semi-circle. There was prolonged and savage fighting. The Egyptian marines, fighting with boarding-pikes and pole-axes, carried five ships by boarding. Both sides were glad, says Herodotos, when sunset ended the battle. The Athenians found half their ships lost or crippled; and the Greek admirals, even the sanguine Themistokles, agreed that they were in no state to give battle next day. They gave their men a good meal on Euboian mutton ('denying it to the enemy'), and after midnight, leaving their camp-fires burning, made off to the south. A despatch boat, held ready for liaison with Leonidas, had been sent to warn him; but Leonidas was beyond reach of messages.

What happened that day at Thermopylai became a great saga; but Herodotos caught it near enough to the source to make sense. Later, it became sadly contaminated with sentimental journalism.

The Persians, experienced mountain fighters, had no doubt been trying to find a way round Thermopylai since their first arrival; the saga as it reached Herodotos makes them noticeably more stupid than in most of his narrative. They duly found a local man, no more anxious than most northern Greeks to have the Persians stuck in his country, and eating it up, who was prepared to show them a path by night. There was a moon; there would be high festival that night in the south, and after that, Greek reinforcements might start. On the other hand, the mountains were covered by thick oak forest.

The secret of Thermopylai is that, above the cliffs, the mountain culminates not in a rocky ridge, but in two ridges with, between them, a wide, shallow, grassy trough, where a tributary of the local river Asōpós flows in slow meanders. Here, 'along the spine of the mountain', as Herodotos says (and not half-way down the forward slope, as in a modern map, reproduced distressingly often), runs a natural route, passable even to jeeps or trucks, by which invaders more than once in antiquity by-passed the coast-road. The problem was to reach it – and to reach it with a formed body of troops, without so much straggling that those in rear could not support the leaders. For this, only a good route would do. There is one possibility, straight up a spur, east of the great gorge by which the Asōpós descends; but since Herodotos says that the Persians went a long way round, it is probable that this shorter way up was guarded, by 1,000 Phokians, who had volunteered to look after the mountain flank. What Ephialtes the Malian (the Judas Iscariot of classical Greek tradition) had to show was how to outflank Leonidas by first outflanking the flank-guard itself.

Xerxes sent the Immortals, whose march-discipline on rough tracks in the dark might be equal to the task. They started at dusk, perhaps up the slope by the modern village of Vardhatés, and 'marched all night ... and it was about break of day, when they came out on the top of the mountain'. The Phokians, alerted by a mysterious rustling – that of fallen leaves under thousands of feet – and then 'shot up' at dawn by troops already *on* the top, not coming from in front, pulled in to a high point and prepared to sell their lives dearly; but the Guards – professional soldiers against citizen militia – ignored this minor objective and 'started down, going fast'. They were through.

Leonidas, perhaps deceived by the heavy frontal attacks into thinking the Persians had no other idea, awoke to the news that his flank was hopelessly turned. There was not a hope of preventing the Persians from getting down the mountain, once they were up. It was no use, either, for his whole force to retreat at once; the enemy cavalry could round them all up within the day. A sacrificed rear-guard must stay, to give the others a start.

Leonidas ordered away his Peloponnesian allies; good troops, who could fight again. He kept his Boiotians, perhaps on the cool calculation that, as their cities were bound to be lost, they might as well be 'expended'; and he stayed, with his Spartans, without whom in any case the reaguard might have collapsed too soon. Some of the Boiotians finally did surrender, after doing valiantly first. No doubt also he remembered the oracle: a Spartan king must fall. With these troops he fell furiously upon the enemy in front, driving many into the sea; and after a mêlée in which two young brothers of Xerxes fell, among hundreds of their men, he and all his Spartans, with probably 900 faithful helots, perished to a man.

A king of Sparta had been defeated and killed; it was daunting news. As an immediate sequel some Arcadians, 'poor men, wanting employment', went over to Xerxes; they were probably among those who had fought under Leonidas, and now felt that a victorious king was better than a dead one. To make the best of it Greek propaganda, fairly enough, emphasised the gallantry shown; and the Thermopylai legend was born. But in its glamour, the real importance of Thermopylai is usually forgotten. The few at Thermopylai made possible the Artemision operations, in which over 60,000 Greeks caused losses to the enemy, directly in battle and still more indirectly, by forcing him to expose his fleet on a dangerous coast, which ultimately decided the result of the war.

Phokis and the coasts of Euboia were devastated with fire and sword; Thebes and most of Boiotia joined Xerxes quickly, Alexander of Macedon making their peace for them. Athens was evacuated, not without haste and panic. The allied fleet, picking up its last reinforcements from Poros, put in to Salamis Sound, to help ferry non-combatants to Salamis and Aigina. A volunteer garrison was left on the Acropolis. Their wooden palisades were soon in flames, from incendiary arrows shot from the Areopagus, but they still held out, and crushed under rolling stones an assault by the only accessible way. Then

Persian rock-climbers, as at Sardis, found a route 'where no one would have thought it possible', and took the defenders of the gates in rear; and in fire and massacre the Acropolis fell.

Xerxes sent home a despatch announcing his victory. It was still only four months since he had crossed into Europe.

4 THE RAZOR'S EDGE

Nevertheless, Xerxes still had his anxieties. It would be difficult to feed his large army in Greece through the winter; and he had not made an end of his enemies' main forces. To attack the entrenched line on the Isthmus, now held by a formidable Peloponnesian army, was unattractive. The position must somehow be turned by sea. Damaratos is said to have proposed detaching a squadron to seize the island of Kythera, Sparta's Achilles heel; but the king's brother Akhaimenes, satrap and admiral of the Egyptians, objected that after its storm losses the fleet was no longer strong enough to divide in face of the enemy. The Persians called up their last reserves, the ships of the Cyclades; but these were not many; moreover their behaviour, with their homes still at the Persians' mercy, suggests that they were not at all sure of Xerxes' victory. The few ships of Paros hung about at Kythnos, which had sent one ship to join the Greeks, and missed the battle; those of Naxos joined the Greeks in a body; and a ship from Tenos deserted, with valuable information, on the eve of the decisive clash.

So the Persian fleet remained massed in Phaleron Bay, and the Greeks still inside the Salamis strait, where they flanked, and could cut off from supplies of water, any Persian seaborne move against the Peloponnese. Salamis itself, holding the Athenian government and army and thronged with refugees, was an important objective, and Themistokles still hoped that the Persians would attack it. Xerxes ordered the construction of a mole, to be completed by a floating bridge of merchantmen lashed together, across the narrows – probably at this point of time, though only inferior sources say so. It was a typical Persian massive engineering project; but its completion would be virtually impossible without control of

the straits themselves. Accordingly, after a conference to hear
the opinions of his contingent-commanders, he finally ordered
the fleet to close up on Salamis next day, and seek out the
Greeks in their lair. A minority opinion, expressed by Artemisia,
half-Cretan and half-Karian, the queen-regnant of Halikarnassos, was for waiting till lack of supplies forced the Greeks out;
but, with autumn approaching, Xerxes was in a hurry.

Themistokles meanwhile had been having his own troubles,
persuading the Peloponnesians, accustomed, like all Greeks, to

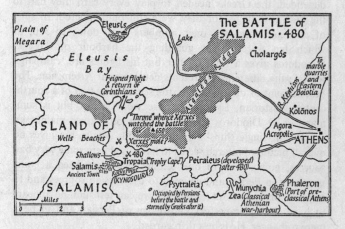

strictly local wars, that the right position in which to defend
their country was at Salamis. He probably succeeded in convincing Adeimantos ('Undismayed'), the Corinthian admiral;
Adeimantos' epitaph claimed, long after, that he 'by his counsel' saved Greece. Athenian accounts, which reached Herodotos, representing him as both a fool and a coward, reflect
merely a later Athenian feud with Corinth and with his family
in particular. But he may have had difficulty in holding his
men, especially when dust on the coast road showed that the
Persians were marching for Megara.

It was now that Themistokles made his contribution to
making up Xerxes' mind for him. He sent him a message
professing readiness to defect, exaggerating the tensions in the

Greek camp (of which the Persians, with many Greek exiles working for them, must have been aware), and saying that they were on the point of breaking up, to flee in the night or, if attacked in the morning, likely to come to blows among themselves. The message fell on already fertile soil.

So Themistokles was to have his Battle of Salamis, fought, as ancient sources agree, *in the Narrows*, and not, as some moderns have suggested, off the eastern tip of the island. In this great battle, on which the existence of fifth-century Athens depended, the Greeks needed to play every card they had to the best advantage, for they were still outnumbered. In spite of all reinforcements, their numbers were down to 310, of which ten were absent guarding the harbour of Aigina; Herodotos gives a total of 380, but his figures are 'campaign totals'; the difference represents nett losses at Artemision. The best account of their line of battle seems to be that of a fourth-century historian, Ephoros, whose work is lost but is summarised by Diodoros of Sicily. Herodotos gives mainly an account of single ships' actions; he adds details, but gives no overall picture. Plutarch seems to have used here some very bad sources, going back to one Ktesias, who had been a court physician in Persia, and claimed to use Persian sources and to improve on Herodotos; wherever we can test him, he appears to have a very imperfect knowledge of Persian and to be a mere romancer. He is best disregarded.

In the main Greek fleet of about 200 ships, Athens still filled the left and centre, though Sparta (sixteen ships) had the post of honour on the extreme right. Their assignment was to meet the enemy when his leading squadrons had passed the Narrows, envelop the head of the enemy column, and destroy it. Aigina and Megara (fifty ships at most, but among the best in the fleet) formed a detached squadron on the right, probably based in the bay below the Narrows, by the ancient Salamis town (modern Ambelaki); they were to hit the tail of the column in flank and prevent it from getting forward. Corinth had a special assignment: at first sight of the enemy, to hoist sails to the morning sea-breeze and 'flee' up the Strait. (Greek ships never fought under sail; the square sail gave no manoeuvrability.) This was to draw the enemy on, suggesting to Phoenician veterans that what happened off Miletos, fourteen years before, was happening again. Prejudiced Athenians told Herodotos that the Corinthians really fled, and took no part in the battle; but he notes that other Greeks said they fought very well, so presumably they returned. An epitaph of some Corinthians, buried on Salamis, is quoted by ancient writers as that of men killed in the battle. Part of the actual stone has been found.

Xerxes detached his hard-fighting Egyptian squadron to block the escape route west of the island, and the whole of his fleet spent the night at sea, ready to cut off a retreat which never took place. In the morning, unable to return to shore for fear that the Greeks might escape before they could get the men on board again, they advanced into the strait as originally planned, while Xerxes watched from a throne above the Narrows.

The best account of the action, streamlined for poetry but given, not ten years later, before men who fought in it, by one who saw it, probably as an Athenian soldier on shore, is that of Aeschylus, in *The Persians*: the only extant example of a Greek tragedy on recent history. A messenger tells the story to the queen-mother Atossa:

> O Queen, the whole disaster first began
> surely with coming of some fiend or devil!

> There came a Greek from the Athenian camp,
> and said to your son Xerxes: come the night,
> the Greeks would wait no longer, but embark
> and sail in secret, scattering for their lives.
> He, not suspecting the deceitfulness
> of that Greek, nor the envy of high heaven,
> forthwith gave order to his admirals
> at sunset to embark, in three divisions,
> and guard the outlets well, while other ships
> encircled all the island round about.
> And should the Greeks escape, their heads should fall;
> – so said he, confident and glad at heart.

Little he knew what the gods had in store!
    Then they in order took their evening meal,
and sailors set in rowlocks each his oar,
and when night fell, each master of the oar
embarked, and every skilful man-at-arms,
and rank hailed rank as the long ships went forth.
    Then all night long the captains kept their crews
patrolling in the fairway. Night wore on,
and still no Greeks came out in secret flight;
but when at last the sun's bright chariot rose,
then we could hear them – singing; loud and strong
rang back the echo from the island rocks,
and with the sound came the first chill of fear.
Something was wrong. This was not flight; they sang
the deep-toned hymn, *Apollo, Saving Lord*,
that cheers the Hellene armies into battle.
    Then trumpets over there set all on fire;
then the sea foamed as oars struck all together,
and swiftly, there they were! The right wing first
led on the ordered line, then all the rest
came on, came out, and now was to be heard
a mighty shouting: 'On, sons of the Greeks!
Set free your country, set your children free,
your wives, the temples of your country's gods,
your fathers' tombs; now they are all at stake.'
And from our side the Persian battle-cry
roared back the answer; and the time was come.
    Then ship on ship rammed with her beak of bronze;
but first a Greek struck home; full on the quarter
she struck and shattered a Phoenician's planks;
then all along the line the fight was joined.
    At first, the torrent of the Persian fleet
bore up; but when the press of shipping jammed
there in the narrows, none could help another,
but our ships rammed each other, fouled each other
and broke each other's oars. But those Greek ships,
skilfully handled, kept the outer station
ringing us round and striking in, till ships
turned turtle, and you could not see the water
for blood and wreckage; and the dead were strewn
thickly on all the beaches, all the reefs;
and every ship in all the fleet of Asia

in grim confusion fought to get away.
 Meanwhile the enemy, as men gaff tunnies
or some great shoal of fish, with broken oars
and bits of wreckage hacked and killed; and shrieks
and cries filled the whole sea, till night came down.*

The detail 'right wing leading', as the Greeks come in sight, shows that they appeared from behind the cape of Mount Aigaleos, to engage the Phoenicians, leading the Persian fleet, as they emerged from the Narrows, where relatively few could sail abreast, and tried to fan out. The Phoenician ship struck on her quarter early on must have been caught turning.

The Greeks are said to have destroyed or captured 200 ships for the loss of forty. Enemy strength was still considerable; most of the Ionians in the rear got away, and the Egyptians may not have been engaged. At nightfall the Greeks, like the victors of Gettysburg, hardly realised what they had done. The shore was still full of Persian troops; work on the mole still continued. But on the second morning after the battle, there were no enemy ships to be seen; and scouts, presently venturing to look into Phaleron Bay, found it empty. They had inflicted crippling loss on the Phoenicians, the flower of the imperial navy; and without them the rest of the fleet was reckoned unreliable. Xerxes ordered it away, to winter at Kyme, whence it could if necessary defend the Hellespont.

5 THE CONSEQUENCES OF SALAMIS

The Greek fleet followed up at leisure; to say 'pursued' would be an exaggeration. They ravaged the lands of Andros, Karystos and Paros and collected indemnities, before returning to their base, to find Xerxes gone too. He is said to have fled in terror, spurred by a second privy message from Themistokles, saying that only his, Themistokles', good offices had prevented a Greek raid on the Hellespont bridges. But in fact, there were good reasons for his withdrawal. He was dangerously out of touch with the east, after losing command of the sea; he had,

*Adapted from the author's own translation in his *Persia and the Greeks*, by permission of the publishers, Messrs Edward Arnold.

after all, taken Athens and killed a king of Sparta. Mardonios is said to have suggested that the king should return home, leaving Mardonios with a picked force to complete the conquest.

As it turned out, Greece was saved. News came from Sicily too that Gelon and Theron had smashed the Carthaginian invasion 'by sea and land', as Gelon's dedication at Olympia said. The decisive battle was on land, before Himera, about the time of Thermopylai; a synchronism apparently 'improved' later to say 'on the very day of Salamis', linking victory with victory. But it still remained to deal with Mardonios.

Mardonios eased his supply problems by 'stream-lining' the army; he dismissed the miscellaneous auxiliaries, who streamed back to Asia, their ranks thinned by dysentery and some failure of supplies. He kept the Iranian troops and a few hand-picked detachments; one Iranian division was detached to escort Xerxes to the Hellespont and come back. From the size of his camp in 479, said to have been 2,000 yards square, he may have had up to 75,000 horse and foot. With these, he evacuated Athens and withdrew to winter in the richer land of Thessaly.

The winter passed, full of strains and stresses among the free Greeks. Themistokles was fêted at Sparta; but at Athens the chief fighting commands for 479 went to the returned exiles. Aristeides, who after the sea-battle had destroyed a Persian garrison on Psyttáleia island, off the east coast of Salamis, commanded the land forces, and Xanthippos the fleet. Themistokles did have a command again in 478; but the fact remains that the elder statesmen in the Areopagus, which played a very important part during the emergency, were mostly hostile to him; they may have seized a chance to 'ease him out'.

Mardonios in Thessaly continued Persia's political warfare. Argos by secret messages confirmed her willingness to join him; and western Arcadia, which had sent 1,000 men to Thermopylai, took no further part in the war. But his chief hope was to win over Athens. He offered her forgiveness of all past injuries, self-government within the empire, and any of her neighbours' land that she cared to annex; with renewed occupation and devastation as the penalty for refusal. Nevertheless the

Athenians did refuse, reassuring the Spartans in the name of 'our common blood and language and religion and ways of life'; a classic statement of pan-Hellenic patriotism.

Athens' main trouble was that the Peloponnesians, with their all-but-island fortress now secure, behaved as if they hoped to avoid sending their main armies outside it at all.

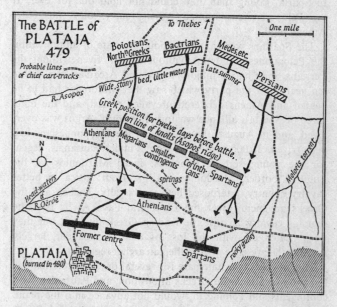

The BATTLE of
PLATAIA
479

Probable lines of chief cart-tracks ====

One mile

To Thebes ↑

Boiotians, Northⁿ Greeks

Bactrians

Medes, etc.

Persians

R. Asopos

Wide, stony bed, little water in late summer

Greek position for twelve days before battle, on line of knolls (Asopos ridge)

Athenians Megarians

Smaller contingents

Corinthians

Spartans

springs

N

Head-waters of R. Oëröe

Athenians

Former centre

PLATAIA
(burned in 480)

Spartans

Moloeis torrent

rocky gulley

Could not the Persians be forced out of north Greece by sea-borne threats to their communications? This perhaps was why Sparta honoured Themistokles more than Athens. There was one such movement, in Chalkidike. Poteidaia (a Corinthian colony), Mende and Skiōne revolted, and held their isthmus against attacks by the division that had escorted Xerxes. To Athens, the Peloponnesians offered economic assistance to maintain their destitute people, and even a new home within the Peloponnese. The Athenians were not amused.

Spring came, and Mardonios marched. No Peloponnesian army appeared, and the Athenians, who had done some autumn sowing and repairs, were compelled in high disgust to evacuate the city again. Mardonios reoccupied it, and signalled the news by beacons to Xerxes at Sardis. Still the Athenians refused his terms; they even lynched a Councillor who proposed discussing them; and Mardonios started destroying the city systematically. In desperation the Athenians sent a protest to Sparta, saying that they could not hold out for ever. If the Peloponnesians wanted Athens' navy, they must save Athens' land.

The Spartans were anxious about the state of affairs within the Peloponnese, and not without reason. Even without the Persians, they had a major Argive and Arcadian war within ten years. But the party which saw that Mardonios had to be beaten and Athens delivered prevailed at last, and the main force of Sparta's alliance was ordered north. Argos was over-awed, and in August, though not all the Peloponnesians had yet arrived, 38,000 armoured troops under Pausanias, regent for the young son of Leonidas, faced Mardonios on the Boiotian border. Mardonios, retiring from Attica to better cavalry country, interposed between his ally, Thebes, and the Greeks advancing over the Eleutherai Pass. At its foot, he sent his cavalry against the leading Greek division, but they were beaten off with the loss of their commander, largely through the presence of an Athenian archer regiment.

Then there was a stalemate for several days. Mardonios was too wary to attack the Greeks in position, and Pausanias, with contingents still coming in, would not advance into the plain. Pausanias did move, however, about three miles to the left into the territory of Plataia. Here he occupied a range of knolls, one to two miles from the foot of Kithairon, in undulating country, between eastward and westward-flowing streams. His supply-line now ran over the more westerly pass called the Oakheads, Dryoskephalai (a name wrongly applied to the main-road pass in some modern maps). The Persians, with northern Greeks and Boiotians on their western flank, faced him across the northward bend of the stripling Boiotian Asopós. Here he found better water-supplies and room for camping; but he proved to be too far from the foot of the pass. Persian cavalry cut in behind his line, destroying a food-convoy in a night raid, and fouling and blocking the springs. They also harassed the Greeks with archery by day. The position was untenable, and Pausanias determined on a withdrawal to the foot of Kithairon by night. This was the move which led to the greatest land battle of classical Greek history.

Herodotos represents what happened as a chapter of accidents; but since Pausanias (he says) gained high credit for the result; since he derived his account from old men who had been young soldiers at the time; and since Athenians in his time, owing to the sad course taken by subsequent history, were disposed to slander their former allies, it seems reasonable to emphasize what he says the troops *did*, and to neglect allegations of misconduct by everyone except the Athenians. The centre (half the army) went back to the hill-foot, where they covered the descent of a food-train waiting behind the Dryoskephalai Pass. The Spartans, on the right, waited till near dawn before retiring, leaving behind a battalion, which drew Mardonios and his native Persian division after them in pursuit at first light; and the Athenians, on the left, after waiting for the centre to get clear, retired under orders to close on the Spartans, who were going to need badly (and did not get) the support of the Athenian archers. The Athenian move drew after them the northern Greeks from the Persian right, and these came across the front of the Persian centre (Medes, Bactrians and 'Indians' from Afghanistan), who, owing to the bend of the Asopos, started from further back. The enemy wings were drawn into a converging advance, and if the Athenians had joined up with the Spartans, the whole of the former Greek centre would have been able to come in on a flank.

The Athenians failed to complete their movement, however. They were brought to bay between the headwater streams of the westward-flowing Oëröë by the northern Greek cavalry, and then attacked by the Boiotian infantry, their old enemies. However, they held the attack; their flanks, which would have been in danger from the cavalry, were covered by the old centre, which advanced in two bodies on their left and right.

Those on their left, headed by the 3,000 men of Megara, drew the attention of the cavalry upon themselves, and were driven back with heavy loss; a sacrifice which the Athenians did not wish to acknowledge. The Persian centre never got into action at all. But the battle was decided on the Greek right, where the Spartans stood stoically under arrow-fire, to which they could make no reply, until the Persians were deeply massed. Then they charged. In a furious fight their armour, pikes and training gave them a decisive advantage, though the Persians fought with desperate courage. Mardonios was killed, his finest troops were cut to pieces, and when the Persians broke, their allies left the field. The camp was stormed, and enormous booty taken; Thebes surrendered after a short siege, and the chief Theban collaborators were taken by Pausanias back to the Isthmus and there put to death.

About the same time (on the same day, says tradition again) Latychidas, King of Sparta, and Xanthippos of Athens, with a fleet of 110 ships, having already liberated Samos, attacked the remnants of the Persian fleet, beached under the promontory of Mykale; its commanders had decided that it was useless to fight at sea. The Greeks landed and, after a tough fight with Persian marines, burned the whole fleet. It was a relatively small battle, but it was followed by revolt in Ionia. The Peloponnesians went home after it; but the Athenians and liberated islanders followed it up by besieging and taking the bridgehead fortress of Sestos. Xanthippos came home in triumph in the spring, towing the huge cables of the bridges as spoils of war.

CHAPTER 9

THE GREAT FIFTY YEARS. I
478–460

1 AFTER LIBERATION

GREECE heaved a huge sigh of relief. But victory too has her problems. Moreover, the war continued; and even while it did, the removal of immediate pressure permitted differences between allies and between individuals to reveal themselves more starkly.

The Athenians (we quote from Thucydides now) 'brought home their women and children and the possessions they had saved ... and prepared to rebuild their city and walls; for not much of the perimeter was standing, and most of the houses were down, only a few surviving, in which the Persian grandees had lodged'. But the Spartans, prompted by Corinth and Aigina, both now thoroughly afraid of Athens' huge naval power, sent an embassy to demur, urging that fortified towns outside the Peloponnese might be of use to the enemy if he came again, and that the Peloponnese itself was the best citadel for all Greece. On the motion of Themistokles, the Athenians got rid of them with a promise to confer. Themistokles himself went to Sparta, where he was still popular, but declined to begin talks pending the arrival of his colleagues, who were 'unaccountably delayed'. Actually, the delay was part of Themistokles' plan; at Athens men, women and children were working like beavers on the walls, using stones from the ruins that lay everywhere, and not inquiring whether any particular piece came from a sacred edifice. Naturally all this activity could not be kept secret, even in winter when there was little travel; but Themistokles assured the Spartans that the rumours that arrived were nonsense, and invited them to send responsible people to report. Meanwhile Aristeides and a third ambassador arrived, and told Themistokles that the wall was now high enough to be defensible. Themistokles then confessed all, and informed the Spartans that they must in future consider Athens capable of taking her own decisions. Meanwhile, the Spartan observers were politely detained, pending the ambassadors' safe return.

The Spartans, who still had friendly feelings for Athens, pocketed their pride and said they had meant well; and plans went ahead for an allied counter-offensive in 478. That is the story of the Themistoklean Wall, from which many worked stones survive as relics; they include the well-known statue-bases with the reliefs of the 'hockey-players', wrestlers (one attempting the 'flying mare' throw), a team ball-game and other sporting subjects, in the National Museum at Athens. It was not a promising beginning to a new era.

In the new year, the commands on land and sea were interchanged. Pausanias and Aristeides, with twenty Peloponnesian ships, thirty Athenian and many allies, won over Cyprus (but not Phoenician Kition, in its south-east corner). They also reduced Byzantion, which had a Persian garrison. Latychidas, the victor of Mykale, with Themistokles, led a fleet and army to reoccupy northern Greece. Collaborationist governments were ejected from Phokis, part of Thessaly, and as far afield as Thasos. Delphoi received the liberators with open arms and a tall story (which, however, no one publicly doubted) that the holy place had only been delivered from sack by a miraculous storm and rock-fall from Parnassos. But the operations in Thessaly were prolonged. The tenacious Aleuadai survived at Larisa, apparently by bribing Latychidas, who is said to have been caught red-handed in his tent, 'sitting on a glove full of money'. He was later brought to trial at Sparta, and fled into exile. We hear of a Peloponnesian fleet wintering at Pagasai, and of Themistokles thinking of burning it; but that the scheme was turned down by Aristeides, back from Byzantion, whom the Athenians nominated to accept or reject Themistokles' secret proposal.

Meanwhile Pausanias too had shown that Spartan discipline left Spartans not less corruptible than other men when they got away from it. Inordinately proud of his achievement at Plataia, he gave great offence by commissioning an inscription for the thank-offering at Delphoi, in which he named only himself as 'destroyer of the Median host'. The Spartan government had it erased, and substituted on the monument – a bronze pillar formed of three intertwined serpents, whose heads supported a golden tripod – the names of thirty-one cities, with the truly 'laconic' statement: 'These fought in the war'. Carried off by Constantine, mutilated by barbarians, the stump of it still stands in Constantine's Hippodrome.

In Ionia, Pausanias' arrogance and lust for gold and women aroused widespread anger. He was recalled and 'disciplined' for offences against individuals, though acquitted on a more serious charge of communication with the enemy. The allies refused to obey his less distinguished successor, and invited the Athenians to lead them; and the Spartans, willing to get this oversea commitment off their hands, and still friendly to Athens, once more acquiesced. So began a new and fateful chapter in Greek history.

Already, on the morrow of Mykale, the Asia Minor Problem had arisen. How could the Greeks of Asia be protected from Persian revenge? The Peloponnesians reckoned that it was impossible, and proposed an exchange of populations, such as, in the steam age and with enormous suffering and loss of life, was actually carried out 2,400 years later. All who did not wish to live under Persia should be resettled in northern Greece, on the lands of those who had submitted. The allies had sworn to expel these with fire and sword; but the enormous scope of such an operation, when the whole north had surrendered, led to its being quietly dropped. In practice the 'Medizers' were not even expelled from the Amphiktiony, the religious league of old Greek states, which had its centre at Delphoi. Themistokles is said to have opposed their expulsion, seeing that it would leave the League, whose political influence was not negligible, dominated by the Peloponnesians. In Asia likewise Athens took a stand, backed by the islanders of Lesbos, Chios and Samos, against the abandonment of her Ionian 'daughter-cities'.

Athens had no such objection as had Sparta to campaigns beyond the Aegean. Her naval counter-offensive must have been financed already at the expense of the reoccupied cities, for her own treasury was empty. Whether the levies were reckoned as eager contributions to the cause of liberation, or fines for having joined the enemy, the money was as good; and the oarsmen, drawn from the landless citizens, knew no more congenial way of earning a living. So a league was formed, including all the liberated Aegean states, under the presidency of Athens, whose general, Aristeides the Just, was an impressive contrast to Pausanias; and he drafted the list of 'cities which were to provide money for the war, or ships; for their programme was to avenge themselves for their injuries by harrying the King's country. A new board of officials was established at Athens, the Treasurers of the Greeks, who received the Tribute, as the contribution was called. . . . Their treasury was at Delos, and the league Congress met in the sacred precinct there. It was as leader, at first, of self-governing allies sending members to a general congress, that Athens conducted her campaigns and negotiations' in the following years.

Aristeides was growing old, and Themistokles, whether because he too was no longer young or because he was losing ground politically, never again commanded the fleet he had fathered. A new, young general was the man of the hour: Kimon, son of Miltiades, who in the darkest hour of 480 had set an example of imperturbability and loyalty to the democracy. He marched through the market-place and up to the Acropolis with a band of other young 'knights', carrying their bridles. At the temple, he hung up his bridle as a dedication to Athena, as men did with tools with which they had done; made his prayer to the Goddess, took down an infantry shield dedicated by some former soldier, and went on down to the sea, to serve as a marine. Kimon had been left by his father's fine still with broad lands, but so short of money that he could not even dower his sister. He was rescued from this humiliating situation by Kallias, hereditary Torch-Bearer of the Eleusinian Mysteries and the richest man in Athens, who not only married her undowered, but paid the fine. Later Kimon himself married an Alkmeonid bride. These dynastic alliances show the

Athenian aristocracy drawing together, to play a leading part within the democratic state.

Under Kimon the Delian League set itself to eliminate Persian advanced posts. In 476 they laid siege to Eion, which guarded the Strymon bridge. The governor Boges resisted with desperate courage; finally, when the place was invested and starving, he had all gold and silver thrown into the river, killed the women of his harem, burnt his residency over his head and stabbed himself amid the flames. The governor at Doriskos, Xerxes' chief supply-base further east, resisted as bravely and with more success; 'no one ever reduced him, though many tried'; perhaps he withdrew finally by permission of the king. Proud Karystos, which had resisted Persia but then stood by her, was forced to join the League. The islanders of Skyros, who had a bad name as pirates, were sold as slaves, and Athenians colonised the island. The prestige of Athens had never stood so high.

2 THE DAWN OF CLASSICAL CULTURE

This was also the spring-time of early classical poetry, sculpture and architecture. The famous Persian War epitaphs, which established a style imitated down to our own times, were by Greek tradition all ascribed to Simonides of Keos; but Herodotos does not actually name him as author even of the most famous of them, that on Leonidas' Three Hundred:

> Tell them in Lakedaimon, passer-by:
> Carrying out their orders, here we lie

– where the Greek is so simple that any soldier might have said it, and it might have been metrical by accident. Herodotos does name Simonides, in the same paragraph, as author of the epitaph on Leonidas' prophet who 'foresaw the coming death, but scorned to leave the lords of Sparta'. His silence about the authorship of the more famous epigram thus amounts almost to a denial that Simonides wrote it. These little poems were produced both during and after Simonides' time by men of many cities, in that high-hearted and simply-spoken age. The very difficulty and high cost of cutting neat letters in stone helped to foster the close-packed, 'lapidary' style. Later, as the stone-cutters developed their skill and as the 'epigram' (which originally simply meant an inscription) became a literary art-form, epigrams became more diffuse.

> We dwelt by Corinth's waters, passer-by;
> But now in Salamis, Ajax' isle, we lie.

> For Hellas and for Megara to raise
> a dawn of freedom, we gave up our days.

This is from an inscription re-cut, with lettering and spelling of the Christian empire, and with the note 'Down to our time, the city sacrificed a bull'.

> Through valour of these men, no smoke on high
> from burning Tegea rose to foul the sky.
> Death in the line, to leave her free for those
> who should come after them, was what they chose.

This was the age of Pindar, the professional poet whose victory-odes, for runners, boxers, wrestlers and owners of racing-chariots, victorious at Olympia or in other great games, span the years 498–446, and commanded high prices. They, with the sculptures, give us best of all the impression of the fleeting high tide of Greek life. They are also almost untranslatable, since, as in Sappho, the golden language is greater than the subject. The best version is Richmond Lattimore's. The theme is usually an ancient myth, belonging to the city or family to which the victor has brought new glory. Pindar wrote his elaborate choral odes also in many other *genres*, but we have only fragments of these. All, including the victory-odes, are formally religious; the Games were sacred occasions, at which men worshipped with the strength of their bodies. He wrote *Paeans* for many cities; Paian was the name of an ancient god, now identified with Apollo as Preserver; it was a traditional Paean that the Greeks sang before Salamis. He wrote Laments or Dirges for funerals, not forgetting the consolations of religion; for an Alkmeonid, who was an initiate in the Eleusinian Mysteries, he echoes the 'Homeric' Hymn: 'Blessed is he who has seen these things, before he goes into the hollow earth'. Elsewhere he has the abode of the blessed not, apparently, inside the earth but at the Antipodes; perhaps a Pythagorean conception. This translation faintly suggests Pindar's rhythms:

> There to light them
> brightly the power of the sun shines
> when it is night up in our world.
> Crimson the roses around their
> mead, the approach to the town-gate;
> shady the cedars around that
> place; the ripe fruit golden grows there.
> Some in the racing of horses,
> some in the foot-race, some the draught-play,
> some the sweet lyre, take delight there,
> blossom aflower beside them,
> plenty and all wealth agrowing.
> Scent sweet in the air of the land
> spreads abroad; always is the incense
> mingled to burn in the bright fire
> kindled to gods on the altars.

It is the first appearance of the earthly paradise; and a very Greek one.

By this time too the skill of the sculptors had almost, not quite, completely mastered the material; their work has to many eyes a charm even greater than that of the absolute mastery which followed. The great pedimental (gable-end) group at Olympia (about 460), where Apollo with outstretched arm dominates the battle of Greeks and Centaurs – civilisation against savagery – marks the culmination of a generation's work, the transition from Archaic to Classical. At Athens in 478, when men were clearing up the Acropolis, they found statues lying smashed on all sides, among them the archaic Maidens (p.102), smiling demurely, in their painted robes. They did not restore them. Not only broken but old-fashioned, they were buried in the 'made ground' above the new citadel-wall, paid for out of the spoils of Kimon's campaigns. Athens was soon fast producing new dedications; and the new statues were different, not only in technique but in spirit. Where archaic art was gay, that of the new age is serious. The mark of it is the disappearance of the 'archaic smile'. The young athletes stand less stiffly, more relaxed and natural than the archaic; but the expression is grave. Life is earnest.

Most of the statues that survive are in marble; but bronze was the material of most of the highly-regarded free-standing works. The introduction of the 'lost wax' process, in which a model was made in clay, coated in wax, buried in sand, and the molten bronze poured in, to melt the wax and replace it, had made possible large, hollow-cast bronzes. The earliest known is the Apollo at Athens, pre-500, found with later works in a ruined warehouse at Piraeus. The great Zeus (not Poseidon) fished up off Artemision, over 2m tall, about to hurl his thunderbolt, is a masterpiece of *c.* 475. The Charioteer at Delphoi was a minor figure in a group commemorating a chariot-victory of Gelon of Syracuse; a concrete illustration to Pindar.

Greatest, in Greek opinion, of all the masters of bronze work of this generation, was one known to us only through copies of his works, in stone: Myron, from Eleutherai on the Boiotian border, whose Discus-thrower vies with the much later Aphrodite from Melos ('Venus of Milo') for the title of the most famous Greek work of art. Less known, undeservedly, is his group of Athena, shown as quite a young girl, and the satyr Marsyas, stealing up to snatch the flute, the 'Phrygian' instrument, which the Greek goddess has discarded. Myron made statues of victorious athletes, and of animals, of which we have no copies; but many charming minor bronzes show with what sympathy animals were treated in early Greek art. Some dozens of epigrams on how his Cow was so lifelike that she deceived her own species may suggest that, by modern canons, later Greece admired Myron for the wrong reasons; but in his work it is clear that the mastery of instantaneous poses, if not yet of facial expression, had been finally achieved.

Most of the original sculpture of this age that we have, however, was to the Greeks only journeymen's work, an adjunct to temples.

The familiar Greek temple, with the low-gabled or pedimented façade imitated in thousands of modern buildings, had evolved from the *megaron*, the oblong hall with entrance at one end through a porch supported by prolongations of the side walls, with two posts, moderate-sized tree-trunks, between. Wide eaves to carry off rain, with the ends of the beams supported on additional free-standing posts, might form a veranda; but early examples of this have so far only been found in rainier regions of Europe.

The translation of this style into stone began in the sixth century; the temples at Paestum are an example. In the east the first huge temple of the nature-goddess Artemis at Ephesos ('Diana of the Ephesians') was 360 feet long. King Croesus paid for many of the pillars; there are pillar-'drums', with fragments of inscriptions recording his munificence, in the British Museum. Equally big was that of Hera at Samos, begun by Polykrates.

Many temples were still of timber and brick on stone foundations; those of the Hera-temple at Olympia remain, well preserved by the mass of mud-brick, which, when Olympia lay desolate in Christian times, gradually melted in the rains and slumped down over them. Its wooden columns were replaced in stone one by one, as they decayed; whence the various thicknesses that may be seen today. Pausanias the traveller, under the Roman empire, saw one wooden column still surviving inside.

The oldest temple in Greece proper whose colonnade still stands is of about 490; that of Aphaia, a goddess later identified with Athena, at Aigina. The internal walls, however, are a product of the restoration or *anastylosis* now in favour with the Greek authorities. Here as in many places, later ages removed the squared blocks for re-use, leaving the less useful columns standing. The pediment sculptures, also rather heavily restored, are in Munich, but some fine fragments are in Athens.

In the new, stone temples, elements of the old wooden structure were religiously preserved. In the so-called Doric style, which prevailed everywhere west of the Aegean, the beam-ends, that rested upon the 'main beam' or *architrave* along the sides of a wooden hall, are represented by the 'triple-grooved' *triglyphs*. For the sake of appearance, triglyphs continue round the ends too. Between them the *metopes*, which originally meant 'intervals' and then the terracotta slabs put in to keep birds out, now afforded an opportunity for sculpture. Fine examples of these too come from the temple of Zeus at Olympia (about 460), showing the Labours of Herakles. Severe in style, there is much refinement in them too; for instance in the First Labour, in the compassionate face of Athena, gazing at the boy Herakles as he stoops in exhaustion, with his foot on the body of the Nemean Lion. Pillar-capitals, communicating the weight of the entablature above to the columns, consist of a plain, square slab, the *abacus*, above a bowl-shaped member called, from its shape, the *echinos* or 'sea-urchin'. This is plump and cushion-like at first, as at Paestum; in the fifth century it becomes nearly a section of a cone. Similar 'slimming' develops in the bulge or *entasis* of the columns, which taper from bottom to top, giving an impression of great sturdiness, again most pronounced in the early temples; at Aigina it is already much more delicate.

East of the Aegean there had developed a more ornate style, the Ionic; it first appears in Greece proper in the 'treasuries' (sixth century) built by eastern Knidos and Siphnos at Delphoi to shelter valuable dedications. Its columns are sometimes ten diameters in height, compared to the four to seven of Doric, and have an ornamental base. The classical Ionic capital, with its symmetrical volutes, is descended from the earlier, so-called Aeolic, foliage capitals (p. 101); here too the development is towards the relative austerity.

3 THE NEW AGE IN SICILY

Some of the finest temples surviving are those at Akragas (Agrigento; pp. 111 f.), especially the splendid series on the south ridge, overlooking the olives of the coastal plain. Akragas had won a particularly rich haul of prisoners in the manhunt that followed the rout of the Carthaginians and their host of European barbarians; and they, as slaves, provided the unskilled labour, hewing and hauling where they had hoped to plunder.

But the Sicilian achievement was not confined to the victors. Western Selinous, which had been forced into alliance with Carthage before the main invasion, also had her great temples, though they have been shaken down by earthquakes; but what she had, and Akragas had not, was a major school of sculptors. A late archaic bronze athlete is kept at Selinunte; the architectural sculptures are at Palermo, and there one may study the development from a plump and smiling archaic to a gracious early classical. The draperies are delicate, the faces begin to show expression, as in the Marriage of Zeus and Hera, or the Amazon falling before Herakles, with a look of despair that sets one wondering if it is really there, or if one is imagining it. It is really there; the parted lips (as in some of the struggling Lapiths at Olympia), still with a trace of their original colour, actually show the teeth, though this detail would have been invisible to any viewer who could only see the metope set high on the building.

In major sculpture, Selinous seems to have stood alone; but the coins of Sicily are almost everywhere splendid, and much sought after by collectors. Finest of all are those of Syracuse, and especially a victory issue, the great ten-drachma Dēmareteion, struck out of a Carthaginian war-indemnity, and perhaps used to repay a war-loan which Gelon had raised. It was named for Dāmareta, the wife of Gelon, who had given her jewellery for the war-chest; and it may be that she sat as model for the goddess (Arethousa, the fountain-nymph?) whose head adorns the obverse.

Theron at Akragas, Gelon and his brother Hieron after him at Syracuse, ended their days in peace, their chariot-victories and their warlike deeds celebrated by Pindar. Hieron also drew to his court the veteran Simonides and his nephew Bakchylides, an agreeable lesser Pindar. Aeschylus of Athens (pp. 205 ff.) also visited him. The sons of the great tyrants failed to hold their positions; it is not surprising, and their alleged violence of character was perhaps due to their being faced by opposition from the first. By 460 most of Greek Sicily had achieved democracy; Syracuse imitated the constitution of

Kleisthenes, even to the institution of ostracism. It was an age of intellectual ferment too; Empedokles of Akragas, already mentioned (p. 141), Pythagorean, great poet and not inconsiderable scientific speculator, author of the theory of the Four Elements which held sway only too long, died in a democratic Sicily; and if he seems to have been tinged with megalomania, a cooler view of philosophic speculations is taken (and a striking impression of the intellectual level of a wide public given) by Epicharmos, son of an eastern refugee, who entertained Syracuse with comic dramas; he parodied not only myths (Herakles becomes a greedy and simple giant of gargantuan appetites) but also the new philosophy. A character, for instance, exploits the Herakleitian doctrine of perpetual change to argue that, if I am not today the man I was yesterday, it is unreasonable to dun me today for yesterday's debts.

4 ATHENS AND AESCHYLUS

Athens so far had had no time to restore her temples. A fine new temple had been begun, on the highest part of the Acropolis (not in its centre, where the old temple had been); but like all else it had been wrecked in the war. On the other hand there was plenty of sculpture. New bronze statues of the 'heroes' Harmodios and Aristogeiton were commissioned, to replace an earlier pair carried off by Xerxes. Later, when Alexander the Great recovered these from Persepolis and restored them to Athens, the two pairs stood together, and stone copies show vividly how art had progressed in one generation.

But the unique glory of Athens was already her drama. Other cities under democracies had developed comedy; but tragedy was the invention of Athens alone.

In the days of Phrynichos' *Fall of Miletos*, as was observed, tragedy was a kind of oratorio with costume. As it changed from rustic religious mime to an independent art-form, poets used it to portray other stories than those of the Dionysos cycle, not without a few murmurs of dissent; it was as though church lessons were drawn from other books than the Bible. Narratives in recitative also became more important, and were delivered by a solo voice, that of a player called the *hypokrites*, 'answerer' (hence 'play-actor'), who also held dialogues with the chorus-leader. He was probably first introduced by Thespis, the primitive of the new art-form, about 520. Between his 'successive entries' or *episodes*, the *hypokrites* could change his costume and mask (a primitive feature) in the dressing-tent or *skēnē* (whence *scene*) and so represent different characters. Meanwhile the chorus ('dancers') sang their elaborate songs and *danced* the emotions suggested by the developing situation. This was still by far the major part of the performance. Phrynichos elaborated it by dividing the chorus into groups; some could represent men and some women, though all voices were in fact male.

Aeschylus, who had fought at Marathon, now turned the development on to new lines. He greatly increased the amount of dialogue, introducing a second actor to take minor parts, while the first actor or prōt-agonist might remain on the stage throughout; and thus a tragedy became truly a drama, or action. Even Aeschylus' development proceeds cautiously, however, and the first impression left on a modern reader by some of his plays is that there is *little* action. For instance, Phrynichos had produced a victory-play (spring, 477) on the receipt of the news of Salamis in Asia. There was a semi-chorus of *Phoenician Women,* from whom the play was named, and another of Persian elders. The news was given immediately, and the rest of the piece, probably quite short, was given to lamentations and reactions to it. Aeschylus in *The Persians,* while paying his predecessor the compliment of many echoes and imitations, builds up the suspense for some 300 lines before giving the great Messenger's Speech; but even so, this climax is over before the play is half done. In *Prometheus* (whose name should rhyme with 'Zeus') the compassionate Titan, who saved men from extirpation under the harsh rule of Zeus by giving them fire, is 'crucified' at the beginning of the play, and still defiant at its end. His reconciliation to a relenting Zeus apparently came in a sequel; for – since poets submitted groups of four plays, the last being comic relief, for the competition – Aeschylus introduced the practice of giving successive phases of one story. In *Agamemnon, The Libation-Bearers*, and *The Furies*, the one such trilogy that we have complete – the great drama of revenge and expiation, as long, in the aggregate, as a Shakespeare tragedy – there is more action. Violence never took place on the Dionysian stage; but the dying cries of Agamemnon are heard, 'off', and through the opened doors his wronged and avenging wife is seen standing over his body; as at the end of the next play, her son and daughter stand over hers. But that is later, when Aeschylus had adopted further innovations, including a *third* actor and painted scenery, from his younger rival Sophocles.

That there is some naïveté in the art of Aeschylus, there is no need to deny. There is also ample evidence that he thought and felt deeply. The protests against a cruel god, put into the mouth of Prometheus, are daring, on any showing. But, as a poet, his function was not primarily to preach or instruct. He *presented* an action. 'Morsels from the feast of Homer', he is said to have called his plays; old stories, which kept their appeal because they dealt with human nature and the human situation.

Perhaps the best example that we have of *typical* Aeschylus, among the seven plays preserved – part of the classical curriculum of Christian Constantinople – is the play *Seven against Thebes*. The Achaians of the south are marching on Thebes. In the centre of the stage stands Eteokles, eldest son of the fallen Oedipus, who has driven out his brother Polyneikes; he is in charge of the defence. Behind him, left and right, stand six splendid warriors – mute 'extras' were allowed *ad libitum* – in the fifth century's idea of ancient armour, which was probably that of their grandfathers; visored helmets, huge crests, emblazoned shields. To him enters the second actor: two columns of the enemy, led by famous heroes – their blazons are described in detail – are reported approaching two of the seven gates. Eteokles tells off two Theban champions against them. They salute and go. The messenger returns. Two more attackers are described; two more defenders go; then two more, and Eteokles is alone. The messenger returns again. The enemy is approaching the seventh gate; and the leader is his brother. Eteokles recognizes his fate, and the fate of his house. 'The gods are weary of us.' *He* goes. While the chorus sing and dance their suspense, the audience knows perfectly well what will happen – what *did* happen, in the *Thebaïd*, ascribed to Homer. Thebes is saved; and the brothers kill each other. Is it past or present? We hardly know. The Greek capacity for dramatization seems to break the cocoon of our one-dimensional time; as when, in a modern Greek tale, the outcast at Christmas begs shelter 'for the love of Christ, who is being born at this hour'. So Aeschylus gives his 'morsel from Homer', with splendid spectacle, language, dance and music; and with the thinning line and the emptying stage comes the unspoken moral for everyman: You are in this too, brother.

The Persians, the oldest surviving Greek play – for the archaic-looking *Suppliants* appears really to be later – brings Aeschylus into contact not only with the Great War but with post-war politics.

In face of the coalition of the great families, Themistokles was losing ground. Occupied with reconstruction and the continuing war, paid for largely by war-booty and the League, the people were not in an experimental mood. They rejected, for instance, Themistokles' proposal to transfer the whole city down to Piraeus, where they could not be cut off from the sea; and he was being attacked by a campaign of scandal (there was no libel law) saying that he had taken bribes during the war, and had even had treasonable communication with the enemy. He is said to have launched an attack on the Areopagus, for usurpation of powers that were not statutory. He failed, and there was talk of ostracism. It was then that Aeschylus produced *The Persians*, with its reminder of wartime unity, and of what Themistokles' communication with the enemy had achieved. And the rich man who paid for the production and dedicated the tripod – the three-legged bronze caldron, which was the traditional 'cup' for a Greek victory – was Pericles, son of Xanthippos, who must lately have died. It was a bold and a characteristic step by this young aristocrat of twenty-two. But it was too late to save Themistokles; in

471 he was ostracized. At best, he would be about sixty-five when he returned; but he did not return.

5 THE BREAKDOWN OF GREEK UNITY

There had been, whatever its limitations, some real transcendence of old prejudices among the allies of 480; but in a few years it was everywhere breaking down. The forces making for change, especially for democracy, are customarily blamed; but we cannot acquit of blame the members of 'establishments', especially in Athens and Sparta, who resisted change in the effort to keep their very enviable positions.

Themistokles settled at Argos, whence he 'made visits to other parts of the Peloponnese'. It is hardly an accident that Argos about this time adopted the Kleisthenean type of democracy; the men of Elis for the first time built themselves a city of that name, to which men migrated from many villages; so did Mantineia; and both, without breaking with Sparta, adopted forms of democracy too.

Then came a great scandal. Pausanias, the victor of Plataia, had been abroad again in a private or semi-official capacity; he held Byzantion for a time, till the Athenians expelled him. Then he was at home again, under suspicion of intrigue both with Persia and (worse, in Spartan eyes) with the helots. But there was no proof, till a messenger of his – a young man from a small town, whom Pausanias had seduced as a boy – having noticed that his messengers to Persia did not return, opened his letter, found that it included the request 'execute bearer', and helped the government to obtain incontrovertible evidence. It was Kleomenes over again ... Pausanias took sanctuary, and was left there till starving, and brought out only to die. But it was reported that the new evidence also incriminated Themistokles, and he was summoned to Athens to stand trial. He did not choose to go; after an adventurous escape, west, north, across the northern mountains to the Aegean, across the Aegean in a merchant ship, through an Athenian fleet (when Themistokles threatened to incriminate the skipper if the skipper did not conceal him), he finally reached Asia; he died a few years later, as governor of Magnesia, and inland Ionian city, under the Persian king. Four coins from his mint there are extant; two of them are solid silver, and two are plated.

The peace between Greeks was breaking down too. In the Peloponnese, Sparta had a war with Argos and Arcadia (except Mantineia) and probably a revolt in Messenia, all about this time. Outnumbered, the Spartans succeeded in defeating their enemies separately; but Argos regained territory lost under Kleomenes, destroying Tiryns and Mykenai and leaving their ancient walls standing desolate. Athens was also faced by her first crisis in the Delian League. War-weariness was growing among the allies, and, perhaps in 467, Naxos, unilaterally, announced her secession. Now when the League was formed, the contracting parties had 'cast lumps of iron into the sea', implying the swearing of oaths, in that time of high enthusiasm, which were to be binding until the iron came up again. It was a serious matter to coerce a free Greek city; but the Athenians took their decision: secessions would not be tolerated. They blockaded Naxos (it was into this fleet that Themistokles' ship was blown by the summer north wind), forced it to surrender, disarmed the people and re-enrolled Naxos as a tribute-paying member. Thucydides notes it as an ominous precedent.

With this question forcibly settled, Kimon, about 466, led a great League fleet into the Levant, where the Phoenicians had rebuilt their navies and Persia had regained Cyprus. Off the river Eurymedon he won a crushing victory, a second and greater Mykale, followed up by a landing, to capture the Persian camp and destroy or capture the entire fleet. But in 465 there was again trouble in the Aegean. Thasos, more powerful than Naxos, objected to Athenian activity among her mainland trading-posts and gold-mining enterprises, and seceded. Defeated at sea and besieged, the Thasians managed to send out emissaries to appeal for help to Sparta; and Sparta promised, secretly for the moment, to threaten an invasion of Attica if the attack was not called off. But before anything had been done, Sparta was hit by disaster. An earthquake brought down nearly every house in the town; there was a great loss of life; and the helots – even those in Laconia now – rose in rebellion. It was widely thought that the earthquake itself represented the vengeance of Poseidon the Earthshaker for some helots who had taken sanctuary at his temple at Tainaron (Cape Matapan), and had been induced to leave it and then put to death; presumably the disappointment of hopes raised by Kleomenes and Pausanias had left a legacy of bitterness. Only the presence of mind of the young king Archidāmos, who ordered his trumpeter to sound the Fall In, and the Spartan discipline, which caused every man who could to get his arms and run to the parade-ground, saved many survivors from being massacred among the ruins by a rush of helots from the surrounding country. Once more the Spartans had to fight for their lives; and even when they had restored order in Laconia (for only a few of the free 'dwellers-around' joined the revolt), they were faced with a regular war against the Messenians, dug in in their ancestral fortress in the mountain amphitheatre of Ithōme.

Meanwhile, the Athenians reduced Thasos after a two-years' siege; and then there came to Athens a Spartan embassy, asking for help under the alliance of 481. The Athenians were held to be skilled in siege warfare. After the promise to help Thasos it sounds extraordinarily cynical; but presumably not all Sparta knew about that.

Naturally, no one at Athens knew. Nevertheless, not all Athens was in favour of helping Sparta; but Kimon, the Spartan type at Athens, as Pericles was to call him – had he not even named one of his sons Lakedaimonios? – turned the debate, with a passionate plea: 'Will you look on and see Hellas lamed and Athens without her yoke-fellow?' He carried the assembly, and was sent to Messenia with a third of the field-army, 4,000 armoured men.

Then came Kimon's great disappointment. The Athenians failed in an attack on Ithome, and presently the Spartans informed them that they were no longer needed, and might go. As the Spartans kept other allies with them, it was clear that their reasons were not military. 'They were alarmed', says Thucydides, 'by the Athenians' daring and revolutionary spirit, and felt that if they stayed they might be persuaded by the defenders of Ithome to change sides.' Many, after all, even of middle-class Athenian men-at-arms were democrats; and in an ancient siege it was easy to shout propaganda across the lines. So the Athenians went; and even those who had warmly favoured Sparta were now bitterly resentful.

It was a turning point in Greek history. In Athenian home politics too, democratic views had of late been regaining ground. The radical leader Ephialtes, poor but incorruptible, resented the traditional functioning of the Areopagus, as 'Guardian of the Laws', to interfere with democratic developments. He undermined its reputation by successful prosecutions of several of the rich men, who now reached the archonships by the luck of the draw, for corruption or other faults of administration. Then, in the absence of Kimon, perhaps at Ithome (the exact sequence of these events cannot be established), Ephialtes and Pericles carried through the Assembly an act formally depriving the Areopagus of all powers for which there was not formal, written warrant in the constitution; the 'added powers', as they were called. What was left to it was chiefly its immemorial function of being the court in trials for homicide. Henceforth the Council of Five Hundred and the people's courts, with juries of 501 (or sometimes 1,001, 1,501, even 2,501 in great political cases), would be their own judges of what was constitutional. The archons, no longer expected to be statesmen, had as their chief function the chairmanship of the jury-courts. Four years later, as a logical conclusion, the archonships were opened to the 'small-holders'' property-class, and later in practice, without formal legal warrant, to any Athenian against whom no positive objection lay.

But in the meantime feeling was very bitter. The democrats sealed their victory by ostracizing Kimon (461). In foreign policy they broke off the alliance with Sparta and made alliances with Argos and Thessaly, which had been pro-Persian. Ephialtes was assassinated by a Boiotian, hired by his enemies – the last political bloodshed in Athens for fifty years. The veteran Aeschylus speaks for reconciliation in *The Furies*, the last play of his Agamemnon trilogy; Athena warns against civil strife; the play celebrates her foundation of the Areopagus *as a homicide court*, and Orestes speaks of the 'Argive alliance' which Athens has won by saving him. But Aeschylus too was sick at heart. Soon after this, he accepted once more an invitation to Sicily. There men made much of him, and there, at Gela, he died two years later. He left the epitaph, so characteristic of his generation:

> Here Aeschylus, son of Euphorion, bred
> in Athens, lies in Gela's cornland dead.
> His fighting prowess Marathon could show
> and long-haired Medes, who had good cause to know.

And not a word about his poetry.

So there was an end of hopes that the union against Persia might be permanent. There was to be no emancipation for Sparta's helots; no future for Themistokles at Athens; no free United States of the Aegean under Athenian leadership; no cooperation between Athens and Sparta. Democratic and increasingly imperial Athens was to 'go it alone'.

CHAPTER 10

THE GREAT FIFTY YEARS. II
IMPERIAL ATHENS

1 THE YEARS OF VICTORY

PERICLES, aged thirty-three, was left by the fall of Kimon and the murder of Ephialtes as already the most influential orator in the Athenian Assembly. He was a man who, if there had been more like him, might have led Greece to an even more brilliant future. An aristocrat, but a convinced democrat; a friend of Archidamos, King of Sparta; an intellectual, who maintained for many years Anaxagoras, one of the last great names in Ionian 'natural philosophy', he had sympathy with all those forces in Greek life which, in the tragic actuality, could not be reconciled. Through the next thirty years he won by devotion, by political sagacity and by conspicuous indifference to increasing his moderate inherited wealth, the trust of the people as no other man did.

But it is important to remember that he was not a Prime Minister or the head of a government. The Assembly was its own government. The Council, chosen by lot and changing annually, prepared its business and looked after routine matters; the Generals, in war and foreign affairs, carried out its policy, but did not make it. Pericles was often one of them; but in policy-making he had no special power, only influence; he had the right, which he was proud to say was shared by the obscurest citizen, to address that formidable Assembly, and to persuade if he could. It is Plutarch, knowing nothing of democracy in action, who constantly says that Pericles (or Kimon, or Themistokles) did this or that; Thucydides, like Herodotos, more correctly says 'the Athenians'. Often Pericles advised; usually, but not always, successfully.

All influential parties in Athens were agreed in determination not to let the Delian League be eroded by secessions;

213

there had by now been a number of these. The usual reasons were, says Thucydides,

failures to provide their quotas of money or ships, or cases of desertion; for the Athenians insisted on exact fulfilment, and were harsh in applying compulsion to people who were neither accustomed nor willing to endure hardship. And in other ways too the Athenians were no longer the popular leaders they had been. They no longer treated the allies as equals on campaigns; and they found it easy to reduce seceders. This was the allies' own fault; for because of their shirking of military service most of them, to avoid campaigning, arranged in lieu of ships to provide their quota in money. So the Athenians increased their navy at the expense of the allies, and the latter, when they revolted, had neither the armaments nor the skill for successful resistance.

The suppression of revolts was accompanied by the reconstruction of governments and the installation of democracies. An inscription shows Athens remodelling the constitution of Erythrai in Ionia. There is to be a People's Council, appointed by lot and changing annually, like that of Athens, though smaller; and its members swear an oath of allegiance to 'the People of Athens and the allies'. Erythrai is to send offerings to the great Panathenaic festival at Athens (an obligation presently imposed upon all the allies); and if the beasts for sacrifice are not good enough, the organizers of the festival will buy others, and debit Erythrai. Commercial law-suits involving Athenians, arising in allied cities, were transferred to the Athenian courts; the resulting congestion of business led to loud complaints of the law's delays and the rapacity of Athenian lodging-house keepers; but none are known against Athenian fairness, though we do not lack anti-imperialist witnesses. Probably Athenians would have had more to fear in courts abroad. An appeal to Athens against capital sentences in criminal cases was also imposed in some treaties. Cities which gave no cause for intervention kept their own institutions, even if undemocratic; but there was no doubt about the trend. Soon, few cities kept up their own war-navies; those that did so longest were the three powerful islands, Samos, Chios, and Lesbos with its five cities. Some time later, Athens even closed local mints, and imposed the use of Athenian silver money, weights and measures; though the 'pale gold' of Kyzikos was still struck. She also planted settlements of Athenians, who, unlike ordinary colonists, kept their Athenian citizenship, in Naxos, Andros, and other 'strategic points'. The tribute of cities whose land was taken was scaled down; but this did little to reduce the resentment caused. The requirement of offerings from subject cities – 'a cow and a panoply of arms' became standard – for Athens' national festival showed most clearly of all that Athens was making herself the capital of an empire.

Pericles hoped – perhaps naïvely, but with the sincerity of a devoted patriot – to make the allies proud of their position as participants in such an empire; and indeed, the fact that there were several isolated revolts is perhaps less remarkable than that, when Athens fell on evil days, many allies stuck to her with impressive loyalty. He claimed, in a famous phrase (p. 263), that Athens was 'an education to Greece'. He was thinking no doubt of Athenian art and literature; but perhaps not only of these. The inscriptions of fifth-century Athens, compared with those of other cities, are revealing. Prose texts, sometimes running to hundreds of words, gradually become common. They record especially treaties, decrees imposing constitutions or regulating the collection of tribute, and financial accounts of sacred funds. Secular accounts, unless of major importance, e.g. of wars, were not yet recorded on stone. The famous Tribute Lists, beginning in 454, which give a gazetteer of place-names of the Aegean and show accessions to and secessions from the empire – fragments of two huge marble slabs, restored to order by the labours of B. D. Meritt and other scholars – are accounts not of the whole tribute but of the quota of one-sixtieth paid to Athena. Meanwhile the relatively few secular inscriptions of other states remain often crabbed and archaic in style, expecting much more 'background knowledge' of anyone who was to understand them. After those of Athens, we seem to be passing from the affairs of a city to those of a village. The contrast shows an aspect of what Pericles meant. Democratic Athens, with a citizen body of perhaps 70,000, had achieved a major 'break-through' in the field of public administration.

Already, Argos, Syracuse and other cities had adopted the Kleisthenic form of democracy. The question was how much further Athens could extend her leadership or her direct control. Twenty years after the defeat of Xerxes, there seemed to be no limit.

However, with Thasos and the Spartan commitment 'liquidated', Athens returned (no less keenly than under Kimon) to the war in the Levant. A League fleet of 200 ships sailed once more for Cyprus; and then a tremendous opportunity opened. A Libyan prince had raised Egypt in rebellion against Persia, and applied for help. Leaving Cyprus, the generals went after the greater prize. They swept enemy ships from the Delta, joined hands with the insurgents, overran the lower town of Memphis, and besieged the citadel. But the citadel, the White Castle, held by Persians and their Egyptian allies, held out strongly, and for some years the war in Egypt became 'bogged down'.

Meanwhile in Greece, during Sparta's embarrassments, Corinth engaged in a border war with Megara; and Megara appealed to Athens. The Athenians garrisoned Megara and its western port of Pēgai – a 'window' for Athens to the Corinthian Gulf – and built parallel walls a mile long from Megara town to its eastern port of Nisaia, to secure their ability to provision the city by sea. Soon after this, they embarked on the much greater task of connecting their own city with Piraeus and Phaleron by two 'long walls', five and three miles in length, later reinforced with a five-mile 'middle' wall, giving additional security to Piraeus.

Athens was now at war with Corinth, which gained the support of Aigina and Epidauros; but, calling in ships from their allies, and without suspending the Egyptian campaign, the Athenians won two sea-fights in the Saronic Gulf. The second was a sweeping victory, and the Athenians followed it up by landing troops on Aigina and besieging the town. The Corinthians in desperation attempted a diversion by attacking Megara, thinking that at least, without relaxing pressure on Aigina, Athens would be unable to man a third front; but the Athenians did. Calling up men from eighteen to sixty to reinforce the

Megarian levy, they first held the Corinthians, and then in a second battle fairly routed them. At the end of the year (459?) one of the Athenian tribes set up an inscription for the dead of its regiment, which survives. The first and last lines are spaced out for emphasis:

OF ERECHTHEIS

these died in the war, in Cyprus, in Egypt,
in Phoenicia, at Halieis, in Aigina, at Megara

IN THE SAME YEAR

The word 'Halieis' refers to an unsuccessful landing on the south side of Argolis. There follows a list of 177 names, including a general, an 'acting general' and a 'seer'. It is a testimony to the vigour of Athens at the height of her power, but also to the cost; 177 from one regiment, in a year unmarked by any serious disaster. Of about the same date is the exquisite little relief of the Mourning Athena, on the Acropolis; it has lost the inscription which must have accompanied it. Athena, in helmet and the thick woollen dress of an Athenian lady, leans on her spear, head bowed, looking at a *stēlē*. She too is reading the casualty-list.

At some time – Thucydides mentions it before the Egyptian expedition – Athenian ships in the Corinthian Gulf also captured the Lokrian stronghold of Naupaktos (medieval Lepanto). The Lokrians were piratical – two of their cities had only recently concluded a treaty promising not to cut out shipping from each other's harbours, while reserving the right to piracy on the high seas! – and this was probably Athens' reason. The long war in Messenia was then drawing to a close. The Spartans never stormed Ithome, but they reduced its defenders to agreeing to leave the Peloponnese under an armistice; and the Athenians handed over Naupaktos to them. They remained there, allied to Athens and a thorn in the side of Corinth, for the rest of the century.

But Sparta could now once more look abroad. She sent an expedition (1,500 Laconians and 10,000 allies) to protect Doris, north of Parnassos, whence the Spartans' ancestors were thought to have come, against attacks from Phokis. The Athenians regarded this as a hostile move and, though still engaged in Egypt and Aigina, sent ships to the western gulf, garrisoned the Megarian mountains, and cut off the expedition's retreat. The Spartans retaliated by restoring Thebes to the position of presiding city in Boiotia, which she had lost in 479. Some Athenian reactionaries also got in touch with them, urging them to march on Athens, before the completion of the Long Walls made the city impregnable. But the Athenians got wind of this and, calling in Thessalians, Argives and Ionians to reinforce their own fully-stretched man-power, attacked first. When they crossed the Boiotian frontier, the exiled Kimon met them, asking to be allowed to fight as a private in his regiment; but the democratic generals, not sure who was loyal, rebuffed him. He left, after passing the word to his supporters to play the man.

In a severe battle at Tanagra, lasting into the second day, the Athenians were beaten; the Thessalian cavalry, unnatural allies for a democracy, changed sides during the night. But the Peloponnesians too had lost heavily, and contented themselves with marching home, wrecking farms on the way, through the Megarid, now left open. Pericles himself carried a measure for the recall of Kimon, whose supporters had fought very bravely, hoping to come to terms with Sparta through him; but nothing came of that for the present. Then, 'sixty-one days after the battle', the Athenians fell upon Boiotia, won a great victory and gained control of the whole country through separate treaties with the cities; many of them were not sorry to be delivered from Thebes. Phokis joined her alliance; hostages were taken from eastern Lokris; and Athens controlled all central Greece up to Thermopylai. Aigina surrendered, and was disarmed and enrolled as a tributary; the Long Walls were finished; and in 455 the Athenians sent 100 ships round the Peloponnese, burning the Spartan naval base at Gythion, winning the alliance of the Achaian cities, and attacking Sparta's allies on the Corinthian Gulf. The ships were left at Pegai, to be a permanent western squadron. Corinth, Sikyon and Epidauros were half-encircled; Troizen came over to the Athenian alliance; and Sparta, at war with Argos, seemed doomed to be confined to the southern Peloponnese.

2 THE YEARS OF CRISIS 454–445

The whole scene was changed by disaster in Egypt. King Artaxerxes of Persia tried first to draw off the Athenians by financing their enemies in Greece – Persia's first use of a policy which was to become standard. Failing in this, Persia made a major effort. A large army under Megabyxos, a veteran of Xerxes' invasion, invaded Egypt in 457 and relieved the White Castle; a Phoenician fleet cut off the League ships in the Nile. Most of Egypt submitted, and the Greeks found themselves besieged on an island in the Delta. There they held out for eighteen months, until the Persians, by one of their huge engineering enterprises, diverted the water from the channel protecting them, stranded their ships and took their position by storm (455?). A remnant escaped across the western desert to Cyrene; several thousand were taken prisoners; and a relief squadron of fifty triremes sailed unsuspecting into the western arm of the Nile and was trapped, less than half escaping.

It is not certain that the force in Egypt had been kept up to its original strength of 200 ships' crews; but certainly it was a huge disaster, and had immediate repercussions. Pericles, embarking with 1,000 marines on the ships at Pegai, raided and showed the flag once more along the Gulf, but thereafter he brought the western fleet back to Athens. The treasury of the League was also transferred to Athens from Delos (454), for the sake of security. In Greece the war languished, and in 451 a five-years' truce was concluded. The sanguine and optimistic people of Athens had found the limits of their power.

In this same year the Athenians took a fateful step in internal policy. They laid down that henceforth none should be an Athenian citizen who was not born of Athenian parents on both sides; an end to the policy of easy enfranchisement that had strengthened the city since the days of Solon. Citizenship of imperial Athens had become a desirable privilege, and citizens, not least the poor but powerful 'naval class', were no longer willing to share it. Sponsors of the bill, which Pericles himself is said to have promoted, might argue that the character of the city was in danger from a flood of immigrants. Resident aliens were given an honourable status. But the enactment fixed a gulf between the people of Athens and their allies.

Sparta made peace with Argos for thirty years; and no doubt the Five Years' Truce was intended to provide a 'cooling off period' with a view to a general settlement. But in the clash of Athenian and Spartan pride, nothing came of it yet. On the other hand, the truce gave Athens a chance to strike once more against Persia. It was desirable both to show Persia that Athens was still formidable and to show Greece that Athens was still concerned for the original purpose of the League. In 450 the veteran Kimon, with 200 ships of Athens and the League, set sail once more for Cyprus and laid siege to Kition.

But the expedition was a disappointment. Kition held out; the besiegers ran short of food – which shows that the Cypriote Greeks, who could have provisioned them, were less than enthusiastic. Kimon himself fell sick; Megabyxos, the conqueror of Egypt, was building up forces in Cilicia for a counterstroke. Then he succeeded in running troops across to the island; and at this point, Kimon died. His death was kept secret; and acting on plans prepared by him on his death-bed, his successors moved from Kition and defeated the relieving forces by land and sea. It was a consolation to Athenian feeling, and gained for the expedition an unimpeded withdrawal; but Cyprus remained lost.

Both Athenian and Persian leaders were now aware that, despite the Eurymedon, despite Egypt, there was no triumph to be won. Both were at last prepared to pocket their pride and make concessions. Kallias, the brother-in-law of Kimon, Athens' foremost diplomatist, was sent to Sousa ('Shushan the palace' of the Bible); and, on terms of which neither side was very proud at the time, peace was made. Athens abandoned the Egyptians still holding out in parts of the Delta; Persia undertook not to send ships of war into the Aegean. There was probably an exchange of prisoners. In Asia Minor, there seems to have been 'disengagement' and a demilitarised zone; neither side was to keep troops or construct fortifications in Ionia or within a belt fifty miles inland; but Athens, there is some reason to think, agreed that the Greeks of Asia should pay their tribute to Persia under the assessment of 493 (p.158). (This would also account for the fact that Athens' own tribute-assessments on these cities are remarkably light.) In fact, without the means of applying force, Persia seems not to have had much success in collecting her tribute; but the mere existence of such a clause helps to account for the fact that the Peace of Kallias was not publicised at the time. A hostile historian later maintained that the whole treaty was an Athenian invention. Athens may later have published exaggerated accounts of its glories, in contrast with the much worse treaties which Persia then became able to impose upon divided Greece; but that there was a Treaty made about 449 is almost certain. So, fifty years after the Athenian raid on Sardis, the great Persian War ended in a compromise.

Peace brought its new problems. Athenian society had been geared to war for so long that many breadwinners had never known a time when they could not earn a summer's income by rowing the triremes. In peace, Athens kept a standing fleet of sixty, which policed the Aegean, collected the tribute and escorted it home. Two hundred or more reserve galleys, some new ones being built every year, lay in the long ship-sheds round the war-harbour of Zea. All, with some help from allies serving for pay, could be manned in a crisis. Nevertheless, peace was going to mean some under-employment. Pericles and his circle had no doubt foreseen this, and among their remedies was a public building programme, beginning with the great temple long projected (p. 204) on the summit of the Acropolis.

First, Pericles proposed the sending out of ambassadors throughout Greece to invite delegates to a pan-Hellenic congress, to discuss '[the rebuilding of] the temples burned by the Persians; the sacrifices on behalf of all Greece, due to the gods under vows made during the war; and the peace and freedom of the seas'. But the congress never met. It was too clear that its lofty proposals had political implications. The temples burned were only those of Attica, Plataia, Thespiai and Phokis;

a pan-Hellenic payment of wartime vows at this juncture would be a recognition that Athens had made peace with honour; and if the freedom of the seas were put on the agenda, Athens could claim that the Athenian navy was performing a pan-Hellenic service. The Peloponnesians were quick to see the point; and the project was dropped.

The proposal was really a manifesto; for it was the intention of Pericles and his supporters to go on, even in peace, collecting the tribute, on which Athens had come to depend. Payment probably was suspended (the allies would hardly wait for Athens to decree it) in the first year of peace; there is a 'quota-list' missing at this point. Then Kleinias, an aristocrat married to an Alkmeonid lady, proposed and carried, as if nothing had happened, a programme of arrangements for improving and systematizing the collection; and forthwith, under protection of Athenian warships, it was resumed. There was great resentment, and considerable passive resistance.

Sparta too was being difficult. In 448, the Five Years' Truce had still two years to run; but, showing that she did not 'recognize' Athens' system of alliances on the mainland, Sparta sent an expedition to liberate Delphoi from the Phokian League. She was granted, for this service, priority in consulting the oracle by the Delphians, who had no wish to share their wealth with their country cousins. Athens, not to be outdone in correctitude under cold-war conditions, did not intervene until the Spartans had gone home; but then immediately Pericles in person led an expedition, which reversed the Spartan arrangement, restored Phokian control, got equal priority voted to Athens, and had the grant recorded on the flank of the great bronze wolf, standing before the temple, whose forehead already bore the record of the grant to Sparta.

The next year showed how precarious Athens' imposing position had become. League receipts were down by a quarter, many of the largest cities not having paid. Most of them resumed thereafter, without incidents recorded in history; but on the mainland, after the end of the summer campaigning season, rebellion broke out in western Boiotia. An expedition of 1,000 armoured men, despatched in haste, against the advice of Pericles, to quell it with the aid of local allies, was ambushed at Koroneia between Helikon and the lake Kopaïs and, after heavy losses, compelled to surrender. Effective support from local allies was conspicuously absent. Athenian power in central Greece collapsed overnight; and to recover the prisoners left in enemy hands, Athens agreed to a treaty promising to respect Boiotian independence.

Among the killed was Kleinias. He left a small son named Alkibiades, destined to fame, who became the ward of Pericles, his mother's kinsman.

Athens' troubles were only beginning. The Five Years' Truce was running out. Exiles from Euboia had taken part in the revolt in Boiotia; and in the spring of 446 the cities there, which had perhaps only lately compounded for tribute in lieu of ships, and now found it required in peace-time, rebelled together. Pericles crossed with the bulk of the Athenian army, only to be recalled by the news that the Peloponnesians were marching and, to make things still worse, Megara had revolted in rear of the regiments holding the mountain frontier. These escaped only by a devious march, by the west coast and over Kithairon to Plataia, with a local guide, whose epitaph in rustic verse survives at Athens. It adds the detail that he killed seven men in battle, and died happy, 'having done no harm to anyone'.

The Peloponnesians reached Eleusis, vastly outnumbering the reunited Athenian army; and then, to everyone's amazement, they turned and went home. As soon as they were away Pericles, with only 5,000 men-at-arms this time, crossed again to Euboia, and in a swift campaign reduced it to obedience. However brilliant his generalship, and however great the dismay caused by Sparta's betrayal, it looks as if some Euboians must have favoured Athens and democracy. Only one city was severely punished, Histiaia in the north, whose people had massacred the crew of a stranded Athenian warship. They were expelled, and replaced by an Athenian citizen colony, strategically placed to hold the straits of Artemision.

What had happened at Eleusis was naturally a secret; but everyone guessed. Pericles had an item in his accounts at the year's end which he did not want discussed. He put down 'To necessary purposes: 10 talents'; and the Assembly, trusting him as it never trusted another man, passed it. The phrase 'necessary purposes' was still good for a laugh on the comic stage in the next generation.

The Spartans did not think the episode so funny. The Laws of Lykourgos had signally failed to render Spartan gentlemen indifferent to money; but it seems unlikely that the highest in the land would have sold out their city's interests under circumstances absolutely certain to erupt in a major scandal. At a guess, Pericles perhaps made perfectly genuine suggestions that Athens was ready to negotiate for a general settlement, and added a handsome *douceur* to the Spartan commanders to withdraw without fighting or devastation. He is reported to have said later, 'What I bought was not peace, but time.' What the Spartans had not bargained for was that between the promise and the fulfilment Pericles would reconquer Euboia. When they saw what had resulted, there was furious indignation. The young king in titular command, Pleistoanax, a son of the ill-fated Pausanias, was impeached and fined a sum which he could not pay; he fled to the grim sanctuary of Apollo the Wolf-God in Arcadia, where it was said that human flesh was mixed with the sacrifices, that he who ate it became a wolf, and that no beast cast a shadow. On that haunted ground he lived for nineteen years, most of the time in a house built half inside the sanctuary limits and half outside. His military adviser, Kleandridas, fled abroad, and was condemned to death in his absence.

Pericles, concerned over the drain on Athenian man-power, was anxious for peace; and the Assembly, chastened by reverses, was now willing too. Kallias went to Sparta, and after tough bargaining Athens withdrew from the two ports of Megara, which she still held, and gave up her alliances with Phokis, Troizen and Achaia. But the Messenians remained at Naupaktos, and Athens kept her naval league, including, subject to a promise to allow local self-government, her old enemy, Aigina. On this basis, in 445, peace was made for thirty years. It lasted for fourteen.

3 THE GOLDEN AGE OF ATHENS

Those fourteen years are the years when they built the Parthenon, with Pheidias, backed by Pericles, the master-craftsman among a great band of sculptors; when Sophocles (born *c.* 495), who had been the chief boy dancer and singer in the thanksgiving for the defeat of Xerxes, brought tragedy to perfection; when Herodotos, the 'father of history', came to Athens and made her the heroine of his work; when there was peace – though even then not completely unbroken – and when Pericles was supreme in politics; the age to which later orators look back with admiration, and Plato, born too late to share in it, with a critical but wistful eye.

Prose writing had begun in the age of the first philosophers. While some of them wrote down their thoughts without resorting to metrical form, other men in many cities, mostly Ionian, recorded in unvarnished prose the myths, customs and traditions of their home towns, often with special reference to the impact of Persia. Hekataios of Miletos wrote a geographical work with many historical details. Herodotos went further, producing a work of epic dimensions and artistic arrangement. His first sentence is worth arranging, as was first done by Sir John Myres, as a title-page:

Herodotos of Halikarnassos
his RESEARCHES
here set down
that the deeds of men may not be forgotten in time
and that the great and notable achievements
both of Greeks and Barbarians
may not be unrenowned;
and more especially the causes of the war between them.

The word for 'research' is *historia,* to which Herodotos in this sentence gave its subsequent meaning.

Owing to the citizenship-law of 451, Herodotos was unable to become an Athenian, and before long he moved to Italy. There Athens organized a colony of men from all parts of Greece, called Thouria (less correctly, Thourioi), to take the place of murdered Sybaris; and there, a rather poor consolation, the exile of Halikarnassos could be a land-owner and citizen. There he wrote up, from notes and memory, most of his great work, stating, not without courage, his conviction that Athens had saved Greece in 480, unpopular as the statement might now be; and to Athens presently he returned – perhaps when the Thourians, rather ungratefully, turned away from Athens to neutrality.

Sophocles, his friend, born into the Athenian 'establishment', had no such troubles. He was an active if conventional soldier and citizen; and from early manhood he wrote plays. At twenty-seven, against the veteran Aeschylus, he won the first prize. He introduced the third speaking actor, which made possible plots of some complexity. He used painted scenery; occasionally there was even a change of scene between acts. He gave up the Aeschylean trilogy, and his triads of tragedies were on unrelated subjects; each one, of about one-third the length of a Shakespeare play, therefore confined itself strictly to the climax of one of the well-known stories. All is done in not much over an hour; and yet there is no sense of haste or excessive compression.

He is good at presenting the tragic conflict, that of right and right, as in *Antigone,* in modern times his most popular play. Polyneikes, the exiled son of Oedipus, has fallen fighting as one of the Seven against Thebes, his own city. Kreon, the new ruler, orders that his body be left unburied – thereby ensuring that his spirit shall find no rest for ever. Death is the penalty for burying the traitor; but his young sister Antigone, loving, passionate and with a will of steel, all alone – for her own sister Ismēne, a softer character, tries to dissuade her – carries out the rites, and pays the penalty. Entombed alive, she does not await death, but hangs herself with her girdle, before Kreon, warned by the prophet Teiresias that he is offending heaven, has time to release her.

Here Kreon too has some right on his side. He is given some fine lines on the claims of the state, which alone preserves the people, to total obedience. Against him, Antigone urges the 'unwritten laws of God', the claims of love. But the two characters are no mere mouthpieces for the state and the individual conscience. Kreon could have been made austere but noble; Sophocles makes him a hectoring bully. Even Antigone is no perfect heroine; under great strain, she is harsh to the gentle Ismene; and it has been too seldom emphasized that, had she not impetuously rushed on her death, she would have been rescued. The piece is not a tract, but a drama.

Sophocles is a great master of theatre and of plot. In *Oedipus the King*, in *The Women of Trāchis* (the chorus in a play on how the loving and much wronged wife of promiscuous Herakles unwittingly caused his death), the end is inevitable only in the sense that the audience knew what did happen. Sophocles shows *how* it happens, to people and through people, who are not mere puppets, but free agents. They may be in situations already bedevilled by the past, by their offences and the offences of their forefathers; so are people in real life; but the drama (the 'action') shows what they try to do about it. The same impetuous energy, which had driven Oedipus long before to leave home, to escape the fate of killing his supposed father and marrying his supposed mother at Corinth, is manifested in his investigation of the question, Who really killed the old King of Thebes? In *The Women of Trachis*, no small part in the catastrophe is played by the mischievous self-importance of a minor character, the messenger who brings the news that Herakles is on his way home, victorious – with another captive princess. The interest is in people. As H. D. F. Kitto has put it, Sophocles has a very strong feeling, not indeed that 'all things work together for good to them that love God', but that 'all things work together'. Terrible things happened in the world of the old heroes; so they do in our world. Usually they are caused by men's sins, which have started a long train of trouble. It remains true that the ways of the gods, who overrule men's lives, are inscrutable; but there is no sense of rebellion in Sophocles, who in his own life was a man of orthodox piety. He presents his dramas and leaves his audience with an enhanced sense of the pity and terror (Aristotle's phrase) of the situation, by which they felt, as it were, 'purged'. Confident, imperial Athens could 'take it'. His plays were immensely popular. He is said to have written over a hundred; as they were presented four at a time, three tragedies and a farce, with chorus of satyrs (the old companions of Dionysos) for comic relief, this means that he presented plays, through his long working life, every two or three years. More than half his output, fifteen sets of plays, won the crown. The great *Oedipus the King*, with its lost companion plays, was among the exceptions.

The Tribute-List for 443 ends with the name, slightly damaged on the stone, '-o-okles of Kolōnos, Treasurer'. Almost certainly it is Sophocles of Kolōnos, the dramatist. He went from that year's appointment to work on his *Antigone*, and fresh from that triumph he was elected general of his tribe. It was not the only time.

The year 440 was marked by a crisis, when Samos, which still had a war-navy of seventy ships, engaged in private war against her old enemy Miletos, refused to obey Athens' order to keep the peace, and revolted, appealing for help on all sides. There was considerable alarm, and all the ten generals were sent on service. But Pericles, striking hard and promptly, without waiting for general mobilisation, pinned down the Samians' main forces; Persia did not move, though the local satrap had given the revolt some initial help; nor, in the end, did the Peloponnesians; Corinth, which maintained overlordship over her minor colonies in north-west Greece, argued that for an overlord to chastise her own allies was an internal affair. Of Athens' other allies, only Byzantion came out, and both cities were reduced at leisure. Samos, under an imposed democratic government, became tributary and was sentenced to pay the cost of the war, 1,400 talents (8,400,000 drachmas), by instalments. It was Athens' only serious campaign in fourteen years. It does not appear that Sophocles saw the slightest incongruity between the lofty idealism of his plays (especially *Antigone*) and serving his imperial city in the taxation and coercion of unwilling allies.

In the years of peace after 439, Athens was by no means inactive abroad. In 437 a major objective was attained, when Hagnon, a friend of Pericles, led a colony, not confined to

Athenians, to a site guarding the only practicable crossing of
the Thracian river Strymon between a lake and the sea. The
place was called Nine Ways; and not only was it such an
important cross-roads; it gave access to the goldfields of
Mount Pangaion, where Peisistratos as an exile had gathered
wealth long ago. For it, Athens had hoped when she besieged
Eion and fought Thasos (pp. 197, 209); but a large colony
sent there about 465 had been cut into pieces by the Thracians.
Hagnon called his new foundation Amphipolis, the City
Surrounded, from its strong position in a loop of the Strymon.
Pericles, who had already secured the Gallipoli Peninsula with
a citizen colony of 1,000 families, also, about this time, led a
splendidly equipped fleet on a flag-flying cruise in the Black
Sea, securing the alliance of Sinope by expelling a tyrant, and
impressing Greeks and natives everywhere with Athenian
power. Phormion, a daring admiral with a winning personality,
aided the backward Greek Akarnanians of north-west Greece
against their enemies, and secured them as loyal allies. In 433
western Leontinoi and Rhegion (Reggio), claiming kinship
with Athens as 'Ionians' threatened by the more powerful
Dorian states of Sicily, sought and were granted an alliance.
Avoiding major hostilities, carefully observing the Thirty
Years' Peace, Athens was expanding again. Some of her late
enemies, indeed, were growing alarmed.

But above all, these years saw the building of the Parthenon
and the Propylaia or Portals of the Acropolis. Already in 447
fragments of the accounts show that work had begun, to continue without a break even through the crisis of 447–5. The
funds in the League treasury, now amounting to 5,000 talents
(thirty million skilled-man days' pay), were used; but this
was not done without a parliamentary battle over the ethical
question. The new conservative leader, Thucydides, a kinsman
of Kimon and of Thucydides the historian, denounced it
fiercely, voicing the complaints of the allies at seeing their
money so used; 'seeing us', he said, 'decking our city like a
vain woman with precious stones and statues and thousand-
talent temples'. Pericles in reply argued that the money was
earned; it was paid by the allies for protection, and so long as

Athens performed this service it was no one else's business what she did with the surplus. The assembly, desirous to be persuaded, accepted this argument.

The conservatives were alarmed, or affected to be, at the dominant position which Pericles was achieving; he was elected general year after year continuously, which was unprecedented, and before 440 the law was actually altered to take account of this. It was provided that one general each year should be elected from among 'all Athenians' and the other nine tribe by tribe; one tribe each year, presumably in rotation, might thus have no general, but it meant that other good officers of Pericles' tribe were not denied all opportunity. Politicians, echoed by the comic dramatists, who were conservatives to a man, complained that he was a tyrant in all but name, which was nonsense; the assembly could have suspended him even from his office of general at any time if they had wished, and at a later time they once did. Finally, in 443, resort was had once more to the expedient of ostrakismós; but it was Thucydides who was the victim.

4 THE GOLDEN AGE OF GREEK ART

The Acropolis was not the only scene of building activity. New temples were built to Poseidon on the promontory of Sounion, whose restored colonnade is still a landmark; to Nemesis at Rhamnous, north of Marathon, which lies in ruins; to Ares the War-god at Acharnai, at the foot of Mount Parnes, which, as the home of charcoal-burners who supplied the city with fuel, had grown into a considerable town. Under the Roman Empire, when the countryside was in decay, this building seems to have been taken down and re-erected in the Athenian Agorá. Fully preserved, on the other hand, though it has lost its sculpture, is the temple of Hephaistos the Smith god (formerly, but wrongly, identified as that of Theseus) on the hill overlooking the Agorá, close to where the metal-workers still beat their copper pans today. A new Hall of the Mysteries was built at Eleusis; and next to the open-air Theatre of Dionysos, where the plays were performed, was built a wooden-roofed covered theatre, for musical performances: the Ōdeion, a name much desecrated in our time. Pericles himself stood as a candidate for the board of directors of the music festival in 442, when the new hall was first used, and drafted the new regulations. It was said that Pericles 'never had time' to go out to parties; but he had time for this.

Pericles was passionately interested in the building of the new and beautiful Athens, but he also certainly regarded these great projects as a 'crash programme' for the relief of unemployment. Plutarch – revealing in his first phrase an attitude to the manual worker, common in late classical literature – writes of them:

Wishing the vulgar throng neither to be without a share in the profits [of empire] nor to be paid for doing nothing, Pericles proposed great building enterprises and projects for the employment of skill, so that those at home, no less than those on naval or garrison or active military service, might have an excuse for being paid out of the public funds. For the materials included stone, bronze, ivory, gold, ebony, cypress-wood, and the relevant trades, carpenters, sculptors, copper-smiths, stone-masons, dyers, goldsmiths, ivory-workers, painters, embroiderers, workers in relief; and then there were the transport services; merchants, oarsmen and helmsmen at sea, and on land wagon-builders, keepers of draught oxen, drivers, rope-makers, weavers, leather-workers, road-makers and quarrymen; and every trade had under its command as it were a disciplined army of the unskilled labouring class to be the tools and muscles of its service; and so the demands set up distributed and disseminated prosperity to men of all ages and conditions. And as the buildings rose, majestic in size and matchless in beauty and grace, while the craftsmen vied with each other to surpass all standards in artistry, the most amazing thing was the speed of the work. Buildings which men thought would hardly be finished in several succeeding generations were all completed within the political prime of one man. . . . [Generally] facility and speed are not conducive to lasting impressiveness and the highest beauty; the time invested in hard work pays its dividend in the permanence of the product. And this is the more cause to marvel at the buildings of Pericles, that were made in so little time to last for so long. Every one of them was venerable for its beauty, immediately, and in freshness to this day they seem as though just finished. Such a bloom of newness is there upon them, keeping them, to the eye, untouched by time, as though the works had, blended into them, an evergreen spirit and a soul of unfading youth.

Plutarch, at school at Athens, learnt to love these great works in his impressionable years. One could not but revere Athens; and this set up an ambivalence of feeling, which stimulated his interest in Pericles and his age; for, as we have seen, according to the prevailing literary tradition, democracy was a Bad Thing.

All was dominated by the great Parthenon, the House of the Maiden, as Athens began to call it in the next century, just under 70 by 31 metres (230 by 101 feet) in plan; Doric, in the new, more slender style, with columns about $5\frac{1}{2}$ ground-level diameters in height, as compared with four in archaic temples, and with the *entasis* or 'bulge' of the shafts reduced so that it disappears, to a casual view; but it is clearly visible if one looks aslant, between two pillars, at a narrow band of sky. Not visible at all to the naked eye are some other famous 'refinements'. There is scarcely a straight or a strictly vertical or horizontal line in the whole exterior. The floor rises slightly in a bulge (not a mathematical curve), to a height of about 4 inches in the middle of each long side and $2\frac{3}{4}$ inches in each end, and this rise is followed by a line of the architrave along the top of the columns, and the whole entablature. The corner columns are slightly thicker than the others, as may be detected with a measuring tape; while the rise of the stylobate can be more easily 'seen' by placing an object such as a hat at one end and noting that it is invisible from floor-level at the other. Even more delicately, all the pillars lean inwards at an angle of less than one degree – those at the angles twice as much, since they are inclined in both planes. It has been calculated that, if produced, all their axes would meet at a height of about a mile. Curvature of the stylobate is found in the archaic temple at Corinth; but it is not universal. In the Hephaistos temple, the floor is flat; and 'flat' is the effect produced by that good but more pedestrian building – the best-preserved of its age in Athens – when compared with the marvellous lightness of the much larger Parthenon.

The great architect Iktīnos, who designed this work of genius in company with Kallikrates, Athens' regularly retained master-builder, designed also another surviving temple, that of Apollo at Bassai (Apollo-in-the-Glens) in the land of south-west Arcadian Phigalía ; small cities as well as great were building in that generation. Of local grey stone, probably stuccoed, it too is Doric ; but within, where taller pillars were needed to support the roof, Iktinos used engaged columns of the more slender Ionic ; and at one end of the central nave, for a special purpose, there was a column with a foliage capital (now lost, but sketched in modern times), such as was later called 'Corinthian'; the first appearance of this more ornate order, very popular later. The special reason was that, owing to the lie of the ground on a mountain col, a temple of this size, 38 by 14 metres, could not be 'oriented'; its long axis runs north and south ; but in order that the cult-statue might face the dawn, it was placed in a chapel at one end, facing a side-door opening to the east, and marked off from the nave by two jutting side-walls with the Corinthian column between them. Here as at Athens, we see how the conventions of Greek architecture still gave scope for ingenuity and originality.

An essential part of a Greek temple was its sculpture. Part of the planned impact on the senses, indeed, is that of the contrast between the entablature, with its broad band of painted sculpture, and the austere simplicity below, where the Mediterranean sun casts strong shadows downward, emphasizing the lines of the pillars and picking them out against the changing pattern of shade and light in the colonnade. Beautiful as the ruins are, much of that effect has gone ; roofs almost everywhere, and usually the walls too. Even where fragments of sculpture remain in place, the gay paint has perished, except for traces in crannies ; and the sculptures of Iktinos' temples, both at Athens and Bassai, are in London.

The master-sculptor, directing the many who must have worked on the Parthenon, was Pheidias, picked, no doubt, from among many strong competitors, and backed throughout his work by the influence of Pericles. The contemporary Aristophanes mentions attacks on Pheidias, inspired by jealousy of his patron. He had already executed the colossal bronze Athena Promachos – 'the Defender' – which stood in the open, facing the entrance to the Acropolis. Thirty feet high, and sixty from the foot of the pedestal to the tip of the upraised spear, it towered above the neighbouring roofs; the glint of Athena's crest and spearpoint could be seen on a clear day from ships off Sounion.

Among the Parthenon sculptures, we cannot be sure that we have a single figure from Pheidias' own hand. He had the great cult-image to execute, in gold and ivory – gold sheets for the draperies, ivory for the face and hands, built up on a wooden core: Athena Parthenos, the Maiden; but, as always, she bore helmet, spear and shield. As one entered the temple, dimly lit through the door only, or by lamps, from the Greek sunlight, one would see nothing at first. Then, as the pupils dilated, we would find ourselves in the overwhelming presence of Athena, forty feet high on her pedestal, reaching to the roof, in ivory and gold, by Pheidias.

For the architectural sculptures Athens, with Pheidias and Pericles no doubt among influential voices, chose for the pediments scenes from appropriate myths: the Birth of Athena, motherless, from the brain of Zeus, and her contest with the Sea-God for the patronship of Athens; for the metopes, the old theme of struggling Greeks and Centaurs, civilisation against barbarism, and no easy victory; in half the panels, the Greek is being worsted. Some of the scenes are still a little archaic; not every worker was a Pheidias. But for the continuous frieze that ran round the wall inside the colonnade, they made a more daring choice: Athenians at worship: the Panathenaic procession, such as every year, and with greater splendour once in four years, passed through the Agorá and mounted the rock, to bring to Athena (not the Pheidian statue, but the holy, no doubt crude, old image that 'fell from heaven') her yearly new robe: the Peplos, woven and embroidered by ladies of Athens, and borne in the procession mounted as a sail on a model ship, on a wagon. As modern life may, sparingly and on occasion, reach a church stained-glass window, and as in the Persian War plays of Phrynichos and Aeschylus, so here, Athenians felt that their own high day was a subject worthy of religious art. Over the west or rear door, the procession was in preparation; along both side-walls it flowed: the maidens with vessels of oil and wine and wheat-cakes for offering, the beasts for sacrifice, musicians, chariots – the war-pageantry of yesterday – the proud young cavalry soldiers on their thick-necked Thessalian ponies, reining them in to the slow foot pace. At the east end, priests and elders have already arrived, and wait, leaning each on his staff, for the rest to come up; and over the east door, the Olympian family, from Father Zeus to young Eros, son of Aphrodite, under his mother's parasol, sit in relaxed graciousness to receive their worshippers.

All was done in ten years. At the Great Panathenaia of 438, the Parthenos was dedicated and her temple was ready, though work on the frieze was still in progress. One would like to think that all was joy and harmony; but alas, it was not so. The great works were done to the accompaniment of what we must unhappily call a normal amount of backbiting and slander, largely from those who were outshone by Pheidias or Pericles in their respective spheres. Pheidias was accused of having stolen gold entrusted to him, probably on the mere presumption that when so much of it had been in his hands, some must have stuck. This was a total failure. Pericles, having perhaps foreseen the possibility, had warned his friend to make the plates easily detachable. They were taken down and weighed. But then someone thought up a more subtle charge. Pheidias had had the idea, devised again and used by many Christian artists, of introducing discreet portraits of himself and his patron, among the warriors on Athena's shield. Apart from jealousy, he might have established the custom; but as it was, somebody raised, as in the case of Phrynichos (p. 159), the cry of 'impiety'. That Pheidias died in prison under mysterious circumstances, as Plutarch says, is a later and unfounded tradition. He left Athens; but so did Iktinos, of whom no similar story is told. Almost certainly it was after his work at Athens, and on the strength of it, that he was given the greatest commission in the whole world of Greek art: that of making another gold and ivory statue, for Zeus at Olympia.

The choice of the Athenian for this work was made when the Peloponnese too had its great sculptors. Polykleitos of Argos, whom classical writers name in the same breath with Pheidias, had already produced, at Olympia, bronze statues of victors, and was reckoned the chief master in this genre. Still famous in marble copies are his Doryphoros or Spear-Bearer, in which he tried to enshrine the standard or 'canonic' proportions of the perfect male form, and the more youthful Diadoumenos, tying the ribbon round his hair. However, Pheidias was chosen; Polykleitos later showed what he could do in this line in a great gold-and-ivory Hera for his native Argos.

The site of Pheidias' workshop at Olympia was still shown to tourists 600 years later, when Pausanias the traveller wrote. At the spot recently a simple red-figure Attic cup, with Pheidias' name scratched on it, and a few slivers of ivory and traces of gold have been found, to mark the place where the prince of sculptors worked on his conception of the lord of Olympos. The statue was seated, and so large that people said Zeus could not have stood up without taking the roof off; but its majesty was such that the disproportion did not shock. The Athena Parthenos seems to have perished in a fire which brought down the wooden roof-beams above it, within the classical age. The Zeus survived to receive the tributes of writers under the Roman empire. Quintilian, the greatest Roman literary critic, said that it added something to the received religion; Dion 'the Golden-Tongued', that there was no misfortune or depression for which a man would not feel comfort when he stood before it. Pheidias himself is said to have said that his inspiration for it came from Homer's lines:

So Zeus spoke and assented, and nodded his dark brows; and the strong locks moved on the King's immortal head; and he shook great Olympos.

At Athens the building programme continued. A new great architect, Mnēsicles, was commissioned to provide the Citadel with a worthy entrance portal; and in 437 the accounts show work on the Propylaia already under way. On the brow of the rock the carriageway passed through a wide-spaced Doric colonnade of Pentelic marble, its foot marked off by a bold line, a 'doorstep' of dark Eleusinian stone. Within, the marble, coffered ceiling of the deep porch between the inner and outer gateways was supported, like Iktinos' roof at Bassai, on taller Ionic columns. On each side of the Gates, symmetrical wings were probably designed. Two square halls would give the effect, externally, of solid massive buttresses, while internally they would serve as picture galleries. But that on the south flank was never finished, for reasons which will appear. Even so, 'the Portals' were perhaps even more famous in Greece than the Parthenon. Other cities also had noble temples; none had such a splendid façade to its whole sacred area.

The Parthenon was 2,400 years old in 1963. For some nine hundred years it was the house of Pallas Athena, for a thousand the church of another Virgin; for 375 years it was a mosque, and now, for over a century, has been an antiquity. It stood perfect, with all its architectural sculptures, until the fatal day in 1687 when Venetian artillery* directed by the German Count Königsmark (fugitive, after a celebrated murder, from the London of Charles II*) blew up a Turkish powder-magazine within its walls. In 1800 Lord Elgin, ambassador to Turkey, began his removal of the sculptures; but if the propriety of keeping these in London now is at least debatable, it must be said for Elgin that he undoubtedly saved them from damage by weather and smoke, which those left on the building have suffered since his time, and are suffering still.

*It is pointed out to me that the above story, which has had some currency in English, is incorrect in two respects. The fatal shot was fired by a French lieutenant, without orders and purely to demonstrate his skill; K. and many of his officers expressed their horror at the time. Also the K. of the 'Ten-Thousand Pound Tom' Haymarket murder was not the general, but his nephew. Both uncle and nephew, who were Swedes of German extraction, died in Greece during the Venetian campaign. – A.R.B.

CHAPTER 11

THE GREAT FIFTY YEARS. III
ATHENIAN SOCIETY

1 THE WORKING OF DEMOCRACY

PERICLES, then, was no dictator, whatever his enemies might say; *they* said it daily. Being annually elected general ensured that he was always near the centre of things, certainly; it also gave him, even in peace time, every encouragement to work long hours in an office on foreign affairs and imperial security. A surprising range of business might be said to affect state security, and scores of Decrees of the Council and People ended with a clause 'Let the Generals see to it that' something be done (or prevented). Meanwhile the sovereign people went home to dinner with a feeling of duty done. But if Pericles' voice was heard about home affairs too, as about the regulations for a music festival or the choice of a sculptor, it was only because he was Pericles, a citizen of Athens, with one vote and some hard-earned influence.

The official centre of the state was not at the Generals' office; *they* were only important executives. Ambassadors or messengers with important news were conducted to the conical-roofed building called the Tholos (Round House) or Skias (Parasol – its official name), next to the Council Chamber, in the corner of the Agorá. There, unless the Council were in session, they would find the Epistates or Duty Officer of the day (p. 156), with his quorum of sixteen other councillors of the tribe 'presiding'. In Pericles' time the Epistates was also chairman of the Council and Assembly. Later, after the Council of 405–4 had incurred suspicion of developing views disloyal to the democracy, the Epistates was charged with drawing lots for a platform-committee of nine, one from each tribe *except* that 'in presidency', and a chairman of the Assembly from among them.

By one of the few rules which Demos always faithfully kept,

no business ever went before the Assembly without going before the Council first. This prevented the Assembly's time being wasted. The Council drew up the *programma* or order-paper, which might include detailed recommendations, though, once the debate was open, amendments might be moved. In an emergency, a mere statement of the situation or of the news received could suffice; the Generals would already have been alerted, and the democracy could move fast. The best account of what could happen comes from the next century; Demosthenes the orator recalls the day in 339 when news came in that Philip of Macedonia had passed Thermopylai:

It was evening, when a man came with news to the Presidents, of the occupation of Elateia. They sprang up in the middle of their dinner, and some went and started clearing the stall-holders out of the market-place ... and others sent for the Generals and summoned the trumpeter, and the whole city was full of tumult. Next day at dawn the presidents convened the Council in its chamber, and you went to the place of assembly, and before the Council had done its business and drafted the agenda, the whole people was already sitting up there.

(Demosthenes waves his hand from the law-court where he is speaking, towards the historic hillside of the Pnyx.) And then,

The Council entered, and the Presidents reported the news they had received and brought forward the messenger, and he told his story; and then the herald asked: 'Who wishes to speak?'

When business was less exciting, there was no rush to take part; in fact, on these occasions the humorous device was adopted of sending the Scythian slave police, whom Athens employed so that no citizen might have to lay violent hands on another, to sweep up voters from the streets with ropes dipped in wet, red paint. There were in each year forty statutory or ordinary meetings for the transaction of routine business, often purely formal; e.g. at the first in each prytany votes of confidence in the magistrates were moved, and usually no doubt passed without discussion. If one were rejected, the magistrate was suspended and would probably be sent for trial by a jury for his alleged malpractices. At another any citizen might take the green bough of a suppliant and humbly petition to have 'any cause, public or private' placed on the agenda; a right of initiative for the obscure. 'Anyone who wished' could, moreover, take up the cause of a widow or orphan, or anyone else alleged to be suffering wrong.

It is clear that, except when business was particularly exciting, most citizens did not attend the assembly – especially the poor, and those who lived at Piraeus or in the country. Athens in 431 counted over 27,000 citizen-soldiers of the hoplite and cavalry classes; and the poor or 'naval crowd' were presumably considered more numerous. But for some classes of business, such as ostracism or other legislation on the status of an individual, it was laid down that at least 6,000 votes were necessary; which indicates that at a routine meeting the attendance might be much smaller. In the fourth century those who attended meetings were paid for their time, but not yet in the fifth. In the circumstances, regular attenders were probably confined to a class of active politicians. There are indications that even councillors, who were paid, tended to be well-to-do or middle-class citizens rather than the poor; but since it was not permitted to sit on the council more than twice in a lifetime (and not in consecutive years), the demand for an average of at least 250 new councillors, and in practice more, per year, meant that some 12,000 or more different Athenians would have this experience within the forty years of a normal active life.

The 'political world', as modern Greece calls its active politicians, naturally included all those who served as financial officials, who had to belong to the top property-class, or as generals, most of whom were of old-established landed families; and many of these were also frequent speakers. But to see that the gentry did not have things all their own way, there also grew up a class of speakers who did not hold office, and who claimed to speak for the masses; the Popular Leaders or *demagogues*. The first famous demagogue (though he had predecessors) came to the front at the end of Pericles' time: Kleon, a master-tanner. He gets a bad 'press' from all our literary sources; Aristophanes calls him a stinking exponent of a malodorous trade; Thucydides (whose career he may have ruined, after Thucydides had failed in a military command) speaks of him as favouring war, because in it his evil deeds were less likely to be found out. He is also said to have introduced a new and vulgar style of oratory, stamping about on the platform, shouting and gesticulating. But Thucydides also shows him as not afraid to criticize his audience; he seems to have been a sincere if ferocious 'jingo' patriot. Under such leadership a crowd of the poorer citizens could, if provoked, turn up to carry measures displeasing to Pericles, and still more to the conservatives. In imperial politics, it was the 'naval crowd' and their leaders who were the quickest to demand strong measures against suspect allies; while the gentry, whose income came from their lands and not from the sea and who sympathized with their class-mates among the allies, stood for comparative gentleness and moderation.

Apart from well-known speakers, when the herald cried 'Who wishes to speak?' the debate was open; but if the speaker was not very much to the point, the Assembly would soon show its impatience. References in Plato and Xenophon show that it expected sound knowledge of the subject of debate, which might be technical, e.g. architecture or ship-building. If the speaker were inadequate, and the meeting thought so, the chairman might order him down, and if necessary tell his Scythian constables to remove him. It is a great mistake to think of the Assembly as a gullible body ready to listen to any smooth-tongued rhetorician; ready though they certainly were to savour and relish a play on words or a well-turned phrase.

Between meetings of the assembly, the Council had a heavy programme of routine work. It was responsible for inspecting new ships built for the navy, the horses of the cavalry – true cavalry, recruited among young men of the ancient 'knightly class', having been introduced recently – and the candidates for the archonships and Council of the following year. In the fourth century, if it chose to reject anyone, an appeal had to be allowed to a jury. It supervised and advised the numerous boards of officials, all chosen by lot, except the military and some important financial officers. There were auditors, inspectors, and collectors of taxes, market-inspectors, police-chiefs, five in Athens and five in Piraeus; their duties included preventing householders from constructing verandas and trellises which obstructed the street, seeing that girl flute- and guitar-players, in demand for men's parties, did not receive more than a fixed maximum payment (twice that for a skilled workman – but to hire the most popular flute-girl was a status-symbol), and seeing that the scavengers dumped the garbage not less than a mile outside the walls. The Council also had powers as a criminal court in matters arising out of its administrative duties. Later, these too were taken away, and it could only commit for trial by a jury. Altogether the Council was on duty on about 300 days in each year, that is on every day except the numerous festivals – one must remember that the Greeks had no Sunday.

Councillors, as has been said, were paid, with additional subsistence allowances when on night-and-day duty; and so were the other officials, who by the later fourth century numbered perhaps 350. Plato and other anti-democratic writers pour scorn on the practice of pay for public service – how much better that of other cities and of the Good Old Days, when gentlemen gave of their time freely! But looking at the matter dispassionately, it is clear that such pay, like pay for members of Parliament, which was introduced first against fierce opposition, was essential if the democratic machinery was to function in a truly democratic way.

This applies particularly to the judicial branch: the 6,000 registered jurymen of any year, who were empanelled in juries of varying size according to the importance of the case – 501 was common – on all working days, up to the number required. Commercial cases and appeals from the Empire, added to those arising in Athens, at this time kept the courts busy. Nevertheless, Aristophanes depicts jurymen getting up before dawn to queue and make sure of a place; by no means the whole 6,000 were employed every day. Moreover their day's pay was, in Pericles' time, a mere subsistence allowance, two obols, a third of a drachma. This would have made little appeal to the strong and active, and in fact, we gather from Aristophanes, it was chiefly old men who did this work. The allies objected to the whole principle of having to bring cases to Athens; but we have few complaints of Athenian commercial justice, and none at all of bribery; there was safety in numbers. Where the courts were open to criticism was in that they were prejudiced – in favour of Athens and in favour of democracy. When they handled cases from the empire, they were defending their own interests; and they too sympathized with their class-mates in the allied cities. There was no better way of keeping a check on aspirations to autonomy than by supporting the natural opponents of local leaders; and for local democrats there was no better way of resisting the rich than by represen-ting them at Athens as disloyal.

There is a fascinating pamphlet, preserved to our time among the works of the later soldier and historian Xenophon, though the situation which it reflects is undoubtedly that of about 425, when Xenophon was a child. It seems to be a talk, given by some Athenian gentleman to a like-minded audience of non-Athenians, as it might have been, say, in Thessaly,, who were sincerely puzzled at the way in which Athens conducted her affairs. It runs to about 5,000 words in an English translation, and the last few paragraphs, after a repetition of the opening 'key-note' remarks, which might well mark the end of the paper, are disjointed – as though they were notes of the speak-er's replies to questions. Who he was, we can only guess. A *possible* candidate would be one Kritias, an intellectual, a collateral descendant of Solon, a cousin of Plato, and a man whose name was to become later, as will appear, one of the most hated in Athenian history. Whoever he was, he is cool, tough, and prides himself on having no illusions.

No, I do not approve of the Athenian constitution, he begins,

but since they have decided to have it, I propose to show that they are going the right way about preserving it – even in matters in which other Greeks think they are off the mark.

First, then, it is *right* that there the poor and the commons have advantages over the nobles and the rich; for it is the commons who row the ships and give the city its power – they and the petty officers and the shipyard workers – rather than the armoured troops and the gentry. This being so, it appears fair that all should have a chance of holding office, whether by lot or vote, and that any citizen who wishes should have the right to speak. Besides, they do not compete for those positions in which good conduct is essential and bad conduct would jeopardise the public interests. They do not demand application of the lot to the choice of the military officers. They realise that it is in their interest not to hold these positions but to let the leading men have them, while *they* go for the jobs that only exist to provide a salary. The very point that surprises people – that in every way they give preferential treatment to the base, the poor, the men of the people, rather than the decent classes – is a fine example of how they preserve the democracy; for if these prosper and multiply, they will strengthen the democracy, but if the rich and the gentry prosper, the democrats are building up the force that is opposed to them. . . .

People say that they ought not to let every man indiscriminately [have the right to] speak or sit on the Council; but here too, they know very well what they are doing. . . . If the gentry did all the political speaking, that would be good for the likes of them, but not of the democrats; but as it is, anyone who 'wishes to speak' gets up – any low type – and devises what is best for himself and *his* like. . . . They realise that his uneducated low cunning and loyalty produces better results than a gentleman's virtue and wisdom and disloyalty. A city so run may not be ideal; but that is how to preserve a democracy. The people do not want a well-organized city with themselves in subjection, but freedom and power. Disorder is a minor consideration; what you consider disorder is the very foundation of the people's strength and freedom. . . .

Slaves and non-citizens are extremely undisciplined at Athens. You are not allowed to hit them, and a slave will not get out of your way. But I will tell you why. If it were allowed . . . one might easily strike an Athenian by mistake for a slave; they are no better dressed and no better in appearance. . . . And if you wonder at their letting the slaves be comfortable, and some of them indeed have quite a high standard of living, there is sense in that too. Where sea-power is important, it is necessary that slaves should work for money, so that we may collect revenue from them, and we must let them be free. . . . Likewise, the city needs its domiciled non-citizens, for the sake of the numerous skilled trades, and for the sake of the navy; and that is why we give equal rights to them too.

Slaves, indeed, worked alongside free citizens and non-citizens at such highly skilled trades as fluting the pillars of the temples – those pillars of such fine workmanship that the blade of a knife cannot be inserted between drum and drum. Many too plied their trades or kept shops, paying their owners a 'royalty'. Lest we idealise Athens too much, we must remember also that several thousand slaves worked ten-hour shifts (as judged by the duration of their oil-lamps) in the shafts of the Laurion silver-mines; and that if a slave's evidence was required in a law-court, it had by law to be given under torture. His master's permission had to be given first, and it seems that it was often refused; also, if a slave received any permanent injury under torture, he had to be paid for. It remains a grim business. Nevertheless, the fact that we have indignant, hostile testimony (there is some more in Plato's *Republic*) that the Athenians were altogether too 'soft' to their slaves is very striking. Many Athenians, moreover, had no slaves, and many only one maid-servant. The view of Athens as a community of leisured citizens whose slaves greatly outnumbered the free is against the evidence.

The Old Oligarch (as Gilbert Murray first called him) also refers repeatedly to the policy of backing the proletariat in the subject cities against the 'best people':

for if the rich and the upper classes prevail in the cities, the rule of the people in Athens will be short-lived. This is why they disenfranchise and fine and banish and put to death the gentry, and encourage the lower classes.

This is the point, he goes on, of compelling the allies to bring legal business to Athens; also, the demand so created for lodgings and transport and slaves for hire was good for trade. The complaint was made that sometimes delegations wishing to approach the Council and Assembly could not get their business done 'though one stay for a year', or had to bribe an official to get it brought forward. Perfectly true, says the speaker, but even if they all offered bribes they could not all be dealt with expeditiously, for sheer pressure of business, especially on the Council.

He comments on what Plutarch calls Pericles' policy of

'educating the city through cultivated amusements'. It is a policy which may fairly be called socialist:

The people, realising that poor men cannot afford sacrifices and feasts and temple-building and a fine and splendid city to live in, have devised a way to provide themselves with these things. The state offers many sacrifices, and the people divide up the meat and feast on it. And athletic-grounds with baths and dressing-rooms are things which some rich men have privately; but the people build themselves many sports-clubs with these amenities, and the masses make more use of these than the well-to-do minority.

He has much to say on the advantages of sea-power, with the greater mobility of sea-borne forces, and on sea-borne trade. All the wealth of the world flows in to Athens, and no trading community can afford to be on bad terms with her; and, he adds, Athens was becoming cosmopolitan: 'other Greeks have their characteristic accents and ways of life and dress, but the Athenians use a mixture of all the accents of Greece and barbary'. It is the beginning of the *koinē* or 'common Greek', which was to be the language of all the Near East after the time of Alexander.

2 THE INTELLECTUAL FERMENT

The intellectual ferment that had begun in Ionia did not cease; but its activity moved out – the intellectuals themselves migrated – from the war-damaged and now perhaps doubly taxed land, to colonies: Elea in Italy (p. 142), Abdēra in the north Aegean, a refugee settlement from Teos, Lampsakos, which like Elea was a Phokaian colony, at the head of the Dardanelles. Leukippos, a Milesian, may have sat at the feet of those ruthless reasoners, Zenon and the aged Parmenides; and moved by their criticisms of the first Ionian speculations on the nature of things, he devised a theory that the primal reality was not singular but plural. This was the birth of the original Greek atomic theory, based not on an attempt to account for physical observations, but on metaphysical reasoning. It became influential later, when taken up by the famous Demokritos, the dynamic leader of a 'school' – a group of friends pioneering in thought – about 420 at Abdera.

Pericles, though immersed in politics, was far too intellectually active a man not to be interested in all this. As has been mentioned, he found a man after his own heart in Anaxagoras of Klazomenai, brilliant, unworldly and unpractical, who – in the admittedly difficult circumstances of war-time Ionia – had failed to combine the claims of the higher thought with the business of a land-owner, and let his inherited estate sink to the condition of rough pasture. Pericles welcomed him at Athens and maintained him at his own expense for many years. There was a touching scene once, when Pericles through press of business forgot to send him his allowance, and Anaxagoras, ageing and too proud to ask for it, lay down quietly to die; but Pericles was reminded in time. He reproached Anaxagoras, who is said to have answered, 'Well, if you want a lamp, you must keep it filled up.'

Anaxagoras was another who felt that the Milesian attempts to identify a single primal matter had failed; he postulated that the forms of matter known to man were made up of particles of many kinds. 'How can hair come from what is not hair, or flesh from what is not flesh?' But none of the familiar forms of matter is quite pure: 'in everything there is a portion of everything'. Our world has arisen out of a chaos in which all the elements were mingled; and not our world alone; at many places and times within the infinite universe, he believed that worlds, with men and other animals and civilisations, must exist or have existed. But he could not imagine that all this had taken place fortuitously, nor that mind could have arisen from what was not mind. Mind too is a substance. It does not mix like the ordinary elements: 'Other things partake in a share of everything, but mind is infinite and self-ruling and is mixed with nothing, but is alone itself by itself.' But it exists *among* the elements of animals' bodies; so 'in everything there is a share of everything, except mind, and in some things there is mind also'. Mind set in motion the revolution of the universe, as a result of which the elements became separated out, producing the forms of matter, all mixtures, but distinguished according to which elements predominate in them.

Anaxagoras was probably much impressed by a physical event which took place in 468–7: the fall of a huge meteorite at Aigospotamoi, 'the Goat-Rivers', in the Gallipoli peninsula; a great mass of heavy matter, from outer space. He propounded that the sun was such another mass of incandescent stone, 'larger than the Peloponnese', and that such were the stars too, so far away that we do not feel their heat. The moon is nearer, and is of the same materials as our earth, 'with plains and rough ground in it'; its light is a reflection of that of the sun, and at the turn of the month it can cause eclipses by blocking off the sun's light – the first appearance of the correct explanation. Winds are caused by rarefaction of the air by the sun, causing it to rise, just as when burnt objects go up in smoke.

Such doctrines were shocking to men to whom the heavenly bodies and the winds were gods, or at least directly controlled by gods. Athens, contrary to uninstructed modern belief, was rather conspicuously conservative in religious matters; it could even be dangerous to propound such ideas, all the more so because the state was democratic; for the masses were less 'advanced' than the leisured intellectuals. However, Anaxagoras' views perhaps might have passed unnoticed had not some of the conservatives tried to use them to discredit Pericles. An expert on oracles and well-known 'holy man' named Diopeithes carried a decree making those who 'do not believe in the Gods, or teach doctrines about heavenly bodies' liable to impeachment. Anaxagoras retired to Lampsakos, where he taught, highly respected, until his death in 428. His last request, when asked by the city council what sort of memorial he would like, was for an annual holiday for schoolchildren on the anniversary of his death.

Athenian intolerance was at worst only intermittent; and we hear that his book, from which the above doctrines are quoted by later Greek writers, was on sale at Athens at the end of the century; price, one drachma.

There was by now an increasing public demand for knowledge about the speculations of the philosophers; and a new class of professional free-lance lecturers arose to supply it. Some of them were themselves original thinkers; but their source of livelihood was teaching, whether their own ideas or other men's; that, and the art of public speaking, much sought after by rich young men, now that the only path to influence and eminence was by persuading the people. They were known as 'sophists', a word, perhaps always a little pejorative, meaning people who *professed* wisdom, or professed to teach it.

One of the most famous sophists, who may (with the warning that the profession was full of interesting individualists) be taken as 'typical', was Prōtagoras, from Abdera; an arch-humanist, whose most famous maxim was 'Man is the measure of all things'. Consequently there is no absolute truth, or not for us; we must do our best with the truth as we see it, and what *seems* good to a man, that *is* good, to him. All disputes have two sides, and can be argued both ways; and Protagoras was prepared to demonstrate how it could be done. In his courses he excluded 'astronomy and geometry and music' and professed to teach arts that would make a man a better manager of his property and politician. Of theology he said, 'Of the gods, I cannot say either that they exist or that they do not; it is a very difficult subject, and life is not long enough.' He was, however, quite prepared to talk about them conventionally. He is represented as a highly honourable man; he claimed that his pupils would 'go home better men' for every day that they associated with him. He is said to have charged 1,000 drachmas – three years' good wages for a workman – for a complete course; but if anyone demurred at the end of a course, he was prepared to go with him to a temple, where the pupil should declare on oath what he thought the course was worth, and pay accordingly. But his moral relativism and his willingness to show how both sides of a case might be argued (plain men complained that sophists taught how 'to make the worse cause appear the better') aroused much prejudice against him, especially among honest democrats, who feared the gods and also could not afford his fees. This was how the word sophist, a title which Protagoras frankly accepted, acquired the connotation of insincerity and anxiety only to sell one's product.

Commonly ranked among the sophists, but apparently more especially a professional rhetorician, was another great figure, Gorgias, who came from Leontinoi in Sicily a little later (427) to plead for aid against Syracuse under the treaty of 433. Rhetoric had first received systematic study in Sicily after the fall of the tyrants there. In the older culture of Athens, young men were still learning the speaker's art imperceptibly from listening to their elders, whose oratory, based on a tradition going back to Homer, was not to be despised. But Gorgias brought something new, and enjoyed a great personal triumph. His speech glittered with verbal brilliance; especially assonance, the use of similar sound to reinforce similar sense, and antithesis, the use of studied contrast to point almost every sentence. Quoted specimens of his style, which survive, sound to us intolerably mechanical; and, indeed, later Greek oratory modified his perpetual use of the same tricks; but when the tricks were new, young Athens was enthralled. Gorgias spent most of the rest of his long life – he is said to have lived to be over 100 – in old Greece, especially since his own city, after receiving some help from Athens, was betrayed to the Syracusans by its own upper class when faced with social revolution, and ceased to exist (422). He lived much among the cultivated nobles of Thessaly, teaching rhetoric for high fees, and revisiting Athens more than once. He is not said to have taught philosophy, and his alleged statement of a total scepticism – (A) that nothing *is*; (B) that if it were, we could not know it, and (C) that if we knew it, we could not communicate our knowledge – was perhaps merely a text for a rhetorical *tour de force*. He too is described as a man of honourable and even austere life; when asked in old age to what he attributed his continued health, he is said to have answered 'I have never in my life done anything for the sake of pleasure'. But as a teacher of the art of defending weak causes, he too came under popular suspicion.

The sophists were and are somewhat unfairly blamed for a growth of scepticism in their time. They were themselves products of their time; and they were supplying a want which had not been felt previously, that for higher education. Mere elementary schools existed in every city; they taught reading, writing, figuring and, for those whose parents could keep them at school longer, literature and music. Illiteracy was by this time practically unknown among Athenian citizens (among women, it may have been commoner); but to be able to accompany one's self on the lyre while singing was a gentlemanly accomplishment. Literature (prose books being still mainly on abstruse subjects) meant poetry, especially Homer, studied with a teacher who explained the archaic and difficult words, and extensively learnt by heart; also lyric poetry with its musical accompaniment, especially that of the patriotic and high-toned Simonides, and elegiac poetry, full of proverbial wisdom. Theognis (p. 113), with his advocacy of eugenics and anti-democratic sentiments, and with his homosexual poems expurgated, was in favour with well-to-do Athenian parents.

It was all the thought of the new age that called in question the ancient myths and traditional morality derived from Homer and other poets. Herodotos, who favoured Athens and democracy, but could not otherwise be called a revolutionary, told a story of how King Darius once found before him simultaneously some Greeks and people from a tribe on the borders of India, whose custom was ceremonially to eat the bodies of their parents. He asked the Greeks how much they would have to be paid to do that, and they said stiffly, not for any money. So then he asked the Indians how much they would have to be paid to cremate their parents; 'and they cried aloud, and bade him not say such things'. Herodotos comments: 'These, then, are their lawful customs; and I think that Pindar was right when he said in his poem "*Nomos* is king of all".'

Nomos: law *or* custom or convention. The widening geographical horizon had indeed brought together a knowledge of many strange customs, and Herodotos is the father not only of history but of comparative anthropology. The Greeks knew too that their own customs had altered, both from the old poems and from observation of what still went on in backward Greek areas. Philosophers, since Anaximandros first propounded his doctrine of evolution, had speculated on the ways of life of primitive man; Protagoras himself does so, in Plato's *Protagoras*; and the conclusion lay ready to hand, that our laws or customs exist not by nature or by the unalterable will of the gods, but simply *by* custom or convention. It was then also a perilously short step, for anyone who found traditional morality troublesome, to appealing from it to the law of nature or law of the jungle, either in power-politics or in personal relations. This is parodied in Aristophanes, where a young man, who has just had a modern humanist education, argues that it is what the animals do, and therefore natural, and therefore right and proper, that he should beat up his old father as soon as he is strong enough. High-minded but sceptical sophists, like similarly-placed people in many ages, were in fact living on their capital, on a traditional morality, the bases of which they were kicking away; and in the next generation, the morality suffered.

It was an age of real progress in thought, and of real dangers, such as new developments in human affairs always bring. All the great men of the last third of the century, Socrates, Thucydides, Euripides, Aristophanes, are very conscious of being caught up in it.

3 PERICLES AT HOME

Two reported conversations show Pericles himself involved in the current debates. When Protagoras, already famous, came to Athens, not only did all the bright young men flock to hear him, but Pericles, who 'never had time' for parties, invited Protagoras to his house. They had a long talk, largely about the question of responsibility for a recent fatal accident in a javelin-throwing competition. Should one attribute responsibility to the thrower, or the javelin itself, or the organizers of the games? To many Athenians it seemed an odd way for the leading citizen to spend so much time. Really it was important; for by primeval custom, a man who killed another, even by accident, was both polluted and exposed to a feud. Nor did ignorance save one; it did not save Oedipus. There is a set of speeches written, a few years later, for a mock trial, in which a similar accident is supposed to have happened in a boys' sports club. The father of the victim, prosecuting without malice, takes it as self-evident that the accidental killer must go into exile; and the killer's father does not attempt to escape the consequences to his son by saying that he is morally innocent; he uses the sophistry that since, when the javelin was in the air, the deceased, a younger boy playing about, had run into its path, *he was 'guilty' of his own death*. When Pericles and Protagoras thought of attaching blood-guilt to the organizers of the games, they took the modern view that the organizers are responsible for safety regulations; but they probably agreed that, before a Greek court, there would be more hope in pleading that the guilt should attach to an inanimate object. This was an expedient actually employed in Athenian courts; and it had been employed from time immemorial after the sacrifice to Zeus of a ploughing ox, the Bouphonia or ox-*murder*. It was felt to be a terrible thing to kill such a friend of man, and it was customary for all concerned in the rite to be prosecuted, to blame each other in a fixed ritual order, and finally to cast the blame upon the knife, which was found guilty and cast into the sea.

Another conversation in which Pericles became involved is recounted (allegedly verbatim) by Xenophon. Alkibiades, Pericles' ward, the son of Kleinias who was killed at Koroneia, was growing up, a handful; spirited, brilliant, very handsome and very thoroughly spoilt by competing lovers. Socrates, then about thirty-five, who used to profess in his deceptively naïve way to be in love with Alkibiades too, and susceptible to the charms of any handsome young creature, tried to save him; but it was up-hill work. Socrates, personally austere, had, however, considerable influence over him, as over many of the rising generation. He was interested, like them, in the new thought, and they found his apparently naïve but really most penetrating approach to its problems fascinating. He was keen on definitions, and his dialectic was lethal to any kind of imprecise thinking. The young men loved hearing him deflate anyone pompous, and took his tricks home to try out on their elders. With them, Socrates was becoming unpopular; but he could not have cared less.

This was the background to Alkibiades' (if we may trust Xenophon) asking Pericles one day:

Could you explain to me what Law is?

P. Certainly.

A. Then please do; because, when I hear people praised for being law-abiding, I think that one could never deserve that praise if one does not know what Law is.

P. Well, that is not very difficult. All enactments are laws, which the People in parliament has approved and published, laying down what shall be done or not done.

A. – resolving that we should do good things? Or bad things?

P. Good gracious, boy! Good, of course, not bad.

A. But then, if it is not the People, but, as happens where there is an oligarchy, a minority assembles and publishes its enactments, what is that?

P. Everything that the government of the city, after deliberation, publishes, as to what is to be done, is called law.

A. But then if a tyrant, in control of a city, publishes enactments as to what the citizens are to do, is that law?

P. Even what a tyrant publicly enacts, as he is the government, is called law.

A. But, Pericles, what is lawlessness and arbitrary power? Isn't it when the stronger compels the weaker, by force and without consent, to do what he pleases?

P. I agree.

A. Well, then, what a tyrant compels the citizens to do by his enactments, without their consent, is the negation of law?

P. Yes, I agree; I withdraw my statement that what a tyrant enacts, without the people's consent, is law.

A. Then what about an oligarchy's enactments, if it legislates for the people without their consent, by compulsion?

P. Everything which one forces another to do without his consent, whether by public enactment or otherwise, seems to me arbitrary, rather than law.

A. Well, then, when the people, being stronger than the rich, legislates for them without *their* consent, is that arbitrary, or is that law?

P. Oh, Alkibiades, I was good at that sort of thing when I was your age. We used to debate and quibble over just that sort of thing.

A. I wish I could have talked to you when you were at your best, Pericles!

Pericles' home life, indeed, had its distresses; even the story of his talk with Protagoras was first given to the world on a painful occasion, in a law-court. Speeches probably gave their first currency to many of the picturesque anecdotes told about famous Greeks.

Pericles had been married, long before, to a kinswoman of his, who had already, Plutarch says, been married to Hipponikos, son of Kallias, the ambassador; but when she had borne him two sons, he divorced her, and she remarried Hipponikos; their son, another Kallias, was younger than Pericles' sons. This curious business was probably due, though we are not told so, to the wife being left an heiress, without brothers; for by Athenian law an heiress had to marry her next of kin, even if at the cost of two divorces. It was a cruel law, as speakers in inheritance cases admitted; but so strong was the insistence that property must descend within the patrilinear clan, that throughout classical times it remained unaltered, even though under it happy marriages might be broken up or children (like Pericles' sons) left motherless. Pericles, moreover, was too busy even to look after his landed property; but it did not occur to him to hand this task over to his sons as they grew up; presumably relations were not of the best already. Instead, he delivered it to a freedman, his trusted steward, with directions to sell the produce of the estates wholesale, and buy what was needed for the house retail in the market. He lost money by it, but it saved trouble. But the system also bore hardly on the sons, especially the elder, Xanthippos, when he was grown up, married to an aristocratic young lady with expensive tastes, and still living, as was customary, under the family roof. A great estate could produce all the daily consumer-goods of Greek life (not least, the wine and food for parties) in abundance, with a surplus for sale; that was what being rich meant; but under Pericles' system, one had to be always watching the expenditure. Short of the means to keep up with his rich friends, and nagged by his young wife, Xanthippos at last borrowed money on his father's credit. When this, in due course, came out, Pericles was furious, and not only refused to pay, but sued the creditor for fraud. Xanthippos, in court, told the Protagoras story as evidence of his father's hopeless eccentricity. The public enjoyed it hugely.

Bad relations between fathers and sons were, alas, not uncommon. Comedy takes them for granted. Sophocles, who lived and wrote splendid poetry up to the age of ninety, suffered legal proceedings in his last years from his son, vainly attempting to get control of the family property on the ground that his father was senile. As the son must have been about sixty, one may spare some sympathy for him on being still financially *in statu pupillari*. The matter is not without importance; it highlights one of the great defects of classical Greek character: its hardness. It appears in the attitude of these old men who would not hand over; also in the relative weakness (by no means total absence) of tenderness towards women and children, characteristic of a society that practises the exposure of unwanted babies (especially girls), and expressed in the slowness of Greek art to make any study of children; though we now have some charming studies of Athenian child-acolytes from Brauron. It is reflected in the cruelty of the law on heiresses, and matched by an equal hardness in the relations between states. The classical world – more, perhaps, than some other ancient civilisations – was deficient in *caritas*. For lack of it, those brilliant, hard and gem-like individualists failed to consolidate and make permanent their social achievements.

What his socially forced marriage may have done to Pericles we do not know; perhaps nothing; perhaps it left him a little more austere, more Olympian, as the comic poets said. After the divorce, he remained, so far as we know, for some years without either wife or mistress. But soon after the peace of 445, Athens was provided with an unfailing source of gossip, when her leading general, at fifty, fell in love with a girl of twenty, who was not even an Athenian: Aspasía of Miletos, a *hetaira* or professional 'geisha-girl' (so all our sources say, though some scholars believe that this too is one of the licensed libels of comedy); cultivated, as the secluded and uneducated good ladies of Athens were not, and possessing not only beauty but a fine intelligence. Socrates is said to have enjoyed talking to her. She was Pericles' 'morganatic wife' for the rest of his days, and bore him, before 440, a son, named Pericles; but since his mother was not Athenian he could not, under the act of 451, be an Athenian or rank as legitimate. To the comic poets and to gossip, Aspasia was a godsend; as Pericles had long been called Zeus – 'God Almighty' – and his oratory the divine thunder, she was his Hera, or alluded to under other parodies of mythology, often obscene. Athens noted it with avidity when Pericles was seen to kiss her on setting off for his office.

Much of what the comedians said was simply fun, delivered on those privileged feast-days when obscenity and exaggeration were in order; but it is hard to believe that there is no venom in some of it. The comedians, like other literary men, were almost to a man conservative, upper class people, who enjoyed despising the masses; and Pericles was to them something of a traitor to his class. Perhaps late in the thirties, Aspasia was attacked in earnest with a prosecution for 'impiety'; what the formal ground for it was we do not know; possibly she had given some of a school of geisha-girls, which she is said to have kept, the names of the muses. The real motive, as in the case of Pheidias, was political; and since, in an Athenian trial, relevance was no object, all manner of other slanders were brought in, including the suggestion that Aspasia was a 'security risk'; she was a foreigner, and she influenced policy; some said she had caused the Samian War by persuading her lover to back Miletos. To save her, Pericles was constrained to lay aside his Olympian calm and plead for mercy. He broke down and wept; and the 501 jurymen, much gratified, voted for an acquittal.

CHAPTER 12

GREECE AND THE TEN YEARS' WAR
431–421

1 WAR RENEWED

THE significance of the date 431 B.C. in our histories of Greece has been compared to that of 1914 in the history of Europe. In 433–1 the Thirty Years' Peace broke down, without having run quite half its course; and the Peloponnesian War – two wars really, separated by a few years of uneasy peace – made an end of hopes that Athens might bring unity to the Greek world under her leadership. With that, many have felt, in the words of a Greek proverb which Pericles once quoted, over the dead of an earlier campaign, that 'the spring is gone out of the year'. But there was still a great harvest to be gathered; and even during the years from 431 to the fall of Athens in 404, much fine creative work was done. To them belong nearly all the surviving plays of Euripides and Aristophanes, and the last plays of Sophocles. On the Acropolis, the south wing of the Propylaia was finished off summarily, perhaps as a measure of war economy; but to these years belong the exquisite little Ionic temple of Nike (Victory; about 426) and later the Erechtheion (p. 297). In them Plato (born 428) places the dramatic setting of most of his dialogues; and they, with the sombre and tragic history of Thucydides, which begins in earnest at this point, make these years some of the best known in the history of Athenian society.

A war broke out between Corinth and her powerful, unfilial and independent colony, Kerkyra. Sparta tried in vain to restrain Corinth from proceeding to extremities. After a defeat, and with help from their Peloponnesian naval allies, they proceeded to outbuild Kerkyra's navy; and Kerkyra in fear abandoned her isolation and appealed to Athens for an alliance.

The Peace permitted either side to make alliance with uncommitted states; but to join in offensive action against

Corinth would naturally be a breach of it. However, Kerkyra was important, both as a sea-power and from her position on the way to the west. After keen debate, the Assembly concluded with her a defensive alliance, and sent a token squadron of ten ships, with orders to take part only, if absolutely necessary, in the defence of the island. When it became clear that Corinth would not be deterred, Athens reinforced with another twenty; and these arrived just in time to save Kerkyra from a complete defeat at sea. After these hostilities, Athens ordered Poteidaia in Chalkidiké, a member of her League but a loyal Corinthian colony, to expel her Corinthian High Commissioners and raze her walls on the seaward side. Poteidaia refused, received a Corinthian volunteer brigade, and was shortly besieged; and Corinth complained to Sparta of Athenian aggression.

Thucydides says that the Athenians acted on a calculation that a Peloponnesian war was inevitable anyhow, and that they had better secure Kerkyra because of its strategic importance. 'Historical inevitability' is unfashionable nowadays, especially among historians, who emphasize the consequences flowing from individual human decisions, which could have been taken differently. The prelude to the war of 431, as to that of A.D. 1914, affords an interesting case-study.

Sparta called a conference of her league, and the complaints of Corinth were backed by others. Megara, which had probably had no diplomatic or commercial relations with Athens since her massacre of the Athenian garrison in 446, complained that she was now (apparently under a recent decree, moved by Pericles) excluded from all ports of the Athenian empire, contrary to the treaty. For this small, eastward-facing, maritime state, which exported cheap woollen goods, it was ruin. Aigina, subject to Athens, made secret representations that Athens was interfering (no doubt on security grounds) with the internal self-government which the same treaty promised her. And then an Athenian deputation, which 'happened to be at Sparta on other business', asked leave to address the meeting. It was granted; but the speech made was not a defence of Athens' recent actions. It was truculent and provocative: Athens had saved Greece in the Persian Wars, and deserved her empire;

she ruled it justly, but had to defend her citizens and her security, through her own courts, against the natural resentment of subjects. Finally, war was a chancy business. Sparta had better be careful.

Now Sparta, the great 'sated' power, to use the terminology of the 1930s, was not at this time bellicose. The veteran king, Archidamos, who knew Pericles well, and knew also better than most what a war with Athens would mean, made sustained efforts to save the peace and negotiate. But the Spartan assembly, meeting alone immediately after the conference, carried by a large majority, against the king, the resolution that Athens had broken the treaty, and must be made to withdraw or fight.

Why the truculent speech, just then? And was the Athenian deputation's presence really an accident? And why the Megarian Decree, just then? It was this decree which was probably the most definite breach of the treaty; the Spartan ambassadors sent to Athens went so far as to say that if it were withdrawn there would be no war. But Pericles spoke against any compromise, saying that concessions would be taken as a sign of weakness and be followed by new demands.

It appears then that it was Pericles who considered that war was inevitable, and that he deliberately took steps to precipitate it while he was there to guide Athens. No one else, as he was sure, and as it proved, could restrain that ever-sanguine and optimistic people from embarking, during a war, upon adventures that would overstrain even Athens' resilient manpower; and he was already over sixty. He had a strategy which he believed would secure a safe draw with little bloodshed: it was not to engage the overwhelming Peloponnesian armies in battle; to evacuate rural Attica, let the Spartans burn every farm in it if they would, and find that, behind her Long Walls, Athens could still feed her people. Athens must meanwhile keep her subject allies on a tight rein, and above all, not attempt new conquests during the war. Sparta would presently have to give up the struggle, with disastrous loss of 'face'; it would be made clear that she could not defend her naval allies. They would have to come to terms with Athens; the route to the west would be in her sole power; the world would be safe for democracy, and for the Athenian empire.

But *was* the war inevitable? On this, if one must take a line, it is that Pericles' judgement deserves respect. What must not be forgotten is the class-struggle endemic in Greece at this time. Athens was securing her position in many of the subject cities by supporting democrats – to some writers, the scum of the earth – against former governing classes, to those same writers the 'decent people'; even in Athens, conservatives felt that this was wrong. Conversely, there were unprivileged classes in some mainland states who looked longingly towards Athens. It was this which made it difficult for the two power-blocs, representing different social systems, to lie down together. Pericles may hape felt, like Lincoln, that the land could not remain indefinitely part one and part the other. In the sequel, this was exactly what it did; but as a result, Greek political history ends in stultification.

Hostile tradition had it that Pericles plunged his people into war because his political position was shaken, and he reckoned that in a war they would have need of him. This accusation, at least, we can dismiss; Thucydides, contemporary and near the centre of things in Athens, makes it clear that he was as unrivalled as ever. Pericles still bears a heavy responsibility.

Greece went gaily to war, the great war of liberation as the Spartans called it. After the long peace there were, says Thucydides grimly, many young men in Greece on both sides who welcomed it, 'because of their inexperience' (1914 again). But there were some things which even Pericles could not foresee.

In the first year everything went according to Pericles' plan. The Peloponnesians devastated parts of Attica, and Pericles restrained his men from rushing out – not without difficulty, when the smoke went up from the burning villages before their eyes. The Athenians harried enemy coasts by sea. There was much burning, but little bloodshed.

At the end of the summer campaign, Pericles was deputed to deliver the customary funeral oration over the fallen. As reproduced by Thucydides, it may be supposed to give the gist of what Pericles said, and some of his striking phrases. He made the main part of it a eulogy of the Athenian way of life, for which these men had died.

... For ours is a constitution which does not imitate those of others, but rather sets them an example. Its name – because power rests not with a few but with the majority – is Democracy; in private disputes all are equal before the law, and in public life, men are honoured for conspicuous achievement in any field, and not for sectional reasons; nor is any poor man, who has it in him to do good service to the city, prevented by his obscurity. Ours is a free state, both in politics and in social life. We do not grudge our neighbour his pleasures, nor treat him to black looks, which may do no harm, but are unpleasant. We are tolerant in our private life, but at the same time we fear and obey the laws and public authorities; especially those laws that are laid down for the protection of the oppressed, and those unwritten laws whose sanction is dishonour.

We have provided ourselves with ample recreation from our work; games and sacrifices at intervals throughout the year, and the gracious fittings of our own homes, our pleasure in which removes all dreariness from the daily round. ...

(Those middle-class Attic cups and bowls – our museum-pieces.)

... and because of the greatness of our city, all the products of the world flow in to her, and we enjoy the good things of other lands as easily as our own.

We are superior to our opponents, too, in the way in which we prepare for war. Our city is open to the world; we are not continually expelling foreigners for fear they might learn or see something of a military importance; for we trust not in secret preparations but in our native valour. In education, *they* seek to inculcate manliness by a laborious training, even from childhood; we are relaxed – and yet we face the same dangers no less readily. ...

We are lovers of beauty with economy, and of intellectual life without growing soft. Wealth we consider an opportunity for service, not an occasion for boasting, and poverty no disgrace to confess, unless we are failing to do anything about it. Among us, the same people manage both private and public business, and men who are immersed in other work form an adequate judgement on political questions.

(Politics are not the preserve of a 'leisured class'.)

For we alone call the man who keeps out of all this not inoffensive but ineffective.... Also, we do not consider that debate impedes action, but rather that to go into action without previous briefing does so. We are the better men in this too, that we, who run the risks, are the same men who calculate them; whereas among others, ignorance is daring, and the calculated risk is shirked. Those men should surely be judged the bravest, who know most clearly what danger is and what pleasure is, and then do not flinch....

In a word, I say that our whole city is a liberal education to Greece, and our individual citizens excel all men in versatility, resourcefulness, brilliance and physical self-reliance; and that this is no empty boast for the occasion, but actual truth, our city's power bears witness. Athens alone when put to the test proves greater than her reputation.... We need no Homer to praise us, no poet whose lines give pleasure for the moment, but whose 'facts' are open to doubt; we have made every sea and land accessible by our daring, and left everywhere the abiding memorials of our enmity or our friendship.

Such, then, is the city for which these men, making the hero's choice, that she should not be taken from them, died in battle; and every one of us who are left ought to be ready to spend himself for her. This is why I have dwelt so long upon the city ... for all those things, for which I praised her, were the glories with which these men and men like these by their courage adorned her....

Thus, then, worthily of the city these men bore themselves; and we who are left may pray indeed for preservation, but must disdain to show a less daring spirit.... Think of the greatness of the city, actually seen day by day, till you fall in love with her; and when you think how splendid she is, remember this: that all this was won by men who faced danger and knew their duty and shunned dishonour, and, when they met defeat in any enterprise, did not think that a reason for failing in their duty, but threw in their lives as the best offering they had. They gave their lives to their country, and won for themselves a fame that shall not grow old, and the finest of sepulchres – not only that in which they lie, but in the memories of men, among whom, in every crisis that calls for speech or action, they will be remembered. For the whole earth is the sepulchre of famous men, and their memory remains, not only graven on stone in their homeland, but unwritten, in lands not theirs – the memory of their spirit, not of their fate. Emulate them now, and believing that happiness is freedom, and freedom is courage, do not shun the dangers of battle.

He ends with words of comfort for the bereaved; cool, realistic, even a little chilly, as when he says to the widows:

... if I must speak also of feminine virtue, I will sum up all briefly: great glory is yours if you do not fall short of the nature that is yours, and hers, who is least spoken of among men either for good or ill.

Strange words from Aspasia's lover; but official Athens was a man's world still.

2 THE WAR, AND THUCYDIDES

The war, which Pericles intended to be a demonstration of his negative strategy, was in its military operations a petty affair. Seaborne brigade or battalion operations, as we should call them, bulk quite large in Thucydides. The Athenian army that invaded Boiotia in 424 (p. 269) numbered 7,000 armoured men plus a horde of undisciplined light-armed; it was beaten by a Boiotian army of about the same size; and that was the greatest battle of the first or Ten Years' War. Physically, by far the greatest disaster of these ten years was a plague which, arising in upper Egypt, ravaged the Persian Empire and was brought to Piraeus by ships trading with the east. It scarcely touched the Peloponnese, which was effectively isolated by the Athenian blockade. At Athens, crowded with refugees during the Peloponnesian invasion of 430, it raged all that summer and the next year, and after a temporary slackening flared up again in 427 before finally burning itself out. No one ever knew how many died. Thucydides had figures only for the cavalry and armoured infantry classes. Of them, 4,400 infantry died, out of 26,000 of all ages from eighteen to sixty (or, as most scholars think, out of the 13,000 of the field army; Thucydides does not actually say which). The figure is swollen by the catastrophe that smote one force of 4,000, in camp before Poteidaia; it lost 1,050 men in forty days. Three hundred knights died; there had been 1,200 of active age. The death-rate among the un-registered poor was probably worse. In all, Athens may have lost up to a quarter (hardly a third, as some believe) of her population; but she showed no sign of collapse.

Pericles, illogically if not unnaturally, was blamed for every-thing; not least for the concentration of the country people in town, which gave free rein to the plague – 'the one thing,' said Pericles bitterly, 'which I did not foresee.' He was suspen-ded from office, and his accounts examined; they were in con-fusion, almost naturally in such a year, and he was fined. About the same time, both his legitimate sons died. Then there was a revulsion of feeling; he was pressed to stand for election as general again, and elected in 429; but he was a sick man. After surviving the crisis of an attack of the plague, he died, ex-hausted, that autumn. Shortly before his death, two meetings of the Assembly, with quorums of 6,000, carried and con-firmed an act to confer citizenship on his son by Aspasia.

The great statesman was irreplaceable; not because there were no talented and even incorruptible men to follow him, but, says Thucydides, because he could resist the people to their face. His successors, being more on level terms with each other, were under the continual temptation to give the assembly its head, for fear of losing in the race for popularity. The result was expenditure of blood and treasure, sometimes in divergent operations backed by sectional interests.

Thucydides, who himself survived an attack of the plague and, thus immunised, nursed many of his sick friends, gives a careful account of it, in spite of which it remains uncertain whether it was bubonic plague (the prevailing view) or some other disease, such as measles, which produced equally horrible disasters among populations with no immunity to it in the Pacific islands. Here, as always, he faithfully describes what has happened once, for the guidance of men involved in future events, 'which, in accordance with human nature, are likely to be of generally similar character'. The feature which most of all makes his work, as he proudly aspires to make it, 'a possession for all time', is not so much his austere and often fine narrative as his reflections, often set in the form of speeches put into the mouths of characters. There is some characterization in these; but the style of a deep and abstract thinker who has heard Gorgias has an awkward way of creeping in, even in those of Spartans! Through it all, Thucydides traces ruthlessly the disaster that the war was, physically (he goes straight from the high idealism of Pericles' Funeral Oration to the horror of the plague) and morally. He is interested in wishful thinking, for instance; but, especially, he chronicles the undermining of Greek standards by a 'war mentality'.

Thus, when Poteidaia, after nearly three years, was reduced by famine, the Athenian generals, to save further expense and hardship to their troops, allowed the inhabitants to evacuate it with the clothes they stood up in and a modest sum in money apiece. They came under criticism on the ground that if they had waited a little longer they could have forced surrender at discretion. An example could then have been made of the rebels. When, in 428, Mytilene revolted and was forced to surrender after a much shorter siege, through a mutiny among the populace when the government (clearly not democratic) served out armour to them for a sortie, the 'tough' party at Athens showed what they had in mind. The fierce Kleon carried a decree that the whole male population, including even the mutineers, should be put to death, and the women and children enslaved; and a ship was sent off to convey the order. But many in Athens (some of whom had not been present) were shocked, and some politicians induced the councillors in office to re-open the question, 'the more easily because it was clear that majority opinion was in favour of this'. In the 'Mytilene Debate', a famous pair of Thucydidean speeches, Kleon shows some courage in opposing the majority; he reprimands them for sentimentality and inconsistency as boldly as ever Pericles could have done, even using some Periclean phrases. 'Not for the first time, I realise how impossible it is for a democracy to govern an empire.... You must realise that your empire is a tyranny, exercised over hostile and unwilling subjects.... Consistency is more important than cleverness ... I am for consistency ... Mytilene has wronged us ... the punishment is just. Let it stand, as an example to others.' Against him, the opposition speaker does not plead for mercy as such, but on the contrary also makes a show of taking a tough and realistic line. We are not concerned, he says, with abstract justice, but with expediency. All experience shows that savage punishments are *not* an effective deterrent; Kleon's stern ethical line is old-fashioned. It is in Athens' interest to keep the goodwill of the allies, and this is not going to be done by killing those who mutinied and caused the surrender along with the guilty. If we do this, every city that revolts will hold out with desperation. So let us try those whom the general has sent to Athens as guilty, and spare the innocent.

By a narrow majority, these arguments prevailed. A second war-ship was sent off in haste; but the one carrying the sentence of death had twenty-four hours' start.

The ambassadors from Mytilene bought wine and meal for the crew, and promised them a great reward if they arrived in time; and they made such haste that the men were fed as they rowed, with meal wetted with oil and wine, and took sleep in relays, while the rest rowed on. They were lucky enough not to run into any contrary wind; and as the first ship had made no haste on its uncongenial errand, while the second pressed on in this fashion, the former arrived first by just long enough for [the general] to have read the decree and be preparing to carry out its orders, when the second came in. . . . So narrowly did Mytilene escape. But as to the men sent to Athens as chiefly responsible, the Athenians, on the motion of Kleon, put them to death. They numbered slightly over 1,000.

One thousand must have been a considerable fraction of all the free males of Mytilene.

Six years later, when Skione in Chalkidiké was starved out after revolting, there was no such revulsion of feeling. Kleon was dead by that time, but even without him the Athenians executed all males from adolescence upwards, and sold the women and children as slaves. They gave the city to the people of Plataia, which, evacuated of civilians, had been starved out and its garrison put to death by the Spartans during the plague at Athens.

Athens did that. What citizens of other cities did to each other, once the fine-drawn 'harmony of opposite tensions' of peacetime politics snapped and revolutionary struggle set in, Thucydides tells in a detailed case-study of events at Kerkyra in 426. This case, he says, 'gained more notoriety because it was the first; for later, almost the whole Greek world was disturbed, with the popular leaders everywhere wishing to call in the Athenians, and the oligarchs the Spartans'. Both sides appealed to the slaves, with promises of freedom, and most of them joined the democrats. These were victorious, and massacred their prisoners, while an Athenian fleet chased off a Peloponnesian fleet which had hoped to intervene. Thucydides appends some famous comments on the psychology and even the semantics of a revolutionary situation:

Many grim things took place in the revolutions, such as happen and will happen as long as human nature remains the same, with more or less exacerbation and varieties in details according to circumstances. In peace and prosperity, both states and individuals are more generous, because they are not under pressure; but war, which cuts down the margin of comfort in daily life, is a teacher of violence, and assimilates ordinary people's characters to their conditions.

Revolution now became endemic; ... even the former prestige of words was changed. Reckless daring was counted the courage of a good party man; prudent hesitation, cowardice in disguise; moderation, a cover for weakness, and the ability to see all sides, inability to do anything.... The bitter speaker was always trusted, and his opponent held suspect. The successful conspirator was reckoned intelligent, and he who detected a plot more brilliant still, but he who planned not to need such methods was accused of splitting the party and being afraid of the enemy. In short, credit went to the man who struck first, or who stirred up those who had no such intentions.

The tie of party took precedence over that of the family; ... and even the solidarity of parties depended not on solemn oaths but on being jointly compromised.... Most people would rather be called clever knaves (if knave is what they are) than honest fools; they are ashamed of the latter label, but proud of the former.

The cause of the whole trouble was the pursuit of power for the sake of greed and personal ambition. ... Leaders everywhere used honourable slogans – 'political equality for the masses' or 'the rule of a wise *élite*'; but the commonwealth, which they served in name, was the prize that they fought for.... And moderate men fell victims to both sides.... And the cruder intellects generally survived better; for, conscious of their deficiencies and their opponents' cleverness, and fearing that they might get the worst of it in debate and be victims of some cunning plot if they delayed, they struck boldly and at once; but the others, contemptuously sure that they would see danger in time and had no need to take by force what they could get by wit, were more often caught off their guard and destroyed.

In 425, Athens won an important success. Her general Demosthenes (not the orator) seized and fortified the headland of Pylos, at the north end of Navarino Bay. A Spartan battalion, landed on the island of Sphaktēria to aid in blockading the fort, was itself cut off by an Athenian fleet. Blockade-runners foiled the attempt to starve it out; but Kleon, after attacking the leading general, Nikias, in the assembly, for letting the operation drag on, and being invited to go and finish it himself if he thought he could, actually went to Pylos and, with Demosthenes, landed an overwhelming force on the island; and the Spartans, after losing 30 per cent of their numbers, and in a state of exhaustion, laid down their arms. Athens secured among the prisoners 120 of the dwindling class of Spartiate full citizens; and the breaking of the tradition that Spartans never surrendered was a shock to all Greece.

Sparta offered peace to recover the prisoners. Peace without concessions was all that Pericles had desired; but Kleon persuaded the assembly to demand territorial gains; and the war continued. Now that Athens held Spartiate 'peers' as hostages, there were no more devastations of Attica; and the Athenians redoubled their coastal raids. Nikias seized the island of Kythera, an important base for these; Sparta was in deep depression. But Athenian attacks on Corinth and Megara produced only indecisive successes, and their invasion of Boiotia was defeated with over 1,000 killed (Battle of Delion, 424). Meanwhile Sparta discovered a better way to hurt Athens; an enterprising general, Brasidas, with a small force largely of enfranchised helots and a few Spartans as officers, marched to the north, raised rebellion in Chalkidiké and, a formidable blow, won over Amphipolis (p. 228 f.). Counter-strokes under Nikias in 423 and Kleon in 422 won back only part of the ground lost; and at last, after both Kleon and Brasidas had fallen in one battle (an Athenian disaster) before Amphipolis, peace was made on the same terms which Athens had rejected after Pylos – less losses in the north.

But it was a worse peace for the Spartans. They got back their men, and a promise of Pylos and Kythera against a promise of Amphipolis and no reprisals against the mainland rebels in Chalkidiké. But they abandoned peninsular Skione, which was cut off and under siege (p. 267). Brasidas' successor heard the terms with dismay, and reported that he was unable to hand over Amphipolis against the will of its citizens. The Athenians then refused to hand over Pylos and Kythera. Also the treaty made no mention of Nisaia, the eastern port of Megara, or of some north-western colonial possessions of Corinth, which the Athenians had captured. To get back her men, Sparta had in short betrayed her allies and totally forgotten her high talk of 'liberation'; and as a result, her league showed every sign of dissolution. The Boiotians refused to return an Athenian border fort, which Sparta had promised over their heads, and Corinth, Megara and Boiotia refused to sign the treaty. In the Peloponnese, Elis had a frontier dispute of her own with Sparta; Sparta's thirty-year peace with Argos was about to expire, and Argos declined to renew it without reviving old border claims; and in Arcadia, Tegea and Mantineia were fighting each other.

Faced with so much discontent, Sparta, even without regaining Pylos and Kythera, actually concluded an alliance with Athens, timed to last for fifty years; while the secondary states, with their own divergent interests, intrigued kaleidoscopically in the effort to form a 'third force'. The war seemed indeed, as Pericles had hoped, to have made the world safe for Athenian imperialism.

3 THE CULTURE OF
THE LATE FIFTH CENTURY

Even in the midst of the war, we have to remind ourselves, there was seldom fighting going on in many places at a time; and though towns and populations could be destroyed in ancient warfare, chiefly by fire and famine, forces had first to get there, on foot or by rowing. Thus, right through this time, the work of classical Greece in art and writing, science and philosophy, continued; just how much diminished as a result of the war, we cannot know. At Abdēra, affected by it only through a drastic increase in Athens' tribute, it was the age of Demokritos (pp. 246 f.); and in Kōs, at the other end of the Aegean (though he also travelled widely) worked another of the greatest Greeks, the physician Hippokrates.

Hippokrates (about 460–377) became the revered 'father' of a school; and of some sixty treatises, mostly short, which survive from its archives, perhaps only about a quarter are from his own hand. But one spirit runs through them all, empirical without disdaining theory, insisting on careful observation but also on general science as a foundation for medicine, and highly ethical. A treatise on dislocations was found useful still in 1850. A case-book records, with names and addresses of the patients, the course taken by illnesses – mostly serious illnesses, recorded *because* they baffled the practitioner; most of the patients are candidly recorded to have died. A treatise entitled *On Airs, Waters and Places*, written in a terse and primitive Ionic (Hippokrates himself?), discusses the effects of climate and environment on physique and psychology; Herodotos would have enjoyed it. A discussion of *The Sacred Disease* (epilepsy, the 'possession by a devil' of the Jews) declares, stoutly rejecting current superstition:

I do not consider that the body of a man is corrupted by God, the most perishable by the most holy of things. Even if it were corrupted by something else, it would be more likely to be purified and sanctified by God.... It seems to me no more divine than other diseases; but it arises, like them, from natural causes; men think it divine because they do not understand it. . . . All diseases alike are divine, and all are human; all have their antecedent causes, and none is beyond the scope of our study.

Probably after the master's time, under influence from the works of Empedokles, the school adopted the theory of the Four Humours, phlegm, blood, yellow bile and black bile, which reflect in the body the four elements of the cosmos, fire, air, water and earth. Their proper balance in the body is the cause of health, and temperaments differ (phlegmatic, sanguine, choleric and melancholic) according to which predominates. This theory was to exercise a thoroughly deleterious influence on medicine for 2,000 years; *because* under it one could account for anything, it blocked the way to further inquiry based on observation. One would like to know whether Hippokrates himself would have seen the danger.

But the most famous document from the Hippokratic collection is the famous Oath, taken on adoption into the 'family' of the school, and in use to this day:

I swear by Apollo the Physician and Asklēpios and Health and Panakeia ['panacea' or 'All-Heal'] calling all gods and goddesses to witness, that I will keep this oath and this [written] bond to the best of my power and judgement:

I will reckon him who shall have taught me this art as dear as my parents. I will share with him my substance . . . if he be in need; I will regard his sons as my brothers, and will teach them this art if they wish, without fee or conditions . . . by example, by lecture and by all other methods.

. . . I will adopt the regimen which in my best judgement is beneficial to my patients, and not for their injury or for any wrongful purpose. I will not give poison to anyone, though I be asked . . . nor will I procure abortion. . . .

Whatever house I enter, I will enter for the benefit of the sick, and will abstain from all wrong-doing, especially from seduction either of male or female, slave or free. Whatever I see or hear, in the exercise of my profession or otherwise, which ought not to be spoken of outside, I will keep secret religiously. And so long as I keep this oath inviolate, may it be mine to enjoy life and the practice of this art, with good repute among all men at all times; but if I break it, may the opposite befall me.

At Athens, the typical poet of this age is Aristotle's 'most tragic' of tragedians, Euripides. Only fifteen years younger than Sophocles, who was still working – he lived ninety years to Euripides' seventy-five, and was active to the end – Euripides belongs intellectually to another generation. No doubt the difference between them is largely personal; but it is worth while also to remember the different circumstances in which they grew up. For Sophocles it was the terror and triumph of the great Persian War; at fifteen, his unbroken voice was the voice of victorious Athens. When Euripides was fifteen, Kimon was sailing against Thasos; then came the breach with Sparta, Ephialtes' exposures of corruption in high places, the fall of the Areopagus. The unity of Greece and of Athens broke down over his adolescent head.

Thoughtful, interested in the philosophy of Anaxagoras, Euripides remained a rather *un*typical Athenian. He took no prominent part in public life; probably his family were poorer than that of Sophocles; it was a popular joke in comedies that his mother had sold vegetables (from her husband's holding?) in the market – a good example of the snobbery of literary Athens. But he could afford to live, across the water in Salamis, largely in a cave fitted up as a study, with a collection of books, and to devote himself to tragedy. In youth he was a good enough athlete to aspire, it is said, on the strength of a prophecy given to his father, to Olympic honours; but he soon gave that up. At twenty-five he had a group of plays accepted for public competition, and he received this honour over twenty times; but only four times, with a fifth after his death, did he win the first prize.

This is not really surprising. 'Everyone' was interested in Euripides' plays, the cleverness of his dialogue and the exquisite beauty of his choral lyrics. But he tended and he probably *in*tended to leave his audience uneasy and dissatisfied. For instance: legend told that Ion, ancestor of the Ionian race and son of Apollo, had also a 'human father', Xouthos. In Euripides' *Ion*, the traditional union of a god and a mortal is described very frankly by the girl concerned – Kreousa (meaning simply 'Princess') of Athens, now fifteen years older – as a rape: 'I was forced into a miserable union with Apollo' – in a cave under the 'Long Rocks' on the north side of the Acropolis. Afraid of her father's wrath, she brought forth the baby in that same cave, and left it there; and it disappeared. She supposed the dogs had got it; but there was no blood. Later she married the soldier Xouthos; but they remained long childless. In the play they have come to Delphoi, where the scene is set, to inquire if there is anything they can do about it. Now there is at Delphoi a happy young acolyte (he comes out singing, to sweep the temple steps at dawn) who had been a foundling, left on those same steps by unknown hands about the same number of years ago. Hermes, the brother of Apollo, explains in a prologue that this boy, now growing up, is Apollo's and Kreousa's son, brought there by Hermes himself at Apollo's request. Apollo in his divine providence will now provide for his own. Xouthos wants a son. The oracle will tell him that the boy *is* his son. (It is, on Hermes' own showing, untrue; but the soldier of fortune when told has no difficulty in accepting it. He can even remember a time at Delphoi, when it might have been; a Dionysiac *fiesta* ... there were a lot of wild girls, and he was drunk; he was young then; always faithful since his marriage.) This will get the boy to Athens; and Kreousa will be told the truth later. Thus, says Hermes blandly, 'Apollo's affair will be kept dark, and the boy will get his due.' Unfortunately this divine plot totally miscarries. Kreousa, hearing that this boy, to whom she had been attracted, is her husband's bastard, and that she is expected to take him home as future King of Athens – for she has no brothers – tries to poison him. She is detected, and runs for sanctuary, pursued by Ion and a mob. The worst is only averted when the Delphic prophetess produces the trinkets which had been left with the foundling, which Kreousa recognizes as hers; and then Athena (for Apollo does not apparently venture to confront the mortals whom he had deceived) appears to clear up the situation and claim, as blandly as Hermes, that 'Apollo has done all things well'. The mortals are silenced; but there is no restitution to Kreousa for the empty years. Ion, who in his earlier innocence had refused to believe that Apollo would do anything wicked, has previously expressed himself forcibly.

This kind of thing, then, was repeatedly 'given a chorus' by the archon who selected plays for the festivals; but when it came to awarding the first prize, the judges usually opted for something less disturbing. Often Sophocles was the victor. In 431, both Sophocles and Euripides, with his famous *Medeia* among other plays, were beaten by Euphorion, son of Aeschylus. In *Medeia*, Jason has brought back with him this eastern princess, without whose help he would never have won the Golden Fleece, has had children by her, and then had to flee from home when Medeia compassed the death of his wicked uncle. Now he has settled at Corinth, and is about to restore his fortunes by marrying the brotherless daughter of the king. The king requires that Medeia be sent away. Jason tries to make her 'see reason'; but Medeia, one of the greatest in Euripides' gallery of wronged and highly articulate women, pretends to be reconciled only in order to murder the 'Kreousa' of Corinth and her own children by Jason, before escaping in a chariot drawn by winged dragons. Here again, the supernatural appears at the end, after a plot developed on an entirely human level, with the characters arguing like intelligent Athenians.

Euripides' women were awful, it was widely felt; people said that his own two marriages must have been awful too. His characters, like Ion, queried the ways of the gods; Aristophanes says that he has taught men to disbelieve in them. Euripides himself, in Hades, in Aristophanes' *Frogs* (405, when Euripides and Sophocles had both recently died) says 'I worship other gods' – philosophers' gods – and this was probably the truth; like Socrates and other thinking men, he could not stomach some of the mythology. He could have said that he was not committed to everything his characters said; but some of what they said was horribly forcible; for instance, in lines quoted from his lost *Bellerophon*:

> Does someone say that there are gods in heaven?
> There are not, there are not – unless one choose
> to follow old tradition like a fool.

Look for yourselves – do not accept my words –
but here is what I say: Tyrants kill men
and rob them of their goods, and break their oaths,
and lay whole cities waste; and still they prosper,
more than the pious and the gentle do.
And I know little cities, honouring gods,
subject to greater ones, not so devout,
held down by their superior force of arms.

No, this was not the sort of thing for the first prize. But men always heard Euripides, and even bought books of the words and read them; and Aristophanes, who laughs at him and parodies him, shows by the parodies themselves that both he and his audience had an astonishing knowledge of these strange, fascinating, possibly dangerous new plays.

Euripides' 'blank verse' is flatter than Sophocles', more prosaic, closer to common speech. His tragedy was more realistic; when he dealt with the plight of the captive women of Troy, the exile or the refugee, he did not content himself with splendid and hieratic gloom; he brought in touches of squalor. His splendid collection of stage rags became another Aristophanic joke. When he produced, in 415, his dreadful and splendid, almost static and almost plotless *Trojan Women* – awaiting disposal after the fall of their city – Athens had just 'liquidated' Melos, the Dorian island that would not join her league; Thucydides gives an account of power politics in negotiation, brushing aside Melian pleas to remain neutral. Failing unconditional surrender, the Athenians besieged the town, took it after long and brave resistance, put all the men to death and enslaved the women. Euripides had produced patriotic plays on occasion, on legends that showed Athens as protector of the oppressed. But as he grew old, he probably became more alienated. At seventy, he accepted from King Archelaos of Macedonia an invitation to his court; and there he wrote his last play, the *Bakchai*, a lyrical study of Dionysiac religion, which won the first prize at Athens after his death.

All the nineteen plays of Euripides that we have belong to his middle age or later. The young poet who flashes upon the scene early in the war is – it is perhaps *not* very surprising – not a radical, but a whole-hearted tory: Aristophanes, the great laugher, who cheered Athens in dark hours. We may regret that we have not also, except in quotations, some of the work of his predecessors, who laughed in the days of Pericles, not sparing the great man. But the scholars and scribes who preserved twelve plays of Aristophanes deserve our gratitude.

Mockery and iambic satire 'for luck', with a strong element of obscenity, had always been a feature of the agrarian rituals. On this basis, when tragedy diverged and became serious, comedy became the licensed vehicle for satire on all and sundry; naturally it concentrated on the conspicuous and the great. Hence the political comedies. Efforts to keep it within bounds by legislation, as by forbidding the naming of living people, seem to have been made, and to have remained a dead letter. Also, the new invites satire, not the old and familiar. It all suited young Aristophanes (born about 445) and he attacks the demagogues, intellectuals, the old men on the juries (who were no intellectuals), town-planners, calendar-reformers, modern music, generals who enjoyed the war and the fat man who threw away his shield at Delion, all with fine impartiality. How far it was taken seriously, it is impossible to say; sometimes, no doubt, more seriously than at others. Kleon once 'haled him before the Council', which could have been a prelude to prosecution; Aristophanes says that he was shouted at within an inch of his life; but as he was still under twenty, the great boss probably only thought to frighten him. The offence alleged was making the government ridiculous before foreign visitors at the Dionysia; Aristophanes returned to the charge at the next *winter* dramatic festival, remarking through one of his characters 'Now we are by ourselves'.

His choruses were got up with an extravagance already traditional. His *Knights*, the natural enemies of Kleon, were probably mounted pick-a-back on human steeds with horse heads and tails; a vase-painting shows such a chorus, long before his time. His jurymen, the *Wasps*, carried large skewers for stings. His *Clouds*, nymphs representing the 'new gods' of the philosophers, were perhaps not funny enough, and the play got only a third prize; but it is famous today, for in it he attacked Socrates. It is the earliest mention of Socrates that we have, for Plato and Xenophon were then (423) small children. Whether there was, even then, any serious ground for depicting Socrates as keeping a 'thinking-shop' where his disciples engage in scientific disputations is open to doubt; Plato and Xenophon insist that he never taught for pay, and was interested in ethical, not physical questions. He may have been interested in science earlier; but strict verisimilitude was not an object in comedy. Kleon, who had opposed peace on honourable terms, is accused in *The Knights* of intriguing with the enemy!

In *The Clouds*, old Strepsiades ('Twister'), caught in the toils of war-time rising prices, with an extravagant wife and son (he had married above his class), after toying with the idea of getting a witch to interfere with the moon and postpone quarter-day, decides to resort to the clever man who can 'make the worse cause appear the better'. Socrates finds him too stiff in his intellectual joints, so his son takes his place; and in one scene the Just Cause and Unjust Cause are personified, competing for the young man's soul. (The word translated 'cause' is *Logos*: Word, discourse or reason.) The Just Cause, who speaks first, represents the education of the Good Old Days, when boys were seen and not heard, and all went to the village school, even if it was snowing; singing the old songs (and no damned modern variations or jazz rhythms, or you would be skelped); respect for parents and old folk generally; lots of healthy athletics; and of course no boy *ever* goggled at girls. That was before the days when children began to wear grown-up clothes and to be so keen on speeches and arguing and hanging about in those immoral places, the bath establishments. Keep out of all that, and you will have a healthy body and keep out of a lot of trouble.

The Cloud-goddesses are impressed; but not so the Unjust Cause, who, after some debating points – Herakles was partial to hot baths; old Nestor was an orator – proceeds in democratic style to ask, what sort of people are the politicians?

Oh, queer! The tragedians? Queer! The audience? Well, I know *him* – and *him* – and *him* – Oh, I give it up! And the Just Cause himself jumps off the stage to join the Majority.

But old Strepsiades regrets that he got mixed up in all this when his son proceeds to beat him up according to 'natural law'; and the end of the play is that he sets fire to the Thinking-Shop and burns it to the ground.

Plato represents Socrates and Agathon, a young poet whom Aristophanes also parodied, as sitting happily with Aristophanes at a dinner-party; but he also represents Socrates, on trial, as blaming the comic poets in part for his undeserved bad reputation.

CHAPTER 13

ALKIBIADES AND THE FALL
OF ATHENS

1 SOCRATES AND ALKIBIADES

SOCRATES was at the height of his popularity, chiefly with young men; his unpopularity with old-fashioned people, including a good many parents, was growing. He is said to have told the story, long after, when he was brought to trial for corrupting the young – shaking their faith, we might say – that his lean and enthusiastic disciple Chairephon actually went to Delphoi and asked the god, Is any man wiser than Socrates? And the oracle, which often gave the answers people 'fished for', answered 'No'.

Perhaps Chairephon was trying to induce Socrates to give, clearly and dogmatically, the 'right answers' to all the deep questions which people asked him. Chairephon was sure he knew, if anyone did; but Socrates, like many a good teacher, was apt to parry a question with another question, beginning 'Now just what do you mean by ... ' (justice, for example). Socrates' reaction to the oracle was to say, in complete sincerity, 'But I know *nothing*.' Then, he says, he embarked on a mission in all humility to 'refute the God' by producing somebody who really was wiser. He went to the leading men of the city first, but he was disappointed; for he found, when he questioned them, that they could not give any clear account of what the final end of all their activity was. So he tried the poets, the composers of great choral hymns, or tragedies; but they were no better. 'They worked by inspiration, like prophets'; but they could not give a rational account of the meaning of their fine words. Then he tried artisans, and they were better; they had a real knowledge – 'know-*how*'; but the trouble with them was that, being master-craftsmen, they thought they knew about everything. So in the end, he had to agree with the oracle that, since he knew at least his own ignorance, 'it was better to be as I am'.

Perhaps too, he thought, the God meant him, like a gadfly, to sting the citizens out of their self-satisfied slumbers; an unpopular duty, but it must be done.

Socrates' favourite question was 'What do you mean by ... ' or, more directly, 'What *is* ... ' justice, or courage, or self-discipline. You claim to be acting in accordance with this virtue, so clearly you must know what it is. His victims, in Plato, usually begin with a concrete example. Socrates explains that he wants a definition. Then comes an answer (sometimes backed with a quotation from a poet), in the form 'Justice is when ... '. Then real definitions are proposed; but they always break down; there always seem to be exceptions; and in dialogue after dialogue we end in acknowledged ignorance. Socrates remains convinced that each cardinal virtue must really exist or, as he says, 'be something', though we see only particular virtuous actions. To Plato, Socrates' insistence on definition plus the Pythagorean emphasis on the timeless and general character of mathematical truths made up the basis of his idealistic synthesis, in which the *form* of each virtue, as also of truth, of beauty, and for that matter of Man or Horse or statesman or other species or classes, more permanent than the individuals, exists in the presence of God; the *idea*, a Greek word which, like the equivalent Latin word *species*, originally meant the visible form. It may seem obvious to us that Socrates' conviction that to each concept there must correspond a 'something', a concrete universal, is due to a naïve view of language; but his insistence on definition and precision was a service to thought, especially in his time, when the rhetoricians were teaching the dexterous use of emotionally toned words. His desire to reach definitions of the virtues, so as to 'know what they are', had a practical aim; for in his opinion, no one who really knew what the good is in any situation could voluntarily do other. 'Virtue is knowledge.' A man of iron self-control himself, he was unfamiliar with the Pauline predicament, 'The evil that I would not, that I do.'

281

It is interesting to note in passing that in Socrates' own time philosophers of the 'School of Names' in China were conducting rather similar studies within the Confucian tradition.

Socrates, as we have mentioned, professed to be in love with Alkibiades, now grown up and entering politics, as well as susceptible to the charms of any handsome youth, especially if he had also 'a beautiful soul' (*psyche*). The right relation of an older to a beloved younger friend was, he said, that of a teacher of all virtue. He tried to deflate the vanity of Alkibiades, fostered by the attentions of a horde of other admirers; Alkibiades was impressed, and as a young soldier had the good taste to choose Socrates for mess-mate, against keen competition, in the campaign before Poteidaia. But in the end the world won. Athens was full of tales of his outrageous insolence; but those who did not actually suffer from it rather liked them. Brilliant as well as handsome and physically intrepid, he seemed able to get away with anything.

Alkibiades wanted glory to feed his vanity. He also needed money, such as easily came the way of a successful general. He was rich by inheritance, but his extravagance would have strained any fortune. He set out to aggrandize himself, and the morality of the means was no object. An aristocrat, he heartily despised the people, though naturally he flattered them in public. His natural party would have been the conservatives; but they mistrusted him. Many respectable people disapproved of his morals. Moreover, the leadership of the gentry and to some extent of the whole city was held by Nikias, religious and 'safe', who imitated Pericles in devotion to duty and meticulous carefulness in any military enterprise. The people trusted him, though they rather enjoyed seeing him baited by demagogues in the assembly. He had won several moderately important successes during the war; and unlike Athens' more adventurous generals, he had never yet met with a defeat.

Alkibiades therefore posed as an extreme democrat. Again, in foreign affairs the 'natural' policy for him might have seemed to be one of better relations with Sparta. His family had old Spartan connexions; even his name had been adopted from Sparta, for his great-great-grandfather. Alkibiades had had a Laconian nurse (a tradition with some Athenian families, like Scotch nannies in modern times); his grandfather had been Sparta's 'official friend' or *proxenos*, but had resigned after some unfortunate incident; Alkibiades had hoped to renew the connexion, and had looked after the interests of the Spartan prisoners of war. But the Spartans preferred to deal with the more staid and senior Nikias. Insulted and seeing no hope of prestige that way, Alkibiades turned against them.

Sparta's treaty with Argos had expired in 421, and war between them was imminent. In 420, both sent ambassadors to Athens. Alkibiades advised the Spartan ambassadors to withdraw a statement which they had made to the Council, saying that they were empowered to deal on the spot with all points of difference, lest they should find themselves under severe pressure; and then, in the Assembly, he publicly attacked them as insincere and unreliable people who could not even stick to the same story. This piece of treachery was completely successful. The Spartans and Nikias were discredited. Athens made alliance with Argos and the Peloponnesian malcontents; and Alkibiades, probably as soon as ever he reached the legal age of thirty, was elected a general for 419. He was a bad general in his young days, thinking that diplomacy and his personal charm, which never failed him at home, could win victories on the cheap. He was not re-elected for 418 (not that this indicated any grave dissatisfaction with him), and thus, perhaps unfortunately for Athens, missed the pitched battle of Mantineia, in which the Spartans routed the Argives and their allies, and 200 out of 1,300 Athenians present were killed, including two good fighting generals.

Alkibiades continued to encourage Argos to resist, and to take credit for having given Sparta a fright. He bought himself a concubine out of the spoils of Melos in 416. He was general again in 415, and in favour of a plan to intervene with larger forces than before in support of Athens' allies in Sicily.

This is the context of a famous work of what we may call historical fiction: Plato's *Symposium* or *The Dinner-Party*. The composition of an author who was only born in 428, it gives, nevertheless, our most vivid picture of the society of imperial Athens in her Indian summer, and of the relations of the two men whose names are indissolubly linked with the disintegration of that society. All the people named in it are historical, and the biographical facts will have been known to Plato from conversation with older men. He makes, indeed, a great point of quoting his (oral) sources for the story; but how far that is to be taken seriously, it is hard to say.

Aristodēmos, a devoted admirer of Socrates, met Socrates 'washed, and wearing evening slippers', whereas he usually went barefoot, and asked him where he was going, all dolled up? Socrates said, 'To dinner at Agathon's.... That is why I have made myself beautiful, to match my host.' The young poet was celebrating the triumph of his life, having won the first prize for tragedy. 'What about coming too, uninvited?' added Socrates. Relations were evidently easy enough to make this possible. Before they had got there, however, Socrates fell into a train of thought; and since for him, if a train of thought coincided with dinner-time, it was the dinner that suffered – a matter on which his wife held strong views – he turned aside off the road and sent Aristodemos on alone. Agathon greeted him with, 'Oh, Aristodemos, you have come just at the right time! We are going to have dinner. I looked for you yesterday to invite you, but could not find you.'

Aristodemos however confesses all and, knowing Socrates' habits, begs Agathon not to disturb him. Dinner proceeds, Socrates arriving, quite unabashed, half-way through. After eating they decide to take their drink gently, especially since several had drunk deep the evening before, when the result was declared; so they dismiss the flute-girl 'to go and play to the women in their apartments if she likes,' and, by way of entertainment, decide each in turn to make an oration in Praise of Love.

The speeches are a brilliant example of Plato's dramatic power. He is said indeed to have written tragedies in his youth; but the possibilities of originality in that art-form were getting worked out. The first speech is sentimental; a mere foil for the better ones which follow. Eryximachos, a leading physician, deals – in suitably light vein – with love's psychosomatic aspects. Aristophanes is Aristophanic; he makes up a myth, to the effect that in the Beginning mankind had eyes in the back of its head, and four arms and four legs apiece, and when they wanted to go very fast, they rolled along on all eight; and they were very strong and very bold, and they thought of storming heaven, and the gods feared that they might succeed. So, rather than destroy them with his thunderbolt, thereby cutting off the source of sacrifices, Zeus split them in half, like flat fish; and since then, men have spent much time and energy in seeking each his other half, and when it is found, they are inseparable. Agathon's speech is a wonderful (and really beautiful) exercise in the New Rhetoric, all antithesis and assonance, causing Socrates, whose turn is next, to protest that he has been turned to stone with the display of the authentic Gorgias' head. But after some Socratic affectation that he has nothing to say, he tells what he professes to have heard from a wise woman, Diotima of Mantineia: of how love is a school of virtue and true wisdom, leading us on from the love of one beautiful body to that of all beautiful bodies; and then to the beauty of the soul, beside which he will come to think the beauty of the body of small account; and then to that of laws and institutions, which train the soul; and thence to the sciences and to contemplation of 'the open sea of beauty' in philosophy, and to the knowledge of the Beautiful itself.

And then at the end of the path of love, he will suddenly see a marvellous beauty, the end to which all his earlier toils were means; which is for ever, and neither comes into being nor passes away.

He ends:

[Diotima said], If it befell a man to see the Beautiful itself, unalloyed and pure and unmixed, not bound up with human flesh and colour and all the nonsense of mortality, but if he had power to see the one divine beauty – what then? Do you think that ... he would bring forth and nurture true virtue, and having done so, become the friend of God, and if any man may become immortal, such would he be?

But just then,

There was a loud knocking on the street door, as though from a band of revellers, and the sound of a flute playing. Agathon said to the servants, 'Boys, go and see what that is; and if it is any of our special friends, ask them in; but if not, tell them that we are not drinking, and are just going to bed.'

Not long after, they heard the voice of Alkibiades in the court-yard, very drunk, and shouting 'Where is Agathon? Take me to Agathon.' So they brought him in, leaning on the flute-girl and others of his company; and he stood in the doorway, garlanded, with a thick wreath of ivy and violets and a lot of ribbons on his head, and said 'Good evening, men! Will you accept a very drunk man to join your party? Or shall we go away, when we have garlanded Agathon, which is what we came for? I could not get round yesterday, but now I have come, with these ribbons on my head, so that from my own head I may garland the cleverest and prettiest head – are you laughing at me as a drunk? Even if I am drunk, I know it's true. Well, tell me, shall I come in on these conditions to drink with you, or not?'

Everyone shouted and said 'Come on'; and Agathon invited him. So he came in, supported by his people, and started pulling off the ribbons to garland Agathon, and with them in front of his face did not see Socrates, but sat down on the dinner-couch between him and Socrates, who moved up to make room for him. Then he kissed Agathon and garlanded him. Agathon said 'Boys, take off Alkibiades' shoes, so that he may have three with us.'

'Yes, do,' said Alkibiades; 'but who is the third here?' And with that he turned round and saw Socrates; and he jumped up, and said, 'Oh, my God, what's this object? Socrates! Lying in ambush for me, and turning up where I least expected you, as usual! What are you doing here? And why are you on this couch, instead of with Aristophanes or some other humorist, having worked things so as to be the next to the best-looking lad in the room?'

Socrates said 'Agathon, defend me.... I am in danger from his jealousy.... Or else make peace between us!'

'There's no truce between you and me,' said Alkibiades; 'but I'll pay you out later. But now, Agathon, let me have some of those ribbons, so that I may garland that amazing head, too, so that he may not complain that I garlanded you and not him, when he beats the whole world, and not only yesterday like you, but all the time.' Then he took some of the ribbons, and garlanded Socrates, and lay down on the couch.

Then he said, 'Now, friends! I believe you're sober. We can't have that; you must drink; that was our agreement. I appoint, as master of the feast, until you have drunk sufficiently – myself. Agathon, kindly send for a *large* cup if there is one – but, no, don't bother. Boy, bring me that cooler' (it was one that would hold over half a gallon). He had it filled up, took a drink himself, and then told them to fill it again for Socrates, adding 'Not that my clever trick will make any impression on him. He can drink as much as anyone asks him to, without ever being drunk at all.'

Someone then tells Alkibiades the game they have been playing, and points out that as he is sitting on the right of Socrates (Greek 'turns' and drinks passed anti-clockwise), it is his turn to speak next. Alkibiades argues that it is not fair, he is drunk and they are sober; also, if he praises anyone else, god or man, in Socrates' presence, Socrates will be jealous and beat him up. ('Will you shut up?' says Socrates. 'No, I won't,' says Alkibiades.) He gets his way, and what follows is Plato's most detailed character sketch of the philosopher:

Well, gentlemen, I will praise Socrates in a simile. He may think I am doing it to make him ridiculous, but I am not doing it for that, but for the sake of the truth. I say that what he is most like is those figures of satyrs that you see in the sculptor's shops, holding pipes or flutes; and they open in the middle, and reveal images of gods within.... You yourself, wouldn't deny, Socrates, that you are like a satyr to look at.

Socrates, he goes on, is like the satyr Marsyas who bewitched men with his flute; but Socrates can bewitch without any instrument.

If you wouldn't think me hopelessly drunk, I would tell you on oath what his words have done to me, and still do – and I see the same happening to other people. When I hear him, my heart turns over, more than if I were in a religious frenzy, and tears pour from my eyes; and I have heard Pericles and plenty of other good orators, but they never did anything to me like this. They never upset me and made me angry with myself, feeling that I am in the condition of a mere slave; but this Marsyas here has many a time reduced me to thinking that life is not worth living, the way I live.... He forces me to admit that there are many things crying out for attention in my own life, while I neglect them and engage in politics. . . . A sense of shame is something that no one would think I had in me; but *he* makes me ashamed; no one else does. I know I cannot deny that I ought to do as he says; but when I get away from him, I cannot resist popularity and applause. So I run away from him like a slave from his master, and when I see him I am ashamed of what I cannot deny. Many a time I would gladly have seen him dead; but if he did die, I know I should be much more sorry; and so I simply do not know what to do about the man.

Warming to his task, he goes on to describe how in youth he had so far mistaken Socrates' motives as to try to seduce him. This had been a total failure.

. . . Well, all that was a long time ago. After that, there was the campaign at Poteidaia, where we served and were mess-mates. First of all, in endurance he surpassed not only me but everyone – if we were cut off from supplies, as is always liable to happen on a campaign, and had to go hungry, for putting up with that, there was simply no one else in it; and when, for a change, we had it good, he was the only man who seemed to enjoy it to the full – and among other things, though he did not drink for choice, if he was pressed, he could beat all; and most remarkable of all, no one has ever to this day seen Socrates under the influence of liquor. (I think we shall see the proof of this before long.)

Then, as to enduring cold – the winters out there are frightful – he was amazing. Once we had a most appalling cold spell, and nobody went outside at all if he could help it; or if they did, they wrapped themselves up in a fantastic way and wore boots and wrapped up their feet in felts and fleeces; but *he* used to go out just in a cloak, as usual; and he walked barefoot on the ice, and got along better than the others in their foot-gear. The men began to give him nasty looks, thinking he was despising them.

And there was another thing that happened on that campaign. 'This too the enduring hero did and bore'*: One day about dawn a thought struck him, and he stood still, thinking about it; and when he made no progress, he did not give it up; he went on standing and searching. Midday came, and people began to notice, and said to each other 'Socrates has been standing there thinking since early morning!' In the end some of the Ionians, in the evening after dinner (it was summer now), brought their pallias-

*Homer, on Odysseus.

ses out, to sleep in the fresh air, and incidentally to watch Socrates and see if he would stand all night too; and he did, until dawn came again and the sun rose; and then he said a prayer to the sun-god and went his way.

And if you want to hear about the battles – well, I must give him his due! In the battle, for which the generals gave me a decoration, it was this man and no one else who saved my life. I was wounded, and he would not leave me and stuck it out and saved both my shield and me. And I told the generals at the time, Socrates, that they ought to give you the decoration - you won't deny it - but they, with an eye to my family connections, wanted to give it to me; and you were keener than the generals themselves that I should have it instead of you.

And oh, men, you should have seen Socrates in the rout at Delion. I was there in the cavalry, and he in the infantry. Well, he was retiring, after the line was broken, along with Laches.* I happened to pass, and told them to take heart, and that I would not leave them. I had a better view of Socrates there than at Poteidaia, having less fear for myself, because I was mounted. He was far cooler than Laches; and I thought of that line of yours, Aristophanes - there he was, marching along just as he does in Athens, 'stalking along like a pelican, gazing all round', casting his eye over friend and foe with impartial serenity, and making it quite clear even from a long way off that if anyone tackled that man he would meet with a very tough resistance. As a result, both he and his companion came off unmolested. That is what happens to a man like that; enemies don't meddle with him; they go after those who are in full flight.

But after a little more backchat, the party is interrupted:

Someone going outside had left the door open, and a passing band of revellers, finding it so, marched straight ahead into the dining-room and sat down. Then there was chaos, and everyone was compelled to drink deep.

Some guests withdrew. Aristodemos, the narrator, put his head down on his couch and had a good, long sleep. When he woke up, it was grey dawn and the cocks were crowing. He looked round,

---

*Laches was a general; he and Nikias both figure in Plato's *Laches, or on Courage*. He was killed at Mantineia.

and saw that everyone was either asleep or gone, except Agathon and Aristophanes and Socrates. They alone were still awake, and were drinking out of a large cup, which they handed round and round; and Socrates was arguing. Aristodemos said he could not remember all of it, being sleepy and having missed the beginning; but the main drift of it was that Socrates was compelling them to admit that it was of the nature of the same man to be able to compose tragedy and comedy, and that the skilled tragic poet could be a comic poet too. But while they were being compelled to accept this – not following the argument very well – they began to nod; and first Aristophanes went to sleep, and then, when day was just breaking, Agathon. Socrates, having put them to sleep, then got up and left, Aristodemos, as usual, following him. Socrates went to the Lykeion ['Lyceum'; one of the sports clubs], where he had a shower, and then spent the rest of the day in his usual manner, and went home in the evening.

2 PARTY POLITICS
AND MILITARY DISASTER

Nikias, like most generals famous in history for great disasters, was a sufficiently imposing figure in his time. He was reckoned 'lucky', which meant more than it does to us. The Hebrew equivalent of it would be 'the Lord was with him'. If the gods favoured him, it was no more than he deserved for being so devout. He was not only very rich (he was said to own 1,000 slaves, which he hired out to entrepreneurs in the silver-mines); he was also the model of an Athenian officer and gentleman. If, as Plutarch says, he carried a shield splendid with gold and crimson, it means that he had some feeling for the glamour of war. He was also physically brave. In moral courage, he showed some deficiency.

His chief rival now was Alkibiades; but when, about 417, the demagogue Hyperbolos proposed an *ostrakismós*, probably in the hope of getting rid of that dangerous young man, who outshone Hyperbolos as a radical leader, Nikias shrank from the danger that he himself might be the victim. In the end he and Alkibiades got together and swung all the votes that they could influence against Hyperbolos himself. Amid loud laughter from the gentry, Hyperbolos 'the lamp-seller', a low bourgeois type, was exiled. It was an ostracism to end all ostracisms. 'Potsherds were not invented for the likes of him,' said a comic poet; and *ostrakismós* was never employed again.

Then, at the end of 416, ambassadors again came from Sicily, this time from Hellenized but non-Greek Segesta, to beg help against Dorian Selinous. Nearer home, Melos had just fallen. Thucydides writes in consecutive sentences:

They put to death all Melians of military age whom they captured, and sold the women and children as slaves. Later they sent 500 colonists and occupied the place themselves.

And in the same winter, the Athenians determined to sail against Sicily again with a larger fleet ... and attempt its conquest, most of them having no idea of the size of the island and of its population, and of the fact that they were embarking on a war not much less serious than that with the Peloponnesians.

There was great enthusiasm, encouraged by Alkibiades and all who hoped for glory and wealth from war. It was voted to send sixty ships under Nikias, Alkibiades and Lamachos, a great soldier. Nikias, who knew the potential strength of the western cities, urged that Athens should avoid adventures and continue reconstruction; but, if they must send the expedition, he added, sixty ships were too few. Pressed to name his own figure, he proposed 100 from Athens, plus allies, and a large land force of all arms. His hope to deter the people by the thought of so much expense was a faint one, and was disappointed. The generals were promptly authorised to ask for everything they judged necessary; and in spring a magnificent armament, carrying over 5,000 Athenian and allied armoured men and nearly 1,300 archers and slingers, was ready to sail. In addition to coercing Selinous, it was to compel Syracuse, if possible, to restore Leontinoi.

And then a scandal broke. 'In one night, nearly all the Hermai in Athens' (square pillars, carrying busts of Hermes, the traders' god) 'which stood throughout the city, in the porches of houses and in sanctuaries, had their faces mutilated.' There was panic, lest this sacrilege might bring divine wrath upon the city, and public opinion jumped to the conclusion that it was part of a plot against the democracy by impious elements. Highly unconvincing as it appears to us, that political conspirators would start operations by advertising their presence and outraging public opinion, this was what a religious and superstitious population easily suspected.

Who really did it was never known; the conclusion finally more or less accepted at Athens was that it was a piece of drunken hooliganism by irreligious young men. But the people who exploited it were the enemies of Alkibiades. His name, as of one who notoriously revered neither gods nor men, was the first to be thought of, and when informers came forward, attracted by the public offer of rewards and an amnesty, they named him too – not specifically in connexion with the Hermai, but with earlier acts of sacrilege, including a parody of the Eleusinian Mysteries at a drunken party; as it were a Black Mass. Alkibiades, presumably entirely innocent of the latest outrage – he would hardly have courted ruin in this way when his highest ambitions seemed within reach – demanded an immediate trial; but his enemies preferred to pursue the investigation without the presence of the army, in which he was popular. They urged that the expedition must not be held up; and Alkibiades was ordered to sail with it.

Arrived in Sicily, Alkibiades proposed to start with a diplomatic campaign in search of allies; a political strategy, typical of him at this period. Lamachos would rather have struck straight at Syracuse, the head of the Dorian forces in the island; Nikias would rather have merely coerced Selinous, and then, unless some special opportunity arose of employing the force for Athens' advantage, have taken it home again. Lamachos, who, not being a rich man and leading politician (says Plutarch), carried less weight, finally gave his support to Alkibiades, and they outvoted Nikias. As a result, the armada wasted the summer to next to no purpose. Even the non-Dorian cities, alarmed at the size of the Athenian force, preferred neutrality; and meanwhile Alkibiades was recalled to answer charges concerning, more particularly, the profanation of the Mysteries. He was not under close arrest; and after starting for home, he gave his escort the slip in south Italy, and made his way to Sparta. He was found guilty in absence, and condemned to death.

In the next spring Nikias, having exhausted all excuses for delay and not daring to go home and report a fiasco, at last moved on Syracuse, which was now better prepared and much less frightened than a year earlier. Even so, with about 8,000 soldiers, including a few local allies, and 25,000 sailors who could be used as labourers, he secured the high ground inland of the city, drove the Syracusans within their walls, and began the construction of a double wall from sea to sea, with a view to a blockade. The Syracusans were at first no match for the war-hardened troops of Athens; but they defended themselves with courage and resource. In this Dorian democracy, Thucydides comments, the Athenians found antagonists all too like themselves. And meanwhile at Sparta, Alkibiades had made men's flesh creep with an account of Athens' dream of conquering and uniting the west. He advised the Spartans to renew the war in Greece; to encourage volunteers to go to the help of Syracuse, and especially to send a Spartan officer to take command. The Spartans were impressed, and chose Gylippos, an officer with western connexions; he was the son of the general who had fled into exile after being bribed by Pericles (p. 224), and who had thereafter won renown among the Greeks of Italy. Gylippos after an adventurous journey with a small force reached western Sicily, refusing to be deterred by rumours that Syracuse was already completely walled in, and, gathering reinforcements locally, marched in and joined hands with the defenders; Nikias, alone in command, for Lamachos had been killed in action, did not venture to engage Gylippos as well as keeping up the siege. Other contingents crossed by various routes to join the 'international brigade'; Nikias, now heavily outnumbered, lost control of the high ground, and the Athenians in their base-camp by the Great Harbour, south of the town, were less besiegers than besieged.

Still Nikias, now a sick man but, as ever, less afraid of the enemy than of the Athenians, would not call off the operation. Instead he sent a dispatch (winter, 414–13) relating his difficulties, and saying that, now that the enemy had been reinforced the Athenians must *either* call off the expedition *or* send another as large as the first. It was the same tactic which he had employed before the expedition sailed; and it failed again. With Sparta preparing to renew the war in Greece, Athens, with the unyielding spirit of a tragic hero, sent another 5,000 armoured men and seventy-three triremes, under officers including her best surviving general, Demosthenes. There seemed no limit to her power, and Syracusan hearts sank again.

Demosthenes launched a full-scale night attack to regain the high ground, as the one hope of making the siege again a reality; but after a good start this operation ended in a bloody repulse. Demosthenes was now in favour of withdrawing; but Nikias, in sick obstinacy, still demurred. He said he would rather be killed by the enemy than by the Athenians, who would be furious and would not understand the necessity; also that Syracuse was on the verge of economic collapse, and that he was secretly in touch with a party which was in favour of surrender. He gave way only when Syracuse was further reinforced, both from Greece and Sicily; and then, when the decision had been taken, there was an eclipse of the moon (27 August, 413). This was, by tradition, a sign that the time was unpropitious for an important enterprise, and the troops clamoured for delay. Nikias, himself much given (Thucydides comments) to such attempts to find out the will of heaven, consulted his soothsayers; and they advised waiting for 'thrice nine days', for another period of the moon.

The result was hideous disaster. The Syracusans and their allies, discovering that the Athenians were contemplating retreat, went over to the offensive; and the Athenians, with their ships, except the new arrivals, in bad condition from the impossibility of maintenance, with much sickness among the crews, and unable to use their skill in the confined waters of the Great Harbour, were defeated at sea. The Syracusans then blocked the entrance to the bay with old ships anchored and lashed together, and in a crowning victory, after very heavy losses on both sides, foiled the last desperate effort of the Athenian fleet to break out. Abandoning their ships, their sick, and everything that they could not carry, the Athenians tried to retreat into the interior; but now the passes leading up out of the coastal plain were held against them too. Forced off the direct route inland, short of food and water, their last formed bodies disintegrated at a river-crossing on the coast road south of Syracuse:

Nikias led on his men again at first light, and the Syracusans and their allies harassed them as before from all sides with missile attacks. The Athenians pushed on to the river Assinaros, under pressure from swarms of cavalry and light troops, thinking that things would be easier for them once they got across, and also tormented by thirst. But once they got there, they rushed into it, all discipline lost and every man wanting to cross first, while the enemy pressure was making the crossing difficult already; for being compelled to cross in a mass, they fell over each other and trod each other underfoot; and some perished pierced by each other's spears, and some, entangled in their equipment, were swept down stream. Meanwhile the Syracusans, lining the farther bank, which was high and rugged, went on shooting from above at the Athenians, most of whom were drinking thirstily, in complete disarray, in the hollow bed of the river. Then the Peloponnesians went down after them, slaughtering especially the men in the river. The water was fouled, but they still went on drinking it, mud, blood and all, and fought in packs to get at it.

At last, when the dead were lying thick in the river-bed, one upon another, and the army was in complete ruin – any who did get across being caught by the cavalry – Nikias surrendered himself to Gylippos, trusting him further than the Syracusans, bidding him and the Spartans do what they chose with him, but to stop the slaughter of his men. And then Gylippos gave the order to take prisoners.

The Syracusans, however, took Nikias and Demosthenes off Gylippos' hands and, to his great distress (for he would have liked to display them at Sparta) put them to death. Those who had been in touch with Nikias across the lines were among the keenest on this step, being afraid that if put to the torture he might reveal awkward facts. Nikias' shield, splendid with gold and crimson, was long displayed in a temple. 'No man of my time', comments Thucydides, 'less deserved to perish so miserably; he had framed his whole life according to the accepted code of virtue.'

The Athenian citizen prisoners – some 7,000, after many had been taken off by individual captors as slaves – were herded into the quarries outside Syracuse, as the safest place in which to keep them; and, packed in these concentration camps, without cover against early autumn sun or winter rain, 'forced to do everything in the same place' and fed on half a slave's ration of meal and water, in the course of eight months most of them died. A few, however, are said to have won easier slavery and ultimate liberation when the Syracusans found that they had a coveted possession: they could recite whole lyrics and other long passages from the plays of Euripides.

3 THE LAST YEARS OF THE WAR

Even now Athens did not collapse. With a permanent Spartan fort established fifteen miles to the north at Dekeleia (as advised by Alkibiades); with the Peloponnesians, financed by Persia and reinforced from Sicily, disputing command of the sea; with Ionia in revolt – the Athenians built new ships and fought on for nine years (412–404). In 411, after a hundred years of democracy, there was revolution. The democratic leadership was discredited, but even so, it was not until several prominent democrats had been assassinated by unknown knifemen and a meeting of the assembly called outside the walls, where many were probably afraid to go, that a gathering calling itself the People of Athens abrogated democracy in favour of a Council of Four Hundred oligarchs. These men promised, but were in no hurry, to draft a list of 5,000 voting citizens. They also tried to make peace, but could get no terms tolerable to any Athenian. The fleet and army off Ionia, based at Samos, declared for democracy; the oligarchs themselves split into an extreme and a moderate wing; and within two years, with scarcely any bloodshed, the democracy was restored.

In the meantime Alkibiades, who was in Ionia, had become homesick for Athens; he had also incurred suspicion of having seduced a Spartan king's wife. He intrigued with both parties, but finally double-crossed the oligarchs and was welcomed back by the fleet at Samos. He had, after all, not been found guilty of mutilating the Hermai, and it was easy to say that accounts of his profanation of the Mysteries had been exaggerated.

He was a much tougher and better war-leader now. Gone were all thoughts of cheap and easy victories; and under his inspiring command the Athenians actually destroyed the main Peloponnesian fleet, with a Syracusan squadron, which was trying to cut Athens' Black Sea life-line in the Dardanelles. Then Athens disastrously rejected an offer of peace, keeping what she still had. Cities in the north which had revolted, including Thasos and Byzantion, were recovered; but even Alkibiades could not reconquer Ionia; and when the exaggerated hopes which had been placed in him were disappointed, his enemies began to whisper that, if he *were* victorious, he would become a military tyrant. An enemy fleet was soon abroad again, under the tough and shrewd Spartan Lysander; and when Lysander won a partial but damaging victory in the absence of Alkibiades, levying desperately needed money from cities still subject, Alkibiades was accused of leaving an incompetent officer in command, and suspended. Once more, he did not choose to risk going home, to face his enemies before a court of inquiry. He retired to a private castle which he had acquired in the Gallipoli peninsula. Once more this man, who had done so much real evil, was felled, it seems, unjustly.

Athens was under desperate strain. Since the occupation of Dekeleia, nearly all food had to be imported. Euboia had been lost during the revolution of the Four Hundred. Cavalry horses were worn out in endless patrolling. Over 20,000 slaves, 'mostly industrial', escaped to Dekeleia, perhaps only to be re-enslaved. The silver-mines could not be worked; Athens melted down statues and other dedications of happier days, and produced for the first time gold and copper coins. Yet she still had many skilled workers, both slave and free; and it was actually at this time that Athens, providing employment for many who would otherwise have been 'on relief', completed the Erechtheion on the Acropolis; the unusual and irregular-shaped temple, built to cover a number of holy sites, with its richly-adorned Ionic pillared porch on the one side and the dainty Porch of the Maidens on the other.

Drama also continued to give spiritual sustenance, and to develop. In tragedy, poets increasingly found the Chorus very much in the way when there was intrigue to be done. Euripides, in some plays, gives it lyrics of escape, only remotely connected with the plot; Agathon is said to have introduced musical interludes not connected with the plot at all. Sophocles in his *Philoktētes* (409, when he was eighty-six years old) on the contrary drastically reduces the choral songs, and weaves what there are closely into the plot. Aristophanes could still laugh. In his famous and Rabelaisian *Lysistrata* of 411, he imagines a general strike of women, who seize the Acropolis and hold out till the men agree to stop the war. Later, political satire being no longer safe, he turns to literature for subjects. The women use their private festival of the Thesmophoria to attack Euripides (who is helped by Agathon) for his shocking studies of female psychology; and in the very last year of the war, 405, when both Sophocles and Euripides were dead, he depicts in *The Frogs* the god Dionysos descending into Hades to beg for one tragedian to be released, as there are no decent ones left. Sophocles, 'always content', does not compete; Aeschylus and Euripides do so, noisily and very amusingly. Aeschylus, the poet of the Good Old Days, wins – of course; but it is taken for granted that none but Euripides is worthy to be named with Aeschylus and Sophocles as one of the Great Three.

Comedy was a service, nothing less; and when Aristophanes' rival Eupolis was killed in action in 412, Athens had the greatness of heart, even at such a time, to decree that thenceforth established poets should not be sent on active service abroad.

But the war dragged on. In 406, scraping the very bottom of their resources, the Athenians won yet one more great naval victory, off the White Islands, Arginoussai, near Mytilene. But once more they refused a peace that would leave them only some rags of their empire. Fierce patriot-demagogues still dreamed of recovering all. Also the victory had cost 5,000 lives; on a stormy evening and amid great confusion, there had been a failure to take adequate steps to pick up men clinging to wreckage. There was great popular indignation. The generals maintained that they had assigned the duty to certain captains, including Thēramenes, a politician, who was now accusing them; and in attack and counter-attack, the tale of negligence was made to sound worse. Theramenes won, and (not on his proposal) six generals were sentenced to death, without proper trial, by a vote of the Assembly. Socrates, doing his duty in rotation as a Councillor, the only political post he ever held, happened to be one of the committee presiding, and tried to refuse to 'put the question'; but he was brushed aside. So perished, among the six, the younger Pericles, son of Pericles and Aspasia.

The end came in the next year, when the main Athenian fleet, incompetently commanded, was caught on the beach by Lysander at Aigospotamoi. Nine ships escaped; 170 were captured; 4,000 Athenian prisoners were executed in cold blood. The Athenians too had been killing prisoners of late. Lysander threatened death to any Athenians caught outside Athens, and from every outpost refugees streamed home, to swell the number of mouths to be fed in the city. Even then, Athens stood a siege, fearing to meet the fate of Melos and Skione, and trying desperately to make terms that would leave the Long Walls intact. With people dying in the streets, the city held out through the winter. But by spring, 404, it was clear that it was useless. Athens offered unconditional surrender.

4 REVOLUTION
AND COUNTER-REVOLUTION

In a congress at Sparta, Thebes and Corinth, among others, actually urged that the fate of Melos and Skione should be meted out. That, however, would have allowed Thebes to dominate the whole of Attica. The Spartans announced their refusal to destroy a city which had 'done good service in the time of greatest danger to Greece', and took Athens into their own system. Athens was 'to have the same friends and enemies' as Sparta (losing control of foreign policy) and receive back the anti-democratic exiles, now numerous. She was allowed to keep twelve ships of war (enough for local police-work) and the walls of the city, but not of Piraeus. She was thus left the means of defence against nearer neighbours, who hated her bitterly, so long as she satisfied Sparta.

On these terms the war ended. 'Lysander sailed into Piraeus ... and the Walls were demolished by eager hands, while flute-girls played, and men thought that that day marked the beginning of freedom for Hellas.'

With Sparta now Athens' protector, the masses cowed and hungry and their leaders discredited, it was clear that the democracy was doomed; but even this business was carried out at first in a comparatively gentlemanly way. 'It was resolved by the People' – so ran the preamble of a decree passed under the cold eyes of Lysander – 'to select thirty men to codify the ancestral laws under which they should be governed.' 'The ancestral laws' had long been the accepted slogan of reaction. In the meantime, the Thirty acted as a provisional government. Lysander then went off to expel the democrats of Samos, who were still holding out; but before long, the Thirty applied to Sparta for a guard to support them until they had purged the city of 'criminal elements'. Seven hundred Laconian men-at-arms were installed on the Acropolis; not nearly enough to dominate united Athens; but Athens was not united. The 'knights' and many of the armoured-infantry class were behind the Thirty. The Thirty destroyed first those extremists who had shouted down opposition, refused peace-terms and had been responsible for such crimes as the execution of the generals; and in the present state of opinion, few regretted them. But as time went on and innocent men were put to death simply as past or potential democratic leaders, while their property went to support the government and pay the Laconians, hostility, still voiceless, mounted. Some democrats fled across the frontier, among them two former generals, Thrasyboulos and Anytos; and Thebes, with no wish to see Athens remain permanently a Spartan satellite, harboured them. At Athens, more and more people had cause to fear the peremptory knock on the door by day or night.

One 'Gestapo story' of these months concerns the very family in whose house Plato stages his most famous dialogue, *The Republic* or *On Justice*. They were wealthy, non-Athenian, arms-manufacturers of Piraeus. Old Kephalos, who had come from Syracuse in the time of Pericles, was now dead, and the head of the family was his son Polemarchos, who also figures in the dialogue. The story was told later before a court by a younger son, Lysias, who became famous as a writer of speeches for other men to deliver.

The Thirty had decided that some of the resident foreigners were disaffected; also, they were again short of money; so they decided to arrest ten, 'including two poor men for the sake of appearances':

They found me entertaining guests; turned them out, and left Peison to guard me while the rest went to the factory and made an inventory of the slaves. I asked Peison if he would let me escape for a bribe, and he said Yes, if it was a big one. So I offered a talent; and he agreed. I knew that he regarded neither gods nor men; but still I thought in the circumstances I must take an oath from him. So he swore, invoking destruction upon himself and his children; and I went into my chamber and opened my strong-box. But Peison saw, and came in, and when he saw what was in the box he called two of his servants and told them to take it. The actual amount was three talents in silver, 400 gold pieces of Kyzikos, 100 gold pieces of Persia, and four silver cups; and I begged him to allow me some money for my journey; but he said I should be content if I saved my skin.

And then, as Peison and I were going out, we met [two others of the Thirty] coming from the factory. They met us just at the door, and asked where we were going. Peison said, to my brother's, to see to things out there; and they told him to go along, but me to come with them to the house of Damnippos. However, Peison came up to me and told me to keep my mouth shut and not lose hope; he would come there.

There we found Theognis, guarding some more prisoners. They delivered me to him and went back. Now I was desperate, and thought I must try everything. So I addressed Damnippos [the house-holder was not one of the Thirty] and said 'You are my friend, and I am in your house. I am an innocent man, and being done to death for my money. Please do all you can to save me.'

Damnippos said he would, but he thought he had better speak to Theognis; he thought he would do anything for money. Now I knew that house well, including the fact that it had another door at the back; so while he was talking to Theognis, I thought I had better try to escape that way, reflecting that ... if I was caught, there was still the chance that Damnippos had succeeded in bribing Theognis to let me go, while if he failed I should die anyhow. So I slipped away, while they kept guard at the court-yard door; and there were three doors which I had to get through, but as it chanced, they were all unlocked. I made my way to the house of Archeneos the sea-captain, and got him to go up to Athens to find out about my brother. He came back with the news that he had been arrested in the streets and taken off to prison. Having heard that, I got a boat on the following night and crossed over to Megara. But to Polemarchos, the Thirty gave their familiar order, to drink hemlock, without so much as telling him what the charge was against him.

They pillaged Polemarchos' property, Lysias goes on, even to his wife's golden ear-rings; and his family had to beg and borrow the things for his funeral, who had been the master of 120 slaves. (This, by the way, is much the largest manufacturing establishment that we hear of in Athens.)

Leader of the Thirty Tyrants, as Athens came to call them, was Kritias. It is probably his aged great-uncle who, in Plato's *Timaios* and *Kritias*, tells the alleged Egyptian traditions of lost Atlantis and of how Athens beat off the invasion of that bull-worshipping sea-power (p. 304, n.); but he comes in the *Charmides*, dated when Socrates was just back from Poteidaia (432), and named after the golden boy of those days, Kritias' cousin and Plato's mother's brother. Socrates gravely recounts how, when Kritias called Charmides to join the group, everyone shoved up so hard that the man at one end of their seat was pushed off on to the ground, and the man at the other end had to get up. Charmides was now one of Kritias' lieutenants in charge of Piraeus.

Kritias had also written poems and tragedies; in a surviving quotation from one of these, on Sisyphos, the legendary wicked king of Corinth, a speaker explains that belief in the gods was invented by an ingenious ruler, so that evildoers might fear an all-seeing eye. Exiled from Athens, he spent some time in Thessaly, where, surprisingly, he is said to have organized a rising of the serfs. Clearly he was no conventional reactionary. On the contrary, he was a devotee of the 'new thought', who believed that a rule of virtue could be imposed by force. (Even Lysias says that this was what the Thirty *professed* to be doing.) But the essential first step was to hold power; and for this, the government must have money, disaffection must be crushed, and the passively well-behaved must so far as possible be compromised on the side of his government. He tried to compromise Socrates by sending him and three others to make an arrest; but while the others obeyed, Socrates simply went home. He might have got into trouble, for all his old acquaintance with Kritias and Charmides; but by now (late in 404) the sands were running out for them.

First Theramenes, a moderate oligarch and a politician, whereas Kritias was a doctrinaire, caused a split in the government by opposing the reign of terror, urging that it was losing support and making enemies. Kritias disposed of him by terrorising the Council, with a display of his strong-arm men below the gangway, into sentencing Theramenes to death by hemlock; but the danger against which he had warned Kritias was already brewing. Anytos and Thrasyboulos, a tough man with a roaring voice, with seventy followers, crossed the mountains from Thebes and seized the ungarrisoned fort of Phyle, ten miles from Athens, on the edge of the hills. The supporters of the Thirty were repulsed in an attack on it, and foiled in an attempt to besiege it by an early and heavy snowfall. Democrats slipped out to Phyle until Thrasyboulos' force mounted to 700, and took the offensive, routing an outpost held by two squadrons of the knights and the bulk of the Laconians, by a surprise attack at dawn. Four nights later, now 1,000 strong, though only 600 had regular arms, they marched on Piraeus and entered it through the breached walls. Kritias marched against them with 3,000 Athenians, whom he had enrolled to form his tame assembly; but the small armoured force of the democrats held their position in the main street leading up Mounychia Hill, supported by hordes of stone-throwers behind them and on the roofs; the harbourside population had risen. After a sharp fight, the oligarchs were swept back down the hill, leaving Kritias, Charmides and seventy more dead in the street.

This was not quite the end. For some months the oligarchs still held Athens, where most of the conservatives lived and most of their opponents had fled or been massacred; and Sparta intervened. But the young king Pausanias took a broadminded view of the situation. He snubbed Lysander, who would have crushed the democrats. Even when his troops became involved in fighting with Thrasyboulos' men, he refused to push things to extremes; and largely through his good offices, peace was restored and the democrats marched into Athens in triumph. Only the oligarchic leaders were outlawed; for all others there was an amnesty. The archonship of Eukleides, who took office at midsummer, 403, marked the restoration of full democracy.

NOTE ON ATLANTIS:

Plato's Kritias tells of hearing this story when he was ten from his grandfather, then nearly ninety, who had it from *his* father, who had it from Solon, who had it from priests at Saïs in Egypt. Atlantis was a vast island in the Atlantic Ocean, which 'nine thousand years ago' had a high civilisation and ideal constitution, and dominated the Mediterranean; but becoming aggressive it was beaten off by Athens (where everything then was also bigger and better), and then, through the anger of the gods, sank in the sea. No writer (not even Herodotos, who had questioned the archivist at Saïs) mentions this story earlier; but it became (like Tolkien's world) immensely popular, and later writers in many centuries have continually looked for history in it. Minoan Crete, with its bull-games, was a favourite for a time; now, with the discovery of a real cataclysm, it is Thera. One would like to believe it; but nothing in their extant records suggests that ancient Egyptians took any interest in events overseas; and Plato's 'oral tradition' is (ironically?) tenuous. For a recent discussion see E. W. Ramage (ed.) and other scholars, *Atlantis: Fact or Fiction?* (University of Indiana, 1978) and (briefly) A. R. Burn and Mary W. Burn, *The Living Past of Greece* (Herbert Press, 1980), pp. 52–7.

CHAPTER 14

THE AGE OF PLATO

1 POST-WAR ATHENS, AND THE DEATH OF SOCRATES

THE restoration of democracy was not the least in nobility among the achievements of Athens. Thrasyboulos and Anytos saw that it was essential that Athens should present a united front, so that Sparta might not be provoked to intervene again; and both of them left confiscated property of their own in the hands of men who had bought it. The amnesty was enforced by the swift punishment of some who tried to take private vengeance. Tolerable economic conditions were not slow to return; the corn grew, untrampled by enemies, and ships could sail again. But bitter memories could not be abolished so easily. Post-war Athens was certainly not a comfortable place. Speeches preserved from law cases show that though events 'before Eukleides' could not be made the basis of a case, they could not, under Athenian rules or absence of rules, be kept out of the pleadings. Andokides, the young aristocrat and brilliant speaker, who by turning state's evidence had stopped the witch-hunt after the affair of the Hermai, had to go over the whole of that story again, as well as that of a matrimonial feud with Kallias the Torch-Bearer, when officially only defending his political rights under the amnesty; and speeches for and against the young Alkibiades (son of the famous one), on a charge of evading military service, range far back into the ancestry of the family. The chequered career of his father is handled at length, with special reference to a racecourse quarrel involving the Olympic chariot-race of 416.

The famous Alkibiades was dead; his last phase as a general of the democracy had not commended him to the oligarchs or to Sparta. After Aigospotamoi he had fled from his castle in the vicinity (where he had vainly tried to warn the Athenian commanders of the risks they were running) and crossed to

Asia. He intended to go up like Themistokles to the Persian court; but Lysander (probably), afraid of the impression which his personality might make, procured an order to the local governor to make away with him. The house where he was lodging was set on fire at night, and he was shot down with arrows as, game to the last, he threw his bed-clothes on the fire in the doorway and charged out sword in hand. His last girl-friend used a robe of her own in which to give him decent burial.

But the trial which overshadows in fame all others of these years was that of Socrates, in 399. The indictment, preserved in the record office which Athens had lately established, stated:

That Socrates does not believe in the gods in whom the city believes, but introduces other and new deities; also, that he corrupts the young. Penalty demanded: death.

Why this trial, just then? Socrates was nearly seventy years old, and had been asking his questions since before most people could remember. No doubt, public life had been embittered since the revolution; but in four years, the worst of that might have been expected to die down. Socrates was in fact a religious man; though he did disbelieve so many of the sacred stories that it could be said that his gods were not the city's. But there was nothing new in this. If he had evolved a religion for a scientific age, so had Anaxagoras; and if Anaxagoras had been chased out of town, ages ago, his book, as Socrates reminded the court, was on sale at the stall 'by the Dancing-Floor'. If he had once been a friend of Kritias and Charmides, he had been in trouble with them before they fell; and anyhow, past history could not be made into a charge.

In 399, the 'climate of opinion' was no doubt unfavourable to him. Most of the young aristocrats who had flocked round him were dead or discredited, and the leaders of the restored democracy were middle-class, 'no-nonsense', rather anti-intellectual business men. They would approve when Melētos (probably a religious bigot; *not* the same Meletos who arraigned Andokides) undertook a prosecution calculated to force Socrates out of Athens.

Exactly among these 'tory-democrat' leaders, Socrates had just made a dangerous enemy: the general Anytos. Anytos was the son of a self-made man, who made a fortune in leather. He appears briefly in Plato's dialogue *Menon*, expressing, on Socrates' favourite question 'Can virtue be taught?', the straightforward bourgeois view that the proper person to teach a young man is his father. Educational experts? Sophists? Bah! 'You seem very down on sophists,' says Socrates; 'has one of them ever injured you?' 'No, I never go near them.' 'But then, how can you know?' 'I know well enough,' says Anytos, and shortly after withdraws from the conversation. But he had a more personal grief than having met Socrates in an argument. He too had a son; and since Anytos was not too old for the guerilla operations at Phyle, it is rather likely that his son was only now growing up. The son talked to Socrates, who considered that he had a fine mind – a mind too good to be confined to the administration of a tannery. Socrates, who did not number tact among the major virtues, said so to Anytos, suggesting higher education. Anytos refused angrily, and insisted that the boy should go into his business. The boy was left with a sense of wonderful things half revealed and then snatched from him; and the end of it was that he became a drunkard. So, when Meletos, 'a young man with a sparse beard and a beaky nose' (says Plato unkindly), brought his accusation, Anytos not only approved but appeared in court to speak on his side.

Plato, then in his late twenties, who worshipped Socrates, makes it clear with great fairness that Socrates asked for trouble. He considered that he had a mission from God to make people think, and he was not going to withdraw an inch, either physically or verbally. Plato wrote, and put into his works immediately before the famous *Apology* or Defence-speech of Socrates, a short and humorous dialogue in which Socrates, actually while waiting at the King's *Stoa* in the Agorá for the preliminary proceedings, catechizes Euthyphron, another religious enthusiast, who has come to court to prosecute his father for homicide. The father had caused by neglect the death of a labourer, having left him too long tied up, after the labourer had killed one of the slaves on his farm in a drunken fight.

Euthyphron is sure that it is the will of God that blood-guilt, even with extenuating circumstances, must be expiated. Oh, says Socrates admiringly, what an expert in theology you must be; you had better instruct me, and then I shall not get into trouble for heretical opinions.

So the catechism starts, and before long Euthyphron is involved in the question whether God approves an action because it is good, or whether it is good because God approves it. Euthyphron, who has never thought this out and wants to have it both ways, is chased twice round his circular argument, and then remembers an engagement elsewhere; whereas a few minutes before he had been waiting, like Socrates himself, for the 'King', the archon for religious affairs, to arrive and open his court. Socrates, in short, is represented as upsetting another pious citizen's convictions on the very eve of his trial.

In the *Apology*, Socrates treats the court with reasonable respect, but absolutely unyieldingly, giving an account of his mission (see above, p. 280), and protesting 'O Athenians, I love and honour you, but I will obey God rather than you' – even if he had to die for it many times over. He was found guilty by 281 votes to 220.

Then came the business of assessing the penalty. Except where this was fixed by law, the condemned had the right to propose an alternative to that demanded by the prosecution, and the jury had to choose between them. If Socrates had proposed banishment, it would probably have been accepted; but withdraw, physically, he would not. After consultation with his friends, who no doubt implored him to be reasonable, he blurted out that what he really thought he deserved was maintenance for life as a public benefactor; but that in deference to his friends, he would propose a fine of 3,000 drachmas. Everyone knew, but for good measure Socrates added, that he did not possess 3,000 drachmas; if all his chattels were sold up, they might realise 100 ; but 'Plato and [other friends] will stand surety for me'. The jury was insulted, and chose the death penalty by a larger majority than had originally found him guilty.

Even then he could have escaped. Kriton, one of his most

loyal friends, bribed the jailer – probably the more easily, because few influential people really wanted him dead. But Socrates refused to go. 'Shall I not obey the laws, which have protected me until now? I stood my ground in the army, where my generals posted me; shall I not stay at my post now, where God has placed me?' Would escaping from death be conduct like that of Achilles in the *Iliad*? After some delay due to a religious season in which no one might be put to death, during which he talked with his friends and versified some of Aesop's Fables, his last day came. To a friend who cried tearfully, 'But it is so dreadful that you should be put to death when you don't deserve it', he replied, 'Do you wish I did deserve it?' He is said to have spent that day proving the immortality of the soul; but the famous dialogue *Phaidon* (named after a young prisoner of war from Elis, whom Socrates had caused Kriton to buy out of slavery, when he was to have been made a male prostitute) seems to reflect the mature metaphysic of Plato; and Plato himself says that he was absent, sick, on that day. He drank the hemlock at sundown, refusing to wait till the very last moment, while the afterglow rested on Hymettos, and Kriton said in vain, 'The sun is still on the mountains, and there is no need to drink it yet, Socrates.'

2 PLATO LOOKS BACK

There were not many left now of the brilliant company who had talked with Socrates; and the younger men scattered. Xenophon, who as a 'knight' had probably served under the Thirty, with increasing scruples at their reign of terror, had already gone. He joined the expedition which the Persian prince Cyrus, the friend of Sparta, led against his half-brother the king, with 14,000 Greeks as a corps in his army. When Cyrus was killed in battle, the Greeks, who had routed the troops facing them, were left leaderless; their generals, invited to a conference with the Persians, were treacherously seized and put to death; but they refused to surrender, elected new generals, of whom the young, educated gentleman-soldier Xenophon was one, marched north from Mesopotamia to the

Armenian mountains, and through those mountains, mapless amid snow and hostile tribes, until one day, amid immense emotion, the leading files were heard shouting 'The sea, the sea!' Xenophon's account of this long march in his *Anabasis* (*Expedition to the Interior*) is one of the greatest Greek adventure stories.

Back in Greece, Xenophon wrote also (not at Athens, for reasons which will appear) miscellaneous works on hunting, horsemanship and other subjects; extensive notes, scarcely attempting to be a systematic history, on the wars of his own times; and *Reminiscences of Socrates*, defending his master against the charge of having been a disintegrating influence. They lack the brilliance of Plato, but are interesting as a check on him, since Plato apparently fathers on Socrates his own idealistic philosophy (p. 281). In Xenophon and Plato, some have said, Socrates had his St Mark and St John.

Plato, whose young manhood had been passed in the last grim years of the war, never bore arms again; but he lived dangerously at times. After other travels, he was invited in 388 to Syracuse to act as tutor to the son of the tyrant Dionysios, one of the most colourful and most disastrous figures of the new age. Dionysios had overthrown the democracy, after military disasters in which the Carthaginians, avenging their defeat in 480, sacked Selinous and Himera; but his own four Carthaginian wars, punctuated by aggressive wars against the Greeks of South Italy, left Carthage still holding a third of Sicily, and a trail of devastation. Between the wars Dionysios also wrote tragedies for the Dionysia at Athens; after many efforts, in 367 he actually won the first prize, and died, it is said, of the effects of his feast to celebrate it. His interest in Plato was no doubt genuine; but Plato did not find life among the western millionaires congenial. He described Sicily as a place where one over-ate twice every day and never slept alone at night; and he gave such offence by free speaking that Dionysios is said to have put him on a ship (Athens being then again at war with Sparta) with a returning Spartan ambassador, 'for disposal'. The ambassador (so at least ran the story) sent him to the slave-market at Aigina, where, moreover, a resolution had been passed to put any Athenians found on the island to death; but one Annikeris, a man of Cyrene, whom Plato had criticized for his hedonist philosophy, found him and bought him out. Back at Athens, Plato soon raised the money to repay him, but Annikeris refused to take it; and Plato, seeking a worthy use for the money that was the price of his redemption, then bought with it a small park a mile outside the western walls, close to the shrine of a local hero, Akadēmos. This was the *Academy*, where for the rest of his life he lived austerely with a group of friends and pupils, devoted to study and contemplation. Women as well as men were admitted, if they could meet the preliminary mathematical requirements. He visited Sicily again after the old Tyrant's death, but found Dionysios II, his old pupil, no ideal philosopher-king, and returned. Dionysios II soon lost his power, and retired to Corinth. He had learned enough from Plato to write a book called *Plato's Philosophy*, to which Plato took strong exception, and to support life by taking pupils – his enemies said, teaching children their ABC.

Plato's Academy lasted for 900 years, until the Christian emperor Justinian suppressed pagan philosophical schools (A.D. 529). Its doctrines varied during the centuries from dialectical scepticism to Neoplatonic mysticism, but always in the name of Plato as father-figure, to whom hero-cult was offered as Founder.

For Plato, the heart of the matter, the truth itself, was not something that could be written down. Philosophy, the Love of Wisdom, meant a way of life. On all books professing to give 'Plato's Philosophy' he comments :

There is no written summary by me, and never shall be. For it is not a thing that can be put into words, like other lessons for learning. But from a long communing over the thing itself and from living together, suddenly as though from a flame leaping a gap, a light kindles in the soul; and after that, it finds its own nourishment.

If it could be done, he goes on, he would be the man to write it; and 'What better could I have done with my life than to

311

write what would be of great service to mankind and lead all their nature to the light?' But he is afraid that the only effect on many would be to fill them with contempt of others or 'a vain conceit, as though they had learned something tremendous'. He has the same fear of evoking spiritual pride as the author of *The Cloud of Unknowing*. What could be done in writing was to give an account of Socrates; to expose error and erroneous ways of thinking; and to deflate the pride and empty conceit already existing.

The fourth century was an age of many great achievements. Isokrates, one of the masters of artistic prose, had his own school of higher studies in Athens, in which he taught *rhetoric*, meaning not merely journalese, but all the arts serviceable to a practical statesman. No doubt many of his pupils despised Plato's. In pamphlets, in the form of speeches but written to be read, he pleaded, though in vain, for the cities to make peace and combine against Persia, which had won back Ionia and used her gold and diplomacy to foster trouble in Greece. In art, it was the age of Praxiteles of Athens, one of whose minor works perhaps survives at Olympia (though good judges have seen even in this only an early copy): the famous Hermes, whose delicate finish at least shows how much is lost in nearly all our later copies. These are all we have of his masterpiece, the first Greek nude Aphrodite, at Knidos, one of the most admired statues of its day. It was the age too of Skopas of Paros, one of the four sculptors who worked on the tomb of Mausōlos, the Karian dynast of Halikarnassos, from which the fine portrait statue and frieze of racing chariots are in the British Museum. Two battered heads from a temple, on which he worked, at Tegea, from a pediment-group of the Hunting of the Boar of Kalydon, show in their deep-cut eye-sockets and knitted brows how Skopas or his fellow-workers could render expression; his work foreshadows the exciting, sometimes thoroughly overdone action-sculpture of later Greece. Of this age is the life-size bronze Piraeus Athena (is she *too* pretty?); and what unnamed sculptors could do may be seen at Athens in scores of grave-reliefs, and in the sculptures from Epidauros, where the sanctuary of Asklēpios the Healer was becoming the centre of a well-appointed spa, with its sports facilities and lovely theatre, the best-preserved in Greece.

But for Plato rhetoric, the art of the sophist (a title which Isokrates did not disclaim), was the quintessence of deception, the elaborate pseudo-science of the unreal; and the art of his time, too, with its air of aspiring to the condition of a wax-work, disgusted him. He condemned it as mere imitation of imitation – for to him even people and objects, as has been seen, have their being only by *mimēsis* of the universal Forms. The people who have managed their art properly, he makes his principal speaker say in a work of his old age, are the Egyptians; *they* worked out in the dawn of their civilisation, 10,000 years ago, the canons of good form both in music and in the visual arts, and then told the artists to stick to them. It was not, in fact, true; Egyptian civilisation was not as old as that, nor was Egyptian art so static. The truth was that *in Greek times* Egypt was archaizing, trying, in intervals of free-dom from foreign domination, to recapture the spirit of an imperial past by imitation of old forms. But Plato's attitude suggests that he would have sympathised with Byzantine art, and with at least some art of our own century.

So also in the famous *Republic*, an early version of which was parodied by Aristophanes in his *Women in Parliament* (392), he has his laugh at liberal democracy. Democracy is represented as an advanced stage in the decay of the state. It succeeds, by a proletarian revolution, a capitalist oligarchy, whose *laissez faire* has made the rich few and the poor numer-ous; oligarchy having succeeded military aristocracy, which is the first and least bad (to Plato's disenchanted eye) of the stages of decay, that succeed even his communist despotism of dedi-cated philosophers, when this ideal state has gone wrong and the rulers begin to batten on the ruled. Democracy in turn falls into anarchy and so gives way to the last and worst form of government, which is tyranny.

The democratic city

abuses those who obey their rulers as slavish and contemptible, and rates the rulers and the ruled exactly on the same footing. ... And the tendency seeps down into the family ... accustoming

313

the father to be on a level with his sons, and afraid of his sons, and the son to be like father; and there is no fear or respect of parents, for freedom's sake; and immigrant is equal with citizen, and citizen with immigrant, likewise ... and altogether, the young are on a level with their elders, and argue with them and compete with them, and the old come down to a level with the young and are full of adaptability and sweetness, imitating the young, in order not to appear sour or strict. In the end ... the very slaves are not a bit less free than those who bought them. As for the equality of the sexes, I almost forgot to mention it.

Once more we have that *indignant* testimony that democratic Athens was absurdly gentle to slaves.

The *Republic*, for all the fantastic conclusions to which Plato's Socrates is led by his relentless following of reason – from the abolition of marriage and the family in his communist state, to the ejection of Homer as unedifying – has never lost its charm and is often reckoned Plato's greatest work; but we cannot summarise it here. It begins, in earnest, after Socrates has made short work of a sophist who blatantly argues that the strong *should* rule in their own interests. Two of Socrates' young friends (they are, in fact, Plato's elder brothers) demand a more convincing demonstration that it really is best to be just, even if the righteous man were misrepresented and not rewarded but punished for it. We must do away with rewards: 'Let him be stripped naked of all things except his righteousness. ... Doing no wrong, let him be thought the greatest wrong-doer.' In that case 'the righteous man will be scourged, tortured, bound, have his eyes burnt out, and finally, after suffering every evil thing, be crucified'. What now, Socrates?

Socrates then sketches in detail his ideal state, in order to maintain that the success of justice is a function of a good society. In the world, the just man may have tribulation; indeed, he may have to keep out of politics, lest he perish with his work undone. But (at the end of the main argument) he will take part in politics 'in his own city'. 'I see,' says young Glaukon; 'you mean the city which we have been constructing in words; it does not exist anywhere on earth, I think.' 'But,' says Socrates, perhaps it is laid up in heaven for an example, for him who will to see, and seeing it to build himself as a city. But it makes no difference whether it exists, or ever will exist; for he will work the works of that City, and of no other.

In his old age Plato wrote another utopia: *The Laws* (quoted above, on art). This republic is not 'laid up in heaven'; it is a suggested code for a small, nearly self-sufficing city, supposedly about to be founded in Crete. Some of its enactments have indeed appeared on earth, on a vast scale, long after Plato's time. Here alone among the Dialogues, Socrates does not appear; indeed, he would have received short shrift in this city. The speakers are a Cretan nobleman, a Spartan and an Athenian, who represents Plato and theory. Everything is minutely regulated, and corrupting influences from the outside world carefully excluded. To this end, only mature and reliable citizens are to be allowed to travel, chiefly on definite missions, in case there is anything significant to be learned; those under forty are normally not to be allowed to travel at all, except that, for the sake of prestige, the state must send the strongest possible teams to the Olympic and other athletic and musical festivals. 'And when they return, they shall tell the others that the ways of other people are much inferior to ours.'

Right religion is of the greatest importance. Citizens must believe in the gods, and in their inflexible justice; we must have no truck with atheism, nor with salvationist cults (such as those of Orpheus), which teach that absolution may be obtained through rituals. Orthodoxy is defended by a Holy Office, the Nocturnal Council, which administers two prisons: a dungeon in a remote glen for the incorrigible, and a House of Correction for those amenable to brain-washing. The atheist of upright life may, for a first offence, be sent to the House of Correction for not less than five years, 'during which no one shall speak to him except the members of the Nocturnal Council, who shall commune with him for the salvation of his soul.' For a second offence, the penalty is death.

There are few more tragic things in Greek history than this tendency to despair of mankind in the aged Plato, before, one morning in 348 or 347, he was found dead at his desk.

3 SPARTA AND THEBES, 400–362

Plato in 403 may have had hopes of Sparta; but Sparta failed to give peace and unity to Greece, more quickly and more disastrously than Athens. Her military governors were both arrogant and greedy, and the Boards of Ten local oligarchic partisans, set up far and wide by Lysander, were in no hurry to resign at the end of the emergency. Even when the Spartan government put Lysander in his place as a private citizen and declared for 'ancestral constitutions' (as at Athens), these oligarchies were soon more unpopular than the democracies which Athens had fostered. Also Sparta was compromised with Persia, having financed her naval warfare largely with Persian subsidies. Spartans may have hoped to escape sacrificing Ionia to Persia by backing their friend, prince Cyrus; but when Cyrus fell and King Artaxerxes II ordered his satraps to restore Persian power over the Greeks of Asia, Sparta was constrained to protect them. From 399 to 395 forces under Spartan command, including 6,000 of Cyrus' mercenaries, campaigned in Asia, confirming the superiority of Greeks over Persians in infantry but not in cavalry.

But Sparta had enemies at home. Preserving the liberties of the Hellenes, and incidentally the supremacy of Sparta, meant checking attempts of the other larger states to extend their power. Thebes resented Sparta's power in central Greece; and Persia used her gold and diplomacy to foment Greek differences. So, a border incident between Phokis and Lokris led to a war between Sparta and the Boiotian League. Persia was also mobilising the Levantine fleets, strengthened by Greek exiles and mercenaries, under Konon, an Athenian admiral, the only one to extricate himself with a few ships from the disaster at the Goat Rivers. Athens thrilled at the news, and made alliance with Thebes. Lysander, invading Boiotia with allies from Phokis, was defeated and killed before the Spartan home army arrived. Argos, Corinth and Euboia joined the league against Sparta; and the Spartans sent to recall their king Agēsilāos and his army from Asia.

While Agesilaos was on the long march home, the allies invaded the Peloponnese. They were bloodily defeated before Corinth; but in the same summer (394) Konon's fleet destroyed that of Sparta and her allies off Knidos, at the south-east entry to the Aegean. Konon sailed to Piraeus, and with the help of his men and money the Athenians repaired the breaches of the Long Walls. Then they began rebuilding their own navy.

Agesilaos fought his way through Boiotia, winning a desperate battle at Koroneia in which the Thebans showed their prowess; he did not attempt any of the cities. Xenophon was with him and, having fought against Athens' ally, was banished from Athens. Thereafter, the war settled to a long-drawn affair of positions and raiding, as it were trench-warfare, round Argos and Corinth. Athens re-established her citizen-colonies in Skyros, Lemnos and Imbros. Thrasyboulos, the liberator of 403, was killed in 389, raiding nearly as far as the Eurymedon (p. 209).

But meanwhile Persia was preoccupied by the revolt of Egypt, and also of the Greeks of Cyprus under an able leader, Euagoras. Spartan sea-power revived, and Persia and Sparta, both somewhat sobered but with something to offer, came to terms. The King's satrap summoned Greek delegates to Sardis to hear them:

King Artaxerxes deems it just that the cities in Asia should be his, and of the islands, Klazomenai and Cyprus; the other Greek cities, small and great, he leaves free, except that Skyros, Lemnos and Imbros shall ... remain Athenian.

And whichever side does not accept this peace, against them I will make war, together with those who accept these terms, by land and sea, with ships and with money.

Argos and Corinth were under great strain, Athens terrified by the threat of a Spartan fleet to the Dardanelles, and at the prospect of Persia supporting it. Thebes saw the federal Boiotian League, in which she presided, dissolved by the 'autonomy' clause; but, left isolated, she too gave way. Sparta's league, depending on separate treaties with the states, was not affected. So by the 'King's Peace' of 387 the verdict of 479 was reversed; and Sparta gained all she wanted at home, by sacrificing the Greeks of Asia.

Sparta proceeded to suppress democracies among her allies and to punish those which had been slack in the recent war. In 382 she went further. The growing and democratic cities in Chalkidiké, of which the largest was Olynthos, had formed themselves into a league which had sided with the allies in the late war, and bade fair to dominate Macedonia. But two Greek cities which did not wish to join appealed to Sparta; and Sparta, hostile to any powerful *bloc* other than her own, and claiming to act as executor of the autonomy-clause in the Peace, brought the ambassadors before a conference of the Peloponnesians. The Peloponnesians agreed to send 10,000 men, but, as it was a distant campaign and might well be lengthy, not citizen levies but mercenaries; a new development characteristic of the time. The force proved insufficient, and had to be heavily reinforced; but by 379, Olynthos was defeated, blockaded, starved out, and her League dissolved. Sparta had once more demolished a rival centre of power; but the ultimate beneficiary of these proceedings was Macedonia.

Incidentally to this war, almost by accident, Sparta achieved what seemed a yet more brilliant success. Her armies for the north passed, in peace and by permission, through Boiotia; but the commander of one force, encamped near Thebes, was approached by a Theban oligarchic leader, who offered, in return for support in suppressing democracy, to put the citadel into his hands. The Spartan, eager to distinguish himself, accepted the offer; and the Spartan government, through the personal influence of Agesilaos, concurred in this piece of treachery and put to death their protégé's chief opponent as a 'war-monger'. But there were many at Sparta who had their doubts; and Xenophon, hostile to Thebes and an admirer of Agesilaos, but a man of simple piety, comments that the sequel showed that the gods are not indifferent to evil deeds.

The Spartan garrison held Thebes for just three years. Then, in 379, seven Theban exiles crossed the frontier from Attica and slipped into the city at dusk with the workers returning from the fields. Two evenings later, they were introduced by a confederate into a drinking party attended by the pro-Spartan leaders, disguised as women, heavily veiled. They promptly knifed those present, while others were sought out and killed at their homes; they gained entry to the jail, liberated 150 prisoners and armed them with weapons hung up as trophies of war; then they called the city to arms. In the morning the Spartan commander in the citadel found himself beset by such a furious multitude that he lost his nerve and agreed to withdraw.

So it was war again; but though the Spartans invaded Boiotia in summer year after year, they never ventured to attack Thebes or even the Boiotian forces in prepared fieldworks. The number of fully-qualified Spartiates had been dwindling for a century, and Sparta, it became clear, was anxious to avoid heavy losses. Between invasions, the Thebans gradually reduced those outlying Boiotian cities which fought for Sparta and autonomy. They produced two great soldiers: the dashing Pelopidas, whose *Life* by Plutarch gives the best account of the conspiracy, and Epameinondas, their best strategist, who from philosophic scruples had refused to join in the cloak-and-dagger murders. At last, in 371, the Spartan king Kleombrotos, operating from a base near Delphoi, got past Epameinondas by a surprise march through the glens of Helikon. Epameinondas fell back, to confront him west of Thebes; and in the open country and with superior numbers, including their Phokian allies, the Spartans clamoured for battle. But Epameinondas was an original tactician. He mustered his Thebans, in a deep mass, on the left, facing the Spartans, while holding back the rest of his line. He advanced obliquely, out to the left, while the strong Boiotian cavalry flung back the inferior Laconian horse upon their infantry; and though Spartan drill was equal to forming front in a new direction, the Theban charge, after a furious and bloody mêlée, burst through their line. Four hundred out of 700 Spartiates present – one-third of all that there were, between eighteen and sixty – and 600 Laconians fell with their king in this action, the Battle of Leuktra; the Flodden Field of the Spartan aristocracy.

Epameinondas, in the following years, invaded the Peloponnese. He liberated Messenia, where the towered walls that surround the stronghold of Ithome commemorate his work; the finest surviving example of classical Greek fortification. He encouraged the Arcadians to build themselves a new federal capital, Megalopolis. He marched clean through Laconia to the sea. Twice he assaulted unwalled Sparta; but he was beaten back from the barricaded streets; and the free Laconians, and even (be it noted) the Laconian helots, showed few signs of wishing to exchange the devil they knew for one they knew not. Several of her smaller allies stood by Sparta still – even some of the Arcadians; and Athens, confronted with Thebes as the most powerful city in Greece, went over, by a new turn of the kaleidoscope, to Sparta's side. It was thus that the ageing Xenophon, driven from the estate near Olympia which the Spartans had given him, was able to return to Athens.

Meanwhile, the Thebans campaigned far afield. They intervened in the internal wars of Thessaly, where Pelopidas fell in battle; and Pelopidas before he died had even arbitrated between parties in Macedonia. He came back with hostages, including Philip, younger son of the king Amyntas; an intelligent boy, who took a keen interest in all that he could learn in Thebes, not least about her army.

The wars in the Peloponnese came to a head in 362 near Mantineia; a great army from Boiotia and all central Greece under Epameinondas, with Peloponnesian allies, faced Spartans, Athenians and other Peloponnesians. Repeating the tactics of Leuktra with further elaborations, Epameinondas after a fierce clash drove through the enemy line; but just as the line cracked and the fighting grew loose, a desperate Spartan felled the Theban general. Speared through the body, Epameinondas sent for his second-in-command, but was told that he had fallen. He sent for the next in order; he too was dead. 'Then,' said Epameinondas, 'you had better make peace.' His men got the spearhead out of him and he died. The advance lost momentum as the news spread; the Athenians at the other end of the line even won some success. It was a draw.

This is where Xenophon, whose son had fallen in the battle, gives up rather than finishes his history of his own time:

The exact opposite happened to what everyone had expected; for when almost all Greece had met face to face, there was not a man but thought that, if a battle took place, the winners would be supreme and the defeated, their subjects. But God so brought it to pass, that both sides set up trophies as victors, . . . and both asked for a truce to take up their dead, as though defeated; and though each side claimed victory, neither of them gained territory nor a city nor power nor any other advantage that they had not before. Only there was even more chaos and confusion after the battle than there had been before in Greece. Enough for me, then, to have written thus far; and what followed thereafter may be some other man's care.

4 BOURGEOIS ATHENS

The Peloponnese was in chaos, though the endless border-fighting and faction-fighting was too intermittent to result in complete economic ruin. Athens and Thebes, on sea and land, were left the most powerful states. They were unfriendly, but both democratic, and for the most part their ways did not cross. Athens, during the wars, had re-formed a naval league, which at one time included seventy cities. Such an organization, to keep the seas safe for commerce, was needed; and it was provided with the built-in safeguard, against a renewal of Athens' imperial ambitions, that any major decision, such as a declaration of war, had to be taken *separately* by a congress of the allies, as well as by Athens. But there were many Athenians who still thought of empire as a source of wealth. They hoped particularly to regain Amphipolis (p. 270); and a promise to plant no more Athenian citizen colonies in the Aegean was not kept. The allies grew alarmed, and in 357 the league partly broke up, with the armed secession of its strongest members.

Nevertheless, Athens was modestly prosperous. The methodical finance of a leader named Euboulos enabled a strong fleet to be kept up, to be manned by the citizens when required; a

Festival Fund enabled the poorer citizens to attend the dramatic and musical performances, as well as looking after other amenities, such as water-points. Speeches written for clients to deliver in the law-courts, especially those of a brilliant young practitioner, Demosthenes (born 384), give vivid pictures of Athenian commercial and middle-class life.

The speech-writer had to adapt his style to the client, concealing the professional hand, and in doing this Demosthenes shows much dramatic power. We hear the tones of injured innocence of an apparently virtuous (and infuriating?) young man, who has had his tent ragged by a party of young bloods when doing his cadet service and afterwards been beaten up during an evening walk below the Acropolis, by the same gang plus their leader's father, who should have been old enough to know better:

They tripped me up and threw me down in the mud, and reduced me to such a state by jumping on me and maltreating me that my lip was split and both my eyes closed, and they left me unable either to get up or speak. And as I lay there I heard them saying many offensive things. Most of it indeed was so bad that I should not like to repeat some of their expressions in court; but, just as an example of the defendant's brutality, ... he started crowing, like a victorious fighting-cock, and the others told him to flap his arms for wings. After that, I was carried off by some passers-by, in my shirt, while they went off with my cloak. And when we got to my door, there were shrieks and cries from my mother and the maid-servants; and at long last they got me to the baths and washed me and showed me to the doctors.

We hear the gruff country tones of a hill-foot farmer, who had built a wall to keep flood-water from the road up the glen out of his land, and is accused of having blocked a recognized water-course, with resulting damage to the next property. 'Who ever saw or heard of a water-course *beside* a road? The natural place for water to flow is *in* the road. Besides, if I get into trouble because water off the road has damaged Kallikles' property, whatever will happen if I let the water into my land and then try to pass it on to the next man from there? Does Kallikles want to make me drink it?'

We hear the voices of a whole range of suave or hearty business men, always, of course, innocent and injured; and stories, sometimes quite exciting, of events on the high seas; for instance, the rascality of two characters from Marseilles, who borrowed money in Syracuse on the security of a cargo of grain for Athens, which they pretended was theirs, sent the money off to Marseilles, and then planned to scuttle the grainship; for if a ship was lost, the loans secured on the cargo were not repayable. Borrowing fraudulently, or more than once on the same security, and then losing the ship thus became the ancient equivalent of barratry at the expense of an insurance company.

Well, when the ship was two or three days out from land, Hēgestratos went down into the hold one night and began cutting a hole in the ship's bottom, while Zenothemis [his accomplice] stayed innocently on deck with the other passengers. But Hegestratos made a noise, which alerted the ship's company to the fact that there was some dirty work going on down below, and they went to have a look. Hegestratos, realising that he was going to be caught and pay the penalty, bolted, with them after him, and jumped into the sea; but he missed the dinghy [towing behind] in the dark, and was drowned; a deservedly bad end to a bad lot, meeting the fate that he had planned for others.

Zenothemis tried to go through with his plot, urging the crew to abandon ship, as she was going to sink at any moment,

but he failed. My company's super-cargo offered the sailors a large reward if they saved her, and the ship got safe into Kephallenia, thanks to the gods first and next to the good conduct of the crew.

A family history, which can be built up from several of Demosthenes' speeches, shows interestingly how slaves could rise to responsibility and affluence in the business world. Phormion, a banker, Demosthenes' client, had been the slave of Pasion, the former owner of the firm. Pasion too had been the slave of two former owners; he had become their indispensable chief clerk, their manager, finally their freedman and heir. Pasion grew rich; he ran an arms factory as well as his bank, and for munificence to the Athenian People, including on five occasions the equipment of a warship, and on one, the gift of 1,000 shields, he received the honour of citizenship. When Pasion grew old, with failing eyesight, and no longer easily able to walk the five miles from Piraeus to Athens, he leased his business to his own manager and freedman, Phormion, of non-Greek, probably eastern origin; and finally, by his will, he provided that Phormion should marry his widow and be guardian of his younger son, Pasikles. Pasikles was content with this arrangement, and continued to be guided by Phormion after he came of age; but the elder son, Apollodoros, who was twenty-four at his father's death, was not. The property was divided, Apollodoros receiving the factory; but he ran through his wealth both by public munificence, e.g. equipping a warship with such lavishness that his prospective successor objected to taking it over, and no doubt by extravagant living. He then claimed more from Phormion and Pasikles. The dispute became bitter, with Apollodoros maintaining that it was all his by right; before the end, he was expressing in court the unsupported suspicion that Pasikles was really Phormion's bastard. It is easy to guess at the background of Apollodoros' poisoned state of mind: the son of the rich Pasion, eager to shine in society and ashamed of his father's humble origins; the old ex-slave banker, mistrustful of his spendthrift son's probable handling of the business. To arrange the marriage of one's widow to one's freedman manager is certainly not like anything that we hear of among freeborn Athenians; but we are told that it was quite normal in the circles in which Pasion and Phormion moved.

Clerks and assistant managers were regularly slaves or freedmen. Free Athenians were not afraid of heavy work; they would dig, plough, hew stone, pull an oar in the navy; but they would not put themselves permanently under another; therefore they would not be domestic servants (even stewards, if they could help it), and they would not be clerks. In one shipping case, both the plaintiff's agent, wintering in a Crimean port, and a whole ship's crew, including the skipper, who had personal savings enough to invest 1,000 drachmas in the venture, are of this class. These men worked under such conditions that if they wished to escape, there was nothing to stop them; but they had no reason to prefer the precarious condition of freemen without citizenship or status. As slaves, they had security, permission to acquire personal savings, and a prospect of liberation for loyal service. Their position was very unlike that of the rough and strictly guarded slaves in the mines. They were, in fact, the 'organization men' of the Athenian business world. That world was full of them, though few, like Pasion and Phormion, were made citizens. It was a cosmopolitan, rootless world; totally cut off from the land, for ownership of real property was not permitted to non-Athenians except as a rare privilege. In it, as the Old Oligarch had remarked, there arose a mixed dialect, the 'common Greek' of most later Greek prose, including the New Testament. In that world, in which slaves might be rich and secure and have slaves under them, we also see a first adumbration of what reached its height in the later 'Caesar's Household', the clerical and sub-clerical grades of the Roman Civil Service; a world apart, to which many of its members were proud to belong, with its own schools and medical service, and its own great men, socially despised but more important than most of the free.

CHAPTER 15

THE MACEDONIANS

1 PHILIP

DEMOSTHENES, with his formidable oratory, was also a keen politician. The son of an arms-manufacturer – though fraudulent guardians had run his property down seriously while he was a child – he favoured the imperialist party. A dour, puritanical 'water-drinker', as an opponent called him, he was prepared to attack moderate men, whose vain search was for a general peace, as little-Athenians, appeasers. But events were to bring him fame, not as the orator of successful aggression, but as the gallant defender of a losing cause.

Macedonia, centred in the fertile alluvium of the lower Axios (Vardar), was a land of stalwart peasants and horse-riding squires, speaking a rough dialect of Greek, unintelligible to Athenians and so reckoned 'barbarous'. Unlike Thessaly, it lay wide open to raids from Thrace and Illyria; but the necessity of defence had resulted in its preserving the 'Homeric' monarchy, instead of a feuding nobility and a population of serfs. King Archelaos, who received Euripides and Agathon at his court, had built forts and military roads; but the land remained beset by enemies. In the 380s, while Illyrians over-ran the upper country, Olynthos had taken its lower regions under 'protection', but the Spartan intervention had ended that; after Leuktra, Athens and Thebes successively intervened between Macedonian factions, and a pro-Theban party handed over the young prince Philip as a hostage. He was back and serving under his brother, King Perdikkas, when, in 359, Perdikkas was defeated and killed by the Illyrians. So, at twenty-two, he was called to power, as regent at first for Perdikkas' infant son. Soon, when the Macedonians had experienced his leadership, they acclaimed him king.

A brilliant soldier, a fine speaker, a man of much personal

326

charm, with a dry and caustic wit, Philip was also the greatest diplomatist in the Greek world, which was full of that craft. That he owed everything to his stay in Thebes is unlikely; to use every weapon and to try to deal with enemies one at a time was an art which his ancestors had had to practise from of old. Philip did it with genius, never better revealed than in his first years.

Enemies from all sides swarmed in upon defeated Macedonia. Philip, whose treasury can hardly have been over-full, bought off two separate predatory raids from Thrace, one of them with a pretender to the throne in attendance. Sated for the moment, the Thracians murdered him. Another pretender, with Athenian backing, marched up from the coast. Judging correctly the feeling in the country, Philip let him reach Aigai (Vergina), the old capital, only to find that no one was joining him. When he started to retreat, Philip defeated and cut off his small army, let all the mercenaries and Athenians go free, on condition that they surrendered the Macedonians with them, and made a virtue of this in treating for peace with Athens. He also placated Athens by withdrawing a force which his brother had sent to help Amphipolis against her. He needed the troops, anyhow.

Then, through the winter, he trained and drilled his army, restoring its morale by his own confidence and fiery oratory. In spring, 358, he invaded and smote the Paiones, one of the late raiding tribes, forcing them to disgorge their plunder; then, turning upon the Illyrians, he inflicted a shattering defeat, using Epameinondas' oblique approach and a marginal superiority in cavalry to smash their second-best troops with his own best, and then to come in on the flank of their strong centre. All the territory lost in Perdikkas' defeat was recovered.

He was now free to resume negotiations with Athens, or rather with Athenian generals in the north Aegean, to whom he secretly offered (a secret offer to the Athenian *assembly* would have been quite impossible) to relinquish Amphipolis if they would acquiesce in his securing Pydna, a Greek town on the Macedonian coast which was a member of Athens' league. The prospect of such a dazzling prize blinded the Athenians to moral scruples over betraying an ally. Their treachery was suitably punished when in 357, while their forces were engaged in recovering the Gallipoli Peninsula, Philip took both towns (Pydna being surrendered by a pro-Macedonian party), and kept them. He did not even have to garrison Amphipolis; with a few pro-Athenians exiled, the goodwill of the citizens, delighted at such liberal treatment, was security enough. Philip was thus able to reach the Pangaion goldfield, where he reinforced a mining settlement from Thasos, naming it Philippoi. Before long, the mines were said to be yielding him 1,000 talents a year; the gold with which he unlocked many fortress gates and added many soldiers of fortune to his army. His service was tough – he is said to have fired a captain for taking a hot bath – but well-paid and interesting.

Athens now declared war on Philip, and both competed for the alliance of Olynthos' Chalkidian League, which had been reformed. Philip, with the offer of rich border territory, won the auction. In 356, he took Poteidaia, south of Olynthos, released its Athenian garrison unransomed, and presented the city to the Chalkidians, thus embroiling them with Athens really thoroughly. Athens was then crippled by the revolt of Rhodes, Chios and other allies, supported by Mausolos (p. 312), vassal Prince of Karia under Persia. It was one of Philip's great strokes of sheer luck; for his up-country neighbours, now alarmed, were combining against him. In 359 he had had to buy them off till he could face them singly; but in 356 he beat the whole coalition. While he beat the Paiones and Thracians, his general Parmenion dealt with the Illyrians. ('A wonderful people are the Athenians,' said Philip; 'they produce ten generals every year; I have only found one in my whole life, and that is Parmenion.') On the same day, somewhere in Thrace, he heard three pieces of good news: Parmenion's victory; the victory of his horse in the Olympic Games; and that his queen, Olympias, had borne a son, Alexander.

Thebes as well as Athens was preoccupied at home. Without Epameinondas, she could not even coerce her neighbour, Phokis; but she tried, and the Phokians, with Sparta no longer able to protect them, 'borrowed', more and more unblushingly, the treasures of Delphoi to hire mercenaries; protesting, the while, that they were only borrowing to protect their liberties and their ancestral sanctuary. Athens and Sparta were willing to accept this excuse, but gave little help. The Sacred War, as the Thebans called it, was essentially a long-drawn struggle of the Phokians, with their rich but wasting asset, against Boiotians and Lokrians (355–346).

Philip was invited south of Olympos first into Thessaly, where there was war between the inland barons and the tyrants of Pherai, with its port of Pagasai, a more *bourgeois* and seaward-looking society. The barons found Philip, a 'horse-lover' (as his name says) like themselves, a congenial ally, and elected him their general. Philip took Pagasai; but Pherai now appealed to the Phokians. Their professional soldiers defeated Philip, who returned to Macedonia; but, said he, 'I draw back, like the ram, to butt harder'. In 352, at the 'Crocus Fields' near Pagasai, his Macedonian and Thessalian cavalry rolled up a flank and drove a Phokian army into the sea. An Athenian fleet picked up swimmers. Pherai surrendered; but the Athenians occupied Thermopylai, to defend Phokis. Philip, ever a realist, did not attack. In the next years he extended his power inland, securing it with colonies of Macedonian peasants and Greek mine-operators and gaining many willing allies, while the Greeks, Boiotia against Phokis, Sparta against Megalopolis, with allies on each side, continued to war interminably among themselves.

By 349, Philip felt ready to deal with his late allies, the Chalkidians. He demanded the surrender of two half-brothers of his, possible pretenders to his throne, who were living at Olynthos. He continued to offer 'peace and alliance', and to the last, Olynthos was not united in resisting him. But it was clear that his alliance meant overlordship. The Chalkidians rejected his demands and appealed, too late, to Athens. Athens sent reinforcements but, despite the fiery oratory of Demosthenes, refused, probably wisely, to commit her main forces close to Philip's base and far from their own. In 348, after overrunning the rest of Chalkidiké, he advanced on Olynthos and, with the help of treachery within, took it. It was razed to the ground -

the site, unencumbered by later buildings, has given to archaeologists their best picture of ordinary Greek houses – and the people sold as slaves. Philip's partisans kept their personal freedom, as his subjects; but they did not find it comfortable. Some of them complained to him that some Macedonians had called them traitors. Philip said 'Yes, the Macedonians are crude people. They call a spade a spade.'

Because Demosthenes used the sorrows of Olynthos to shame and fire his people, we hear a little more about these captives; we seldom do, when Greek combatants 'enslaved the women and children'. An Athenian envoy in Arcadia saw about thirty women and children, under escort, trailing along a road, and was told they were Olynthians whom Philip had presented to an envoy from Megalopolis. One group of girls was begged for by name by an Athenian actor at Philip's court, when the king at his victory celebrations was distributing favours; they were daughters and nieces of a friend of his, who had been murdered at Pydna before Philip took it; already refugees, in Olynthos. Satyros the actor considered it his duty to dower them for honourable marriage. Most were not so lucky. Philokrates, an Athenian ambassador to Philip two years later, brought home another batch, also a royal gift; and, says Demosthenes, who hated him, no one who knows *him* will ask if his intentions were honourable. And he tells a tale of a party given to that same mission by an Athenian exile living in Macedonia. 'I', he says, 'did not go'; but he heard about it from Iatrokles, one of his colleagues. After dinner,

When they came to the wine, the host brought in an Olynthian girl, pretty, but well-bred and modest, as the sequel showed. First, as I heard from Iatrokles next day, they only made her drink quietly and eat some dessert; but as things went on and they got heated, they bade her recline on a couch and sing them a song; and when the poor girl was in confusion, and did not want to and did not know how, [two of the Athenians] said 'Insolence!' and called it intolerable that one of these god-forsaken Olynthians, a wretched captive, should give herself airs. 'Call a servant,' they said, 'Bring a strap, someone.' A slave came with a whip, and – drunken as they were, and ready to fly into a rage over a trifle – when the girl said something and burst into tears, the slave ripped off her tunic and lashed her again and again across the back. She, frantic with pain and dismay, jumped up and threw herself at the knees of Iatrokles, knocking over his table; and if he had not rescued her, they would have killed her in their drunken brutality.

There were 'parliamentary questions' about this incident, we hear, in other states besides Athens; chiefly, probably, because of the indecency of Athenian ambassadors being concerned in an outrage against a daughter of a lately, though briefly, allied city. More often, such things were nobody's business.

Philokrates' embassy was the one which made peace with Philip, after protracted negotiations, two years after the fall of Olynthos. During them, Philip conquered more of the east-central Balkans. He refused to make peace with Phokis, but invited Athens to send troops to join his at Thermopylai and bring the Sacred War to an end. The Athenians refused – it would look too much like turning against their late ally; but Philip knew that having had the prospect of peace, they would be slow to go to war again. He probably also reckoned that rumours about these negotiations and the prospect of being left isolated would undermine Phokian morale; and so it was. Amid quarrels between the Phokian federal government and its chief general, Phokis collapsed and Philip marched in through unguarded Thermopylai. On Athenian intercession, the Phokians were spared the extreme penalty of massacre and enslavement; but their league was broken up, they were disarmed, and the Amphiktyonic League, which met at Delphoi, allotted Phokis' two votes to Philip. Controlling also the votes of Thessaly and the surrounding mountain peoples, he could sway a majority on the League synod. The Phokians were sentenced to repay all that they had taken from the Delphic treasury during the war, which would have taken them about 200 years. Philip was now guardian of that great sanctuary and champion of Apollo, as well as king of his expanded Macedonia and overlord of Thessaly; and even recent enemies, even in Thessaly and Phokis, looked to him as a protector against the more virulent enmity of immediate neighbours. With Thebes as an ally, he could invade Attica by land if he chose.

But this he never did. He always protested his desire for good relations with Athens, and his attitude when, later, he had Athens at his mercy, suggests that he was perfectly sincere. Many in Athens believed him; already Isokrates had published his pamphlet *Philip*, urging the king to unite the Greeks and lead them against Persia. Philip needed no urging; his armaments were so expensive that ultimately only a great empire in Asia could save him from debt. For invading Asia, the seapower of Athens would be of immense value. But also he respected the civilisation of Athens. The man whom he chose as tutor for Alexander, Aristotle, a philosopher and scientist of encyclopaedic range especially in natural history, was a doctor's son from Stageira in Chalkidiké, now subject to him; but one who had spent most of his adult life in Athens and been a member of Plato's Academy.

But to Demosthenes and others an alliance, in which Athens would be subordinate to (as he still thundered) a barbarian king, was anathema. His oratory in the later 40s may remind a modern reader of Churchill:

If anyone thinks that this policy is going to involve heavy expense and much toil and trouble, he is quite right. But if he reckons up the consequences to Athens if he refuses, he will find that it pays to do our duty voluntarily. If some heavenly power could promise (it is beyond human power) that if you stay passive and let every point go, That Man will not attack you at last, then before Zeus and all the gods, it is shameful and unworthy of you and of the history of Athens and the achievements of your fathers, to let all the rest of Greece fall into slavery to save yourselves trouble, and I at least would rather be dead than propose such a thing; but never mind, if someone else proposes it and convinces you, let it be, do not defend yourselves, let everything slide! But if no one thinks this – if on the contrary we all know that the more territory we let him control, the more dangerous and formidable an enemy we shall have in him – then how much further are we drawing back or what are we waiting for?

And at the end of the same speech:

Now let me sum up all in brief and leave the platform. My advice is that you must raise a capital levy; keep together the land-force you have – making good any deficiencies, but not disbanding it altogether because of criticisms; send out ambassadors in all quarters, to tell people the facts, warn them, concert action; above all, punish and hate corruption in public life, so that decent men who have shown themselves honest may be seen to have chosen the best policy both for others and for themselves.

If you will take things in hand like this, and give up refusing to take them seriously, then perhaps – *perhaps,* even now, they may show an improvement. But if you are going to sit there, full of zeal as far as cheering and applauding go, but trying to back out of actually doing anything, I do not know of any oratory which, without YOU doing your duty, will be able to save our city.

Gradually and unwillingly, majority opinion came over to him. Taxes were levied, moneys diverted from the Festival Fund to military accounts, an unrivalled navy built up to keep open the vital Straits. The speech quoted, called *On the Chersonese*, was delivered in 341, urging the people to support their general in the Gallipoli Peninsula, in frontier incidents for which he was probably to blame. War was renewed, and Philip suffered reverses; he attacked Perinthos on the Sea of Marmara and breached its walls, but was beaten back from among the narrow streets and tall blocks of the old town. Persia sent mercenaries and supplies to aid the defence; Byzantion sent troops and also beat off a surprise-attack by Philip in their absence. Athens sent 100 ships, which Philip's outnumbered fleet evaded only by a ruse. A migrating Scythian horde had crossed the Danube. Philip turned north; he defeated the Scythians, but had to fight his way home through the land of the fierce Triballoi, losing much of his booty and being himself wounded. Meanwhile the Athenians liberated Megara and Euboia from partisans of Philip and of Thebes.

But once more a quarrel in the Amphiktyonic synod gave Philip his opportunity. The western Lokrians of Amphissa proposed a fine on Athens for re-dedicating, when Delphoi was in the hands of the sacrilegious Phokians, a trophy of arms taken 'from the Persians and Thebans when they fought against the Greeks'. Aischines the Athenian, a fine orator and a patriot in intention (though Demosthenes accuses him of having 'sold himself to Philip' in 346), turned the tables by accusing the Lokrians of having cultivated land dedicated to Apollo. With Athens and Thebes (which had turned Philip's garrison out of a fortress guarding Thermopylai, during his troubles in Thrace) both holding aloof, operations against the Lokrians languished until, late in 339, one of Philip's Thessalian partisans, as chairman of the synod, carried the proposal that Philip be requested to take command. Philip came south, winter though it was (his disregard for campaigning seasons was a practice which Greek citizen soldiers regarded as unfair), and, with a Theban garrison blocking the coast-road at Thermopylai, got his veteran mountain-fighters over the range further west. Then, instead of going straight for Amphissa, west of Mount Parnassos, he occupied Elateia, a dismantled Phokian fortress on the road to Thebes.

There was alarm at Athens when the news came in (it has been described, p. 239); but Demosthenes, taken less by surprise than most, was ready with his proposal. There must be immediate general mobilisation; and Demosthenes offered to go with an embassy to Thebes, to offer alliance to that old enemy.

So an army from Athens, Thebes and other allies, including Corinth, Megara, Achaia and Euboia, faced Philip on the western border of Boiotia, while 10,000 mercenaries paid by Athens held the pass covering Amphissa. Philip however surprised that strong position, after lulling the alertness of its defenders by letting them capture a false dispatch, to the effect that he was having to withdraw troops to deal with a revolt in Thrace. He shattered the mercenary division, took Amphissa and then concentrated against the main foe. He offered peace, on terms which the allies refused. Then, in late summer, 338, took place the decisive Battle of Chaironeia.

This has often been pictured as a victory of the new, thirteen-foot Macedonian pike over the six-foot infantry spear of classical Greece; but no ancient author says so, and it would have been remarkably naïve of the Boiotians and Athenians to fail to match a weapon which could hardly have been kept a secret from them. Where the Macedonians did have an advantage was in drill and experience. Philip himself took post with

a defensive wing on his right, under the acropolis of Chaironeia, where a stone lion, restored in modern times, still marks
the battlefield. He faced the Athenians, who charged in gallant
style; Philip bade his veterans keep close under their serried
shields, giving back foot by foot slightly up-hill, waiting for
them to tire. 'Keep it up!' shouted the Athenian general;
'drive them right back to Macedonia!' 'Amateurs!' growled
Philip. But also, the advance of one end of the line may, it has
been suggested, have drawn the whole line askew (since it was
important to keep physical touch), causing some derangement
at the other end; and there the young Alexander, with the main
force of the Macedonian and Thessalian cavalry, led his first
great charge, sweeping away the weaker Greek cavalry and
turning the flank of the Theban infantry. The allied line was
rolled up with heavy losses, and when Philip himself went over
to the offensive, the Athenians broke and ran. It was the end
of Greek independence. Isokrates, Milton's 'old man eloquent',
who had hoped to see Philip leader of a willing Greece, is said
to have died of shock after hearing the news.

Even now, Philip treated Athens with surprising gentleness.
Once more he released his Athenian prisoners. He sent home
the ashes of the Athenian dead, escorted by Alexander himself.
He took from Athens only the Gallipoli Peninsula, and even
gave her 'frontier rectifications' (his usual trick, it must be
said) at the expense of Thebes. Thebes, which had turned
against him after being his ally, on the other hand suffered the
execution of many leaders, the sale of prisoners as slaves, and
a Macedonian garrison in the citadel.

Philip organized affairs in the Peloponnese to his satisfaction – Sparta alone defied the lightning, and was contemptuously shorn of some border territories; and in a congress at Corinth, where the old League against Persia had met, a new one
was formed. Philip was acclaimed its captain-general. He was
still under forty-five; and in 337 Parmenion crossed into Asia
to secure a bridgehead for the invasion.

But Philip was not to lead in that enterprise. Frankly poly-
gamous, he had long been on bad terms with Olympias, Alexander's mother; and when he married a niece of one of his

generals, and a son was born to him, whom the proud queen may have imagined as a possible rival to her son, his cup was full. Soon after that, at the acme of his power and glory, he was stabbed while walking in a triumphal procession by a young man with a grievance. It is easy to suspect Olympias or even Alexander; but the assassin was killed on the spot and his evidence thus (conveniently?) lost. He *may* have been a 'loner'.

The gold from Philip's tomb at Vergina, found miraculously intact, has now revealed the opulence of his court art; and in 1980 another (royal?) tomb near by awaited excavation.

2 ALEXANDER

Alexander, still the obvious and intended heir of Philip, despite the late troubles, had no difficulty in obtaining the necessary acclamation from the assembled Macedonians. Olympias seized and murdered the young queen and her baby, and an assassin sent by Alexander disposed of her uncle, who was at the front in Asia. But the accession of a 'mere boy', as Demosthenes optimistically said, encouraged every enemy.

An immediate march into Greece, cutting steps in the steep side of Ossa when the Thessalians demurred at letting him through the gorge of Tempe, ensured his election in Philip's place as general of the Hellenic League; but in 335, when he was away securing the north Balkans, Thebes rose in earnest. Alexander, who had already that summer stormed the Shipka Pass across the main Balkan range, defeated the half-Scythian Getai, crossed the Danube, interviewed fair-haired Kelts near Belgrade and routed the Illyrians after being apparently trapped in their hills, came south again with formidable speed. He stormed Thebes, his troops entering the city on the heels of a sortie, sold the whole population into slavery and razed the city, sparing only the temples and the house of Pindar. Greece was horrified, and cowed.

Alexander had already proved to be a soldier no less than his father, though he did not have to create his own army as he went along. Nevertheless, Philip's murder was a disaster. A few more years of diplomacy might have done something to unite Greece. Alexander remained almost unknown in

Greece; he was in a hurry to proceed with the invasion of Asia, where Parmenion, during the troubles, had held a foothold in the Troad with difficulty. Philip's generals, indeed, urged him to marry and leave an heir to the throne first, but Alexander brushed them aside. He seems to have been abnormally uninterested in sex; we may guess, through being caught in childhood by his adored mother's comments on his father's infidelity. It looks like a case of 'mother-fixation', which appears, very charmingly, in courtesy and chivalry to other royal ladies of his mother's age. For the rest, all his daemonic energy poured into war and government and exploration. What should happen when he was gone, he did not care. Throughout his life, which he continually risked, he made no provision for the orderly government of his people in the event of his death. When he did die, not yet thirty-three, he left just one unborn child; and the whole near east suffered grievously for his lack of normal paternal instinct.

Alexander pointed out later that Philip, for all his victories and his gold-mines, died in debt to the tune of 500 talents – enough for a fair-sized summer campaign. His army could only be kept at its present strength by making greater conquests to pay for past ones. Philip's right-hand men, Parmenion and Antipatros (the trustworthy man whom Alexander left in charge at home), evidently thought the financial position could be held; but Alexander proceeded to borrow another 800 talents, pledging the whole of his crown lands. He did not choose to wait; and the situation was indeed favourable, for the ruthless and able Artaxerxes III of Persia, who had reconquered Egypt with the help of Greek troops and suppressed revolts of his western satraps, had lately been murdered. The new king, a distant cousin, who took the royal name of Darius, was an unknown quantity. Without command of the sea, and financially 'on a shoe-string', Alexander plunged into Asia in 334, and demolished the forces of the local satraps at the river Grānikos, in a cavalry mêlée in which he narrowly escaped being killed. A fleet from Greece and Macedonia covered his crossing of the Dardanelles and helped in liberating Ionia; but it was inferior to the Levantine navies which entered the Aegean, and in the winter, being unable to pay it,

Alexander sent it home. In 333 he entered Syria, marching on Phoenicia, to eliminate the enemy fleet by capturing its home bases. Darius came down to the coast behind him to cut his communications; but he thus gave Alexander the chance to fight with his flanks covered by the hills and the sea, and was routed at Issos.

Most of 332 was taken up with a desperate siege of Tyre, on its inshore island. Alexander was repulsed in an attempt to bridge the sound; meanwhile the Persian fleet regained several of the Aegean islands; Sparta, but not Athens, raised the banner of freedom in Greece; and a Persian army marched to regain Asia Minor, but was kept from reaching the sea by Alexander's line-of-communication forces, Greek and local, under a great general, Antigonos One-Eye. But Sidon and the other Phoenician cities, jealous of Tyre and lately harshly subdued by Artaxerxes, submitted to Alexander; when the news reached the Aegean, their fleets deserted and went home; and with their help Alexander took Tyre by storm after seven months and destroyed it. Gaza, on its high *tell*, with a Persian garrison, held out for two months; but Alexander was able to winter in Egypt, where he founded Alexandria to replace Naukratis (p. 96), and where the oracle of Zeus Ammon saluted him as son of God – i.e. as rightful Pharaoh of Egypt.

In 331 he fought his greatest battle, at Gaugamēla, beyond the Tigris. Hugely outnumbered, he moved obliquely to threaten the enemy's left (Epameinondas' and Philip's old tactics), holding off with flank-guards the enemy's outflanking cavalry. His Thracian javelin-men broke up a charge of scythed chariots intended to disorder his line. All the time he kept his Macedonian heavy cavalry and phalanx in hand, until the Persian attempts to match his movements opened a gap in *their* line. Then, changing direction, he swooped with horse-guards, foot-guards and phalanx upon the Persian guards and Greek mercenaries in Darius' centre, and after a brief but murderous struggle drove the king once more in flight.

Darius retired east through the mountains to Ecbatana. His prestige was shattered, and his chief nobles began to turn against him. Mazaeus (Mazdaï), who had commanded his right wing and taken Alexander's camp, in the vain attempt to divert Alexander from the main business in hand, gave in and surrendered Babylon. Alexander rested his troops for six weeks there, where he received news that Antipatros had broken the rebellion in Greece. He let the rumour get about that his army was demoralised by wine and women, and then marched out *south*-east, fighting his way through the mountains in winter, first against tribesmen to whom the Persian kings had paid blackmail for safe passage and then against the home-levy of Persia proper. He occupied the old Persian capitals, burnt their palaces (probably an act of policy, for the sake of the moral effect), captured the huge imperial gold-reserve and, even more important, rounded up the young men of Persia and set them to be trained under Macedonian drill-sergeants as soldiers of the new king. By this tremendous exploitation of victory, Darius was left with no army in 330 except the forces of eastern Iran, dominated by Bessus, Satrap of Bactria, of royal descent, who had commanded the left wing at Gaugamela. They, in retreat from Ecbatana, put Darius under arrest and, when Alexander's pursuit grew hot, murdered him. Alexander sent his body to be buried in the tombs of the kings. Later, when he captured Bessus, who had been acclaimed king of Persia in Bactria, he put him to death with torture and ignominy as a murderer and rebel; he himself claimed to be the legitimate king.

Even so, it took Alexander three more years of strenuous marching and fighting to conquer eastern Iran, where provinces rose again in his rear and mountain castles of the north-east frontier had to be taken – in one case by a mountaineering operation with ropes and iron tent-pegs, driven as *pitons* into frozen snow. And during these years severe tension grew up between Alexander and his officers. He as the Great King wore Median dress, employed Persians and Medes as governors and desired to be saluted with low obeisance, as he was by his Persians. Macedonian officers were accustomed to treat their king as first among social equals, and they and the Greeks prostrated themselves before gods, but not before any man. Philōtas, commander of the horse-guards and son of Parmenion, was convicted of failing to report a conspiracy, and put to death; and his old and loyal father, who had been left in charge at Ecbatana, was then murdered as a preventive measure. Alexander's foster-brother Kleitos, who had saved his life in the first cavalry battle, taunted him over the wine at a banquet with assuming glory won by his troops and with his oriental dress and despotism; and Alexander, after enduring much provocation, seized a pike from a guard and killed him – an act which cost him an agony of remorse. Kallisthenes, nephew of Aristotle and official historian with the expedition, was arrested and probably died in a cage (his movable prison) after a conspiracy against Alexander's life by some of the royal pages. One of Kallisthenes' duties had been to look after the boys' education, and he had talked of constitutional government, and of tyrants and tyrannicide. Smarting under an unjust whipping, one of the boys had remembered all too well.

Nevertheless, by personal leadership in charge and escalade, by glamour and efficiency, generosity and ruthlessness, he kept the loyalty of his troops. It was not till 326, when he was in the Punjab, that the men at last refused to go further; they had won a very severe battle against the warrior rajah 'Pōros' (really a racial name, Paurava), who had 200 trained elephants, and they flatly refused, perhaps fortunately for Alexander, to march against the Ganges kingdoms, which were reported to have 5,000. Alexander perforce contented himself with taking in the Indus valley. Accompanied by a flotilla which he had built on the Jhelum, he marched to the sea, in a campaign marked by frightful slaughter; for the Indians refused his demands for surrender (and provisions for a large army) and held their mud brick walls with desperate courage. A city of Brahmans resisted so fiercely that scarcely any were taken alive; at a city 'of the Malloi' (it is only a guess that identifies it with Multan), Alexander, first up a ladder when his weary troops hung back, was wounded so severely that his life was in danger for days; his men avenged him with indiscriminate massacre. At the mouth of the river he left his friend Nearchos, a Cretan, to explore the sea-route back to the mouth of the Euphrates when the monsoon permitted (325). He sent back the bulk of his army, less garrisons, to Persia by the main route, inland, but himself set out with a lighter column, hampered however by a train of wagons with the troops' women, children and baggage, to explore the desert coast and dig wells for the fleet. He got through only after frightful sufferings and with heavy loss, partly from thirst but still more, including nearly all the women and children, when his camp, pitched in a nearly dry water-course, was overwhelmed by a sudden flood in the night.

Back in Persia, he distributed decorations for valour, and also executed several governors who, probably never expecting him to return, had conducted themselves as tyrants. Harpalos, his treasurer and boyhood friend, fled with 5,000 talents and a private army to Greece, where he tried to induce Athens to revolt; he was finally murdered in Crete by one of his officers. There was more trouble when he prepared to pay off and send home the older of his Macedonian veterans, replacing them with the young Persians, who had now had five years' training and garrison-duty; for the men, fearing the consequences when they should be only one-third of the standing army and thus no longer indispensable, raised a cry of 'No! Let us *all* go, and stay and fight your battles with your Persians and your father Ammon!' But when Alexander prepared to take them at their word, the 'strike' collapsed and he had his way as usual. Pressing on with his attempt to unite Macedonians, Greeks and Iranians, the master-races of his empire – there is no evidence of such a policy towards any other races – he then celebrated the famous 'marriage of east and west', at which he took to wife a daughter of Darius; he had already married Roxānē, daughter of a Bactrian noble who had submitted after brave resistance. Many of his officers were assigned noble Persian ladies as brides (nearly all put them away after Alexander's death); and the marriages of 9,000 soldiers to Asian women are said to have been celebrated on the same day. Probably most of them were really the official recognition of unions already contracted. Greek priests and Persian Magi led the prayers that the races might be 'united in empire'. He was preparing a sea-borne campaign to take in southern

Arabia when, his splendid constitution undermined by wounds and exertions, he fell sick of a fever at Babylon and died in ten days (summer, 323).

Alexander's genius certainly had its constructive side. He explored as well as fought; he is said to have richly endowed Aristotle's researches in natural history, which probably owed much to him in facts as well as in money. He naturally took thought for the organization of his empire – but for the most part he simply took over the Persian system of satrapies, with Macedonians and Greeks in key positions; any improvements which he may have intended were frustrated by the maladministration of such men as Harpalos. He was a great founder of cities; but most of his Alexandrias, other than the famous one, had a purely military purpose; they were settlements of his Greek mercenary soldiers (who were far from pleased at finding themselves planted out for good, far from home and the sea) to act as garrisons; this is why there were as many as four in the north-east frontier provinces. That the history of south-west Asia after his time was much more unstable than it had been under the Persian peace was no doubt due to his early death. But we are brought back to a point mentioned already. It must be held against him that, while continually hazarding his life, and finally dying young, probably as at least an indirect effect of his wounds, he had made no arrangement for the welfare of his subjects in that event. For all his many acts of spectacular generosity, and some of chivalry to women, he was a selfish man; and even his military genius had the effect of scattering Greek colonists, unevenly but nowhere thickly, from the Mediterranean to Bactria, instead of (say) only as far as the Euphrates. This was a frontier, which Darius had offered him after Issos, which Parmenion had advised him to accept, and which covered an area that might have been more permanently attached to the Mediterranean world.

3 ATHENS AND THE
NEW EMPIRE: ARISTOTLE

Athens meanwhile had had thirteen years of unwonted peace,

while men heard, amazed, how the Great King of Persia had been brought under the new power. To that power, as has been said, Athens remained on the whole unfriendly; yet, when Sparta went to war in 332, Athens did not, and while Antipatros defeated and killed King Agis III, Athens was re-fighting old battles in the courts of law. Aischines had impugned on a technical point a proposal to garland Demosthenes with a golden wreath. The case came to trial in 330, and Demosthenes vindicated his whole career in his great speech *On the Crown*. Even if we had known that we should meet defeat, he says,

not even so ought Athens to have abandoned this course, if she took thought for her honour and her history and the ages to come. Now indeed she seems to have failed, which is the common lot of men when God so wills; but if, having aspired to lead, she had resigned her position to Philip, she would have incurred the blame for betraying all. If this cause had been let go without a struggle, the cause for which our fathers faced any danger that might come ... how could we have looked in the face the foreigners who visit us here? – if the result had been exactly what it is, ... but if the struggle to prevent it had been fought by others without us.

The most important man living in Athens at the time was not an Athenian. Aristotle, who had retired from the Academy when its presidency passed to a second-rate man (Plato's nephew Speusippos), and had later tutored Alexander, returned in 335 and founded his own school in a park near the temple of Apollo Lykeios (whence Lyceum, *lycée*; cf. p. 290).

No Greek is more difficult for us to 'bring to life' than Aristotle. His encyclopaedic learning makes him seem inhuman; and the facts that his biological theory is teleological (or purposive) and that his views on science in general later became an orthodoxy and were defended as dogma have given him an undeserved bad name with scientists. Really, the early modern scientists, observing phenomena for themselves, had much more in common with Aristotle than had the scholastic 'Aristotelians'. His style too is bald and dry; the reason being that most of what we have from him consists of lecture-notes, while what he wrote for the public, including dialogues and some poetry, has perished. Encyclopaedic he certainly was. Logic,

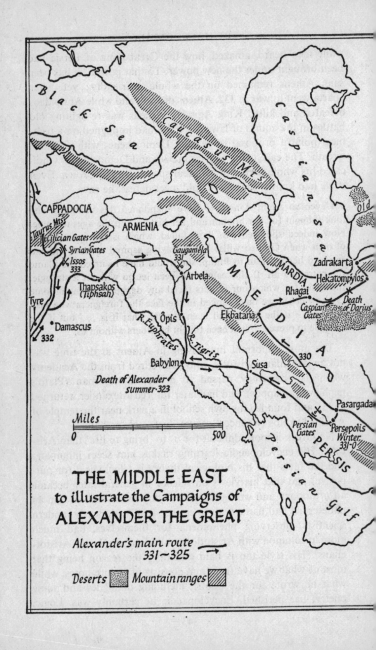

THE MIDDLE EAST
to illustrate the Campaigns of
ALEXANDER THE GREAT

Alexander's main route
331~325

Deserts [shaded]   Mountain ranges [shaded]

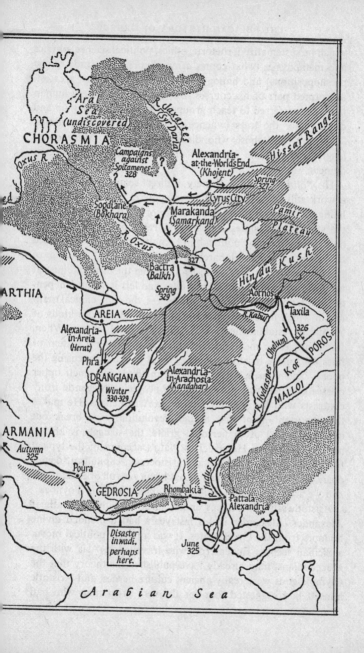

Aral
Sea
(undiscovered)

CHORASMIA

R. Jaxartes
R. Syr Darīa

Hissar Range

ed of Oxus R.

Campaigns
against
Spitamenes
328

?

Alexandria-
at-the-Worlds End
(Khojent)

Spring
327

"Cyrus City"

Soodiane
(Bokhara)

Marakanda
(Samarkand)

Pamir
Plateau

R. Oxus

Bactra
(Balkh)

327

Hindu Kush

Spring
329

ARTHIA

PARTHIA

AREIA

Aornos

R. Kabul

Taxila

326

POROS

Alexandria-
in-Areia
(Herat)

Phra

DRANGIANA

Alexandria-
in-Arachosia
(Kandahar)

R. Hydaspes (Jhelum)

K. of

MALLOI

Winter
330-329

ARMANIA

CARMANIA

Autumn
325

Poura

GEDROSIA

Rhombakia

Indus R.

Pattala
Alexandria

Disaster
in wadi,
perhaps
here.

June
325

Arabian Sea

which he systematized, rhetoric, ethics, political science, physics and metaphysics (what comes *after physics* – the study of the presuppositions) and biology, in which he was at his greatest, all formed part of his courses. But he was also a very human man. He preferred to teach groups of students walking up and down under the trees (whence they were called Peripatetics, 'Walkers'); and those who disliked him as pro-Macedonian laughed at his taste for smart clothes, jewellery and elegant dinners.

His *Politics* – Man in Society, a direct sequel to his *Ethics* – a work still studied by students of politics and education, relating as it does to the endless variety of political experience of the small Greek states – treats, naturally, of the City, as the only form of truly political life known to him. Uncivilised tribes and oriental monarchies seemed to have nothing to teach. Thus it was his fate to be analysing the city-state just at the time when Philip and Alexander had left it, as an independent unit, no longer viable. Nevertheless, the cool, clinical manner in which he discusses the working of the various kinds of 'set-up' or 'establishment' (*kathestōs*) has much charm. When, for example, he mentions the practice of having a system of fines for failure to attend meetings, but of kindly excusing the poor – and classifies it among the methods by which upper classes get their way, 'deceiving the people' – his gentle irony contrasts with the solemnity of some Aristotelians. He makes the important point that though revolutions may break out over small and often personal griefs, the struggle is always *about* great issues. He criticizes Plato's account of the typical life-cycle of the state (military aristocracy, capitalism, democracy, despotism), pointing out that history is full of exceptions; and we are reminded of modern scholars criticizing Toynbee.

Aristotle's life in Athens ended abruptly with the death of Alexander. Alexander in his last years had demanded divine honours from the Greek states. It was a purely political move; a Sicilian sceptic, Euhēmeros, who travelled in Asia with the Macedonians, may already have published his theory that the Olympic gods were really ancient culture-heroes, and Aristotle himself had suggested that for the very great man who had achieved everything it remained only to 'become a god'. Never-theless, it was resented, especially as it was accompanied by a demand that they should receive back exiles – a move intend-ed to bring stability, but involving awkward problems of restor-ation of property. Athens admitted the deification in a cynical spirit. Then, Alexander's death seemed to give the signal for driving Macedonian garrisons from Greece (there was one, for instance, at Corinth) and the recovery of full freedom. Threat-ened with prosecution for 'impiety', Aristotle fled to Chalkis, a Macedonian stronghold, where he died (322).

Most of Greece united in a new, anti-Macedonian, Hellenic League. Highland Aitolia, where population had been grow-ing, emerges as a major force. But Sparta stayed out this time (Antipatros had taken hostages); and with Sparta doubtful and Corinth garrisoned, Argives and Arcadians could not march north. Even so, a league army under Leosthenes of Athens defeated Antipatros and besieged him in Lamia, north of Ther-mopylai. But reinforcements from Asia were on the way. The Greeks had to turn against them; and Antipatros slipped past and joined them.

The really decisive operations of the 'Lamian War' took place at sea. Alexander had built up a formidable navy, pro-bably including quinqueremes, the new heavy fighting ships. The Athenian fleet, after heavy losses in an attempt to force the Dardanelles, went down fighting with 170 ships against 240, off Amorgós island. With Piraeus blockaded, only a decisive victory on land could restore the balance; and when another brave effort against the odds was repulsed near Krannon in Thessaly, Athens surrendered.

This was the end of Athens as a sea-power. Antipatros gar-risoned Piraeus; and the democracy was abolished, or, as it was euphemistically (and falsely) expressed, 'a return was made to the constitution of Solon'. Citizens not possessed of proper-ty to the value of 2,000 drachmas – six years' wages for a hop-lite or craftsman – were disenfranchised; 22,000 were thus struck off the rolls; 9,000 were left. Antipatros offered land-holdings to any who chose to join the Macedonian colonies in Thrace, and many went. Athens was weakened permanently;

and this time the leaders of the war-party were not spared. Demosthenes, run to earth by Antipatros' men in the sanctuary of Poseidon, on the saddle of the hill at Kalauria (Poros island), took there the emergency dose of poison that he had long carried.

Similar treatment was probably meted out to other insurgent cities. Only the tough, highland Aitolians – the stronger because none of their villages nor even their sanctuary-capital at Thermon was a vital objective – survived truly free.

CHAPTER 16

THE LEGACY OF ALEXANDER

1 THE SUCCESSORS

As it turned out, the Greeks would have done better to wait on events before striking for freedom; for almost immediately a naked struggle for power broke out between Alexander's generals. Twenty years of war followed, fought out from Egypt to Thessaly, but chiefly in western Asia; a story full of exciting incidents and kaleidoscopic shifts of fortune, but monotonous in its record of bloodshed and not a few betrayals. In the course of it perished most of Alexander's marshals, his tempestuous and bloody mother, his infant son, and Roxane, who had herself murdered the daughter of Darius.

Not strictly part of the history of Greece, these struggles need not be treated in detail. During them Athens lay for ten years (317–307) under the rule of Demetrios of Phaleron, an Aristotelian, anti-democratic, backed by Kassandros, son of Antipatros, as ruler of Macedonia. A doctrinaire, like Kritias (pp. 302 f.), Dēmētrios legislated in a puritanical spirit; among other things, he limited expenditure on funerals and monuments; and the gracious series of Attic sculptured tombstones now comes to an end. He was ejected by another Demetrios, son of Antigonos One-Eye, who went through a form of restoring democracy, was welcomed with wild enthusiasm, 'deified' as 'the Saviour-God', and kept his mistress in the Parthenon on the strength of it. This is the Demetrios who won the title of 'Besieger' by an elaborate but unsuccessful siege of Rhodes in 305; who, like a Rupert, pursued too far at Ipsos in Asia Minor, where his father was killed (301); and who, after further adventures, was captured by Seleukos (below, p. 351), who treated him chivalrously – and let him drink himself to death. But all was not lost; he left a son, another Antigonos, cool and intelligent, very unlike him; Sir William Tarn suggested that he took after his mother, the trusty Antipatros' daughter. The younger Antigonos, nicknamed Gonatás ('Knee-cap', from a piece of armour – we do not know why), had some of his education at Athens, and met there one of the great men of the new age; a man without form or comeliness or wealth – not even a Greek, but a Phoenician of Kition: Zenon the Stoic (below, pp. 354 f.). By his father's fall, Gonatás was left master only of a few thousand mercenaries and a few half-disaffected cities in Greece; but events were to call him to the throne of Macedonia.

Out of the dust of conflict emerged three chief succession-states: Macedonia, Egypt, and the empire in Asia, soon sub-divided. Ptolemy (Ptolemaios, 'Warlike'), who had been bodyguard, personal staff-officer and intelligence officer to Alexander, set himself from the first a limited objective – unlike the other chief marshals, who played for the earth, or as much of it as they could get. He secured the appointment of governor of Egypt, worked against anyone who tried to keep the whole empire together, and founded the most durable of the Hellenistic kingdoms; it lasted till the defeat of the last Cleopatra and her Roman husband Mark Antony in 31 B.C. It was a purely Greco-Macedonian kingdom, drawing vast wealth from the unregarded peasants through a highly organized bureaucracy; Cleopatra was the first and last of her line who ever learned Egyptian. Ptolemy also hijacked the body of Alexander, which was being taken to Macedonia, and gave it a tomb at Alexandria. He was an educated man, and wrote his memoirs of Alexander's campaigns, a chief source of the best surviving account (that of Arrian, p. 389). He probably planned, and his son founded, the greatest of all ancient institutes for scholarship and research, the 'Temple of the Muses' ('Museum') at Alexandria, with its vast library containing everything of note ever written in Greek. Demetrios of Phaleron, driven from Athens, helped him to plan it. Ptolemy assumed, or was given by well-organized 'spontaneous acclamation', the special title of Saviour (for saving Egypt from rivals?); his grandson was known as Ptolemy the Benefactor (*cf.* Luke xxii, 25).

Alone among the major contenders for power, Ptolemy I also died in his bed (283).

The most resplendent success was that of Seleukos, commander of Alexander's footguards; he gained nearly everything that the Persians had ruled in Asia, and was on the point of winning Macedonia too when he was murdered by an exiled son of Ptolemy, whom he had befriended (280). His son, and most of his important successors, bore the name Antiochos; hence the towns named Antioch, the greatest of which was the Seleukid capital in north Syria. Towns called Apameia or Laodiceia (several of each) commemorate Seleukid queens; the first Apámē was the Persian wife of Seleukos. But Alexander's dream of a fusion of Greeks, Macedonians, Medes and Persians was. rejected; and with no imperial nationality to give it a patriotism, and with never enough Greek man-power, despite some colonisation, the empire proved too large to be manageable. Through most of its history it was shrinking (pp. 363 ff.).

Macedonia, with the extinction of its royal house, was seized by general after general; among them Pyrrhos, King of Epeiros and second-cousin to Alexander, who also fought the Romans in Italy (p. 377). Weakened by the drain of its man-power to the east, invaded by migrating Kelts, whose fathers Alexander had met on the Danube, Macedonia was at last given peace under Antigonos Gonatás. Methodical, efficient, one of the noblest men of his age, Antigonos gets no very good 'press' from Greek writers. The reason is that he and his successors, for security, especially against attempts to dominate Greece on the part of the Ptolemies, kept garrisons at strategic points in Greece (Piraeus, Corinth on its isthmus, Chalkis on its strait, Demetrias, founded by Antigonos' father, near modern Volos) and supported tyrants in other cities. They were called the Fetters of Greece. Plutarch wrote lives of the spectacular Pyrrhos and Demetrios, but not of him; but he preserves some of his sayings, which characterize the man. To a poet who hinted at his divinity he replied, 'The man who carries my chamberpot knows better'; to a son of his own, guilty of some piece of oppression, 'Do you not understand, boy, that *our*

351

kingship is a noble servitude?' He was also probably the first man to call a retreat a 'strategic movement to the rear'.

Athens in 266–2 made a last brave attempt to regain her freedom with help from Ptolemy II. But the powerful Egyptian fleet did nothing effective; a Spartan king was killed trying to force the Macedonian lines on the Isthmus; and Athens was starved out. This is the episode called Chremonides' War, after the Athenian democratic leader. It was not till 229, when Macedonia was again attacked by northern barbarians, that Athens, making a great financial effort – it included the pawning of the official copies of Aeschylus, Sophocles and Euripides to Ptolemy III – managed to buy out the garrison-commander. Athens then proclaimed that she would be friendly with all powers: a neutral state.

2 HELLENISTIC CULTURE IN ATHENS

The Lamian War finished Athens as a naval, the Chremonidean as a military power; but as the city of the philosophers, the university city, her career was only beginning. Already many young men – Aristotle for one – had come from afar to hear Plato and others who had known the 'sainted' Socrates. Diogenes, from Sinope in the Black Sea, attached himself, in spite of every discouragement, to one Antisthenes, who imitated, perhaps with exaggeration, Socrates' austerity, and would regularly 'try the vocation' of would-be disciples with harshness and rudeness. Diogenes outdid the severities of his master, sleeping out in the streets or in the public colonnades or in an upturned clay storage-jar (the famous 'tub'). He mocked at men who studied the deceits of Odysseus and did not cure themselves of the like, or who could produce harmony in the lyre but had none in their souls. To Alexander himself, who visited him in 335 at Corinth and asked 'Is there anything I can do for you?' he was said to have answered, as he lay on the ground, 'You and your friends can stop keeping the sun off me'. Alexander, as he walked away, is said to have commented, 'If I were not Alexander, I would like to be Diogenes.'

In an age in which ambitious men competed for wealth,

power and influence in the service of kings, Diogenes' way of life, the Cynic or 'dog-like' way as it was called, made an appeal to many. The Cynic philosopher, in his homespun plaid, and bearded, whereas the 'polite' now went clean-shaven, became as conspicuous a figure as the Franciscan later. The street-corner *diatribe* or *homily*, meaning a straightforward, unrhetorical 'talk' (in Latin, *sermo*), full of pungent sarcasms against the insincerity of the world, was their medium of communication. Far into the Roman age, with the devotion of St Francis but without his charity, they upheld their ideal of non-attachment, and were by no means without influence. But their 'beatnik' attitude was less influential than those of two other new philosophic schools.

The new age confronted men, nowhere more than at Athens, with the question how to conduct one's life among its overwhelming forces. One answer was to keep out of politics and, as Voltaire was to say, 'cultivate one's garden'. This was the life actually lived by the gentle Athenian Epikouros (Epicurus), born in Samos, who lost his land when an Athenian colony in that island was turned out, and supported life at first by keeping a school for boys. Later, in his garden in Athens, he discoursed to a circle of friends on the way to attain true pleasure, as the only rational goal. Sensuality was rejected – he himself lived very simply. Men should cultivate their higher sensibilities, be good to their friends and attain freedom from worry. They should not worry, in particular about the alarming doctrines of a hell for sinners and the non-initiated, preached by the mystery-religions. Epikouros did not avow himself an atheist; but he adopted the materialist atomic theory of Demokritos (p. 246), and preached that the gods, with bodies of the finest atoms, live 'in the spaces between the worlds' and have no care for man. It was an unheroic philosophy; but the Epicurean societies, which came to exist in many cities, have been described as 'societies of friends'. Epicureanism became the typical philosophy of the unpolitical gentry, not least of the Roman world. Horace professed himself 'a sleek pig of Epicurus' sty'. The most famous epicurean book is Lucretius' great poem *On the Nature of the Universe*, a tract in favour of a scientific world-view, against superstition and its consequences, anxiety and fanaticism.

But the philosophy or religion of many of the more active late Greeks and Romans was Stoicism.

To Athens soon after the death of Alexander came a tall, gaunt young Phoenician of Cyprus, Zēnon, son of a merchant of Kition (Chittim, Larnaka). Attracted at first by the Cynics, he abandoned their major eccentricities, though he yielded to none in following an argument to its logical conclusion. Shy and unprepossessing, discoursing in the public colonnades (*stoai* – whence 'stoics') for lack of the means to hire a lecture-room, he impressed by incisiveness of reasoning and by sheer integrity. He too was interested primarily in practice, in how to live; and he too, therefore, went back to the pre-Socratics for a view of the world. He adopted *en bloc* the philosophy of Herakleitos (pp. 143 ff.), inevitably adapting and reinterpreting it. Fire is the primary substance; the world is the self-expression of God, whose sphere is the empyrean, the *fiery* sphere, beyond the stars and enclosing the universe. The spirits of men too are fiery particles, and those who guard the fire faithfully will return to that heaven. What is natural, therefore, is good and right; and the goal of life is not pleasure, but the preservation of the being, whether plant, animal, man or society, in its natural state; pleasure is a by-product, which occurs when natural functions are properly performed. The function of man is to do his duty faithfully in that place where, as Socrates had said, God has placed him, in the family, in the city and, if that is his destiny, in power.

Stoics therefore would not avoid trouble by keeping out of politics. When challenged with the question whether the good man would still be happy if the path of duty led to torture and death (the old question, posed in Plato's *Republic*) the sterner logicians among them did not hesitate to answer Yes; but Stoics generally allowed that, if one's position was painful and hopeless, it was permitted to retire by suicide. The doctrine that the world is the self-expression of the divine reason, *logos*, led to strong emphasis on destiny, and so sometimes to fatalism; stoics, like other people, were not always consistent. Interest in the stars, as in divine fires, also led to a feeling that they too must have significance for man; and later stoicism was not untinged with one of the superstitions of later antiquity, Babylonian astrology.

Zenon remained at Athens for the rest of his long life. Antigonos invited him to Macedonia to be his spiritual adviser; Zenon would not go, but sent a disciple, also from Kition. The Athenians honoured him in a decree, inscribed on stone, as one who had taught the young goodness and self-discipline, by both word and example. He died in Athens in 264, while Antigonos was besieging it. Antigonos said he had lost his 'audience' – the 'gallery' he had always played to. But when he took the city, there were no reprisals.

The culture of the new age is called Hellenistic, in distinction from Hellenic; the culture no longer only of the Hellenes as a people, but of the Hellenizers, from *Hellenizo*, meaning to speak Greek or side with the Greeks. For this culture, stoicism provided an ethic no longer needing the city-state for its environment; an ethic for a world-commonwealth, *cosmopolis*, even if, like the city of Plato's *Republic* or the holy church universal for John Knox, it might be unrealised on earth and 'invisible'. Its citizens were all good men, whether Greek, Semite, Scythian, bond or free. Several of Zenon's followers came from the Seleukid empire, three actually from Tarsos, the city of St Paul, which was developing as an intellectual centre in its own right. Among Stoic rulers, the first was Antigonos, the last Marcus Aurelius, who died in A.D. 180; and Marcus revered a stoic of a hundred years earlier, Epiktētos, by origin a Phrygian slave.

Athenian drama still flourished modestly, even with a king's garrison at Piraeus. Old tragedies, especially those of the great three, were now regularly revived. Thousands of new tragedies were also written in the succeeding centuries, not a few of them by Roman nobles; but so far as we can tell they became more and more literary exercises, hardly more actable than those of Shelley or Swinburne. Creative dramatic work was more modest: that of the New Comedy, now known to us directly from papyrus finds in Egypt (showing that Greeks scattered over the world read these plays) as well as through the Latin adaptations (much free translation, plus a peppering of crude Roman jokes), made in the next century by Plautus and Terence. We may regret that the Roman drama, which is second-class stuff, has survived rather than its immediate ancestor; Julius Caesar himself remarked that Terence (who incidentally was a slave from Carthage) had successfully Latinised the pure Attic style, but just was not so funny. However, it was this Roman version of New Comedy which reached Renaissance Italian, French and English dramatists, including Shakespeare (his *Comedy of Errors* is a free adaptation from Plautus); and from it thus the whole modern theatre is directly descended.

New Comedy was a social comedy of manners, escapist to the extent that all stories have a happy ending. Young men, amorous but good-hearted, win their girls with the help of a clever man-servant (a Jeeves or Figaro), in a world of irascible but not irredeemable fathers and uncles and villainous slave-owners and brothel-keepers. Sometimes the villain is the legal owner of the heroine, and is duly outwitted and discomfited, while the girl turns out to be someone's long-lost daughter, kidnapped as a child, and thus socially 'suitable' after all. Another stock character is the Braggart-Soldier, home from making his fortune in the east.

The greatest name in this genre is that of Menander (Menandros, *c.* 343–291). A well-to-do man, reckoned pro-Macedonian, he was not very popular in his own days, but immensely so later, as we see from the number of quotations and of papyrus finds. Among the titles of plays recovered in great part are *The Arbitration* (between two peasants who have picked up a foundling with trinkets on it), *The Rape of the Locks*, *The Shield* (or *Missing, Believed Killed*); while *The Surly Man* (*Dyskolos*) is nearly complete. This character lived for choice on a hill farm up at Phyle, making things difficult for the matrimonial designs of his young people; but he was converted when he needed help, after he had dropped a dish down the well and then fallen in himself. But Menander has, along with his humour, much compassion too. Both in this and in his style, he owes as much to Euripides as to Aristophanes. One of his famous 'quotations', used by St Paul among many others – 'Evil communications corrupt good morals' – may actually have been quoted *in* Menander *from* Euripides. 'Who runs away will fight again' was another of his lines. The following, with its theme 'Blessed is he who has seen these things', reads like an epicurean riposte to the claims of the mystery-religions:

> I call him happiest
> who, having seen without pain, Parmenon,
> *these* noble things, goes swiftly whence he came:
> the sun that lights us all; stars, water, clouds
> and fire. Whether you live a hundred years
> or a few seasons, you shall see the same;
> and greater things than these shall you see never.

The same Greek melancholy is in the line, perhaps his most famous: 'He whom the gods love, dies young'.

Menander himself did not reach old age. He is said to have been drowned when out swimming off Piraeus.

3 THE ALEXANDRIAN ACHIEVEMENT

Zenon had declined to go with Antigonos to Macedonia; for philosophers, Athens was still the mother-city, where thought was free if political life was not. Menander likewise was invited by Ptolemy to Alexandria, and would not go; the 'pro-Macedonian' still had his own integrity. At Alexandria, the princely endowments of the Ptolemies did however collect a notable fellowship of poets and scientists. Those who valued their freedom of speech jeered at them as 'fowls in a chicken-coop'; but for many scholars, good minor poets and some major scientists, salaried leisure meant opportunity. Euclid (Eukleides), an original mathematician in his own right, gave geometry a system under Ptolemy I. Aristarchos of Samos, perhaps taking up a guess made in the Pythagorean school, evolved in about 280–265 the theory that the sun is the centre of the universe and the earth revolves about it. He tried to measure the relative distances of the sun and moon but, having no means of measuring angles with the necessary precision, made the sun only twenty times the more distant. At Athens Kleanthes, head of the Stoic school in succession to Zenon – an ex-professional boxer, who supported himself by market-gardening, and author of an impressive *Hymn to Zeus* – found the theory shocking; it was incompatible with the cosmology to which the Stoics were committed (p. 354). He said that Aristarchos ought to be tried for impiety. The tension between science and religion thus long antedates Christianity; but the reason why Aristarchos' theory was not accepted until it was taken up again by Copernicus was the more creditable one, that he could not support it by sufficiently precise observations and measurements.

More successful was the more modest enterprise of Eratosthenes, librarian and head of the institute after 250, who measured the earth. Having observed that the midsummer sun shone right to the bottom of a dry well at Assuan, i.e. that it was vertical, he measured the shadow cast by a vertical pole at Alexandria at the same season, and thus found the angle subtended by the distance between the two cities. His calculation of the circumference gave a result only about 10 per cent too large. At Alexandria too Apollonios of Perga, *c.* 236, worked out as a branch of pure mathematics the theory of conic sections, which was to prove long after to have applications both in astronomy and in ballistics.

Eratosthenes was an encyclopaedic scholar; pure mathematician – he devised a method for finding all prime numbers, known as Eratosthenes' Sieve; chronographer – the traditional date for the fall of Troy, still often quoted, derives from him; geographer, critic. He was the first to call himself a *philologist*, a lover of learning. Some others called him the Pentathlete, or less kindly Beta, 'Number Two', as being second-best in so many fields.

In literary scholarship, the librarians did a great work of classification and criticism. The Ptolemies aspired to possess every significant work ever written in Greek; and to this end the librarians made lists of the major authors, the Three Great Tragedians, the Ten Attic Orators, etc. Many of the works preserved in our manuscripts of Plato, Demosthenes and others, but believed on grounds of style or of inconsistency not to be theirs, probably owe their preservation to persons who succeeded in selling them to the library as works of the great. When a society begins to list certain writers of the past as classical, or in Greek, 'canonical', it indicates a feeling that something has been lost. However, the library rendered a service in directing the attention of later scholars, including those of the East Roman or Byzantine empire, to whom we owe all the manuscripts (except papyri) of Greek literature that we have.

With literary criticism came its occupational disease, the literary quarrel. A celebrated one was that between Kallimachos, from Cyrene, who catalogued and classified the library under its first librarian, and another Apollonios, who had been his pupil. Kallimachos was in favour of short poems, in an age of short poems; though his aphorism, A Big Book is a Bad Thing, perhaps refers rather to the labours of an assistant librarian. It was the Alexandrians who divided Homer, Herodotos and other long works into the 'books' that we know, each short enough for one papyrus roll. Apollonios thought there was still room for new epics. But what really embittered things was the question of the Librarianship, to which, on the retirement of Zēnodotos, the Homeric critic, Apollonios was appointed over Kallimachos' head. Kallimachos rejoiced when, under Ptolemy III, Apollonios lost his post and retired to Rhodes. There he wrote his epic on the Argonauts and the Golden Fleece (with love-interest, in the modern manner); hence he is usually called Apollonios of Rhodes, though born in Egypt. Kallimachos refers to him as 'the Ibis', the sacred Egyptian scavenger bird, alleging that he had 'scavenged' ideas and phrases from his old master.

Kallimachos apparently never got the big post at all – it went to Eratosthenes; but he won great fame by his poetry. The few relatively long pieces that survive are marked by obscurity and learning, and it was apparently exactly this that Alexandrian literary circles liked. His readers, like those of the Roman Propertius, who admired Kallimachos and was admired by Ezra Pound, were expected to enjoy their own cleverness in being able to understand the esoteric allusions. But in very short poems he can be exquisite, as in the six lines on hearing of the death of Herakleitos of Halikarnassos, an old friend. The nineteenth-century version of this by William Cory is one of the best known of all English translations; but it is too long and too 'sweet'. A less pretty version may perhaps be nearer the mark.

> They told me, Herakleitos, you were dead;
> They brought me tears. How often you and I
> At Halikarnassos talked the sun to bed –
> Your home – where now, long cold, your ashes lie!
> But your sweet nightingales are living still;
> Something not even greedy Death can kill.

Even the 'nightingales', presumably Herakleitos' poems, are long lost now; only his friend's little poem preserves his name.

Among critics and coteries the stream of worth-while Greek poetry shrinks to a trickle of sometimes pretty or witty epigrams. But one new vein was struck in the third century: the pastoral.

Theokritos of Syracuse, after failing to win the patronage of the current military boss there, came east, bringing something new: hexameters in the Doric dialect, reproducing in literary form the love-songs, satires, traditional songs and improvisations, with which Sicilian shepherds helped to pass their time on the hill. Away from home, with the charm of the exotic to help him, he won more attention. 'Sweet is the wind in the branches' begins his first poem; and precisely in Alexandria, where Greeks grew homesick, sometimes, for rocks and clean air and the wind in the pines, he had his success. He was able to spend time too in Kos, which was within the Ptolemies' island empire, and where there was a circle of poets; and he won a modest but lasting place in the hall of fame. He is no Robert Burns; he has less underlying seriousness; but he plunged or sank happily into the literary coteries which accepted him, and which adopted the pastoral as a convenient, escapist convention. 'Pastoral' poems could carry references to

recent events; births, marriages, deaths and literary contro-
versies. Here started the convention honoured by many greater
poets, a convention leading to the pastorals of Vergil, Spenser
and Milton; to the Little Trianon and the Dresden shepherdess,
and to *Adonaïs* and *Thyrsis* in the nineteenth century.

The thirty poems preserved are not all pastoral; some of
the *idylls* ('pictures', or vignettes) are of the eastern, Hellenistic
scene. One of the most attractive describes a picnic in Kos;
members of the literary circle walking out to the harvest
celebrations on a farm, and some perhaps amusing themselves
by dressing up in country clothes. The most famous of all – one
could wish there were more like it – is about ladies of Alexandria. Gorgo calls on Praxinoa, who has some acid things to
say about her husband's reasons for living so far out and
then is rather shaken to find that her little boy is taking it in –
but really, you know, the great lump can't do the simplest bit
of shopping without making a blunder. Nor can Gorgo's. Men
are so unpractical. Then they go to see the royal show at the
Festival of Adonis. ('Take Baby and play with him, Phrygia.
Call the dog inside, and lock the front door.') They make their
way with difficulty through the swarming crowds (but at least
the new king has suppressed those native Egyptian footpads
nowadays), rush squealing out of the way of a troop of the
royal war-horses, elbow their way through the jam in the doors
with the help of a kind stranger; and the idyll ends with a girl
soloist singing the hymn for the spring-time resurrection of the
Dying God.

Another 'sketch', of great verbal beauty, is in the form of a
monologue by a girl whose lover has left her. Under the moon,
she first tries sympathetic magic to win him back, and then,
while she waits, pours out to the Moon-goddess (who is also
Artemis, protector of women, and Hekate, queen of hell) the
story of her disaster. The magical part is of great interest, in
that almost every part of her technique can be paralleled in
almost every part of the world: 'As my bay-leaves burn in the
fire, so may Delphis be consumed by love. As this wax image
melts, so may he melt. As my wheel turns, so may he turn and
turn about my doors.' She shreds into the fire a piece of fringe

from his cloak. Something belonging to the destined victim, as well as an image representing him (or her), is a standard magical 'property' everywhere. Finally she sends her maid to smear the juice of herbs over his door, and spit (for luck; giving up something of one's self) and say, 'It is Delphis' bones I smear.'

The techniques of witchcraft are much the same the world over, among both literate peoples and savages, and it seems virtually impossible that they have spread everywhere by diffusion; rather, like the multiple invention of agriculture (applied to different food-plants in the New World and in the east and west of the Old), this nonsense of magic is the expression of a common human nature. It arises from the fact that when the way to doing what one very much wants to do is barred, it gives relief to do *something*, especially something *like* what one wants to do; hence the images, which may also be pierced with pins, with hostile intent. Black magic was known in classical Greece; it is forbidden in Plato's *Laws*, and the Superstitious Man in a set of *Characters* by Theophrastos, the naturalist and pupil of Aristotle, is afraid of it. But it receives scarcely any other mention. The classical writers, and their public, had risen clear of it; though we do find, even in classical times, another product of malevolent superstition, in the shape of 'curse-tablets' usually of lead, transfixed by a nail and fastened originally to a tomb, inscribed with the formula 'I bind' or 'fix' so-and-so; sometimes 'I bind X, his name and himself'. If so and so *is*, by name, X, it follows at this level of reasoning that the name X *is* the man, and by a curse-tablet it is hoped to 'bind' him to the grave. (The 'real name' of the city of Rome is said, therefore, to have been kept secret, for security reasons.) Contemporarily with the great achievements of Alexandrian mathematics and science, the ways of thought of pre-rational man creep back out of oblivion into a twilight where we occasionally catch sight of them.

4 THE GREEKS IN ASIA

Christianity emerged in a Greek-speaking Syria; farther east and earlier, the first Buddhist monumental art is Greco-Bactrian. These are the most abiding achievements of Greek rule in Asia. Politically, the House of Seleukos soon lost control of the east, chiefly because of their western preoccupations – especially wars with the successors of Ptolemy over south Syria. Seleukos himself ceded the Punjab to the Indian empire-builder Chandragupta, in return for 500 trained elephants, which he used to defeat Antigonos One-Eye.

In Bactria and the north-east frontier region, the Greek mercenaries, settled by Alexander in four Alexandrias and other cities, tried to march home after his death, but were forced back by a Macedonian general with Iranian cavalry. Under Seleukos' grandson, their descendants acclaimed their own general Diodotos as king and 'Saviour'. The kingdom of Bactria, controlling central Asian trade-routes, lasted for a century (250–140?) and produced some of the most splendid of Greek coins. King Demetrios, after 200, wears a headdress in the shape of an elephant's head with uplifted trunk; it commemorates his reconquest of the Indus basin, after the break-up of Chandragupta's and Asoka's empire. He is the 'great Emetrius, Lord of Ind', known through the Roman Justin's *Outline of History* even to Chaucer. But meanwhile another general, Eukratidas, made himself king in Bactria; he wears a helmet looking like a modern *topee* – but metal. So there were two kingdoms, and the available Greek or partly Greek man-power was split again. A generation later, Bactria was overrun by central Asian nomads.

The Greek power south of Hindu Kush lasted longer, perhaps reinforced by refugees from Bactria, and displayed remarkable vigour. A king Menandros, about 175–140, marched far down the Ganges. He too, on his coins, bears the title Saviour; for headdress, he reverts to the simple Macedonian diadem or head-band. He figures in a Buddhist classic, *The Questions of King Milinda*; Milinda, king of 'the fierce Ionians', in his town-planned and well-watered capital in the Punjab, holds dialogues with the sage Nagasena, ending in his conversion to Buddhism.

This is the context of the rise of the first Buddhist monumental sculpture, in the province of Gandhara, round modern Pesháwar. Hitherto Buddhists, like the earliest Christians, had not portrayed their master. The motifs are Indian, both free-standing statues and reliefs with, for instance, the birth-stories of the Buddha; the technique is Greek. From it descended all Buddhist monumental art, though it swiftly assumes its own character both in southern Asia and in China. After 'Milinda', the petty kingdoms into which his empire fell apart become increasingly Indianised. Coins go over to the square shape, and one of these, for example, with the name of a King Sileinos in Greek, has Indian motifs on the reverse. Indian Hellenism was already much diluted, before the nomads penetrated the mountains to found their 'Indo-Scythian' or Kushan empire in the last century B.C.

In central Iran, where there were no Greek garrisons, the relapse was swifter. Soon after Diodotos' revolt a nomad chief named Arsakes, coming from Bactria, entered the old province of Parthia, killed its Greek governor, alleging insults and injuries to the people, and seized power. Thus began the kingdom of Parthia, at first a mere buffer-state for Bactria against the Seleukids, but destined to outlast them both. Antiochos III (223–187) indeed restored Seleukid overlordship from the Aegean to the Oxus, over both Parthia and Bactria; but he was drawn back to the west, to meet defeat by the Romans in Greece and Asia Minor in 191–90 (p. 381). Even in Parthia, coins bear Greek legends; probably all documents were in Greek. Greek plays were performed at court; some kings used the title 'the Phil-Hellene'. By 130, with the Seleukids further weakened by Rome, the Parthians had won Mesopotamia, with the apparent goodwill of the people; Seleukid government was more alien and, probably, more expensive. The reputation of the Parthians has suffered, through our knowing of them mainly from their enemies – not least, their successors, the great Sassanid dynasty, who, emerging from Persia proper about A.D. 200, denigrated the dynasty they had overthrown as nomads, not good Persians nor good Zoroastrians. However, the House of Arsakes governed Iran for over 400 years.

Most of Asia Minor was lost soon after the death of Seleukos.

The Gauls or Galatai who overran Macedonia (p. 351), killing Ptolemy Keraunos who had murdered Seleukos, also invaded Greece. They by-passed Thermopylai by the west and thought to sack Delphoi; but the Greek highlanders (especially of Aitolia) rose and destroyed most of them in guerrilla warfare. Others, joined later by remnants from Greece, reached the Sea of Marmara and got ships from Greeks who wished to be rid of them and from the king of Bithynia (north Asia Minor) who hoped to use them against his enemies. Though probably numbering only a few thousand warriors, by sheer ferocity and fighting qualities they then 'held up' Asia Minor for years. Antiochos the son of Seleukos, with elephants in his army, beat them in 275, but was then drawn off by a war with Ptolemy II. The main credit for stopping their raids on Ionia went to Philetairos, captain of Pergamos, a eunuch, left in charge of that fortress and a great treasure during the wars of the Successors. His chief, Lysimachos, had been defeated and killed by Seleukos, who had been murdered by Keraunos, who had been killed by the Gauls ... leaving Philetairos under no moral obligation to anyone. He passed on his power to a nephew, Eumenes, who defeated an invasion by Seleukos' son and ruled nominally as governor for Ptolemy II; the Ptolemies were concerned to hold as much of the Greek coastal and island world as possible, for the sake of access to Greek man-power and ships' timber. *His* successor, Attalos, a cousin, took the title of king.

Attalos and a second Eumenes beat off further raids of the Gauls, now settled inland in the Asian Galatia, and adorned their capital with vigorous though florid sculptures, symbolizing the struggle of Hellenism against barbarism. Some famous stone statues in Italy are probably copies of bronzes dedicated by Attalos on the Acropolis at Athens, after a state visit in 200: Greeks and Gauls, Greeks and Persians, Greeks and Amazons (an Athenian legend). Famous among them are the Dying Gaul (so-called Gladiator) and a Gaul slaying his wife and himself to avoid capture, both in Rome. The sympathy shown for the defeated enemy, noble after his fashion, is in the tradition of Homer. Eumenes II set up at Pergamos, about 180–160, the huge Altar of Zeus and Athena, with its flanking colonnades and approach stairway, now (once more, after a sojourn in Russia) in the Berlin Museum. Its reliefs show the War of the Gods and the Giants. The citadel thus adorned became the centre of Caesar-worship under the Roman Empire and thus the 'Satan's Seat' of the Apocalypse.

Employing the best sculptors of Greece, this royal patronage produced some of the most admired work of the age. The only school to vie with Pergamos in reputation was that of independent Rhodes, with such works as the famous group of Laokoön and his sons destroyed by serpents and the great bronze Colossos of Apollo, 105 feet high, set up about 280 and overthrown by an earthquake about 224. It stood on two rocks at the harbour-mouth, so that men in boats (*not* ocean-going ships, as legend had it) could 'creep under his huge legs'. All this work may seem to us too grandiose for good taste; but the Hellenistic world did also produce more modest work of greater charm. Portraiture (to which that of Roman Italy perhaps owes more than is commonly recognized) reached a high level; children were sympathetically studied, as seldom in classical art; and the Aphrodite of Melos ('Venus de Milo'), unrecorded in antiquity, may have been the cult-statue of a temple in that small island.

As patrons of culture, the Attalids prided themselves on their friendship to Athens. Eumenes adorned the south slope of the Acropolis with a colonnade, 180 yards long, of which the rear wall survives, and a second Attalos (159–138) built the east colonnade of the Agorá; rebuilt to serve as a museum for finds from that area, it shows what a Greek *stoa*, providing space for shops and a sheltered walk for philosophers and other citizens, was like in its prime. Pergamos had also its great library, second only to that of Alexandria; and when the Ptolemies, who resented the existence of the Attalids as parvenus and rebels, meanly refused to supply papyrus, their craftsmen perfected the ancient method of preparing skins for writing ('pergamene', whence 'parchment').

So too Seleukid Antioch had its royal library, and as late as the last century B.C. there arose a school of Syro-Greek poets, who wrote their short elegiac love-poems, occasional poems and epitaphs with a voluptuous sweetness reminiscent of the Song of Songs. Of their more ambitious efforts nothing remains. Meleagros of Gadara, in the Decapolis, the Ten Towns east of Jordan (Greek towns – hence the Gadarene swine, an abomination to the Jews), the best of these poets, also collected the first nucleus of our Greek Anthology of such 'epigrams'. He called it his *Garland* and, in an introductory poem, compared the work of each author to a different flower, with the famous phrase 'of Sappho few, but roses'.

In Melagros' time the Seleukid kingdom, reduced to Syria and rent by faction, was in final disintegration; what was left of it was briefly taken over by a king of Armenia, before Pompey made it the province of Syria (64–3 B.C.) in his organization of the near east for Rome. Its Hellenism lasted on through the Roman occupation, only gradually fading after the Muslim conquest in the seventh century. In the Roman east, Greek remained the language of civilisation; native languages, such as 'the speech of Lycaonia', Galatian, Aramaic, were spoken, but comparatively little written. Already in Ptolemaic Egypt, the Jews of the 'dispersion' spoke Greek, so that the scriptures had to be translated for them (the version of the Seventy scholars, or Septuagint). The general use of Greek was of enormous importance to the spread of Christianity. The Apostle Matthew is indeed said to have written down the *Logia* or Sayings of Jesus 'in the Jews' language'; but our 'Matthew', a combination of the *Logia* with the Gospel of Mark and other matter, made probably at Antioch before 100, was written, like the whole of our New Testament, in Greek. The Greek Church was, indeed, all too slow to translate it into the language of the peasants, and the first versions in Syriac (eastern Aramaic) were made east of the Euphrates, outside the empire. This and the subtleties and wrangles of Greek-speaking theologians help to account for the fading of Christianity in Syria in face of Islam. The Semitic peasants were never Hellenized; and they outlasted the Greeks in the end. Under the Seleukids and the Romans, Syrian cities bore Greek names: Aleppo was Beroia, after the Beroia (modern Verria) in Macedonia; Gerasa was another Antioch, Hamath an Epiphaneia (after

Antiochos IV, Epiphanes, 175–164 B.C., whose attempt to Hellenize the Jews provoked the rising of Judas Maccabaeus), Rabbah of Ammon a Philadelphia; but today they are again, and have been for centuries, Halep, Jerash, Hamah and Amman. Only ruins, and the patriarchate of Jerusalem with its monastery, still staffed from Greece, commemorate the thousand years of the Greek occupation.

CHAPTER 17

THE SHADOW OF ROME

1 THE FEDERAL LEAGUES
AND THE SPARTAN COMMUNE

GREECE was important to the Hellenistic kingdoms as a source of trained man-power: poets, doctors, philosophers, engineers and, above all, soldiers. Ultimately, much of the population seems to have been drained away. In the third century B.C., a united Greece could still have been powerful; but the same disintegrating competitiveness which had lost better chances in the past was still operative. Nevertheless, steps were taken which were intelligent, and remain interesting: federalism among small communities, modernisation at Sparta; only too late.

The Aitolian and Achaian Leagues, in the third century, improved machinery and enrolled members beyond their original borders. Both were federal states, in which self-governing communities shared a common citizenship, foreign policy and defence system. Each elected annually a federal general to execute policy and direct strategy, with the proviso that the same man might not be general two years running. Each had a large advisory Council, meeting periodically, but not sovereign; Greeks never developed representative government, not because they were not clever enough but because they did not trust one another sufficiently. Sovereignty remained with general league assemblies, meeting once or twice annually for some days, and in emergencies, which all citizens might attend, but the poorer citizens from the remoter places naturally could not do so often; and votes were counted, not individually but by communities, with some attempt at 'weightage' according to population. Unfortunately, these two interesting states remained bitter rivals, and frequently at war.

The importance of Achaia dates from about 250. It was

largely the creation of one man, mobilising the impatience of the Peloponnesians at Macedonian domination.

Dorian Sikyōn, Achaia's eastern neighbour on the Corinthian Gulf, was one of the cities ruled by tyrants, *protégés* of the now aging Antigonos; but in 251 a young exile named Arātos, with a band of comrades, liberated it by a 'commando' operation and, with constructive imagination, brought it into the Achaian League. Aratos was a strange, neurotic character; a brilliant politician and speaker, with no formal rhetoric – the Achaians elected him their general in alternate years for a generation – but so nervous that he was not only afraid in battle, but unable to disguise the fact; and at the same time so brave that, being so afraid, he not only began his public career with a commando raid but crowned it with another. In 243, without a declaration of war, he attacked Corinth with its Macedonian garrison, by a night surprise. He was admitted with a hundred men, 300 more following, by a Syrian Greek whom he had bribed, and made for the citadel, the towering Acrocorinth; the Syrian had observed a place where the rocks were scaleable and the wall at the top was only fifteen feet high. Surprise was lost and the alarm was given; but the 300 men in support, who had lost touch and halted in the shadow of the rocks, by luck found themselves perfectly placed to ambush and rout the Macedonian troops from the town below. The guide came down and led them on, shouting now, to give the impression of an army; and thus reinforced, Aratos forced his way over the wall, just as dawn was breaking and the main Achaian army appeared in the plain below.

Corinth joined the League and city after city followed, in Argolis and Arcadia; though Aratos failed to win Piraeus and Athens. But the men of Elis preferred to join Aitolia, with which they had ties of blood and dialect. The Aitolians had extended their power over Phokis (with Delphoi) and Boiotia; now they had Olympia too; but the Achaians regarded them as rough, highland marauders. So there was federalism *in* Greece, but no federal Greece. And there was high tragedy soon to follow.

Sparta had always remained in proud isolation; but the

ancient 'constitution of Lykourgos' was far gone in decay. The number of full Spartan 'peers', fallen to 1,200 even before Leuktra (p. 319), was down to about 700 now. The provision that made the Spartan's lot of land inalienable had long been evaded; and the landless man had no citizen rights. It was a narrow oligarchy, with vast inequalities between rich and poor, even among the free.

Inequality of wealth, indeed, seems to have been increasing in Greece generally. Alexander's dispersal of the gigantic gold-reserves which the Persian kings had accumulated, with serious deflationary effects on their own empire, started a long-continuing inflationary price-rise in Greece, as mercenary service and trade brought much of it thither. Meanwhile wages remained at traditional levels, or actually fell, perhaps through increased competition from slave-labour. Many poor men were feeling desperate. There had been a number of small uprisings, notably in the islands – always suppressed by the overlord-power, whether Macedonia or Egypt – before events took a dramatic turn, when a king of Sparta declared for revolution.

Young Agis IV, aged about twenty-two at the time (241), was influenced by Stoic philosophy, by the tradition of ancient Spartan history, considerably mythologized, and perhaps by Utopian romances, of which several were circulating. One, by a certain Iamboulos, was a tale of adventure and shipwreck in the southern ocean, leading to an account of a Fortunate Isle where the people lived in ideal communism; they finally expelled the Greek castaways as insufficiently virtuous. But Agis' basic desire was clearly to restore the strong ideal Sparta of the Good Old Days.

Agis proposed, with backing among a circle of younger men, the regular Greek revolutionary programme: a cancellation of debts and a redistribution of the land; there were to be 15,000 lots, inalienable, held of the state for as long as the male line lasted, for Laconian 'dwellers-around', and 4,500 nearer the city for Spartiates, to be recruited from landless men and Laconians; foreign residents (mercenaries?) who would accept the Spartan discipline were to be eligible. Agis and his family offered their own lands and fortunes, amid great enthusiasm.

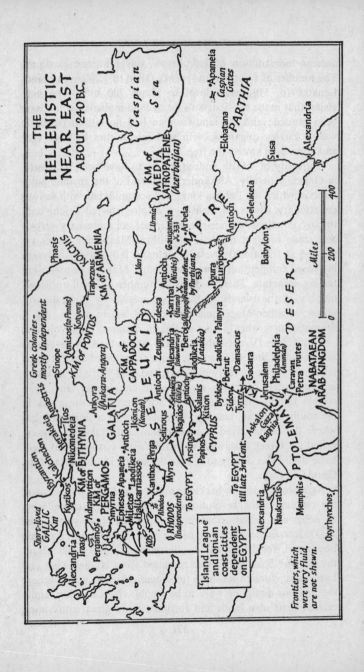

THE
HELLENISTIC
NEAR EAST
ABOUT 240 B.C.

Caspian Sea

*Apameia
Caspian Gates

KM of
MEDIA
ATROPATENE
(Azerbaijan)

PARTHIA

•Ekbatana

Alexandria

•Susa

KM of ARMENIA

KOLCHIS

Phasis

L.Urmia

Gaugamela ×331
•Karrhai (Nisibis)
(Haran)
Edessa

E M P I R E

•Seleukeia

Antioch

Berois(Aleppo)Roman defeat
by Parthians, 53

•Doura
Europos

R.Tigris

Babylon

R.Euphrates

Trapezous

KM of
PONTOS

Amisos(toPontos)

Kotyora

Sinope

GALATIA

S E L E U K I D

Zeugma
Antioch

KM of
CAPPADOCIA

Ankyra
(Ankara-Angora)

•Ikónion
(Koniah)

Alexandria
(Iskenderun)

Antioch

Seleukeia
(Sulefie)

Laodikeia
(Latakia)

L.Van

Palmyra

•Laodikeia
•Damascus

Byblos
Sidon
Tyre•

DESERT

•Gadara

•Philadelphia
(Ammān)

Jerusalem

Caravan &
Petra routes

NABATAEAN
ARAB KINGDOM

 Askalon•
Gaza•
Raphia•

PTOLEMAIC

Beirut

Greek colonies—
mostly independent

Amastris

Herakleia

Chalkedon

Byzantion

Short-lived
GALLIC Km

Kyzikos

KM of
BITHYNIA

Nikomedeia

Tios

•Adramyttion

KM of
PERGAMOS

Pergamos•

Alexandria
Troas

Smyrna

Ephesos Apameia •Antioch
•Miletos •Laodikeia
to •Halikarnassos
RHODOS

KOS

ⓄRHODOS
(independent)

Xanthos• Perga

Myra

To EGYPT

Selinous

Arsinge?
Nagidos

Paphos•
Salamis
Kition

CYPRUS

To EGYPT
till late 3rd Cent.

"Island League"
and Ionian
coast cities
dependent
on EGYPT

Memphis•

Alexandria

Naukratis•

•Oxyrhynchos

Frontiers, which
were very fluid,
are not shewn.

Miles
0   200   400

But the land bill was blocked by a majority of one among the twenty-eight old men of the Senate (p. 115), under the presidency of the other king, Leonidas. The ephors, Agis' friends, impeached and dethroned Leonidas; and when in the next year the reactionaries (since only the privileged could vote) carried the election of ephors, who reversed the sentence, Agis' young friends expelled them by force and appointed a congenial board. But then Agis was outwitted by his wicked uncle, Agesilaos, who persuaded him to go ahead with the cancellation of debts first; Agesilaos was himself heavily in debt, but a great land-owner. Then, when Agis had been sent north with the army, to support the Achaians in an Aitolian war, Leonidas came home with some mercenaries; and when Agis returned, he found himself faced with impeachment for his unconstitutional action. The unenfranchised Laconians, disappointed at the shelving of the land-bill and accustomed to the government of the oligarchs, made no move. Agis' soldiers, it is said, would have supported him; but he refused to engage in civil war, and took sanctuary. He was trapped outside it, and judicially murdered, by hanging, together with his mother and grandmother, who were reckoned responsible for his ideas. That the grandmother of a grown man should still be active is surprising to us; but women married early; she was not much over fifty.

Fourteen years later the revolution was carried through by a king of the other line, Kleomenes III, son of the very man who had foiled Agis. Leonidas had forced Agis' young wife Agiatis to marry his own still younger son, in order to secure her large fortune; but from his wife, no doubt among other influences (he had also a Stoic tutor), Kleomenes became imbued with Agis' ideals. Taught by Agis' fate, even when king (237) he kept his own counsel, until a favourable moment came. In 229, when old Antigonos' son and successor was defeated and killed by northern Thracians – the same year in which Athens bought back Piraeus – he picked a border-quarrel with the Achaians. Mercenaries were hired to reinforce Sparta's Laconians; and with them, leaving his Laconians on the frontier after winning a victory, Kleomenes in 227 marched home, killed four of the ephors (one escaped), proclaimed the revolutionary programme and carried it through.

There was enthusiasm again among the Laconians, who received land, and 4,000 of them Spartan citizenship; moreover a thrill ran through the Peloponnese, and city after city went over from the League to his side – even one in Achaia itself. The rich were alarmed. A papyrus discovery shows us one of the best League leaders, Kerkidas of Megalopolis, urging them in verse pamphlets to share their wealth with the poor lest it be taken from them. Kleomenes had won the city of Corinth and was besieging Acrocorinth and Sikyon, when the League, which had already made overtures to Macedonia for help, in desperation accepted Macedonia's terms. Antigonos Dōson, the new king, who had restored the situation in the north, demanded the cession of Corinth; and Aratos himself accepted the bitter pill.

Also, Kleomenes was not carrying through social revolutions in the cities now allied to Sparta. It became clear that he was not thinking in terms of social revolutions as such; he aspired to lead the Peloponnese. He had already offered to join the Achaian League – as its permanent general. The popular enthusiasm for him collapsed, and while he faced the Macedonians on the Isthmus, his lines were turned by sea. There were still fierce campaigns; Mantineia was destroyed and its women and children sold by the Achaians, and Megalopolis (most of the people escaping) by Kleomenes; for Antigonos could not keep his Macedonians in the south all the time. But in 222 Antigonos invaded Laconia, and the Spartans, after a brave resistance with about 20,000 against 28,000 men, were broken at Sellasia, six miles from the city, near where the hillroad from Tegea comes within sight of Sparta's lovely plain.

Kleomenes, whose courage no one doubted, though urged by at least one friend to join him in suicide, determined on flight; he might yet do something for Sparta. He fled with other friends to Egypt, which had given him some financial aid. But the young Ptolemy IV would do nothing for him beyond keeping him, as a card that might be played some time. In 219, grown desperate, he tried to raise Alexandria in revolt. Its civilian population did not move, and in despair the Spartans killed each other; Ptolemy's men then killed their women and children. Kleomenes' queen had died before the defeat. Sparta became once more an oligarchy, with annual ephors but without kings; but the land-reform was not wholly undone. Antigonos kept Corinth, and formed a new Hellenic League, with the Achaian League as part of it; but Aitolia stood out, holding Elis and most of central Greece, and Aitolian privateers, treating those not in league with them as traitors to the national cause, became the scourge of the Aegean. Both Macedonia and Egypt had let their sea-power fall into decay; but southern waters were policed to some extent by Rhodes, a cultivated, civilised state, in which a merchant oligarchy kept the people content with social services, and developed a code of sea-law, still used in Byzantine times.

Antigonos Doson died soon after Sellasia, after defeating another barbarian invasion; he was probably consumptive. Philip V, grandson of Gonatas, was then a youth of seventeen; but he soon showed high ability, and hammered Aitolia, sacking Thermon, the federal meeting-place, in 218; it was a general war of the 'Hellenic' and Aitolian Leagues.

Rhodes offered to mediate, and was joined by Byzantion, Chios and Egypt; and in 217 a great conference met at Naupaktos. Agelaos of Naupaktos, welcoming the delegates, spoke eloquently of the need for peace. He pointed to the titanic struggle proceeding in the west, between Rome and Carthage. It was time for all Greeks to join hands, 'like men crossing a torrent; for', he said, 'if the cloud now rising in the west should overspread Greece, we shall, I fear, be praying the gods to give us back the chance ... of calling our very quarrels our own'. All men applauded; Philip himself was well alive to the danger, and peace was made. But in the sequel, no Greeks could endure to see a rival gain an advantage. Within five years there was war again; Philip allied with Carthage, and Aitolia with Rome.

2 ROME AND THE WESTERN GREEKS

The conquest of Italy by Greek culture, of which Roman poets speak, had begun in the early days of Greek colonisation. Our Roman alphabet is derived from that of western Greeks. Rome's first great temple was built in the Greek manner. Etruscans and other Italians who could afford it adopted the costly Greek armour. South Italian Greeks and natives developed their own florid styles of vase-painting, imitating Athenian red-figure, and continuing all the more actively when Athens (it seems) lost interest in this worked-out field of art, after 400.

But as the native peoples increased in numbers, and their armies in weight of metal, they pressed the colonies hard. Cumae and Paestum fell under native rule before 400, continuing to exist with some coarsening of their culture. The southern cities suffered disasters around 390, when Dionysios of Syracuse made alliance with their enemies in order to extend his own power. To Dionysios also, it is said, came envoys from the Gauls who in that year sacked Rome.

This is the first mention of Rome in literature, all the native Roman historians being much later. A fourth-century Greek, Herakleides, mentioning this event, called Rome 'a Greek city'; a mistake, but there were probably Greek traders settled there; from a Greek point of view, there was at this time little difference between Rome and Cumae.

Taranto (Greek Taras, Latin Tarentum), nearest to old Greece, held her own awhile under Archytas, philosopher, general and friend of Plato; but later she too was hard pressed. She asked for a general from her mother-city, Sparta; King Archidamos III came, and fell in battle in 338. Alexander, King of Epeiros, uncle and brother-in-law of Alexander the Great, won several victories and even liberated Paestum; but his evident intention to carve out an empire for himself alienated the Tarantines, and he too fell (330). The south, however, was saved for a generation. Then came more appeals from Taranto, to King Kleonymos of Sparta (303), who likewise

quarrelled with his allies and departed baffled; then to Agathokles, tyrant of Syracuse. Agathokles, a potter's son who had
risen as a soldier and become tyrant with popular backing, was
able and ruthless. When besieged in Syracuse during a Carthaginian war, he had had the nerve to create a diversion by invading Africa; and in Italy he won some successes. But after his
death, old and prosperous, in 289, Thouria, the successor of
ancient Sybaris, having had bitter experience of Taranto and
her friends, appealed for help not to Taranto but Rome: to
the rising and Hellenized city, which had lately defeated Gauls,
Etruscans and the Samnite hillmen and emerged as the greatest
power in Italy. Rome sent a garrison. The Tarantines, considering the south their protectorate, marched out and forced it
to withdraw. Soon after this they attacked ten Roman warships
which appeared off Taranto, 'east of the Lakinian Cape' near
Thouria, contrary to an old treaty, and sank several. Then,
growing alarmed, they applied for aid to another king of
Epeiros, the great soldier Pyrrhos (p. 351).

Pyrrhos was delighted. He would carve out an empire among
the barbarians, and then use it to crush Antigonos Gonatas and
other rivals. But when, out on personal reconnaissance, he saw
from a hill the square blocks and ordered lines of a Roman
camp, he commented '*That* does not look barbaric.'

Pyrrhos won two victories over the Romans, in 280 and 279,
but only by using everything he had, especially elephants,
which the Roman horses would not face. The ranks of his well-
trained professional soldiers were sorely thinned. A few more
such 'Pyrrhic victories' and he would be ruined. The Romans
lost twice as heavily; but, from among citizens and allies, they
could replace casualties out of a pool of some 700,000 potential
fighting men.

Having however driven the Romans from south Italy,
though they refused to make peace, Pyrrhos transferred himself
to Sicily, where the Greeks were again in trouble with Carthage. Again he won successes, but no final result. Carthage
and Rome made an alliance against him. Back in Italy, to face
the Romans again, with an army now chiefly of allies, he haz-
arded a night march, to attempt surprise. It failed, and he was

squarely beaten (Benevento, 275). He returned to Greece, to renew his old feud with Antigonos; and there, in 272, he was killed in Argos, felled by an old woman with a tile from a house-top, in the chaos of a street battle, after his largest elephant had got stuck in a postern gate. In the same year Taranto surrendered.

Pyrrhos, leaving Sicily, had said 'What a battlefield I am leaving for Rome and Carthage'; and there indeed Rome and Carthage clashed within ten years. Hieron, the latest military chief to be acclaimed King of Syracuse, set out to suppress a body of Italian mercenaries, the Mamertines or 'men of Mars', as they called themselves, who had seized Messina. The Mamertines asked for and received help from both Rome and Carthage, each anxious to deny the other control of the Straits; but, preferring the alliance of fellow Italians, they presently expelled their Carthaginian garrison. Carthage and Hieron were thrown into uneasy alliance; but when full-scale war broke out, Hieron soon found it prudent to forget the *casus belli* and go over to the Roman side.

Rome's First Punic (i.e. Phoenician) War, fought out from 264 to 241, chiefly in Sicily, ended with most of the island under Roman occupation. The beautiful city of Akragas (Agrigento) had been captured and recaptured, twice sacked, once burnt, permanently crippled; but Syracuse had suffered only the strain of a war-effort. Hieron, Rome's good ally, kept his little kingdom, and his long reign (he lived until 216) saw the city's last golden age. Middle-class houses in Sicily, as in the Hellenistic east, show a rising level of comfort. Sicily had its poets and historians – though Hieron had earlier failed to retain Theokritos – and among his subjects was also one of the greatest Greek mathematicians: Archimedes, who had studied at Alexandria. Great both in pure mathematics, and in engineering, he spoke slightingly of the latter, which was admired by the public. Highest in his own eyes stood the demonstration of a method for showing the relation between the volumes of a sphere and its circumscribing cylinder; but the most famous story about him refers to his discovery of the principle of specific gravity. Hieron presented him with the problem of determining whether the gold of a crown made for him had, as some-one alleged, been adulterated. Archimedes, with this on his mind, was baffled until, noticing the displacement of water by his body in the public bath, he realised that he could solve it by comparing the displacement of water by the crown and by an equal weight of pure gold; whereat he is said to have run home naked (the term could also mean 'scantily clad', in a bath-wrap) shouting ecstatically 'EURĒKA' – 'I've got it!'

But when Hieron died, late in 216, disaster was near. Hannibal had marched to Italy from Spain, and won his early, sensational victories; the opportunity to restore the power of Syracuse seemed too good to be missed. A democratic party made alliance with Carthage: but Rome's vast man-power was far from exhaustion, and soon the city was under siege. The great walls built by Dionysios, taking in the high ground where Nikias had sought to extend his lines, defied all assaults; cata-pult artillery and other engines, directed by Archimedes, as-sailed the Roman ships and siege works with devastating effect. But after months of blockade and the failure of Carthaginian relief operations, the outer wall fell to a night attack, and then the inner city by treachery (212). There was much looting and massacre, despite the order of the Roman general Marcellus that the citizens should be spared; and Archimedes himself was killed, unrecognized – it is said, by a soldier irritated at his refusal to answer to a shout, as he contemplated a diagram in the sand.

3 ROMAN CONQUEST

Philip V of Macedonia had made the same miscalculation, and made alliance with Hannibal; but the Romans neutralised him by sending modest forces to support his enemies, the Aitolians. With Carthage beaten (201), the Roman government deter-mined to render him harmless. Very unwillingly, the war-weary people were induced to vote for the campaign. Legions were raised, consisting of volunteers only; and after three indecisive campaigns a new, young, and brilliant commander, Flamininus, beat the Macedonian phalanx by sweeping away its flank-guards, with the help of Aitolian cavalry, and taking it in rear

(Battle of Kynos Kephalai or 'the Dog-Heads', a ridge in Thessaly, 197). Philip was forced to withdraw all forces from Greece and become Rome's ally, an alliance which he loyally kept; and in 196, amid scenes of great enthusiasm, Flamininus announced the withdrawal of Rome troops also: Greece was to be free.

One Greek state detained Flamininus for two years longer: Sparta, where after a defeat by the Achaians revolution broke out again under a leader named Nabis. Our accounts of Nabis, which make him a monster, are exclusively those of his enemies; 'one must', wrote Sir William Tarn, 'look fairly at what he did. He carried out all the four points of the social revolution.' He abolished debts, redistributed land (leaving some for the wives and children even of exiled opponents), freed slaves and helots, and used money taken from the well-to-do to defray state expenses (including perhaps the ancient Spartan institution of common meals). 'Certainly', says Tarn, 'in getting rid of the class-state, as he claimed to have done, he for the last time restored Sparta's strength in an extraordinary way.... He raised 10,000 citizen troops, partly liberated Helots.' Altogether 'he had in Sparta 18,000 men when Rome declared war on him; and when Flamininus, the conqueror of Macedonia, attacked Sparta, they beat him off. One can see that they must have fought for *some* sort of an idea, anyhow.'

Sparta could not resist such odds indefinitely, and Nabis then accepted Flamininus' terms. He lost Argos, which had been put in his hands by Philip; but Flamininus left Sparta's internal arrangements alone. But the revolution could not survive in a hostile world. Nabis was murdered by some Aitolians, who had come as his allies against the Achaians; the Spartans rose and avenged him, but their remaining leaders quarrelled, and in the confusion the Achaians and exiles swooped upon them. All the new citizens were expelled. Philopoimēn, the Achaian general, offered them homes in Achaia (the wars had evidently left room); but no less than 3,000 rejected the offer and endured the grim alternative of being sold as slaves (188).

Peace had already broken down elsewhere. The Aitolians, disgruntled at the mild terms granted to Philip and considering themselves the true victors of Kynos Kephalai, called in Antiochos III, who had for the last time restored Seleukid over-lordship over Parthia and Bactria, and had designs on Egypt and Pergamos. A Roman army forced the pass of Thermopylai, storming the hills inland (191), and in the next year, with allies from Pergamos and Greece, broke his main army in Asia Minor and forced him to give up all claims west of the Taurus mountains. Aitolian power was cut short after two stern campaigns in their hills. Rome was clearly the mistress, even without direct occupation ; and a miserable feature of the following years is that Greeks sought advantages against their rivals by complaining to the world power. Complaints from Pergamos about alleged designs of Macedonia led to a war in which the Macedonian kingdom was destroyed and broken up into four republics (168) ; its last king, Perseus, died a captive in Italy. The Roman senate, a council of great land-owners, feared and mistrusted democracy and favoured oligarchies. Achaian democrats had hoped for a Macedonian victory ; and the Romans now carried off 1,000 Achaians as hostages. One of them was Polybios, the last Greek historian, son of a general of the League.

Polybios was received into the house of the Scipios, the leading family in Rome and one of the most cultivated. He became a great admirer of Roman character as he saw it, in some of its finest representatives and not yet corrupted by power. He was impressed to see how Roman officers could handle public money honestly, without the apparatus of seals and witnesses which Greeks needed and even then evaded. These were men, he felt, who could give the world peace. His chief patron was Scipio Aemilianus, son of Aemilius Paulus, the poor and upright conqueror of Macedonia, and adopted by the wealthy and childless son of the conqueror of Hannibal. His work was planned as a history of the fifty years down to 168, which had seen Rome emerge from Italy to dominate the Mediterranean world ; but he continued it later for another twenty-two years, which cost him much grief. The Achaian democrats, continually reported on to Rome by their rich opponents, became desperate. 'We want you as friends,' said one of them to a Roman delegation – sent in answer to an appeal from Sparta against Achaian interference – 'but not as masters.' A hopeless war, in which central Greece joined the Achaians, ended in 146 with the total destruction of Corinth, as a warning to others. At the same time there was a people's rising in Macedonia. Rome placed Macedonia under the direct rule of a governor with an army, who also supervised Greece. Later, central and southern Greece became the Province of Achaia.

It is of the sack of Corinth that the story is told, how, when the art-treasures of centuries were being stacked on the quay for transport to Rome, the consul Mummius insisted on the usual clause in his contracts with the shippers; that, if any of these goods were lost in transit, they should be replaced by others as good.

The Roman Senate, like nineteenth-century British governments, was *not* eager for annexations; rather, it regarded oversea commitments as a nuisance and an expense. But with the loot of Greece and Carthage (also destroyed in 146) flowing in, Rome was also a great capitalist power. Italian businessmen were everywhere; some of them simply traders, but not a few also financiers, backed by senators, who were forbidden by law to engage in trade themselves. Prominent among their operations was the lending of money, largely representing the spoils of war, at high interest. With the increase of wealth there also set in a feverish competition between senators, for money with which to give gladiatorial and wild-beast-killing shows, to gain popularity, to gain votes, to be elected to high office in the hope of getting a command in which to make, it was said, three fortunes: one to pay one's creditors, one to bribe the jury if prosecuted for extortion, and one to live on for the rest of one's life in a style befitting a nobleman. In these circumstances it is not surprising if the Italians, who relied on protection from their government, were rapacious and generally hated. Their Roman 'principals' might be cultivated gentlemen, even phil-Hellenes. In 51 B.C. Brutus, the high-principled Stoic who later killed his friend Caesar for conscience's sake, arranged with a proconsul to give Brutus' agent in Cyprus a military commission and troop of horse with which to dragoon the people of Salamis (near Famagusta) into paying a loan, with 48 per cent compound interest. It was an illegal loan, since a recent governor, trying to protect the provincials, had fixed the maximum rate at 12 per cent; but Brutus had also used his influence to procure a directive to the governor of Cilicia, saying that this did not mean him. Cicero, a decent man, taking over the province, ordered the cavalry out of Cyprus, and declined to give military commissions to financiers. But he did not allow the Salaminians to deposit the sum legally due, and close the transaction. To quarrel with Brutus was politically inexpedient.

Italian trade also extended beyond the frontiers; and moreover, in her own supposed interests, Rome set herself to weaken independent states; the resulting chaos then repeatedly made annexation necessary. The shrunken Seleukid kingdom was further disrupted by Roman 'moral support' for the Jews under the successors of Judas Maccabaeus. Rhodes, which had shown an independence of spirit unwelcome in a small ally, was ruined by the establishment of a free port at Delos. It specialised in the slave trade, never so active as in this age; it was claimed that its market could handle 10,000 bodies a day. Most of the elegant houses, well preserved at Delos, are those of Italians and others who were doing well on it. Many of those who took part in the great slave revolts in Sicily (139, 134–1, 104–1) and in Italy (Spartacus, 73–1) must have passed this way. With Rhodes and the Seleukids crippled, moreover, piracy, based on the rocky coast of 'rough Cilicia', flourished as never before, until even coast roads in Italy were unsafe.

In Pergamos the last king, Attalos III, on bad terms with his relatives, and perhaps also hoping to prevent worse by accepting the inevitable, in 133 left his kingdom by will to the Roman Republic; but the hand-over was not accomplished smoothly. A people's rebellion, led by an illegitimate brother of Attalos, who proclaimed a utopian 'City of the Sun', was suppressed with the active help of neighbouring kings. Worse still the wealth of Ionia and Lydia, now the Province of Asia, became a counter in Roman politics. To gain the support of the Roman commercial class, the reformer Gaius Gracchus saddled Asia with an iniquitous system of taxes; Roman syndicates bid for the privilege of 'farming' them, paid the treasury and set out to collect as much more as they could, while Roman troops kept order. It was after a generation of this that, when Mithradates, King of Pontos (north-east Asia Minor), overran the province, during a civil war in Italy, the Asian Greeks are said to have massacred 80,000 Italian men, women and children in a day.

Mithradates' Greek admirals also sacked Delos; it never fully recovered. He crossed over to Greece proper; and in the war that followed, Athens itself suffered a siege and storm by the Roman Sulla (86). The century about 130 to 30 B.C. was the most miserable that Greece had ever seen; for there were still the Caesarian civil wars to come, thrice fought out in Greek lands between the forces of east and west. In the last, before the defeat of Antony and Cleopatra in 31, Greek civilians were mobilised, when mules ran short, to carry sacks of corn (their own corn) 100 miles over the mountains to Antony's huge naval camp. Before that, in 45, a friend of Cicero writes in a letter to him:

At sea ... on my way back from Asia, I was looking at the shores round about. Astern lay Aigina, before me Megara, on my right Piraeus, on my left Corinth; all once teeming cities; and now they lie in ruin and wreck before our eyes.

It was a ruined land that received at last the qualified blessing of peace without honour.

4 ROMAN PEACE

Roman Law and the Roman peace were institutions which kept the ring while, with order and dignity, the richest grew richer and the rest grew poorer; until the government no longer trusted the people, and the poor regarded with apathy or worse the coming of barbarians other than those in the imperial forces. The Empire carried the seeds of decay from its birth. However, not everyone, even of the poor or the decaying middle classes, was conscious of being squeezed all the time; and with the triumph of Caesar Augustus, with salaried governors and officials, fixed taxes replacing tax-'farming', and an administration no longer bedevilled by politics, there was a certain recovery. Already in 46 Julius Caesar had re-founded Corinth as a colony of retired veterans; this city, growing rapidly more Greek and cosmopolitan, is the Corinth of St Paul, the account of whose adventures is, among other things, a first-class document on travel-conditions in the Empire.

Within the provinces, cities retained local self-government; some, which had come into Rome's orbit as allies, were nominally free. Such were Rhodes and, in the far west, Marseilles, both cities to which well-to-do Romans repaired to study literature or philosophy. Sparta, with her archaic institutions, remained a museum-piece, and tourists went to see the celebrated contests of adolescents in the endurance of flogging; for this sadistic spectacle a theatre was provided. But tourists also travelled to see the Olympic and other games (now thoroughly professionalised) and the temples of Greece with their paintings and sculpture. Pausanias, from Asia Minor, in the second century A.D. wrote a travel-guide to central and southern Greece, which is still invaluable, telling us what stood in many places where there are now only foundations and fragments.

Plutarch, from Chaironeia in Boiotia (c. A.D. 45 to 120?), had heard tales from his great-grandfather about carrying corn for Mark Antony. He could appreciate peace. Also he had been to Rome, apparently to plead in a boundary dispute between Chaironeia and a neighbour, which was better than fighting about it, and been invited to give philosophy lectures, both there and in north Italy – in Greek, of course; being indeed kept so busy that he had no time to learn more than a tourist's requirements in Latin. He was honoured by emperors, and dedicated books to elder statesmen, including the famous *Lives*, written at home in his little country town in his later years. Civil archon and priest at Chaironeia, an initiate into the Mysteries of Dionysos, a frequent visitor to Delphoi –

some of his dialogues record conversations he had had there – he may remind us of a scholarly, eighteenth-century English dean. Yet he looks back with some wistfulness to the glorious if tragic past. In his *Parallel Lives* (the title is his own) of great Greeks and Romans he seems to be compensating himself for what saddened him in the present, as well as reminding his Roman friends of what Greece had been. Literary eminence was all very well; but where, he asks in one essay, would the poets of Athens have been without the soldiers and sailors? Today he doubts (in another essay) whether the whole country could raise an armoured brigade. Now there certainly had been much emigration, as also from central Italy in his time; but Plutarch's '3,000 armoured men' does not mean simply *men* but men of substance, land-owning citizens. Evidently, as in other parts of the empire, most countrymen were poor peasants, tenants, not of hoplite class. The estates of land-owners, as in Italy, or Gaul, were large; but correspondingly few.

In one thing Greeks were recognized by Romans to be still their masters: in higher education, the teaching of philosophy (including scientific theories; but not experiment) and rhetoric, for which the modern catchword is 'creative writing'. Here Athens, far outshining Rhodes, Marseilles and other educational centres, remained the premier university for centuries. There were no degrees and no organized examinations; but we recognize the authentic undergraduate in a guilefully pious letter from the son of Cicero to his father's old secretary. Young Marcus professes regret for slackness in correspondence and some more serious but unspecified misdemeanours, and devotion to his studies; a subject on which Father, reading (like the experienced barrister he was) between the lines of rather qualified praise in reports from his tutors, had expressed misgivings, such as to suggest the desirability of a personal visit. Four hundred years later Libanios, a pagan scholar respected by the Christian emperor Theodosios, found even student clubs and their rivalries; groups of devotees of particular 'sophists', or literature-professors, would waylay new arrivals and try to secure them by force. There was even some attempt by the civic authorities to impose discipline, through Kosmētai, Athenian magistrates with jurisdiction over the gymnasia. There is a series of busts of these 'moderators', of Roman date, grave, bearded and looking sufficiently formidable; though one would imagine that they were as little inclined to interfere with the sons of Roman grandees as were the authorities of eighteenth-century Oxford to discipline a young lord. Libanios knew all about facing a blasé student audience, which would refuse to be impressed by his attempts at brilliance; some trying to disturb those who were attending, others counting up the audience or gazing out of the windows.

There was much building in Roman Athens. The centre of the old Agorá, no longer needed for the purposes of a democracy, was occupied by an Odeion or covered theatre with seating for 1,000, the gift of Augustus' general Agrippa. Later, when Hērōdes Attikos, of whom more below, had built the larger and finer Odeion on the other side of the Acropolis, about A.D. 150, that in the Agorá (rebuilt, smaller, after its roof fell in) was used for lectures. North of it stood the Temple of Ares, transferred probably from Acharnai in the now thinly inhabited countryside (p. 230). A new, colonnaded market-place was laid out further east, by the munificence of Augustus himself. Near it was the little, octagonal *Hōrologion* or Clock-tower, built earlier, which also carried a weather-vane. It was a public water-clock; a post, supported by water in a pipe, sank gradually during the day as the water was let out through a small aperture, and markings on the visible shaft indicated the hours. There were also sundials on the outside walls, under the reliefs representing the gods of the Eight Winds (whence 'Tower of the Winds', the building's popular name). Near by, one Pantainos' public library (*c.* 100) bore an inscription saying that it will be open every forenoon, and that books may not be taken out. Hadrian added a grander one.

Hadrian, the restless genius, 'the Grecian' as some Romans called him with a touch of resentment, loved Athens and stayed there in 125 and again in 129. He was initiated into the Eleusinian Mysteries; he accepted the position of Archon; he aspired to be a Founder, and to that end added the new quarter, east of the elegant little Hadrian's Gate, with its inscriptions, on one side THIS IS ATHENS, CITY OF THESEUS, and on the other THIS IS THE CITY OF HADRIAN, NOT OF THESEUS. Its centre was the vast Temple of Olympian Zeus, by the Ilissos, where Peisistratos long ago had planned a temple and where Antiochos Epiphanes had begun to build, but through his misfortunes been unable to finish. Fifteen of its hundred Corinthian columns, ninety feet high, still mark the spot. Loving Greece, too – as, indeed had his more disreputable predecessor Nero, sixty years before – Hadrian founded a new Hellenic League, which might have been a step to self-government; but it was too late; the heart was out of the country. Greece still had intellectuals, millionaires and a fine though poor, despised and ignorant peasantry; but, as Plutarch had complained, as far as citizens of the old type, modest land-owners, were concerned, the population was gone.

Millionaire and rhetorician too was Hērōdes, from Marathon, called Atticus by the Romans, who about 150 built the Odeion at the foot of the Acropolis, used for classical plays and concerts today. He also restored, in Pentelic marble throughout, the Panathenaic stadium, with a seating-capacity of 50,000, restored again for modern Olympic games by the northern Greek Avéroff. There was scarcely a historic site in Greece, indeed, which did not receive some of his architectural benefactions; an attempt to make up in stone for the ills of a land 'where wealth accumulates and men decay'. He was a patron of literary men too, such as the Roman Aulus Gellius, who knew well Hērōdes' villa at Kēphisia, and named his miscellany, written at Athens in winter evenings, *Attic Nights*. The most famous story which it preserves is that of Androcles and the Lion; though it seems to have been Bernard Shaw's idea to make the runaway slave of the story into a Christian confessor. Hadrian's successor Antoninus called Hērōdes to Rome, as tutor to his adopted son, Marcus Aurelius, rewarding him with the consulship, as it were with a peerage; and it was in Greek that Marcus, the Stoic emperor, wrote his *Meditations*, largely in camp on the Danube, when barbarians were bringing to an end the peace of the Antonine 'Silver Age'.

Greeks, often of Asia, were at the same time becoming more prominent in the imperial government and army. Greek names appear among legion-commanders as far afield as Britain. Arrian, a Greek with a Roman name, who had learned Stoicism under the ex-slave Epiktetos, governed Cappadocia, reconnoitred the Black Sea and wrote reports on it to Hadrian, which survive, and commanded an army repelling raiders from the Caucasus. The experience fitted him to produce the best history we have of Alexander the Great, based largely on Ptolemy's lost memoirs. Appian, from Alexandria, another second-century Greek with a Roman name, wrote the best surviving account of Rome's eastern and civil wars (all original memoirs having perished except Caesar's). Cassius Dion, son of a Greek of Asia Minor who had been governor of Cilicia, wrote a history of Rome down to A.D. 229; he had been a senator under Severus. Syrian Lucian wrote his amusing essays.

Even in science, after the long, lean years of the Roman wars, Greeks produced some notable achievements. Hērōn of Alexandria, of uncertain date, designed a steam-engine – and proposed its use to impress the ignorant, by causing temple doors to open, untouched by hands, when a fire was lighted on the altar outside! That it was never put to practical use has often been attributed to lack of interest in labour-saving devices among the dominant classes in a slave-owning society; but in fact, the Roman world was at this very time developing the use of one such invention, the water-mill; and with the end of Roman conquests, the number of slaves was diminishing. The failure to build a practical steam-engine may have been due rather to inability to produce boilers that would not burst.

Two great names of the second century owe their fame partly to their position at the end of the long line of Greek scientists. Both bore the Roman family-name Claudius; their ancestors had received Roman citizenship probably under Claudius or Nero, between 41 and 68. Galēnos, Galen (the

'Gallien' of Chaucer), c. 130–210, was brought up a Stoic and trained as a physician at Pergamos and Smyrna. He worked in his native country, though also at Rome, as physician to Marcus Aurelius. He was a prolific writer, and systematized the knowledge of his time (including that gained from dissection, long practised at Alexandria and elsewhere) in a comprehensive, psychosomatic account of man in health and disease, intended to serve as a basis for further observation and experiment; the exact opposite to the influence which it actually exerted. Claudius Ptolemy at Alexandria, mathematician, astronomical observer and systematic geographer, an older contemporary of Galen, mapped the heavens and the earth, doing his best to give latitudes and longitudes from observations reported, e.g. on the length of the day; one of the furthest north (not accurate) is from the Winged (i.e. Battlemented) Camp in Caledonia, Inchtuthil, near Perth; it must have been made during the brief occupation by Agricola about 83. Like Galen, Ptolemy systematized his subject, accounting for the movements of the planets by his ingenious theory of epicycles (circular orbits whose centres move on greater circles). Through the Arabs and then at first hand, Ptolemy was long studied as 'the authority' in western Christendom, and reverence for him froze astronomical theory until the days of Galileo.

It was not the fault of these two great observers and thinkers, that later centuries chose them to represent ancient and unquestionable authority. If their work had not existed, something, probably less good, would have been found. For when they died, almost everywhere, for social reasons, the lights of ancient Greece were going out.

EPILOGUE

THE END OF ANCIENT GREECE

WHEN did ancient Greece come to an end?

Various conventional 'closing dates' could be suggested, and some are given below; but the century which saw the most profound change in the spirit of Greek-speaking upper-class culture was the third of our era. Being in the Antonine period, very much the culture of a small upper class, it was vulnerable; and when disaster struck again, it did not recover. Its legacy, essentially the legacy of a classical education, was preserved especially in Constantinople, the New Rome founded at Byzantion in 330 by the first Christian emperor, and in Christian Asia Minor.

The murder of Commodus, Marcus Aurelius' unworthy son, was followed by a struggle for power between the generals of the chief army-groups, during which Byzantion. notably, stood a long siege and was destroyed. Its destroyer, Severus, a senator from Phoenician Tripolitania in Africa, with a Syrian wife, was the final victor. He rested his power nakedly upon the army, and when the last of his family was murdered in 237, there followed forty years of military coups and civil wars, while barbarians began to raid across the neglected frontiers. The Heruli, a tribe akin to the Goths, having migrated from Germany to south Russia, took to the sea and plundered the Black Sea colonies. Then, in 267, though some of their boats were sunk by a naval patrol, they passed the Bosporus, raiding far and wide in the Aegean, burning Ephesos with its great temple and then Athens itself. Athens did not fall entirely unavenged; Dexippos, a rhetorician and historian, with a military engineer sent, too late, to restore the ancient walls, took to the hills and, with an improvised 'home guard', struck back, burning many of the attackers' boats and killing some of their

391

crews while they were celebrating. But the Heruli merely marched off, burning and plundering, north by land.

Athens survived; but the rough fortification-wall (miscalled after Valerian, a slightly earlier emperor), now built of marble and other fragments from the wrecked buildings, and incorporating the fire-blackened ruins of the Stoa of Attalos, is eloquent of disaster. So is the fact that the ancient Agorá itself, littered with ruins, was left outside. The shrunken city huddled in a small area round the Acropolis; a spectacle of decay, repeated in many parts of the late empire.

The fourth century saw some recovery, even some slight expansion. The nine-hundred-year-old Panathenaic procession was still occasionally revived. University life went on; Libanios (p. 386) was still to give his picture of it. Among the students were at one time two young men from Cappadocia, destined to be numbered among the saints and Fathers of the Church, Gregory of Nazianzos and his friend, the great Basil; and with them, ironically, for a few months in 355, a prince of the imperial house, Julian, nephew of Constantine the Great and cousin of the reigning emperor Constantius. It was this Julian who, his father and other kinsmen having been massacred by their Christian relatives as possible rivals, reacted against the Christianity in which he had been brought up. He made, as emperor (361–2), the last attempt to check the new faith and restore the Olympic gods.

The attempt was foredoomed, even had not Julian, the lover of the classic past, soon fallen in a skirmish after a victory over the Persians. The rumour that he was murdered by a Christian in his own army was soon current, and could be true. Christianity, with its appeal to the poor, had long since been showing far greater vitality than the religion of the ancient cities; and such vitality as remained in paganism belonged less to the Olympians than to Persian Mithras, Egyptian Isis, and other gods of the mystery-religions. Delphoi, sacked perhaps by the Heruli, had made no recovery when, so at least a legend says, Julian sent men to consult the oracle. The response said to have been given by a priest living among the ruins sounds like a literary composition; but it may serve as a swan-song of ancient Greece:

> Say to the king: in ruin the once gay courts of the temple
> lie; not a shelter of boughs has the god, nor speaks in the laurel
> nor in the fountain; silent is even the voice of the water.

The universities, the Senate at Rome, some outlying peasants – '*pagans*', meaning country people – were the last adherents of the old gods; and pagan philosophy, even at Athens, in the fourth and fifth centuries bore the marks of a new age. Stoics and Epicureans are no more heard of. The prevailing philosophy was Neoplatonism, a movement which, taking up the strain of mysticism present in Plato, had developed it out of all recognition. Its first great master was Plotinus, from Egypt (204–270), an austere ascetic, of whom it was said that 'he seemed ashamed to be dwelling in the body', and whose book, the *Enneads*, is loved by many Christian scholars; its last, Proklos of Athens, a gentle scholar, about 450. One of its most gifted defenders was a woman, Hypatia, mathematician and philosopher, of Alexandria, whose atrocious lynching by a mob of Christians, including many monks, in 415, shocked the Christian historian Socrates.

There was little popular resistance when the emperor Theodosios (379–395) proclaimed the closing of the heathen temples. The Olympic Games, an offence to strict Christians, who discountenanced athletic nudity, were suppressed in 393; Pheidias' gold and ivory Zeus, like Praxiteles' Aphrodite from Knidos and many other famous cult-statues, was carried off to adorn Constantinople. At Athens, Pheidias' statue had probably perished in an accidental fire much earlier (p. 236); and it is not known just when the temple itself was handed over to the Christians. It was the church of the Christian Virgin for a thousand years, before Turks made it, for 365 years, a mosque. But in neoplatonist asceticism and mysticism, the spirit of classical Greece could scarcely be said to live, long before Justinian, builder of the Church of the Holy Wisdom at Constantinople, closed the schools of heathen philosophy in 529.

BOOKS FOR FURTHER READING

The following highly selective bibliography includes only books not requiring a knowledge of the ancient languages. + indicates paper-back.

I – GENERAL

Standard histories, not always as thrilling as might have been expected, include:

The Cambridge Ancient History: volumes I and II, now re-written, include chapters on Aegean prehistory. They are authoritative, but the authors do not always agree; *e.g.* in Vol. II, part 2 (on the Dorians), details given as history on pp. 694f. are described on p. 813 as 'probably fictitious'. The present writer would take the latter view.

J. B. Bury, *A History of Greece*, 3rd edn, skilfully edited and brought up to date by R. Meiggs (Macmillan).

N. G. L. Hammond, *A History of Greece* (O.U.P., 1959). Rather uncritical of the ancient sources. Companion volumes, *Studies in Greek History* (O.U.P., 1973).

+ A. Andrewes, *Greek Society* (Pelican, 1971).

George Grote, *A History of Greece* (1849–56), though completely out of date for the early period, is still, with its nineteenth-century liberal enthusiasm, worth reading on Athens.

Bury, Hammond and Grote end in 323 B.C.

A. R. Burn, *The Warring States of Greece* (Thames & Hudson, 1968) contains what might have been the author's selection of illustrations for this *History*.

+ Sir Alfred Zimmern, *The Greek Commonwealth* (O.U.P.; 1st edn 1911 revised later), chiefly about classical Athens, is firmly based on a first-hand acquaintance with the Greek country and ways of life.

+ W. G. Forest, *The Emergence of Greek Democracy* (Weidenfeld & Nicolson, 1966), is thoroughly original and 'debunks' some ancient and modern debunkers.

+ Sir Maurice Bowra, *The Greek Experience*, now available in a Mentor edition, gives an appreciative treatment of the whole of Greek civilisation.

Two deservedly famous essays on the whole subject are: G. Lowes Dickinson, *The Greek View of Life* (Methuen; 1st edn, 1896)

+ H. D. F. Kitto, *The Greeks* (Pelican, 1951).

+ R. V. Schoder, *Greece from the Air* (Thames & Hudson, 1974). 140 air photographs of sites with key-plans. Invaluable, despite some errors in the letterpress.

A. R. Burn and Mary W. Burn, *The Living Past of Greece* (Herbert Press, 1980) is an introduction to about 70 historic and pre-historic Greek sites, with plans.

II–SOURCES IN TRANSLATION

+ Most of the standard and most readable sources (Homer, Herodotos, Thucydides; Xenophon, *The Persian Expedition* [i.e. the *Anabasis*], and *History of My Times*; Arrian's *Campaigns of Alexander*; Plutarch's Athenian lives, *The Rise and Fall of Athens*) – are in Penguin Classics (some now out of print); so are most of the famous works of the Attic drama, and of Plato, including those quoted in this book. Most are also available in reliable translations, though in an older idiom, in Dent's Everyman's Library (many out of print, but available second-hand) and in the O.U.P. World's Classics, Loeb Library, etc.

+ *Hesiod and Theognis* (Penguin Classics, 1973).

+ *Greek Lyrics*, tr. R. Lattimore (U. of Chicago, 1949) supplies a long-felt want.

+ *Pindar*, tr. R. Lattimore (U. of Chicago).

III–SPECIAL PERIODS AND SUBJECTS
A. THE PREHISTORIC PERIOD

S. Marinatos, *Crete and Mycenae* (Thames & Hudson, 1960).
History of the Hellenic World, I (Heinemann, 1972); tr. from Greek authors.

The above are good, massive, illustrated books.

+ S. Alexiou, *Minoan Civilisation* (Heraklion Museum, Crete).

+ R. W. Hutchinson, *Prehistoric Crete* (Pelican; illust.).

J. D. S. Pendlebury, *Handbook to the Palace of Minos* (Macmillan) and *The Archaeology of Crete* (Methuen); old but unreplaced.

+ R. Higgins, *Minoan and Mycenean Art* (Thames & Hudson, 1967).

P. Warren, *Aegean Civilisations* (Phaidon-Elsevier, 1975).

G. Cadogan, *Palaces of Minoan Crete* (Barrie & Jenkins, 1976).

+ John Chadwick, *The Decipherment of Linear B* (Pelican).

C. W. Blegen, *Troy and the Trojans* (Thames & Hudson).

Lord William Taylour, *The Mycenaeans* (Thames & Hudson).

Colin Renfrew, *Before Civilisation* (Thames & Hudson, 1973).

+ Denys Page, *History and the Homeric Iliad* (U. of Calif., 1963).

Sir Maurice Bowra, *Heroic Poetry* (Macmillan).

+ Jan de Vries, *Heroic Song and Heroic Legend* (O.U.P.).

+ M. I. Finley, *The World of Odysseus* (Pelican).

Nancy K. Sandars, *The Sea-Peoples* (Thames & Hudson, 1978).

A. M. Snodgrass, *The Dark Age of Greece* (Edinburgh U.P. 1971).

V. R. d'A. Desborough, *The Greek Dark Ages* (Benn, 1972).

J. N. Coldstream, *Geometric Greece* (Benn, 1977).

B. MYTHOLOGY, RELIGION, THE IRRATIONAL

+ Robert Graves, *The Greek Myths* (Pelican, 2 vols.). A very learned work; but often extremely speculative.

+ G. S. Kirk, *The Nature of Greek Myths* (Pelican, 1974).

+ E. R. Dodds, *The Greeks and the Irrational* (Beacon Press, 1951).

H. J. Rose, *Primitive Culture in Greece* (Methuen, 1925).

A. R. Burn, *The World of Hesiod*, chaps. 2 and 3 (2nd imp., Blom, New York, 1967).

C. COLONISATION, THE OUTER GREEK WORLD, TYRANTS, LYRIC POETS

+ John Boardman, *The Greeks Overseas* (Pelican, 1964, 2nd edn, 1974; illus.).

+ Sir Leonard Woolley, *A Forgotten Kingdom* (Pelican, 1953). The long-unsuspected evidence on early Greeks (and Mycenaeans) on the coast of Syria.

A. G. Woodhead, *The Greeks in the West* (Thames & Hudson).

J. M. Cook, *The Greeks in Ionia and the East* (Thames & Hudson).

A. R. Burn, *The Lyric Age of Greece* (rev. imp., Arnold, 1967).

A general history *c.* 750 to 510, including thought and literature.

Sir Maurice Bowra, *Greek Lyric Poetry* (2nd edn, O.U.P., 1960).

Sir Maurice Bowra, *Early Greek Elegists* (O.U.P., 1938).

A. Andrewes, *The Greek Tyrants* (Hutchinson's University Library, 1956). Short and 'meaty'.

+ M. Cary and E. H. Warmington, *The Ancient Explorers* (Pelican).

L. H. Jeffrey, *Archaic Greece: the City-States, c.* 700–500 B.C. (Benn, 1976; illust.). Excellent on details; a little short on general development.

D. EARLY GREEK THOUGHT

G. S. Kirk and J. E. Raven, *The Pre-Socratic Philosophers* (C.U.P., 1957), designed for serious students, is the most recent authoritative work on its subject in English. Among the best of the many shorter works are

F. M. Cornford, *Before and After Socrates* (C.U.P., 1932).

E. Schrodinger, *Nature and the Greeks* (C.U.P., 1954).

+ B. Farrington, *Greek Science* (Pelican).

+ Rex Warner, *The Greek Philosophers* (Mentor Books, 1958), runs through the whole history down to Roman times, with many extracts in translation.

E. CLASSICAL ART AND ARCHAEOLOGY

The literature is enormous. So is the output of picture books, some of them (not always the most expensive ones) good.

Authoritative on their subjects are

J. D. Beazley and B. Ashmole, *Greek Art and Architecture* (chapters from the *Cambridge Ancient History*, vols. IV, V; also issued as separate book).

B. Ashmole, *Architect and Sculptor in Classical Greece* (Phaidon, 1972).

C. M. Robertson, *A History of Greek Art* (C.U.P., 1975). A massive library book.

+ J. Boardman, *Greek Art* (Thames & Hudson, 1964).

+ G. M. A. Richter, *Sculpture and Sculptors of the Greeks* (Yale U.P., revised edn, 1970).

A. W. Lawrence, *Greek Architecture* (Pelican History of Art, 1956).

Arthur Lane, *Greek Pottery* (Faber, 1948).

R. E. Wycherley, *How the Greeks Built Cities* (Macmillan, 1949).

I. T. Hill, *The Ancient City of Athens* (Methuen, 1953).

+ R. J. Hopper, *The Acropolis* (Hamlyn, Spring Books, 1971).

C. M. Robertson, *The Parthenon Frieze* (Phaidon, 1975).

F. THE FIFTH AND FOURTH CENTURIES

This is the great classical period, to which general histories (see I, above) give pride of place. To books listed above add

A. R. Burn, *Persia and the Greeks* (Arnold, 1962).

R. M. Cook, *The Greeks till Alexander* (Thames & Hudson, 1962).

A. R. Burn, *Pericles and Athens* (Hodder, 1948).

R. Meiggs, *The Athenian Empire* (O.U.P., 1972); a work of massive scholarship, discussing all the numerous questions.

A. H. M. Jones, *Athenian Democracy* (Blackwell, 1957).

G. de Ste Croix, *The Origins of the Peloponnesian War* (Duckworth, 1972). Vigorous and controversial.

T. R. Glover, *From Pericles to Philip* (Methuen); a large, pleasant, readable book, which does for the later classical period something of what Zimmern (see I) did for the period down to Pericles.

Sir William Tarn, *Alexander the Great*, Vol. I, Narrative (C.U.P., 1948), is a reprint of his chapters in the C.A.H.; a fine narrative, but he worships and whitewashes his hero excessively.

A. R. Burn, *Alexander the Great* (1947; Pelican, 1973).

G. PLATO AND ARISTOTLE

A. E. Taylor, *Plato, the Man and his Work* (Methuen), is old, but still unsurpassed. His view, that practically everything in Plato's philosophy is traceable to Socrates, is not widely shared.

G. C. Field, *Plato and his Contemporaries* (Methuen), and *The Philosophy of Plato* (Home University Library, O.U.P.), give a more middle-of-the-road view.

M. Grene, *Portrait of Aristotle* (Faber, 1962), deals with Aristotle as a human being, and

D. J. Allan, *The Philosophy of Aristotle* (H.U.L., O.U.P.), is authoritative on his thought.

H. THE HELLENISTIC AGE

Sir Arnold Tarn and G. T. Griffith, *Hellenistic Civilisation* (Arnold; 3rd edn), is brilliant and authoritative.

M. Cary, *A History of the Greek World, 323–146 B.C.* (Methuen), covers the same ground attractively, more as a conventional history.

Bury, Bevan, Barber and Tarn, *The Hellenistic Age* (C.U.P., 1925), containing four lectures on the age in the history of civilisation, its literature, its popular philosophy and revolutions, is short, masterly and brilliant, especially the last two contributions.

Sir R. W. Livingstone, *The Mission of Greece* (O.U.P., 1928), a sequel to the same author's *Pageant of Greece*, an anthology of classical Greek literature in translation, is perhaps the best introduction to the neglected later Greek literature, written mostly under the Roman empire; it includes extracts from Plutarch's little-known Essays, the philosophers down to Marcus Aurelius, our accounts of Herodes Atticus, the still amusing Lucian, etc.

For daily life in the Greek-speaking world under the Empire, two of the best sources are the letters of the younger Pliny from his province of Bithynia (+ Penguin translation) and the latter half of the *Acts of the Apostles*.

ADDENDA

The following could not easily be fitted in above:

By Professor Peter Green, already well known for translations and historical fiction (which may account for a certain sensationalism in his otherwise serious and learned historical work):

A Concise History of Ancient Greece (Thames & Hudson, 1973). Some errors in details.

The Year of Salamis (Weidenfeld & Nicolson, 1970).

Armada from Athens (Hodder & Stoughton, 1970); on the Sicilian expedition.

Alexander the Great: Historical Biography (Weidenfeld & Nicolson, 1971). Green's full text, drastically cut in the above picture-book, appears in full, with notes, in *Alexander of Macedon* (Pelican, 1974).

Robin Lane Fox, *Alexander the Great* (Allen Lane, with Longmans, 1973) is both learned and readable; though it may be regretted that his bibliography ignores all earlier general books on his hero. He shares, for instance, some original ideas with Green, who, however, gets no mention.

INDEX

412